FOURTH EDITION

Composing with Confidence

Alan Meyers

Harry S Truman College

 LONGMAN

An imprint of Addison Wesley Longman, Inc.

New York • Reading, Massachusetts • Menlo Park, California • Harlow, England
Don Mills, Ontario • Sydney • Mexico City • Madrid • Amsterdam

To Ann, Sarah, and Bradley.

Acquisitions Editor: *Ellen Schatz*
Developmental Editor: *Susan Moss*
Project Coordination and Text Design: *Ruttle, Shaw & Wetherill, Inc.*
Cover Designer: Kay Petronio
Electronic Production Manager: *Angel Gonzalez Jr.*
Manufacturing Manager: *Willie Lane*
Electronic Page Makeup: *Ruttle, Shaw & Wetherill, Inc.*
Printer and Binder: *R. R. Donnelley & Sons Company*
Cover Printer: *The Lehigh Press, Inc.*

For permission to use copyrighted material, grateful acknowledgment is made to the copyright holders on pp.455–459, which are hereby made part of this copyright page.

Library of Congress Cataloging-in-Publication Data
Meyers, Alan, 1945–
    Composing with confidence / Alan Meyers. — 4th ed.
       p.   cm.
    Includes index.
    ISBN 0–673–99708–1 (instructor's ed.). — ISBN 0–673–99707–3 (student's ed.)
    1. English language—Rhetoric.   2. English language—Grammar.
  I. Title.
PE1408.M519   1996   96-18208
808'.042—dc20   CIP

ISBN: 0-673-99708-1 (instructor's ed.)
0-673-99707-3 (student's ed.)

12345678910—DOW—99989796

Contents

Unit Two   Composing Types of Paragraphs   65

Unit Three   Revising to Strengthen Your Writing   185

Unit Four   Composing Compositions   249

Unit Five   Editing to Improve Grammar and Mechanics   311

Preface

Reflecting current practices in basic writing courses that stress process as a means toward product, this fourth edition of *Composing with Confidence* fully lives up to its name. To a far greater extent than ever before, the book guides students through the recursive process of composing paragraphs and themes, erects platforms for gathering and organizing materials, and emphasizes individual choice at each stage. The new five-unit organization expands the treatment of planning, drafting, and revising; broadens its advice on composing on a word processor; amplifies its coverage of style, sentence variety, and concision; and, for the first time, includes lively end-of-chapter readings by such writers as Amy Tan, Garrison Keillor, Bill Cosby, Judy Brady, and Judith Viorst. The chapter content has also undergone a near complete overhaul. Explanations are clearer, language is simplified, and exercises and examples in virtually every chapter focus on a single topic or theme. The treatment of sentence-level matters has been streamlined, with shorter exercises that require student production and manipulation of sentence elements. Thus, in appearance, organization, and scope and type of coverage, this new edition departs significantly from its predecessors while retaining their most successful features.

NEW FIVE-UNIT STRUCTURE

Like its predecessors, the underlying premise of the fourth edition continues to be that writing, while partially a talent, is largely a skill that improves with practice, imitation, and experimentation. The new structure is designed to facilitate that improvement. Unit One examines composing, unifying, and developing the paragraph. Unit Two explores the process of composing, unifying, and developing the paragraph. Unit Three stresses revision for consistency, clarity, liveliness, variety, and accuracy. Unit Four examines the process of composing expository, persuasive, and essay examination or impromptu compositions. And Unit Five includes editing to improve grammar and mechanics.

This new structure provides great flexibility. For the student, the book introduces a variety of approaches to invention, composing, revising, editing, and proofreading—done individually or collaboratively, by hand or by computer. For the instructor, the five units allow simultaneous or separate treatment of paragraph-, theme-, and sentence-level matters of grammar, mechanics, and style. For both the student and instructor, the book's varied exercises, model paragraphs, and end-of-chapter readings create a practical and enjoyable learning and teaching tool.

NEW CHAPTER CONTENT

Like its predecessors, this new edition is based on the assumption that good form demands good content. Writing must not only be clear, but also informative and engaging. To these ends, the subject matter of the model paragraphs and exercises has been adapted from high-interest sources such as *Extraordinary Origins of Ordinary Things, Imponderables, The Dictionary of Misinformation, Significa,* and *The People's Almanac.* For example, an entire chapter may discuss legendary figures and events in American history, the unusual origins of commonplace practices or objects, or the bizarre behavior of dogs, cats, opossums, fish, bears, snakes, and wolves. A chapter may discuss how the American flag, Uncle Sam, Nike sneakers, Ray-Ban sunglasses, or the engagement ring, wedding ring, and wedding cake entered our popular culture.

ADDITIONAL NEW FEATURES

The most significant changes to this new edition include the following:

- **Expanded Coverage of Writing and Revising Skills.**   The new five-unit organization devotes four chapters to the composing process; seven chapters to composing specific types of paragraphs; four chapters to revising; three chapters to composition and theme writing; and eight chapters to editing.

- **End-of-Chapter Readings.**   Two engaging selections—one short and one long—present models of each paragraph genre in Chapters 5 through 11; a longer reading selection fulfills the same roles at the end of both Chapters 16 and 17, on expository and persuasive compositions. Selections are preceded by headnotes, accompanied by marginal vocabulary definitions, and followed by reflective questions.

- **Expanded Coverage of Composing on a Word Processor.**   In addition to a full section on word processor use in Chapter 1, new Computer Tips throughout Units One through Three facilitate student use of word processors for composing and revising.

- **New Chapters or Chapter Sections.**   New or significantly refocused chapters include Chapter 3: *Developing a Paragraph Through Explanations, Examples, and Details;* Chapter 5: *Composing Descriptive Paragraphs;* Chapter 6: *Composing Narrative Paragraphs* (description and narration were formerly treated in the same chapter); Chapter 14: *Achieving Sentence Variety;* Chapter 15: *Strengthening Modifiers;* and Chapter 18: *Composing an Essay Examination Answer or an Impromptu Theme.* Also new is the section on consistency in quotations or reported speech in Chapter 12.

- **Unified Thematic Content of Chapter Exercises and Models.**   As the first book of its kind to introduce high-interest connected discourse in exercise content, the fourth edition of *Composing with Confidence* carries this practice a step further: In most chapters, all model paragraphs and exercises focus on a single theme.

- **Concise Treatment of Grammatical Topics.**   Explanations have been tightened and the number of items in exercises decreased to facilitate quick mastery.

- **Increased Focus on Student Production of Sentences.**   Most exercises in Unit Five generate student-written sentences or sentence elements. Exercises requiring rote identification of sentence structures have been largely eliminated.

- **Increased Opportunities for Sentence Combining.**   Additional sentence-combining exercises on various coordinate or subordinate structures are included in Chapters 14, 15, and 20.

- **Greater Emphasis on Composing from Outside Sources.**   All chapters in Unit Two except one contain a section on composing paragraphs using outside sources.

◆ **Expanded Opportunities for Collaborative Work.** In addition to the popular Revision Guidelines from previous editions, many new exercises throughout the text can be performed collaboratively at the instructor's option.

◆ **Fully Descriptive Exercise Headings.** Specific heads that clearly indicate the outcomes of each activity have supplanted the generic heads from previous editions.

◆ **Concise End-of-Chapter Paragraph-Editing Exercises.** These exercises, again in connected discourse, have been shortened and made more approachable for students.

◆ **New Photographs.** These visual cues serve as prompts for certain short writing assignments within chapters and extended assignments at the end of chapters.

CONTINUING FEATURES

The following features have been retained from the third edition:

◆ **Realistic Writing Assignments.** All end-of-chapter writing assignments are placed within a context that specifies the subject, purpose, audience, and occasion within the working world, school, or larger community.

◆ **Chapter Previews and Summary Boxes.** These popular features facilitate quick reference and review by students.

◆ **Model Paragraphs and Essays of Each Stage of the Writing Process.** Chapters in Units Two and Four illustrate the development of paragraphs and essays from planning through editing stages.

◆ **Instruction in Free Writing, Brainstorming, and Clustering.** Chapter 1 explains and illustrates these three invention techniques, which are also included in the initial stages of all writing assignments throughout Units Two and Four.

◆ **Predicting Exercises.** Each chapter in Units Two and Four includes one or more exercises in which students read the opening sentences of their early drafts and predict the content and organization to follow. The exercises emphasize not only the topic sentence and thesis statement, but also unity, coherence, and audience awareness.

◆ **Instruction in All Rhetorical Types.** Unit Two explores the composing processes for each of the traditional paragraph organizations.

◆ **Lists of Useful Terms.** These include transitions appropriate to each rhetorical type (Unit Two), important irregular verbs (Chapter 17), and commonly misspelled words (inside back cover).

ANCILLARY MATERIALS

A number of ancillaries accompany the fourth edition of *Composing with Confidence*. The *Instructor's Edition* includes chapter objectives, answer keys, and advice on using the text, especially with students whose first language is not English. The *Test Bank,* written by Judy Boles of Chattanooga State College, contains a variety of instruments for evaluating student progress and mastery. The objective quizzes may be used in a Mastery Learning approach (discussed in the *Instructor's Edition),* as pretests and posttests in classrooms or writing laboratories, or as unit tests. The paragraph-editing quizzes may be used in a similar manner.

ACKNOWLEDGMENTS

I am indebted to many people who have contributed significantly to the form and content of this revision: my students; my acquisitions editor, Ellen Schatz; my developmental editor, Susan Moss, whose advice, guidance, cooperation, and attention to details were invaluable; and reviewers of the manuscript whose thoughtful and practical suggestions led to numerous improvements:

Marguerite Brunner, *McHenry County College*
Gail Caylor, *Phoenix College*
Jeffrey Curtis, *Essex County College*
Cheryl K. DeWaard, *Hawkeye Community College*
Phyllis Donovan, *Bryant-Stratton Business Institute*
Mary Lynn Gehrett, *Clovis Community College*
Julie Hawthorne, *Sacramento City College*
Kevin Hayes, *Essex County College*
Carol N. Ischinger, *NVCC, Annandale Campus*
Joseph R. Kern, *Stratton College*
Sybil M. Patterson, *Hillsborough Community College*
Linda Whisnant, *Guilford Technical Community College*
Phyllis W. Willis, *Northeastern State University*

Finally, I lovingly thank Ann, Sarah, and Bradley—my support network, my source of pride, and the true center of my life.

Alan Meyers

Engaging in the Composing Process

Examining the Composing Process

Before beginning to write, you should understand what is involved and why. The word *writing* comes from a verb, so it is an action—and a complex one at that. Learning to write requires the mastery of a number of skills for discovering and assembling ideas, putting them on paper, and reshaping and revising them. This chapter presents an overview of the writing process—or, more accurately, the composing process. The chapter compares writing to speaking, since both explore and communicate ideas. It examines why and how you write, looking at the entire process from *invention* to *drafting* to *revising* and *editing*. Specifically, this chapter discusses the following matters:

- the relationship between speaking and writing, the reasons for writing, and the goals of writing;
- procedures to follow during each stage of the composing process: discovering and planning, composing a first draft, and then revising, editing, and proofreading your work;
- ways to determine your most efficient practices; and
- how a paper takes shape within the process.

COMPARING WRITING TO SPEAKING

You speak to communicate with an audience—and with yourself, since you cannot know your thoughts exactly until you put them into words. You discover, change, and clarify ideas as you say them aloud. In fact, if you heard a tape recording of your informal speech, you would probably be surprised at how often you repeat yourself and drift from one subject to the next. Such disorganization is natural when exploring and composing your thoughts.

In more formal speech, however, you are more aware of purpose, audience, and subject. You should be better organized and polished, for, as a person with serious (or perhaps humorous) things to say, you would like yourself and your ideas to be taken seriously. You want people to see and hear you at your best. The words you choose and the way you express them tell people who you are, what you think, and what you think of yourself.

Your formal presentation should be organized and clear, but the early stages in preparing it usually aren't. You may think silently for a while, free-associating until your ideas take form. Then you probably speak or write them out, experimenting and changing your mind along the way. In the last stages of preparation, you rehearse until you feel comfortable with both your content and delivery. During a speech, however, you are aware of your audience and adapt to their responses. You read their faces, answer their questions, restate what isn't clear, give examples, speed up or slow down your delivery, raise or lower your voice for emphasis, and pause for effect.

Writing and formal speaking are alike in many ways. Both involve discovering, shaping, and communicating ideas; both address a subject, a purpose, and an audience. But writing and formal speaking also differ in several ways. When you write, your audience can't ask questions or state their objections. They can't hear your voice, see your face, or be charmed by your good looks. Your only tools for communicating are your words and the way you arrange them. You must therefore anticipate the audience's questions and objections. You must consider the occasion, the subject, and the purpose for your writing. You must choose a subject that will interest your audience and then present it interestingly. Because you cannot emphasize and clarify ideas through your voice and body, you must pay attention to each word, each sentence, and the way you arrange them. You must revise until your words strongly and clearly express the meanings you intend. You must compose and polish until you can meet your reader or readers on good terms. This page, for example, is the finished product—the last version—of many hours of work. You don't see the false starts, the early drafts, and then the later ones. You also don't see the changes that occurred in response to suggestions from readers and editors.

ANALYZING OCCASION, SUBJECT, AUDIENCE, AND PURPOSE

The first stage of the composing process, therefore, involves some planning. Here are four questions to keep in mind as you begin. The questions are interrelated, so consider them simultaneously and not separately.

1. What Is the Occasion for Writing?   Since writing is communication, you must have a reason to communicate. Are you composing a term paper or an essay examination in school? Are you composing a letter to apply for a job? Are you composing a memo to a supervisor or colleague at work? Are you composing a letter to a client or letter of complaint to a store manager? Are you preparing a sales presentation to customers? Are you writing an informal note to a friend? Are you composing a newsletter for a business or community group? Are you composing an article for a newspaper or magazine? Each of these occasions involves choices about what to say, how much to say, and how to say it.

2. What Is Your Subject and What Do You Know (or Need to Know) About It?   You will probably write most effectively about subjects you know best. You may not consider yourself an "expert" on anything, but you are an expert on your own experiences. Write what you *care about* and *know about* (or can find out about). Then you can say a great deal, and you can say it clearly and confidently.

In business or everyday experience, the subject of the writing connects naturally with the reason for writing. (An advertising brochure, for instance, may explain what services your company can provide its clients.) In school assignments, where the reason for writing is so closely tied to grades and curriculum, choosing a subject may be more difficult. Students are often given general topics and asked to discuss something that fits within them. For example, in an introductory business course, you might be asked to describe a past or current job. You should choose one that elicits your strongest feelings and opinions, one you can describe in detail because it was interesting or challenging (or, for that matter, even tedious and boring).

You can then search for that detail and explore your ideas. Where did you work, when did you work, and what kind of work did you do? What were your duties on a typical day? How did you perform each task? What was fun or dull or infuriating? You should take notes on specific moments or details you remember and use them later when you start to write.

3. Who Is the Audience for Your Writing?

What you say about your subject depends greatly on who reads it. For example, suppose you describe your part-time job at a carry-out chicken restaurant in an entertaining article for the school newspaper. Your readers already know such restaurants well, so you should focus on something they may not know: perhaps what happens behind the counter and in the kitchen. You can describe the steps in preparing the chicken: dipping it in those magical herbs and spices, popping it in the deep fryer, and laying it out on the trays. You can describe the crackpots and cranks who order you around as they order food. You can describe your co-workers who belong in cages. You can define the jargon words you use on the job. You may really like your work, but you have to think of ways to convey that enthusiasm to your readers.

However, if you write about the same topic for a group of specialists—owners of such restaurants, for example—you would completely redirect the focus of your paper. Since the owners already know what happens behind the counter and in the kitchen, you can discuss what they haven't considered: your suggestions for improving working conditions for the employees, increasing efficiency and profits, or better satisfying the customers.

4. What Is Your Goal or Purpose?

Related to your reason for writing is the goal you hope to accomplish. In other words, is your primary purpose *to inform, to persuade,* or *to entertain?* (Almost all writing is a combination of all three purposes, although one is usually more important than the others.)

- When you *inform, you* are *explaining or describing an idea, a process, an event, a belief, a person, a place, or a thing.* You are providing facts and information, analyzing the facts, defining terms, and explaining causes. If you inform readers about your job, for example, you should mention facts they don't know, describe routines they are unfamiliar with, or define job-related terms they haven't heard. Informative writing is also called *expository* writing because it exposes the meaning of things.
- When you *persuade, you* are *trying to convince your readers that they should believe something or do something.* You are trying to make readers change their minds or behave differently, so you appeal to their logic or emotion or both. In a persuasive paper, you might argue that your job performs a useful role in feeding people who are too busy to cook or who simply want to eat out inexpensively.
- When you *entertain, you* are *trying to make readers laugh, smile, or be fascinated, surprised, or even angry.* Of course, virtually everything you write should be entertaining, but sometimes entertainment is your main goal. In an entertaining paper about your job, you could focus on the funniest moments or funniest people at work.

After forming tentative answers to these four questions, you can experiment with ways of communicating your subject to your audience and accomplishing your purpose. You can consider what to say first, second, third, and tenth. You can consider what terms to define and when to define them. You can consider what to include and what to leave out. In the limited space of a paragraph, a letter, or an article, you can't say everything, so you must choose the most important, most relevant, and most interesting information.

1   Discussing the Occasion, Goals, Audience, and Point of a Paragraph

Read the paragraph and then answer the questions that follow it.

❑   Since people make language and since the needs of people change over time, so must the meanings of words change. A perfect example of this process is the word *awful.* Consider it for a moment. What do its two syllables seem literally to mean? If you guessed "full of awe," you are right. Originally, the word meant that something was impressive, powerful, even fear inspiring. In these senses, the voice of God speaking to Moses through a burning bush was certainly awful, as was the eruption of Mount Vesuvius that destroyed Pompeii. But a poorly drawn painting or a tune sung off-key was not. However, sometime in the nineteenth century, the term came to mean not fear inspiring but unpleasant. A dictionary published in 1818 reported, "In New England, many people would call a disagreeable medicine *awful,* an ugly woman an awful-looking woman. . . ." At about the same time, *awful* and its adverb form *awfully* began to show up as intensifiers—words such as *very* or *really* that add force or emphasis. In this new sense, people might say, "It was an *awfully* beautiful day." That is the meaning of the word today—if it has any meaning at all, for people now use *awful* and *awfully* so frequently that the words have lost their force. Why else would someone say, "That painting is *really* awful"—as if the word *awful* by itself doesn't say enough? *Awful* is now so far removed from its fearsome heritage that people must convey its former meaning through the words *awesome* and *awestruck.*

1. What seems to be the occasion for this piece of writing? That is, would you expect to find it in a technical book, a business memo, or a magazine article? What evidence can you cite to support your answer?
2. Who is the primary audience for this piece? (Does it seem addressed to English teachers or people with less knowledge about the history of words?) Again, what evidence would support your answer?
3. What is the primary goal of this paragraph: to inform, persuade, or entertain its audience?
4. What point is the paragraph making? Why does it discuss the word *awful*?

2   Analyzing Topics and Audiences

For each topic provided, list two or three points you would include if you were writing persuasive letters to the various audiences specified. The lists for the first topic have been completed as an example, as will be the first part of exercises throughout the book. (This exercise could be done collaboratively, in groups of three to five students.)

1. the pros and cons of having two phone lines in the home

   a. parents of teenagers   *Pros: children not tying up your phone, fewer arguments about their using the phone, no longer serving as the children's personal secretary for phone call messages. Cons: higher phone bills for you, lower grades for children who are always talking on the phone, and perhaps more arguments about talking on the phone.*

   b. teenagers   *Pros: your parents not nagging you to get off the phone, making and receiving calls whenever you want. Cons: parents making you pay for the additional line.*

2. the pros and cons of owning a car

   a. an adult who works some distance from home _____
   _____
   _____

   b. a high school student _____
   _____
   _____

3. the benefits of speaking more than one language

   a. a business major who wants to work in a foreign country _____
   _____
   _____

   b. a liberal arts major who doesn't want to work in a foreign country _____
   _____
   _____

4. the benefits of living in your city or town

   a. an unemployed person _____
   _____
   _____

   b. a person who wants to go to college _____
   _____
   _____

   c. a person with several children _____
   _____
   _____

BUILDING ON YOUR WRITING VOICE

Students sometimes produce unsuccessful papers because they put on airs, trying to sound "literary." You should build instead on your natural style, the voice you hear in your head while composing a paper. (Or it may be the voice you hear with your ears—many writers say their sentences aloud.)

To be sure, your writing voice is more formal (and grammatically correct) than the one you use in casual speech. You must learn to build on this voice—strengthening, varying, and polishing it to be graceful, confident, and clear. But a strong writing voice emerges only when you experiment with words and ideas. You must *compose with confidence,* trusting your insights and language, not censoring yourself or trying for perfection while first putting words on the page. As with formal speech, the composing process is part discovery, part revision, and part restatement. You can change your ideas and your wording many times, but first you must produce something to change. Then, having learned the principles of revision, you can revise with confidence, discarding what doesn't work, but reshaping and refining what does.

LOOKING AT THE COMPOSING PROCESS

When we talk about the process of composing, we generally refer to four steps: invention, drafting, revising, and editing and proofreading. However, most teachers also describe the composing process as *recursive;* that is, the steps in it recur, or loop back on themselves. For example, after planning and composing a first draft, you may begin revising it only to discover that you have omitted some important information. Thus, you need to stop and draft that section, which you will probably revise again later. Even in the late stages of editing and proofreading, you can rearrange, remove, or add some information. Therefore, while the following description of the composing process seems to outline a series of steps, don't regard these steps as completely separate from each other. You may repeat some steps many times—and not necessarily in the same order.

Discovering and Planning Your Paper in the *Invention Stage*

The invention stage of the composing process is mostly for yourself, a time to explore your ideas and the way you express them. (That exploration can be in your head, on paper, or on the computer screen.) No two writers compose in exactly the same way, and the same writer may employ different methods with each new task. Nevertheless, during the invention stage, you should experiment with what to say and the order in which to say it (although, no doubt, you will continue to make changes as you rewrite and revise). You should begin to *plan* your paper: What point should it make? What main ideas would develop that point? What explanations and details would support those main ideas? The plan will continue to evolve and change as you draft and revise your work, but a preliminary plan gives direction to the drafting and revising.

With some plan in mind, you can then *write freely* about a topic, recording ideas as they occur to you. For example, in a paper about your job, you could describe two or three memorable qualities of each one of your co-workers, go step by step through the preparation of the chicken, or list the spices included in the chicken coating. Sometimes you may write notes, sometimes only partial sentences or paragraphs. Many people like to push straight through, quickly putting the words on paper or keyboarding them into the computer without worrying about spelling or punctuation or exact meanings because they know they will change their minds and their phrasing many times before they publish (that is, make public) the final draft. Many people also return to this stage more than once if time allows, adding new ideas that occur to them.

The methods for exploring ideas in the invention stage are varied. You can simply list your thoughts in a process called *brainstorming,* discover and organize them in a process called *clustering,* or simply write them out in a process called *free writing.* (All three processes are illustrated later in this chapter.) In any event, however, you should plan, experiment, and play, but not try to rewrite each line at this point.

Drafting Your Paper

During this stage, your paper begins to take a more formal shape. Your ideas about what to say and in what order to say it are clearer. You may write more slowly and make changes more often than you did during the invention stage. Even so, you still needn't worry about getting things exactly right, for you will make additional changes in later drafts of the paper.

Revising Your Paper

In this stage, you write further drafts of your work. You read each draft to see if it says what you want it to say. Does it make a point, and does it stick to the point? Does the organization clearly and logically develop the point? Does the paper need more—and more interesting—details? This is the time to discover additional ideas and reshape or discard earlier ones. You shift around sections of the paper, substitute a few words here and there, and draft new sentences or parts of sentences. You reread and rewrite the paper until you are satisfied that it is interesting and clear. Instead of constantly asking yourself, "Can this be understood?" you ask, "Can this be misunderstood?" You can't sit next to your readers to tell them, "Well, what I meant was. . . ." However, you may want to read your paper to someone at this point in the process. Even if your listener doesn't offer suggestions or advice, the sound of your words spoken aloud to an audience makes you aware of strengths and weaknesses in your paper. Don't worry too much about spelling, grammar, and punctuation as you revise, though, for you will address these matters fully in the final stages of the composing process.

Editing and Proofreading Your Paper

Because you want people to judge your ideas, not your mistakes, this final stage is the time for careful editing and proofreading. You must force yourself to look for misspelled words, words left out or repeated, incomplete sentences, and incorrect punctuation. You must read what you have *actually* written—not what you *think* you have written. Perhaps you should show your paper to someone whose judgment you trust, who can notice small details you may have overlooked. At any rate, after correcting any errors, you should make a clean copy of your paper—and then proofread this final revision as well.

Notice how all the steps in the composing process overlap. As you draft, you also revise by striking out words or sentences and adding new ones. As you revise, you also draft new sentences or sentence parts. And as you do final recopying and proofreading, you continue to change and refine your work. In fact, this drafting and revising process stops only when you show your paper to your audience.

DEVELOPING YOUR PERSONAL COMPOSING PRACTICES

No two writers approach the composing process in the same way, so you should discover what works best for you. Matters such as what kind of pencil, pen, typewriter, or word processor to use may seem unimportant, but they aren't. Your physical comfort increases your mental comfort and, therefore, your ability to compose. For example, if you change your mind and erase often in first drafts, a pencil may suit you best. If you press down hard, a ballpoint or felt-tip pen may feel better. If you are impatient because your hand can't keep pace with the speed of your mind, you should type or, better yet, compose on a word processor. (You will see some advice about using word processors later in this chapter.) Decide on some other matters, too. For example, do you write best in the morning or at night, at the library or at home? Can you write with music on or do you concentrate better in quiet surroundings? Do you prefer to make small changes while composing, or do you delay them until you have completed the first draft?

The following general advice should increase your efficiency.

Tips on Drafting and Revising

For composing the first draft by hand or typewriter

1. Write or type on only one side of the page so later you can cut and paste sections you want to remove or replace.
2. Double-space and leave wide margins on both sides of the page so you can write changes and additions.
3. Say your sentences aloud as you compose, listening for what sounds natural, graceful, and clear.
4. Circle or underline words you think you have misspelled or might change later.
5. When you think of an idea that you should have included earlier, write it on a separate page, and then tape or staple it where it belongs.

For revising the paper

6. If possible, wait a few hours or days to approach the revision with fresh thoughts and eyes—more like the reader than the writer of the work.
7. Make small changes directly on the first draft, and write new sections on separate pieces of paper to tape or staple to the original (copy over only when necessary—in the later stages of revision).
8. Read your paper aloud, preferably to someone else, or let someone else read it to you.
9. Make a clean, neat copy of your final draft, and then proofread it carefully.
10. Take pride in your work—it does, after all, carry your name.

Composing on a Word Processor

Most schools and businesses, and many homes, have computers with word processing programs for a simple reason: Word processing greatly facilitates the drafting, revising, and editing process. Every program includes commands for removing, shifting, and copying anything from single words to whole sections of your paper. Almost every program also includes an on-line spell-checker and a thesaurus (a dictionary of synonyms), and many programs contain grammar-checkers. Computer-generated printouts produce clean, good-looking copies of your work, and the computer allows you to save each draft to revise later. Hardly anyone who learns word processing wants to return to composing by hand.

However, not everyone uses a word processor effectively, so keep in mind the following advice:

1. Learn to use the computer and the program before beginning to compose.   Although the different computers and software are becoming more and more alike, each requires some training and practice. Most programs are user friendly, but any computer can also erase from its memory all the work you have done. Don't be intimidated by a computer, however, and don't be frightened if you can't type. Take advantage of any available tutorials and training, hunt and peck on the keys until you become proficient, and plan to take a typing or keyboarding course soon. (You will be happy you did.)

2. Compose on the computer, not on paper, but don't try to write perfect first drafts.   A computer is not a glorified typewriter; the ability to cut, shift, copy, and add allows you to compose and revise quickly. You may wish to do some composing by hand, especially during the invention stage, although some computer programs are designed to make even this task easier. However, don't let the computer entice you into trying to fashion perfect first drafts. Too much revising as you compose is time consuming; besides, you still will need to revise and edit the paper later.

3. Save your work as you compose.   Computers have two kinds of memory: temporary and more permanent. A power outage or system failure can erase everything in temporary memory—including everything you have written. You should therefore save your work to more permanent memory every five minutes or so, and, when you finish for the day, make a backup copy of your work on a removable floppy disk or diskette.

4. Print your drafts and then edit them by hand.   Since most computer screens show one page (or less) at a time, they don't allow you to read your words in a steady flow. Double- or triple-space each draft of your work, print it out, read it aloud, make changes directly onto the page, and then enter the changes into the computer. If you find yourself drafting new sections or extensively revising others, however, you can return to the computer to compose.

5. Don't rely too heavily on spell- and grammar-checkers.   These programs are wonderful tools, but they aren't perfect. Spell-checkers only identify possibly misspelled words; they suggest new spellings, but you must make the corrections. Spell-checkers also can't correct sound-alike or look-alike words substituted for the ones you intend. And most spell- or grammar-checkers don't identify words accidentally omitted or included. In short, don't let the computer make you lazy; continue to proofread your papers yourself.

6. Discover what practices work most efficiently for you.   Just as no two writers compose and revise by hand in the same way, no two writers employ computers in the same way. Note how you write most efficiently, and then try to repeat those procedures each time you write.

Getting Started Through *Brainstorming, Clustering,* and *Free Writing*

Let's examine how a paragraph might take shape during the composing process. Suppose, again, that you want to write an informative and entertaining description of your part-time job at a carry-out chicken place. You can discover and explore your ideas on the subject in at least three easy ways: listing them, grouping them, or writing them out more completely.

Using Brainstorming.   The first process—making a random list—is called *brainstorming.* You simply put down whatever comes to mind about the subject, and then later choose what to include or leave out. Here is an example:

work behind the counter sometimes
often prepare the food
location: Washington Avenue and Main Street
types of food: chicken, french fries, mashed potatoes and gravy,
    corn, rolls, coleslaw, potato salad
hours: 4-9 three nights a week
eat dinner at work—tired of the food
my co-workers: Bill, LaVerne, and Tommie—funny people
my boss: Mr. Williams, another Hitler
cooking the chicken: unpacking it, washing it, adding the breading,
    putting it in the deep fryer, then putting it on the trays
packing an order: which pieces to include and how it's done
strange customers, especially the regulars: (1) Mrs. Bilge, who

wants catsup, cheese, and gravy on her french fries; (2) Mr. Stupor, the local drunk, who takes coffee with eight sugars; (3) Mr. Blob, who orders a huge dinner with all the trimmings for himself every day; (4) Oscar the Grump, who always has a nice word for everyone—like, "drop dead, please"

Such a list includes too much information for one paragraph, so you might focus on one main idea—the oddballs you work with and wait on—and put a check mark next to the details that fit into this narrower topic:

✓ *my co-workers: Bill, LaVerne, and Tommie—funny people*
✓ *my boss: Mr. Williams, another Hitler*
✓ *strange customers, especially the regulars: (1) Mrs. Bilge, who wants catsup, cheese, and gravy on her french fries; (2) Mr. Stupor, the local drunk, who takes coffee with eight sugars; (3) Mr. Blob, who orders a huge dinner with all the trimmings for himself every day; (4) Oscar the Grump, who always has a nice word for everyone—like, "drop dead, please"*

You might also put a check mark next to the details that help establish the setting:

✓ *location: Washington Avenue and Main Street*
✓ *hours: 4-9 three nights a week*

Now, having narrowed the topic, you might brainstorm a few more details that further develop your ideas:

my co-workers: Bill, the jokester, tells dumb jokes; LaVerne, always pretending to be offended; Tommie, tough and cool, but really a good guy

Finally, before composing the first draft, you might outline the details informally in an order that makes sense. (The setting would probably come first.)

I. *location: Washington Avenue and Main Street; hours: 4-9 three nights a week*
II. *my boss: Mr. Williams, another Hitler*
III. *my co-workers: Bill, the jokester, tells dumb jokes; LaVerne, always pretending to be offended; Tommie, tough and cool, but really a good guy*
IV. *strange customers, especially the regulars: (1) Mrs. Bilge, who wants catsup, cheese, and gravy on her french fries; (2) Mr. Stupor, the local drunk, who takes coffee with eight sugars; (3) Mr. Blob, who orders a huge dinner with all the trimmings for himself every day; (4) Oscar the Grump, who always has a nice word for everyone—like, "drop dead, please."*

Using Clustering.   A second method of getting started is called *clustering*. Like brainstorming, it allows you to generate a great many ideas and details, but it also permits you to visualize and organize them quickly. You begin the process by jotting down a central idea in the middle of the page and then circling it:

You then can branch off of the circle in whatever general directions occur to you:

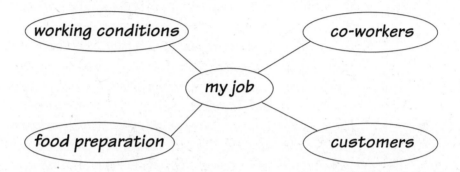

You can continue adding branches off of branches and filling up the page. At some point in the clustering process, however, you will probably discover (or stop and decide) that one or more main branches of the diagram is generating the most interesting details. Here, for example, is the part of the diagram with *customers* at its center.

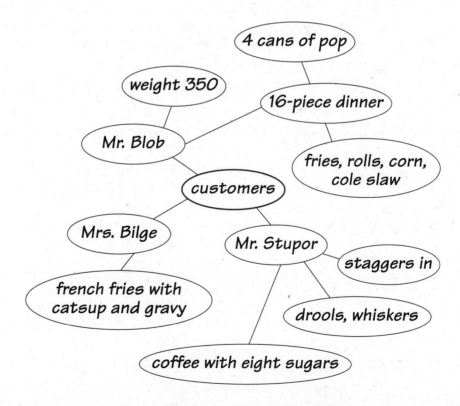

This part of the diagram can form the basis of a plan. Not only has it generated details, but it has begun to arrange them as well. The "Mr. Blob" circle, for example, branches off into two supporting-detail circles about his weight and his dinner choice, and the dinner choice circle branches off into its own supporting-detail circles. At this point, you may decide to begin a new clustering diagram with *customers* (and perhaps *co-workers*) at its center. Then you can compose the first draft of your paper.

Using Free Writing.   You can also get started by *free writing*—that is, putting down whatever comes to your mind about the subject without excessive concern for spelling, complete sentences, and the like. Here is an example:

> My part-time job. I'm a cook at a carry-out chicken place, on Washington and Main Street. Don't like the hours—4 to 9, three nights a week. Travel is a pain—an hour each way on three buses. Hard to study later, I'm too tired. My job is to cook the chicken, fries, and onion rings. Sometimes work behind the counter. Funny people: Bill always telling the dumb jokes, which he thinks are hilarious, and LaVerne, who's always pretending to be offended. Tommie tries to act tough and be cool. Wearing muscle tee shirts and talks tough, but he's really a good guy. Cooking chicken is really simple, just unpack the chicken from the crates, unwrap the plastic bags, and dump the whole mess in the sink. Then turn on the water and let drain. Take pieces and toss into big can of breading, turn on motor that shakes the can. Remove pieces and place in deep fryer. Eight minutes later, there it is, the Colonel's finest. Customers are nice, but some weird. One lady, we call her Mrs. Bilge, because of the garbage she eats—always orders french fries with cheese and catsup. That's not so bad, but she also wants gravy on them, too. Yuk. The local drunk, Mr. Stupor, with his lovely drool and four-day-old whiskers, usually comes in about 8 P.M. to get some coffee—with eight sugars in it! Double yuk. And the all-time eating champ, Mr. Blob. Must weight 350. Every night, he orders a huge dinner and three or four cans of pop. Talk about cholesterol! Hate my boss, Hitler without a mustache, Mr. Williams. Have only a half hour for dinner, but am tired of chicken, chicken, chicken.

Free writing, like brainstorming and clustering, lets you discover specific details and ideas as they come to mind. Although much of the information in a free writing may be disorganized or unusable, you will probably retain some phrasing for later drafts of the paper. But first you must narrow and organize your topic much as you would after brainstorming: Circle or put a check mark next to the parts you want to keep, and then choose a logical order in which to present them.

3   Exploring and Organizing Ideas

Assume you are composing an entry for a journal published each term by the Business Department of your school. The purpose of the journal is to present one-paragraph descriptions of career opportunities and interesting part-time jobs for students. Choose a job that you found (or would find) unusual or challenging. Do some brainstorming, clustering, or free writing on the subject. Then narrow your focus, decide which parts to keep for a first draft, and think about a way to organize them.

Composing Your First Draft

Now you can compose a first draft, something more structured than your earlier brainstorming, clustering, or free writing. The first sentence of the draft may be a challenge, since you want to draw the readers' attention at the beginning. If you can think of a good opening sentence, that's fine. (Often, one occurs to you when you are doing something else: taking a walk or a shower, tossing in your sleep at two in the morning, or watching a soap opera. If a sudden inspiration strikes you, write down your idea immediately before you forget it.) But you really needn't worry. You can add the opening sentence at any point—in your second draft, third draft, or even in your final draft. Remember that you should not try to compose a "perfect" first draft; you will rewrite and revise it later—adding to it, subtracting from it, changing some words and whole sentences. Here is an example of a first attempt based on the illustrations you have seen earlier:

I'm a part-time cook, and I work from 4 to 9 P.M. three days a week. It takes me an hour to get to work since I have to take three buses. My job is at a carry-out chicken place on Washington and Main. My job is to cook the chicken, fries, and onion rings. I meet more interesting characters than the Colonel. I don't particularly like my boss, Mr. Williams, he's Hitler without a mustache. But my co-workers are a riot. Bill goes to a local community college and considers himself another Eddie Murphy (Rodney Dangerfield is more like it), he always has some dumb jokes to tell. LaVerne thinks that she's very sophisticated, so she always gets offended by Bill. Tommie tries to act tough and be cool. Wearing muscle tee shirts and talking tough, but he's really a good guy. Some of our regular customers are a bit weird. One lady, we call her Mrs. Bilge, because of the garbage she eats, always orders french fries with cheese and catsup. That's not so bad, but she also wants gravy on them, too. The local drunk, Mr. Stupor, with his lovely drool and four-day-old whiskers, usually comes in about 8 P.M. to get some coffee—with eight sugars in it! And our all-time eating champ is the incredible Mr. Blob, who must weight 350. Every night, he orders a huge dinner and three or four cans of pop. Talk about cholesterol, fat, and sugar! It's a good place to work, in fact, it's better than the zoo.

✎ **4   Composing Your First Draft**

Now compose a first draft of a paragraph based on the brainstorming, clustering, or free writing you have done. Make sure that you write on one side of the page only and that you leave wide margins for later changes.

Revising Your Draft

After taking a break, you can criticize and make changes on the first draft, and then rewrite the paper one or more times. Perhaps you noticed the following problems in the preceding example (all of which are discussed in later chapters):

1. The point of the paragraph isn't very clear, and the relationships between ideas could be clearer.
2. Some of the information probably is irrelevant to the point.
3. The language is repetitious, too informal, or even babyish.
4. Some of the sentences are incomplete, and the boundaries between some sentences aren't clearly established.
5. More details could be added in a few spots. (For example, what does Mr. Blob order for dinner?) Details could also be omitted in other spots. (For example, we don't need to know how long the writer spends traveling to work.)

Here is a possible revision, with changes written above the line and in notes at the end. (Notice that some of the information has been omitted because it doesn't develop the point.)

> As
> ⌗ ~~I'm~~ a part-time cook, ~~and I work from 4 to 9 P.M.~~ three ~~days~~ nights a week. ~~It takes me an hour to get to work since I have to take three buses.~~ My ~~job is~~ at a carry-out chicken place on Washington and Main, ~~My job is to cook the chicken, fries, and onion rings.~~ I meet more interesting characters than the Colonel. ~~I don't particularly like~~ Although my boss, Mr. Williams, ~~is~~ acts like Hitler without a mustache, my co-workers ~~are a riot.~~ lessen the pain of his tyranny. Bill goes to a local community college and considers himself another Eddie Murphy (Rodney Dangerfield is more like it), ~~and~~ so he always has ~~a couple of~~ at least ten dumb jokes to tell. LaVerne, who thinks that she's very sophisticated, ~~so she~~ always ~~gets~~ pretends to be offended by Bill. Tommie ~~tries to act~~ talks tough and ~~be cool~~ acts in his ~~wearing a~~ muscle tee shirt ~~and talking tough,~~ but he's really a good guy. Some of our regular customers are a bit weird. One ~~lady,~~ woman (we call her Mrs. Bilge) because of the garbage she eats ~~and~~ —and always orders french fries with cheese and catsup. ~~That's not so bad, but she also wants~~ gravy ~~on them, too.~~ ! Next, the ~~The~~ local drunk, Mr. Stupor, with his ~~lovely~~ drool and four-day-old whiskers, usually ~~comes~~ staggers in about 8 P.M. to get some coffee— with eight sugars in it! ~~And~~ Finally, there's the all-time eating champ, is the

incredible Mr. Blob, who must ~~weight~~ *weigh 350* *pounds*. *Every night, he orders a 16-piece dinner with fries, rolls, slaw, and corn, and tosses it down* ~~huge dinner~~ *with three or four cans of pop. Talk about cholesterol,* ~~fat,~~ *Although I'm usually exhausted when I get home, I really like my job; in* ~~and sugar!~~ *It's a good place to work. In fact, it's better than the zoo.*

(Add above: she yells, "Bill, that's disgusting," as she turns her back and laughs.)

5 Revising Your First Draft

Go back to revise your first draft one or more times. You may need to rewrite the paper after making changes on the original version, and you may even change the rewritten version further. At various stages in the revising process, read your paper aloud—and have someone else read it, too.

6 Analyzing Your Draft

Respond to the questions on the form provided to guide you in revising your paper, or ask a reader to respond to the questions. You may wish to discuss these questions in a small group, in which you share responses to each other's work. Each participant should read his or her paper aloud twice, the first time so group members may simply listen, the second time so they may respond to the questions.

Revision Guidelines

1. What was the goal of this paper? _____

   Was the goal accomplished? _____ If not, what must be done? _____

   _____

   _____

2. What is the main point of the paper? _____

   _____

   _____

   Is the point clear? _____ If not, how could it be clarified? _____

   _____

   _____

3. Who is the audience for the paper? _____

   Does the paper speak to the audience's knowledge and interests? _____

   If not, how could it do so? _____

   _____

4. Have any important ideas been omitted? _____ If so, what are they and

   where should they be included? _____

   _____

   _____

5. What other weaknesses does the paper have? (Ignore this question if there are none.) _____

_____

_____

How could those weaknesses be corrected? _____

_____

_____

Editing and Proofreading the Final Draft

When you feel satisfied with your revisions, you can edit your paper, checking for misspelled words, errors in punctuation and grammar, and keyboarding errors if you have composed and revised on the computer. Make a clean copy of the final draft according to the format your instructor recommends—and proofread the draft to make sure you haven't overlooked anything. Here is the last version of the paragraph:

As a part-time cook three nights a week at a carry-out chicken place, I meet much more interesting characters than the Colonel. Although my boss, Mr. Williams, acts like Hitler without a mustache, my co-workers lessen the pain of his tyranny. Bill, who goes to a local community college and considers himself another Eddie Murphy (Rodney Dangerfield is more like it), always has at least ten dumb jokes to tell. LaVerne, who thinks she's very sophisticated, always pretends to be offended by Bill. She yells, "Bill, that's disgusting," as she turns her back and laughs. Tommie, who talks tough and acts cool in his muscle tee shirts, is really a good guy. Some of our regular customers are also a bit weird. One woman (we call her Mrs. Bilge because of the garbage she eats) always orders french fries with cheese and catsup—and gravy! The local drunk, Mr. Stupor, drooling into his four-day-old whiskers, usually staggers in about 8 P.M. to get some coffee—with eight sugars in it! Finally, there's the all-time eating champ, the incredible Mr. Blob, who must weigh 350 pounds. Every night, he orders a 16-piece dinner with fries, rolls, slaw, and corn, and then tosses it all down with three or four cans of pop. Talk about cholesterol! Although I'm usually exhausted when I get home, I really like my job; in fact, it's better than the zoo.

That, basically, is how the composing process works. You first explore and begin to organize your ideas. You compose a first draft. You revise it as many times as necessary to make it clear, lively, logical, and legible. And then you edit the paper for errors. The exact methods you follow will be yours to decide—and, no doubt, you will change them with each writing task or as more efficient steps occur to you.

IN SUMMARY

In the composing process you should

1. consider the occasion for writing, the subject, your audience, and your purpose;
2. discover your ideas by putting them into words;
3. decide what to include and how to organize it;
4. compose a first draft (and don't worry about making it perfect);
5. take a break; then criticize and revise the first draft (making changes on the original if you wish);
6. read your paper aloud, preferably to another person;
7. edit and then recopy final draft; and
8. proofread the final draft.

7   Proofreading and Polishing Your Final Draft

Recopy your final draft, and then proofread it for words left out, words repeated, spelling errors, and punctuation errors.

Composing a Paragraph

The best way to begin any new activity is by mastering small tasks before attempting larger ones, so each chapter in Unit One concentrates on composing paragraphs—the smaller divisions of a composition. This chapter begins our activity by examining some of the most important traits of the paragraph:

- the topic sentence;
- general and specific ideas;
- the point of a topic sentence; and
- paragraph unity.

THE PARAGRAPH DEFINED

At various times during your college and working careers you will be required to compose a single paragraph on some topic. Some essay examination questions require a one-paragraph answer. Some homework assignments require one-paragraph definitions or explanations. And, in the business world, many companies and organizations require one-paragraph memorandums or reports. Therefore, learning to compose a clear, well-organized, and well-developed paragraph makes practical sense.

A *paragraph* is a group of sentences that discuss one main idea. To be effective and clear, a paragraph must have *unity*—that is, each sentence must stick to and develop the paragraph's point. For the same reasons, a paragraph must also have *coherence*—that is, each idea must be logically related to the ones that precede and follow. A paragraph usually contains three parts:

- ◆ *The introduction* attracts the readers' interest and usually states the point of the paragraph in *a topic sentence* that helps readers predict and make sense of the ideas that follow.
- ◆ *The body* of the paragraph fulfills readers' predictions by developing the topic idea through explanations and specific examples, arranged in a clear and logical way.
- ◆ The *conclusion* (usually one sentence) brings the paragraph to a graceful end.

When you compose single paragraphs in this and later chapters, you should treat each paragraph as a self-contained unit. After (or while) mastering this smaller unit, you can focus on the larger one—the multiparagraph composition.

Examining the Physical Appearance of a Paragraph

Take a look at the paragraph you are reading right now, for it demonstrates the physical traits of most paragraphs. Note that it begins with the first line indented; that is, moved to the right (usually about a half inch, or five spaces on a typewriter). Note, too, that a paragraph contains at least three sentences and often many more, and note that each sentence follows directly after the preceding one on the same line, not necessarily on a new line. Finally, note that the topic sentence generally (but not always) comes at the beginning of the paragraph.

IN SUMMARY

> **A paragraph**
>
> 1. is a group of sentences that discuss one main idea, or topic;
> 2. often states the main idea in *a topic sentence,* which usually (but not always) comes at the beginning of the paragraph;
> 3. has *unity*—all sentences develop the topic idea;
> 4. has *coherence*—all the ideas are logically related and connected;
> 5. generally includes at least three sentences, but often many more, that explain and illustrate the topic idea;
> 6. begins with the first line indented; and
> 7. requires that each sentence follow directly after the previous sentence, not on a separate line.

1   Analyzing a Poorly Written Paragraph

The following group of sentences does not constitute a properly written and logical paragraph. List several reasons that explain why. (This exercise could be done collaboratively, in groups of three to five students.)

The Origins of Sunglasses

❏   Tinted eyeglass lenses were first used in China in the early fifteenth century. Many people wear sunglasses today. Chinese judges wore them to conceal their eyes. In the 1930s, the United States Army Air Corps asked the optical firm Bausch & Lomb to produce eyeglasses that would protect pilots from the dangers of glare at high altitudes. Sunglasses are very popular now.

1. _____

2 _____

3. _____

4. _____

Employing the Topic Sentence as a Guide for Readers

A topic sentence usually begins a paragraph, but it can be placed elsewhere as well. It can follow an attention-getting opening sentence or even summarize the details of the paragraph at the end. In fact, some paragraphs may not even contain a stated topic sentence if the main idea is implied. At this point, however, you should concentrate on drafting a topic sentence at or near the beginning of each paragraph. Doing so will help you focus on a single idea, organize and structure your thoughts. Doing so will also help your readers follow your thoughts through that organization and structure. Consider for a moment how your mind works as you read. You don't read a paragraph passively, absorbing ideas like an old sponge soaking up ink. Your mind is actively at work making sense out of the words on the page. You predict what will come next, based on what you have already read. Suppose, for example, that you encounter the following opening sentence in a paragraph:

> Going to the beach on a Sunday afternoon is hardly a peaceful experience.

What would you expect the rest of the paragraph to say?

A logical answer might be: "An explanation of why the experience isn't peaceful." And the rest of the paragraph does explain precisely that:

> It is everybody's day off, and the place is crowded, noisy, and busy. First, you have to maneuver through the mass of sand-covered blankets and sticky bodies to find a few square inches to spread out your blanket and set up your equipment. Second, you have to contend with the dueling boom boxes. Every blanket sports a radio or tape machine playing a different song, loudly enough to drown out the sounds from the other boom boxes, of course, but also loudly enough to make you want to drown their owners. Third, you have to put up with the thousands of preschoolers freed by their parents to terrorize everyone in the vicinity. They trample sand all over your blanket, spill water from their buckets on your head, and fight each other for possession of every toy on the beach. Fourth, you have to endure the macho morons who kick sand in your eyes as they dive for rubber footballs or Frisbees that land on your blanket. The whole experience is enough to make you want to pack up your boom box and Frisbee and take your own preschoolers somewhere else.

Thus, you can see the importance of the topic sentence. It helps your readers in predicting and understanding the main ideas of the paragraph. It also helps them perceive the logical relationships among the sentences of the paragraph.

2   Identifying Topic Sentences

Underline the topic sentences in the following paragraphs. Be careful: Not every topic sentence comes at the beginning. The topic sentence of the first paragraph has been underlined for you as an example. (This exercise could be done collaboratively.)

The Origins of the Engagement Ring

Paragraph A.   (1) The diamond engagement ring seems to have originated 500 years ago. (2) A wedding document from Venice, Italy, dated 1503 lists "one marrying ring having diamond" belonging to Mary of Modina. (3) That gold wedding ring was among the first engagement rings which held a diamond.

Paragraph B.   (1) By the seventeenth century, the diamond ring had become the most sought after statement of engagement throughout Europe. (2) The process began with the Venetians at the end of the fifteenth century. (3) They discovered that the diamond is one of the hardest, longest lasting substances in nature and that fine cutting and polishing increase its brilliance. (4) Therefore, wealthy Venetians exchanged engagement rings of diamonds set in bands of silver and gold. (5) The rings were rare and very expensive, however. (6) So, although their use did not quickly spread throughout the rest of Europe, their natural appeal guaranteed them a future.

Paragraph C.   (1) King Francis I of France and Henry VIII of England wished to ensure a strong alliance between the two countries. (2) Therefore, when the son of King Francis I was born on February 28, 1518, he was immediately engaged to Princess Mary, daughter of Henry VIII of England. (3) The infant Mary was presented with the latest fashion in rings, which doubtless fit the tiny royal finger for only a short time. (4) Thus, one of history's early diamond engagement rings was also its smallest, worn by a 2-year-old bride-to-be.

Paragraph D.   (1) Although we know the origin of the diamond engagement ring, we know less about the origins of engagement rings themselves. (2) Well before the fifteenth century, an Anglo-Saxon custom required that a prospective bridegroom break some highly valued personal belonging. (3) Half the broken object was then kept by the groom, half by the bride's father. (4) A wealthy man was expected to split a piece of gold or silver. (5) Exactly when the broken piece of metal was symbolically replaced by a ring is unclear. (6) Historical evidence seems to indicate that the engagement ring existed before the wedding ring in Europe, and that the groom gave the ring to the bride a second time during the wedding ceremony. (7) One accurate description of the engagement ring's purpose is its original Roman name, *aarhae,* which means "earnest money."

Paragraph E.   (1) For Roman Catholics, the engagement ring's official introduction is well established. (2) In 860 C.E., Pope Nicholas I ordered that a man demonstrate his intent to marry a woman by giving her an engagement ring. (3) Nicholas firmly believed in the holiness of marriage, and once even excommunicated two archbishops who had been involved in the marriage, divorce, and remarriage of a king. (4) And for Pope Nicholas, the engagement ring could not be cheap. (5) It had to be of a valued metal, preferably gold, which for the husband-to-be represented a financial sacrifice.

Paragraph F.   (1) Two other customs began in the same century: A man who did not honor a marriage pledge had to forfeit the ring; and a woman who broke off an engagement had to return it. (2) The Church became unbending about the seriousness of a marriage promise and the consequences if the promise was broken. (3) For example, a church council excommunicated for three years the parents of a man who broke an engagement. (4) Moreover, if a woman backed out for reasons unacceptable to the Church, her parish priest had the authority to order her into a nunnery for life. (5) For a time, "till death do us part" began weeks or months before a bride and groom were even united.

ENGAGING IN THE COMPOSING PROCESS

While the final draft of a paragraph has a certain form and shape, the process of arriving at the final draft can vary a great deal. Sometimes, you start with a clear plan of what to say and then follow it closely while composing; other times, your ideas take shape only while composing and later through extensive revision. No matter how you plan, draft, revise, and edit your work, however, the composing process will almost always include the following steps:

1. Limit the topic.
2. Consider the occasion, audience, and purpose, and the point you wish to make.
3. Make a preliminary plan.

4. Draft the topic sentence and body of the paragraph.
5. Revise the paragraph for unity and clarity.
6. Adjust and perhaps add to the topic sentence.
7. Edit, recopy, and proofread the paragraph.

Let's take a look at each of these steps.

Step One: Limiting the Topic

As you have already seen, most topics are too broad to discuss in a short amount of space, so you must limit your discussion. For example, suppose you wanted to compose a one-paragraph description of a memorable experience in your life as a way of introducing yourself to your classmates. You might consider any number of important moments—a serious illness, a special trip, someone's death, your marriage, the birth of a child—each of which could be the subject of a long composition or even a book. Therefore, after choosing one topic—perhaps a special trip—you would narrow it to a more manageable size. Begin by listing a few possibilities:

the airplane flight
the moment when my grandparents met me at the plane
dinner the first night
the car ride through farm country
tending the animals on the farm

Then select one of these narrower topics—for example, tending the animals on the farm—and brainstorm, cluster, or free write your ideas on the topic: feeding the chickens and gathering their eggs; overcoming your reluctance to milk the cows; feeding, grooming, and saddling a horse; and feeding and hosing down the pigs. If you decide your ideas would take more than one paragraph to describe, limit the topic even further, perhaps to a description of milking the cows.

3 Limiting Topics

Suppose in a social science course you were asked to compose a short description of a contemporary problem that would provoke a lively debate. Limit each of the following broad topics so you could develop it in a single paragraph.

1. Problems created by taxes *the unfairness of the sales tax for poor people*

2. Problems created by television _____

   _____

3. Problems created by guns _____

   _____

4. Problems created by drugs _____

   _____

5. Problems in family life _____

   _____

Step Two: Considering the Occasion, Audience, Topic, and Purpose

Chapter 1 discussed the need to consider why you are writing, what you will be saying, who your readers will be, and what you hope to accomplish with them. Writers who ignore these matters often produce dull, unclear, and incoherent paragraphs. They write "about" a topic, but compose with no direction or goal in mind. They put down a sentence or two and then, not knowing what else to say, and then ask themselves, "What's next?"

Writers who have thought about the occasion, audience, topic, and purpose are much better focused. They usually know where they are going in a paper and why they are going there. You should, therefore, explore these issues before you begin to compose.

✍ 4   Analyzing Your Audience and Purpose

Suppose you were preparing a half-page magazine advertisement for a new fat-free, low-salt cereal called Wonder Bran. Consider the following questions. (You may wish to work with one or more classmates in generating ideas.)

1. Who is the primary audience for this advertisement? _____

_____

2. What is my purpose in writing this advertisement? _____

_____

3. What points would best accomplish my purpose with this audience? (Which

points would have the most appeal?) _____

_____

Step Three: Making a Preliminary Plan

After limiting your topic and considering who will be reading it and why, you can make an informal outline to help organize your ideas. Go back to your free writing, brainstorming, or clustering, and see if a leading idea emerges. It could be, for instance, the hard work involved in milking the cows at your grandparents' farm.

Then examine your invention materials for details or examples that would support that leading idea and list them in an order that makes sense:

I.   *Getting up at sunrise*
Dressing and eating quickly
Walking to the barn in the morning cold

II. *Milking the cows*
Moving Bessie into position to hook her up to the milking machine
Overcoming fear of touching her udder
Grabbing her four teats and attaching them to the suction hoses
Repeating the process with Esmiralda and Lulabelle

Remember that this outline is a guide. Depart from it if a better organization occurs to you as you draft and revise the paragraph. And don't worry if your outline is not as specific as the example here; you may think of more details later in the composing process.

Step Four: Drafting a Topic Sentence and the Body of the Paragraph

Look again at the topics you composed in Exercise 3. They could be titles for compositions—but not topic sentences—because they are incomplete statements. At some point in the composing process, therefore, you must draft a topic sentence. Don't worry about fashioning a perfect one; you will revise it later as the paragraph takes shape. Compose a preliminary topic sentence and first draft of the paragraph, and expect to revise both.

Making a Point in the Topic Sentence.   A good topic sentence *makes a point* about its subject; it shouldn't just say what the paragraph is "about." For example, recall the sample paragraph in Chapter 1 "about" the writer's part-time job in a carry-out chicken restaurant. But so what? What point does the writer want to make about that part-time job? What can the readers predict will be said throughout the rest of the paragraph? Notice that the following topic sentence (a very poor one) doesn't answer those questions:

I want to write about my job at a carry-out chicken restaurant.

This sentence only announces the subject of the paragraph. It doesn't state or even suggest the writer's viewpoint toward the subject: that the job is fun, or boring, or a little of both; that the job is dangerous, or easy, or complicated; that she works hard or hardly works; that she likes her co-workers, or hates them, or is indifferent to them. The sentence simply doesn't inform readers of what she thinks about (or what they should think about) her job. Narrowing the focus of the topic sentence doesn't help.

I want to discuss the people I work with and meet on my job at a carry-out chicken restaurant.

The sentence is more specific—it mentions people, not just the job—but it still doesn't make a point; it doesn't answer the question, "What about the people?" By contrast, the following topic sentence makes a point:

> At my job at a carry-out chicken restaurant, I meet much more interesting people than the Colonel.

The point is that the *people* at work are *interesting*. Now readers can predict what they will probably encounter in the remainder of the paragraph: details about what makes each person interesting.

Expressing an Attitude in the Topic Sentence.   Another way to view the topic sentence is to think of its point as *an attitude toward the topic.* The word *interesting* in the previous example expresses an attitude. Compare the following sentences:

No attitude: Abraham Lincoln was president of the United States.
Attitude: Abraham Lincoln was our *greatest* president.

No attitude: I'm taking business administration courses.
Attitude: I'm *enjoying* my business administration courses.

Many topic sentences, therefore, follow this pattern: *subject + stated attitude*. Here are some further examples.

Subject		Attitude
Returning to school	has been	*exciting and a bit frightening* for me.
Ms. Kim	is	quite a *competent* attorney.
Juan Gonzalez	displays	*unusual musical talent.*

Since a good topic sentence expresses an attitude, it can be disagreed with:

Ms. Kim is quite a competent attorney. (Well, perhaps *you* think so.)

A weak topic sentence, however, provides no statement of attitude with which to disagree:

Ms. Kim is an attorney. (Who can argue with that?)

A topic sentence, and the paragraph it is in, should answer the question, "So what?" If the topic sentence can't answer that question, the paragraph may be aimless, pointless, just a collection of vaguely related facts.

IN SUMMARY

A topic sentence

1. is usually the most general statement in the paragraph, and the remaining sentences develop that statement specifically;
2. usually comes at the beginning of the paragraph, but can appear after an introductory statement or even at the end of the paragraph;
3. can be implied (omitted from the paragraph);
4. should make a point about the subject of the paragraph, not simply announce the subject; and
5. should express an attitude toward the subject.

Deciding When to Compose the Preliminary Topic Sentence.   Although the topic sentence usually appears at the beginning of the paragraph, you can actually draft it at any time during the composing process, and you will probably revise it more than once. In fact, the point of the paragraph (and, therefore, the topic sentence) sometimes emerges only in the final stages of composing—after you have examined your materials, questioned your ideas, and revised them several times. While the finished product of the composing process should be clear, the composing process itself is often far less tidy. Depending on the method you choose for getting started, at least three different options are available to you:

◆ If you already know what you want to say, you can draft a preliminary topic sentence first and then add the supporting sentences.
◆ If you need to discover your ideas, start with brainstorming, clustering, or free writing. You can draft a preliminary topic sentence next and then organize the supporting ideas in the first draft of the paragraph.
◆ If you want to draft and revise the entire paragraph without worrying about the topic sentence, you can add the topic sentence (and revise it) later when you feel sure of your point and comfortable with the supporting ideas.

Of course, you needn't use the same method each time; most writers do what works best at the moment. Furthermore, no matter when you draft the topic sentence, you should expect to modify or change it during revisions—a practice we return to shortly.

5 Composing a First Draft

Assume your instructor in a photography course has asked you to compose a short analysis of what the famous photographer Walker Evans was trying to "say" in the following photograph. Use your first reaction to the photograph of the barbershop as a preliminary topic sentence expressing an attitude or point ("The barbershop is . . ." or "The barbershop looks . . ."). Then complete a paragraph that describes the barbershop, using only details that support the topic idea.

6 Drafting Topic Sentences

Choose one of your topics from Exercise 3 and compose a topic sentence expressing an attitude or making a point, and then compose a first draft of a paragraph that develops the topic idea.

7 Revising Weak Topic Sentences

Each topic sentence here merely announces the subject of the paragraph. Revise the topic sentences so each one makes a point about or expresses an attitude toward the subject.

1. This paragraph will discuss the Great California Gold Rush.

   The Great California Gold Rush was a period of greed and near insanity.

2. There are a lot of commercials on television.

   _____

3. The topic that I want to discuss is my job at a bank.

_____

4. An issue that people argue over is capital punishment.

_____

Step Five: Revising the Paragraph for Unity

Remember that the opening sentences—and especially the topic sentence—of a paragraph allow readers to predict and therefore make sense of the paragraph's content. Of course, some readers may be bad predictors, but a paragraph that doesn't fulfill the reasonable expectations of good readers will not successfully communicate its point. Therefore, a good paragraph has unity; that is, all the sentences in the paragraph develop the topic idea. As you brainstorm, cluster, or free write, you may include some information that is related to the subject but doesn't develop the topic idea. What information, for example, would you expect to learn in a paragraph that began with the following sentence? List five or six ideas and compare your predictions with those of your classmates:

The Origins of the Second Leaning Tower of Pisa

❑ (1) Believe it or not, a man built a remarkable copy of the Leaning Tower of Pisa right here in the United States, and it still stands today.

_____

_____

_____

_____

_____

_____

Now as you read the rest of the paragraph, identify the sentences that probably don't belong, that don't fulfill reasonable predictions. See if you have made any predictions that the paragraph doesn't fulfill.

❑ (2) The man was a Chicago millionaire, Robert A. Ilg, head of the Ilg Electric Ventilating Company, who constructed the tower in Niles, Illinois, in 1933. (3) He did so after falling in love with the Leaning Tower on a visit to the Italian town of Pisa. (4) The marble tower leaned because it had sunk 7 feet below the ground at an uneven angle. (5) And, as many people know, it had been the site of Galileo's greatest experiment. (6) He proved that the pull of gravity is uniform when different sized stones that he dropped from the top of the tower landed at the same time. (7) Ilg was so in love with the beautiful 177-foot marble tower that he was determined to construct a half-scale duplicate of it in Niles, and his was 96 feet tall and made of cement. (8) He even added imported Italian bells like those in the massive Pisa original. (9) In 1960, he gave his tilted tower to the Niles YMCA. (10) Ilg spent his final years in the San Francisco Bay area. (11) Although the tower has been closed to the public since the 1960s because of structural problems, Robert Ilg's love for the tower was recently consummated in an unusual marriage. (12) In 1991, Niles and Pisa formed an alliance as sister cities.

Which sentences don't belong? _____

Which of your predictions does the paragraph not fulfill?

_____

_____

You probably noticed that sentences 5, 6, and 10 don't belong, since they concern Galileo's experiments and Robert Ilg's move to California—not how, where, and why the tower was built, and what has happened to it. In a single-paragraph composition, these sentences should be dropped. In a multiparagraph composition, however, these sentences (or their information) might be included in separate paragraphs. One paragraph could provide history of the original Leaning Tower and another could provide more personal information about Ilg.

Did you predict that the paragraph would provide more specific information about the tower and its construction—for example, the cost of building the tower, the problems with making it tilt, the design of the tower, or the number of steps to the top? These are all valid predictions, and a more extensively developed paragraph might have fulfilled them.

IN SUMMARY

A unified paragraph

1. specifically develops the point of the topic idea and meets the readers' reasonable predictions; and
2. omits any information that does not develop that topic idea or meet those predictions.

8 Unifying Paragraphs Through Revision

Circle the number of the topic sentence of each paragraph. Then draw a line through the sentence or sentences that do not support the topic sentence. (This exercise could be done collaboratively.)

The Origins of the Wedding Ring

Paragraph A. (1) There are two main theories about the origin and original meaning of the wedding ring. (2) One theory claims that the modern ring symbolizes the chains or ropes used by barbarians to tie a bride to her captor's home. (3) If that theory is true, today's double ring ceremonies truly represent the equality of the sexes! (4) The other theory centers on the bands exchanged in a marriage ceremony. (5) The first finger ring used by the Egyptians around 2,800 B.C.E. might have represented a circle. (6) The Egyptians believed a circle, having no beginning or end, signified eternity—the length of the marriage bond.

Paragraph B. (1) The tradition of the golden wedding ring, which began among wealthy Egyptians, continued with the Romans 3,000 years later. (2) Many of the golden rings unearthed at Pompeii (a Roman city buried in ash after a volcanic eruption in 79 C.E.) depict the wedding bonds. (3) For example, one band showed two hands clasped in a handshake, perhaps signifying the joining together of hands in marriage. (4) In America in the 1960s and 1970s, the so-called flower children decorated their wedding or friendship rings in this way.

Paragraph C. (1) Some evidence suggests that young Roman men of moderate financial means often went for broke in purchasing rings for their future brides.

(2) Tertullian, a Christian priest writing in the second century C.E., observed that "most women know nothing of gold except the single marriage ring placed on one finger." (3) Tertullian also noted that the average Roman housewife proudly wore her gold band in public, but at home "wore a ring of iron." (4) Diamond engagement rings evolved many centuries later.

Paragraph D.   (1) In earlier centuries, a ring's design often communicated a meaning. (2) For example, a miniature key is welded to the side of several Roman bands. (3) This was not a sentimental suggestion that a bride had unlocked her husband's heart. (4) Instead, it symbolized a central principle of the marriage contract: A wife was entitled to half her husband's wealth. (5) She could, therefore, help herself to a bag of grain, a roll of linen, or whatever rested in his storehouse. (6) Women had to wait another 2,000 years to achieve such rights again.

Step Six: Adjusting and (Perhaps) Adding to the Topic Sentence

In the final stages of unifying the paragraph, look at the topic sentence again. On the one hand, an overly general sentence won't give the readers a clear understanding of your point and may lead them to make false predictions. For example, the topic sentence of the following paragraph suggests too much:

The Origin of Modern Sunglasses

❏ *Both the military personnel and the public have benefited from products designed for the military.* In the 1930s, the Army Air Corps commissioned the optical firm of Bausch & Lomb to produce eyeglasses that would protect pilots' eyes from the dangers of the glare at high altitudes. The company's physicists and opticians perfected a special dark green lens that absorbed light. They also designed a slightly curved frame to shield pilots' eyes when they glanced downward toward the plane's instrument panel. Fliers were issued the glasses at no charge, and the public soon was able to purchase this model that banned the sun's rays when it was marketed as Ray-Ban Aviator sunglasses.

Although you predict the paragraph will discuss many products designed for many branches of the military, it discusses only one: sunglasses for Army Air Corps pilots. A discussion of many products and military branches would require a much longer discussion—perhaps a full composition, or even a whole book.

On the other hand, a topic sentence shouldn't be too specific, for it will also lead to false predictions, as in the following example.

The first sunglasses were issued to Army Air Corps pilots for free.

This topic sentence doesn't suggest who invented the glasses or for what purposes.

Compose an appropriate topic sentence for the paragraph, one that is neither too specific nor too general. _____

_____

You probably wrote something like this: "Both the military personnel and the public benefited from a set of eyeglasses designed for the military."

You can also change the topic sentence in another way: by adding a short phrase to help readers predict what will follow. Let's return to a topic sentence you saw earlier in the chapter: "Ms. Kim is quite a competent attorney." Suppose while drafting a paragraph that developed that idea, you thought of three reasons to explain Ms. Kim's competence. You could easily revise the topic sentence to include that number:

> Ms. Kim is a competent attorney *for three important reasons.*

The other topic sentences you saw earlier could be revised in similar fashion:

> Returning to school has been exciting and a bit frightening for me *in several ways.*
> I enjoy playing field hockey *for three reasons.*
> Juan Gonzalez displays unusual musical talent *as a composer, singer, and guitar player.*

Sometimes these guiding phrases occur to you as you draft the preliminary topic sentence. Other times, they emerge in the late stages of composing. Although you needn't add a guiding phrase to every topic sentence, try to do so when the ideas of the paragraph are complex.

✍ 9 Analyzing and Revising Your Draft

Choose one of the paragraphs you drafted in Exercises 6 or 7 and revise it, guided by the responses to each of the following questions. (This exercise could be done collaboratively, with each person reading his or her paper aloud twice and the group responding to the questions.)

Revision Guidelines

1. What is the topic sentence of the paragraph? _____
   _____
   _____

2. What word or words express the point of the topic sentence?_____
   _____
   If the point is not clear, what words should be added? _____

3. If the topic sentence is too specific or too general for the supporting details, how
   should it be changed?_____
   _____
   _____
   Would a guiding phrase added to the topic sentence increase the clarity and unity
   of the paragraph? _____ If so, what should it say? _____
   _____

4. Does the rest of the paragraph directly support the topic sentence?_____
   If not, what should be omitted or revised?_____
   _____

5. Does the unity of the paragraph need to be strengthened? _____
   What should be done? _____

6. What, if any, important ideas have been omitted? _____

_____

_____

Where should they be included? _____

_____

_____

7. What was the greatest problem in composing this paragraph? (Ignore this question if the writer experienced no significant problems.) _____

_____

_____

_____

If the problem was not resolved, what should be done? _____

_____

_____

_____

Step Seven: Editing, Recopying, and Proofreading the Paragraph

The last stage of the composing process involves applying the finishing touches to the paragraph: changing some phrasing; correcting grammatical, spelling, and punctuation errors; making a clean copy of your work; and then proofreading it. Later chapters discuss further improvements you can make during the editing and recopying stages.

This step-by-step analysis may make the composing process seem mechanical and inflexible—but it isn't. You needn't follow each of the seven steps, and you needn't follow them in the same order. For example, you may have a clear idea of your point during the early stages of composing, so you needn't reorganize the paragraph extensively later. Or your first draft of a topic sentence may need no or only small adjustments later. The six steps discussed in this chapter should serve as guidelines rather than rules—advice to help you in composing a paragraph, not orders to follow blindly.

IN SUMMARY

A paragraph

1. is a group of sentences that discuss one main idea, or topic;
2. often states the main idea in a topic sentence, which usually (but not always) comes at the beginning of the paragraph;
3. has unity—all sentences develop the topic idea;
4. has coherence—all the ideas are logically related and connected;
5. generally includes at least three sentences, but often many more;
6. begins with the first line indented; and
7. requires that each sentence follow directly after the previous sentence, not on a separate line.

A topic sentence

1. is usually the most general statement in the paragraph, and the remaining sentences develop that statement specifically;
2. usually comes at the beginning of the paragraph, but can appear after an introductory statement or even at the end of the paragraph;
3. can be implied (omitted from the paragraph);
4. should make a point about the subject of the paragraph, not simply announce the subject;
5. should express an attitude toward the subject;
6. should be limited—made neither too general nor too specific; and
7. should often contain a phrase to guide readers in predicting and understanding the main ideas of the paragraph.

 10   Proofreading and Polishing Your Paragraph

After completing the revision, edit the paragraph, checking for correct spelling and punctuation, complete sentences, and clarity of ideas. Then make a clean copy of the paragraph and proofread it carefully for errors.

SUGGESTED TOPICS FOR WRITING

Assume you are writing for a magazine published by students at your college. Compose an entertaining paragraph about a subject from the following list. Include a topic sentence and at least three—but, if possible, even more—sentences that develop it. Limit the paragraph to the topic idea and unify the paragraph around it.

1. a description of the dog in the photograph
2. a description of an interesting public place (a park with many people, a room in an art museum, an outdoor café, a beach, a skating rink, etc.)
3. a description of a rainstorm or a sunset
4. a description of a favorite place away from home
5. a description of your family at the dinner table
6. a description of an old building or part of the building

3

Developing a Paragraph Through Explanations, Examples, and Details

You know that a paragraph discusses one central idea or point. The previous chapter examined drafting, limiting, and unifying paragraphs around topic sentences that state the point. In this chapter we examine how to develop the point further:

- ✏ by drafting and organizing the specific statements that explain and illustrate the point;
- ✏ by providing examples and details from your own experience; and
- ✏ by using facts and figures from outside sources.

EXPLANATIONS, EXAMPLES, AND DETAILS DEFINED

Remember that writing is communicating your ideas to other people. Those ideas must be clear; they must be understandable. You must explain what you mean, illustrate it, and examine it in detail. An *explanation* clarifies a general statement by discussing the reasoning behind it. An *example* illustrates the idea; it provides a specific "for instance" that makes the general statement easier to visualize or understand. And *details,* which come from a French word that means "to cut something into pieces," quite literally show readers the small parts included within the larger idea.

Here's how explanations, examples, and details make ideas more understandable. Suppose you were composing a publicity brochure for a nearby local zoo and began with this topic sentence:

> If you want to see many fascinating and unusual animals from all over the world, come visit the Wilson Zoo.

The topic sentence contains a number of generalizations that readers would expect you to explain and illustrate:

> The zoo is home to over 500 different species of animals of all sizes and shapes, **ranging from elephants, hippopotamuses, and water buffaloes to chipmunks and woodpeckers.** *Of course you'll want to see the **lions and tigers** in the Feline House, but*

specific details

examples

specific example

*while you're **there**, take a look at their less commonly known relatives such as the **margays.***

The last specific example begs for even more specific explanation, since most readers won't know what margays are (in fact, neither would you if you hadn't visited the zoo and taken notes):

These spotted felines, which range from Argentina up through Central America and into the southern tip of Texas, are about the size of ordinary house cats but have enormous ears and tails as long as their bodies. That resemblance to domestic animals certainly disappears when they rip apart raw meat at feeding time, so come to the Wild Cat House and witness the show.

You then might describe two or three other unusual animals in the remainder of the brochure—perhaps a *tapir,* an *emu,* and a *gnu.* (Do these examples attract your interest? Good! Then visit a zoo—or at least a dictionary—and find out more about them.)

EXAMINING THE REASONS FOR SPECIFIC DEVELOPMENT

Some beginning writers struggle to think of specifics. They compose generalizations—the bones of a paragraph—but leave the specific meat off the bones. However, they can learn to flesh out a paragraph by anticipating the questions that readers would ask. The following paragraph, for example, is weak in specific development:

A French king once commanded an abbot to invent a ridiculous musical instrument for the amusement of his guests. After thinking about the possibilities for a while, the abbot then came up with an ingenious solution: an apparatus for making hogs sing. The invention worked, and the king's friends were greatly entertained.

The idea of the paragraph is interesting enough, but it raises many questions that need answers. Let's examine these questions.

Developing for Clarity

The writer of the paragraph know what he means, but he can't be sure his readers will. He must anticipate and try to clear up possible misunderstandings. After reading the previous sample paragraph, someone might justifiably ask: Which French king was it? Which abbot did he ask? When did he ask him? Who were the king's guests? What kind of apparatus did the abbot invent, and how did it make the hogs sing? Explanations, specific details, and examples can answer these questions.

Developing for Interest

The sample paragraph is limp and lifeless; it doesn't motivate readers to care about the subject. The writer must therefore enliven the discussion. A description of how the pigs sang is certainly a good possibility.

Developing for Proof

The writer of the paragraph also offers opinions but no evidence to back them up. He claims the abbot's solution to the problem was "ingenious" and that the guests were "greatly entertained," but doesn't prove either claim. Another version of the paragraph, this time with enough explanation, details, and examples, makes it more informative, interesting, and convincing.

> Around the year 1450, King Louis XI of France commanded an abbot from the monastery of Baigne to invent a ridiculous musical instrument for the amusement of the king's courtiers—noble men and women—at a party. After thinking about the possibilities for a while, the abbot came up with an ingenious solution: an apparatus for making hogs sing. He gathered a herd of hogs, ranging from nursing piglets to full-grown swine. He lined them up under a velvet tent with low-voiced porkers on the left, middle-range sows in the middle, and soprano piglets on the right. Then the abbot constructed a modified organ keyboard and attached the keys to a complicated device that ended with a series of small spikes, one poised over the rump of each pig. At the party, the abbot played his keyboard, causing the spikes to prick the pigs in sequence. The pigs naturally let out piercing squeals, each in its own particular voice range. The tunes were actually recognizable, and the courtiers applauded and congratulated the king on his fine entertainment.

Although this second version is much longer than the first, don't draw the wrong conclusion. The paragraph isn't better because it contains more words. It is better because of its lively and clear details and examples.

Thus, no matter what your purpose—to inform, to persuade, or simply to entertain—you can generate specifics by anticipating the questions and reactions of your readers. Of course, you aren't a lawyer defending each statement you make. If you care about your ideas and want them to be taken seriously, however, support your generalizations with specifics.

✍   **1**   **Predicting the Development of Individual Paragraphs**

Consider paragraph development from the reader's viewpoint. Read each of the following topic sentences and then list two or more questions you want the rest of the paragraph to answer for you. (This exercise could be done collaboratively.)

1. During the Civil War, the commanding generals of the Union army and the Confederate army differed in many ways, but they also had some surprising traits in common. *Who were the commanding generals? How were they different? What did they have in common?*

2. Studying for a test involves far more than simply reading your notes. _____

   _____

   _____

3. The space shuttle is more than a rocket ship; it is a temporary house for seven astronauts. _____

   _____

   _____

4. Recent advances in medicine have greatly altered traditional ideas about conceiving children, becoming biological parents, and delivering babies. ____

_____

_____

GENERATING EXPLANATIONS, EXAMPLES, AND DETAILS

You will develop a paragraph most easily when you feel comfortable with both your subject matter and your writing voice. Choose a subject you know well, and then explore your ideas freely—without stopping to ponder each word. Begin with free writing, brainstorming, or clustering so one fact suggests another, and soon you will fill up a page with details. Suppose, for example, that you were writing about a college student's lifestyle for a magazine such as *Seventeen, Redbook,* or *Esquire.* Part of the article might describe your bed in your room at home or in a dormitory. Look at the bed and jot down your first reaction:

> *It's a mess.*

This preliminary topic sentence (you will draft a more complete and formal one later) will guide you in explaining and illustrating that reaction. Don't generalize as you record the details; write down exactly what you see, as in this brainstorming list:

> *it's unmade, dirty sheets, covered with school books, clothes, and a banana peel in a rolled-up napkin*

You can use some of this material and discard the other parts later, but you now have a good starting point for a well-developed paragraph. While shaping and reshaping the paragraph in later drafts, you might notice or think of even more details to include—especially if you consider what your readers should visualize about your bed and what you haven't told them yet. Here are some other specifics:

> *it's old (I've had it since I was three), light brown wooden headboard, spongy mattress, a red-and-white checked spread that never gets put on, a gray blanket, clothes on the bed: pair of jeans, blue shirt, red sweater*

Part of your brainstorming should also search for explanations of *why* the bed is such a mess:

> *I eat on the bed and leave food and dishes on it.*
> *I dump my clothes on the bed.*
> *I spread out my books and papers on it to study.*

A later draft might then combine explanations with details that illustrate them.

My bed serves as a makeshift dining room table. **For example,** *there is a banana peel in a rolled-up napkin on top of the bed now, left over from a snack I had earlier.*

How many explanations and examples should you include? Although there are no hard-and-fast rules, the answer depends on four related issues:

1. *How complicated is your subject?* The more complicated, the more you must explain and illustrate.
2. *What don't your readers know about the subject?* The less they know, the more you must say.
3. *How persuasive or entertaining should you be?* The more of either, the more you probably must say.
4. *How much (or little) space have you been given to explain your point?* In this case, the less space you have, the less you can say.

Keep these issues in mind as guidelines, but use your own good judgment. Let them aid you, but don't let them lock you in a mental cage.

EXPLORING TWO WAYS OF FITTING THE SUPPORTING MATERIALS TO THE TOPIC SENTENCE

As you learned in Chapter 2, use the method of composing that feels most comfortable. You may either draft the topic sentence first and then generate the specifics or draft the specifics first and then generate a topic sentence. Here's how the paragraph about the bed might develop in either case.

Moving from Topic Sentence to Supporting Materials

One way to proceed to the next step in the composing process is to revise your initial reaction ("It's a mess") into a more complete topic sentence:

> *My bed, like the beds of so many college students my age, is a mess.*

Then you can support the topic sentence with specific statements based on the brainstorming list you had prepared. Here, for example, is a first draft of supporting details that explain and illustrate your point:

It's always unmade, and the sheets are usually dirty. The faded red-and-white checked bedspread is usually on the floor. And the bed is covered with a variety of objects. Right now, there are the clothes I've worn and then taken off—such as the jeans, blue shirt, and red sweater. There is a banana peel in a rolled-up napkin on top of my pillow right now. And there are my school books and papers.

If some details from the list don't fit, don't use them:

it's old (I've had it since I was three), light brown wooden head-board, spongy mattress

2 Exploring Ideas for Your Paragraph

Assume you are composing a letter to a friend in which you describe the terrible state of the building in the picture. Record your initial reaction to the picture as a preliminary topic sentence. Then list the details you observe that explain or illustrate your reaction.

Moving from Supporting Materials to the Topic Sentence

Another way to proceed with the next step is by drafting specific statements based on the list first, and then stating the general idea that emerges from them later. This approach is often rather untidy (you may cross out sentences and add others above the lines or in the margins of the paper), but many writers feel most comfortable exploring specific ideas before drafting generalizations. Either of these two approaches leads to further revisions of the paragraph, in which you reorganize the details, explain more ideas, and adjust the topic sentence to help your readers predict the content of the paragraph. Here is a final draft of the paragraph about the bed, unified around such a topic sentence.

My bed, like the beds of so many college students my age, is a mess because it serves as my temporary clothes closet, informal dining room, and study area. It is always unmade, and the sheets are usually dirty. The faded red-and-white-checked bedspread lies on the floor and hasn't been put on the bed since my grandmother came to visit last fall. Instead, the bed is covered with a variety of objects reflecting the various roles it plays. As my temporary closet, it holds the clothes I have taken off after returning from school or work. At the moment, for example, some jeans, a blue shirt, and a red crew-neck sweater lie at the foot of the bed. As a makeshift dining room table, it holds the remains of whatever snacks I have eaten as I read, studied, or listened to music. Right now, for example, a banana peel in a rolled-up napkin rests on top of my pillow. And as my study area, it holds the books and papers I have used to complete my homework assignments. Of course, the top of the bed isn't messy all the time. I must remove some of this junk before I go to sleep.

3   Generating a Topic Sentence from Specifics

Assume you are composing a caption to be placed next to the following picture at the local art gallery; your purpose is to help viewers understand the message the artist was communicating symbolically. Begin by listing as many details as you can about the picture; you needn't compose complete sentences. Then look over these details and see if some or most of them lead you to a conclusion about the picture. State that conclusion as a preliminary topic sentence. Finally, return to the list, putting a check mark next to the details you would use in a paragraph developing that topic idea.

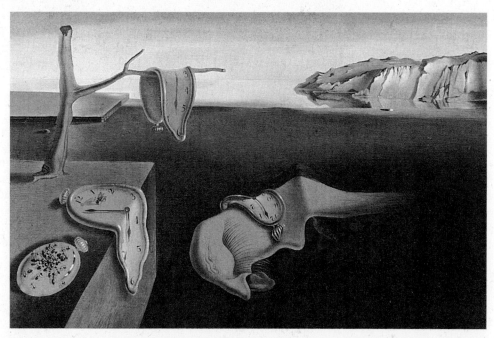

The persistence of memory (1931), by Salvador Dali. Collection, The Museum of Modern Art, New York.

4   Generating Specifics from a Topic Sentence

Assume you are composing a note to prepare a friend for what he or she will encounter when visiting your home. Begin by drafting a preliminary topic sentence for each of the following subjects to guide you in listing supporting explanations and examples. You need not write this list in complete sentences.

Subject A.   the kitchen table

Topic Sentence: _Our kitchen table after lunch is usually a disaster. 1. half-eaten_ _food 2. example: my son's plate with the peanut butter and jelly sandwich sliced_ _in fours, only one side of which has been nibbled at 3. example: my daughter's_ _plate with 3/4 of the hot dog bun left, dripping mustard 4. spilled drinks_ _5. examples: a small puddle of juice next to my son's orange juice cup, and the_ _ring of apple juice left by my daughter's cup 6. wrappers, containers, and garbage_ _7. examples: ice-cream bar wrappers and leaky push-up containers on the plates,_ _peach pits, banana peels, and empty yogurt container in front of my place_

Subject B.   a possible guest room

Topic Sentence: You should probably stay in _____

because _____

_____

_____

_____

_____

Subject C.   your house or apartment building

Topic Sentence: The _____ looks (seems, feels, is)

_____

_____

_____

_____

_____

_____

Subject D.   a place to visit while in town

Topic Sentence: A (or The) _____ is interesting (fun,

 exciting, beautiful) because _____

_____

_____

_____

_____

_____

_____

✏ 5 **Composing a Draft**

Compose a first draft of a paragraph based on one of the topic sentences and list of supporting materials from Exercises 2, 3, or 4. Begin the paragraph with the topic sentence, but expect to revise the topic sentence later while adding, deleting, or reorganizing supporting information.

✏ 6 **Analyzing and Revising Your Draft**

Read the paragraph you drafted in Exercise 5 and respond to each of the following questions. Use the responses as guidelines for revising the paragraph, and then do the revision. (This exercise could be done collaboratively, with each person reading his or her paper aloud twice and the group responding to the questions.)

Revision Guidelines

1. Is the topic sentence clear? _____ Does it make a point? _____

   If it is not clear or makes no point, how should it be revised? _____

   _____

   _____

2. Is the purpose of the paragraph clear? _____ Does the paragraph

   address the interests and needs of its audience? _____ If not, what should

   be added, eliminated, or revised? _____

   _____

   _____

3. Does the paragraph explain its main ideas fully? _____ If not, what

   more could be explained? _____

   _____

4. Does the paragraph provide enough examples of its main ideas? _____

   If not, what other examples could be included? _____

   _____

5. Is the paragraph well unified? (That is, do all the explanations and examples

   develop the topic sentence?) _____ If not, which explanations or

   examples should be omitted, or where should the connections between ideas be

   clarified? _____

   _____

6. What was the greatest problem in composing the paragraph? (Ignore this ques-

   tion if the writer experienced no significant problems.) _____

_____

_____

If the problem was not resolved, what should be done? _____

_____

_____

_____

✍ 7   **Proofreading and Polishing Your Paragraph**

After completing the revision, edit the paragraph, checking for correct spelling and punctuation, complete sentences, and clarity of ideas. Then make a clean copy of the paragraph and proofread it carefully for errors.

EMPLOYING OUTSIDE FACTS AND FIGURES

Many of the details and examples in the sample paragraphs in this and earlier chapters are specific *statements of fact*—that is, they are statements that can be proven. Facts often come from personal observations, but a few, such as those in the paragraph on singing hogs, come from outside sources such as books, magazines, and pamphlets. Some sample paragraphs you have read also include *figures*—numbers and statistics—that can be especially persuasive because they sound scientific and authoritative. Notice how the figures in the following paragraph dramatically support the point of the topic sentence:

❏ *There are more insects in the world than people.* More than 80 percent of the animals in the world are insects. The current population of the world is over five billion (5,000,000,000) people. Yet, in one year a single cabbage aphid can produce 16 full generations of offspring—over 1,560,000,000,000,000,000,000,000 little bugs—to easily surpass that total. While a queen termite may live only a few weeks, it lays one egg every two seconds, 24 hours a day during her lifetime—that is, over 600,000 eggs. Other insects produce similar numbers of descendants, and only the opposing forces in the ecology—disease, predators, and the like—keep these crawling, flying, stinging, and biting creatures from overrunning the planet.

Although outside facts and figures can be valuable tools, remember that your papers should be based primarily on your own ideas and written in your own words, even when you borrow some information. Therefore, keep these guidelines in mind:

◆ *Know your stuff.* Write about a subject with which you are familiar so you will be able to judge the accuracy of outside facts (and be more comfortable writing about them).

◆ *Be in control of the material; don't let it control you.* Write about your ideas and include only a small amount of information from outside sources, which you state in your own words. Otherwise, you will end up rewriting what someone else said—or, worse yet, copying another author's words.

◆ *Acknowledge your sources; tell where you found the information.* That is not only a courtesy you owe the original author but is also required by the copyright laws. You don't have to use footnotes if you mention the author and title of the work somewhere. (For example, to see a list of sources for many of the model paragraphs in this book, look at the acknowledgments on the copyright page.)

Composing Based on Outside Sources

Compose a paragraph for an article in *National Geographic,* based on some—but not all—of the facts and figures supplied here. (You might base it only on those about the elephant's trunk or the comparative sizes of elephants, but these aren't the only possibilities.) Provide your own topic sentence that unifies the information; for example, "The elephant's trunk is a very unusual object." Again, arrange the information logically and compose complete sentences. Also, read through the material several times before you begin composing. Then revise, polish, and proofread the paragraph.

1. locale: Africa and Asia
2. size: African elephant generally bigger than Asian elephant
3. tusks: rare in female Asian elephants
4. ears: large on African elephant; small on Asian elephant
5. tusks: large on African elephant
6. skin: darker on African elephant
7. trunk: more wrinkled on African elephant
8. trunk: end functions almost like fingers; is very sensitive
9. height: about 11 feet tall at shoulder of average African male
10. weight: as much as 14,000 pounds with average African male
11. trunk: as much as 6 feet long; weight as much as 300 pounds
12. use of trunk: to carry food and water to mouth, to take a shower, to measure temperature, to feel objects, to fight, and to show affection
13. tusks: ivory
14. trunk: can grasp peanut, carry a 650-pound log, or drag two tons
15. tusks: used for fighting, digging, and carrying objects

IN SUMMARY

A paragraph can be specifically developed by

1. **explanations of the main idea;**
2. **examples and details, which illustrate important ideas; and**
3. **facts and figures, which support or prove ideas.**

SUGGESTED TOPICS FOR WRITING

The best subjects are those you know well because you have experienced them firsthand. However, the following list may suggest some topics to choose. In each paragraph you compose, include a topic sentence and supporting details and examples. Include facts and figures taken from outside sources when necessary. Assume you are composing a caption to be placed next to an exhibit in an art or science museum. Your purpose is to interpret the exhibit or tell visitors something interesting about it. Provide a photograph of your subject along with your paragraph if possible.

Describe:

1. the room in the photograph

2. a painting or piece of sculpture
3. an unusual object or exhibit at a science museum
4. an old movie poster
5. a valuable or unusual baseball card
6. an unusual postage stamp
7. an unusual coin
8. any other unusual object you have collected

4

Achieving Coherence

Previous chapters have shown how a well-developed and unified paragraph creates interest, clarity, and persuasive power for readers. This chapter demonstrates how *coherence*—the establishment of clear links between ideas—further strengthens a paragraph. The chapter helps you explore a number of ways of achieving coherence:

- *parallelism* (the repetition of sentence structures);
- the use of *pronouns;*
- the *repetition* of key words and terms;
- the use of *synonyms and other substitutes* for those key words or terms; and
- *transitional words and phrases.*

COHERENCE DEFINED

Remember that reading is an active process. With your topic sentences and unified paragraphs as a guide, readers predict what they will find as they travel along the journey of your ideas. Nevertheless, topic sentences and paragraph unity are not enough. A well-written paragraph must also *cohere*—literally hold together—so one idea is linked to the next. Conversely, a paragraph whose ideas are not clearly linked is said to be *incoherent.*

Coherence is partly automatic and partly planned. During the invention stage, you explore your ideas by selecting some, discarding others, and organizing what remains. Sometimes the ideas emerge easily, and the final draft holds together without much further change. Other times you must write and rewrite, organize and reorganize, and add and remove words until the paragraph takes on a logical form. In any case, coherence involves many elements: *sentence structure, consistency in word choice,* and *transitional expressions.* One final element, paragraph organization, is too complex to discuss here, so we examine it in Chapters 5 through 10.

ESTABLISHING COHERENCE THROUGH *PARALLELISM,* OR REPEATED SENTENCE STRUCTURES

One way to achieve coherence is through *parallelism*—that is, the repetition of sentence structures. Parallelism (also called *parallel construction*) signals to readers that ideas are related and of equal importance.* See, for example, how parallelism helps you recognize the supporting details of the topic sentence in the following paragraph:

*For a more extensive discussion of, and practice with, parallelism, see Chapter 12

topic sentence ❑ *Contrary to the popular belief that the American flag has always inspired patriotism, the existence of many flag designs demonstrates the casual attitude people had toward the flag at first.* Some stars came with five points. Some stars came with six. Some stars came in white. Some came in silver.

The repeated pattern of *Some stars* (or just *Some*) + the past tense verb *came* shows the equality of the ideas. You can quickly recognize this pattern and expect its repetition.

Parallelism occurs not only between sentences but within them as well:

> Samuel Adams gained fame as an inspirational *writer, speaker, and leader* during the American Revolution. (nouns linked in parallel construction)
>
> His personal life was less glamorous. He *squandered* his inheritance, *ruined* his father's brewery, and *failed* as a tax collector. (past tense verbs linked in parallel construction)
>
> This hot-headed member of the famous Adams family was far better at *brewing* rebellion than *brewing* beer. (-*ing* words linked—and repeated to create a surprising contrast)
>
> Adams signed the Declaration of Independence *during the war,* held a variety of state offices *after the war,* and then disappeared from the national scene *afterwards.* (repeated—and contrasted—time expressions at the end of phrases)

These repeated structures help you perceive and understand the relationships between complex ideas.

✍ 1   Identifying Parallel Structures

Underline the parallel structures between and within sentences in the following paragraphs. (This exercise could be done collaboratively.)

It's a Grand Old Flag—Sort of

Paragraph A.   We salute our flag, fly it proudly, and sing to it at the beginning of sports events. It's an almost sacred symbol of patriotism today, but it was far from sacred to our country's first citizens. In fact, many Americans—including top government officials—didn't know what it looked like. More than a year after its official adoption by Congress, Benjamin Franklin and John Adams, in a joint letter to the king of Naples, said it "consists of 13 stripes, alternately red, white, and blue."

Paragraph B.   These original Americans may be forgiven for their ignorance, for they seldom had the chance to see the flag. It didn't fly from buildings, wasn't put in the schools, wasn't reproduced in the newspapers, and didn't appear in any pictures painted at that time. Wilbur Zelinsky, reporting on a search of major catalogs of art from the Revolutionary War, says he could not find a single depiction of the American flag.

Paragraph C.   The mistaken idea that Old Glory appeared everywhere in the Revolution is because it appears everywhere in the paintings of the Revolution done a century later. But the fact is, not a single land battle of the Revolutionary War was fought under the Stars and Stripes. There was no American flag at Bunker Hill, no flag at Trenton, and no flag even at Yorktown. In fact, American soldiers first fought under Old Glory during the Mexican-American War—75 years later. Even then the use of the flag in battle was limited. The marines did not adopt the flag until 1876; the U.S. Cavalry did not adopt it until 1887. Forget those pictures of George Custer and the Stars and Stripes during his famous last stand. His men never carried that flag.

Paragraph D.   Soldiers did not go flagless, of course. They carried battle flags to keep up their spirits. But nobody cares about those flags. What we want is Washington crossing the Delaware with the Stars and Stripes. And what we want was exactly what the artists in the nineteenth century gave us, for pictures that include American flags have always sold well.

Composing Parallel Structures

Composing parallel constructions isn't difficult. If you feel confident in your ideas and writing voice, parallelism will flow naturally from your pen, pencil, typewriter, or word processor. You need only sharpen and polish these parallel elements during revisions. However, if you don't find any such elements, you might look for equal ideas to rewrite in repeated sentence structures. For example, suppose that you compose a first draft of a paragraph with this topic sentence:

> There wasn't much to do on Saturday night in my hometown, so almost everyone ended up in the town square.

And, in the next sentence, you provide supporting detail about one group of people and their activities in the square:

> The **bikers were there** in their black leather jackets, **looking** tough and menacing as they circled around the fountain in the center of the square.

As you revise (or even as you continue to compose the first draft), you can attempt to repeat this sentence pattern to describe additional groups and their activities:

> The **punks were there, cruising** the square in their convertibles with radios blasting away and horns honking at the people who sat around on the steps of town hall, sat on the grass around the fountain, or stood on the sidewalks in groups. **The preppies were there, discussing** Friday night's high school basketball or football game, who was dating whom, or where everyone would meet for hamburgers or pizza and beer later in the evening. **The girls were there, gathering** in groups or **driving** their parents'

cars. The girls were the main reason that boys hung around.
Eventually, at least some of the girls would pair up with boys, and
by 2:00 A.M. the square would be almost empty.

✍   **2   Working with Parallel Structures**

Complete each of the following paragraphs by drafting at least three more sentences
of supporting detail. Begin by reading the sentences already supplied and finding a
pattern you expect to be repeated. Then repeat that pattern in the sentences you
write.

1. *My English classroom is typical of the rooms in the school.* There are win-
    dows along the left wall. There is a row of coat hooks on the right wall. *There is*
    a blackboard on the front wall. There is a clock above the blackboard. There is
    a teacher's desk in front of the blackboard. There are movable student desks
    arranged in rows in the middle of the room. And there are 25 brilliant stu-
    dents sitting at those desks, eagerly awaiting the wise pronouncements of
    our teacher.

2. *During the summer months, I try to be outdoors as much as I can.* I walk
    along the river or pedal down the bike paths. _____

    _____

    _____

3. *My morning routine is about the same each day.* I wake up slowly, dragging
    my reluctant body out of bed. _____

    _____

    _____

4. *The behavior of* _____ *is full of contradictions.* (Establish
    your own pattern and repeat it.)_____

    _____

    _____

✍   **3   Planning and Composing a First Draft**

Assume you are composing a paragraph to appear in an article in *Reader's Digest*
about life in various cities and towns in the United States or other countries. Begin by
brainstorming, clustering, or free writing about an activity that occurred in the place
where you grew up. For example, you could discuss what people did on weekends,
at night, during particular seasons, or on special occasions such as weddings or festi-
vals. Then complete a first draft of the paragraph. Draft a preliminary topic sentence
that states the point, such as, "Friday night high school football games were the most
important event in my hometown," or "On Saturdays during the summer, my friends
and I usually ended up at the beach for tanning, loafing, people watching, or even
swimming." Develop the topic sentence through specific details arranged in parallel
structure. Revise the first draft to strengthen or add parallelism to achieve coherence.

ESTABLISHING COHERENCE THROUGH PRONOUNS, REPEATED KEY WORDS, OR SYNONYMS AND SUBSTITUTIONS

Repeating sentence structures isn't the only way to achieve coherence among ideas. You can also make ideas cohere by carefully using *pronouns, repeated key words,* or *synonyms and substitutions for words.* All these methods relate ideas to ones you have mentioned earlier in your piece of writing.

Using Pronouns

Pronouns refer to their *antecedents*—previously mentioned words or phrases that the pronouns replace. Thus, if pronouns are used properly, the relationship between pronoun and antecedent establishes coherence.* For example, in the model paragraph you read earlier, the pronoun *their* refers to the *punks,* and the pronoun *who* refers to *people,* allowing readers to identify the cast of characters:

> The **punks** were there, cruising the square in **their** convertibles with radios blasting away horns honking at the **people who** lounged on the grass. . . .

However, notice the problem with *they*, which could refer to any of three antecedents.

> The **girls** were there, gathering in **groups** or driving their parents' **cars. They** were the main reason that boys hung around.

The passage will be clearer if a repeated noun replaces the pronoun:

> The **girls** were the main reason that boys hung around.

4   Achieving Pronoun-Antecedent Agreement

Improve the coherence in the following passage by circling the antecedent of each missing pronoun, and then supplying a pronoun that agrees with its antecedent.

Oh, Say: Was the Flag Still There?

❏   (1) The popularity of the song "The Star-Spangled Banner"—if the song can still be said to be popular—is due as much to the unusual circumstances under

which _____*it*_____ was written as to the appeal of its lyrics. (2) Probably only

one person in a hundred can recite _____ , but almost everybody remembers how the words came to be composed. (3) Francis Scott Key actually was fortunate enough to watch the bombardment of Fort McHenry (which guarded Baltimore) in the War of 1812, and Key actually waited through the night to see if "our flag was still there."
    (4) There are several myths about the song itself. (5) _____ did not

immediately become popular; and _____ did not become the national anthem until 1931. (6) Many people know that the tune came from an old

English drinking song, but _____ don't realize that the English song celebrated not only wine but love. (7) If Key ever felt embarrassed about

_____ origins, he never said so.

*For more discussion of, and practice with, pronouns and antecedents, see Chapter 23.

Repeating Key Terms

Just as improperly used pronouns cause problems with clarity, pronouns used too often cause monotony. Therefore, another way to achieve coherence is to *repeat key words or terms*. Notice, for example, how repeated terms (boldfaced in the first use, then italicized) tie ideas together in the following paragraph:

Where Was That Flag?

❑   (1) Did **the flag** that Francis Scott Key saw at "dawn's early light" during the War of 1812 fly through the night? (2) As anyone can testify who has seen *the actual flag*, which is on display at the Smithsonian Institute in Washington, it is huge: 30 feet by 42 feet. (3) The stars alone measure two feet across from point to point. (4) For the banner to have survived **the night** the fort was under attack—a stormy, rainy, windy *night*—is almost unbelievable. (5) If there was a flag **on the pole** in the **morning,** as there undoubtedly was, it was probably hoisted up *the pole* that *morning*. (6) And that is precisely what an eyewitness says happened. (7) According to the testimony of Midshipman Robert J. Barrett, as the British fleet sailed away after the battle, the Americans "hoisted a most superb and splendid ensign on their battery." (8) If there was a banner that flew all night, it would have to have been the fort's so-called **storm flag,** a small *flag* designed expressly for bad weather. (9) But how Key could have seen it is a mystery. (10) He was eight miles away—possibly near enough to see the big flag, but not the smaller one.

Of course, key terms repeated too often can be as monotonous as repeated pronouns. Use good judgment, therefore, and (as you will see shortly) consider substituting synonyms for key words as an alternative.

✍ **5   Editing for Coherence**

The following passage is incoherent in places because of carelessly used pronouns. Replace the italicized pronouns with repeated key terms.

The Beginnings of the Revolutionary War

❑   (1) The colonists hated the taxes Britain imposed on them against their will, and *it* __that hatred__ eventually led to the Revolutionary War. (2) "Taxation without representation is tyranny," they protested when the British Parliament passed the Stamp Act in 1765. (3) Then two years later, *they* _____ created the Townshend Acts, which imposed further taxes on key imports—especially tea. (4) Even when *they* _____ were collected, British tea was relatively cheap. (5) But the colonists opposed *them* _____ on principle, and some angry residents of Massachusetts dumped 342 cases of *it* _____ into Boston harbor in 1773—an act of rebellion they called the Boston Tea Party. (6) The British Parliament promptly responded to *it* _____ by closing the port of Boston. (7) When further protests and punishments in 1775 grew into armed conflict at Lexington, Concord, and Bunker Hill, *they* _____ chose "liberty or death" rather than "slavery" as part of the British Empire. (8) Therefore, armed with high principles and deadly rifles, *they* _____ banned together to secure their rights in the modern world's first revolutionary war against a mother country.

Employing Synonyms and Substitutions

Too much repetition can become boring, so you may wish to replace some key terms with synonyms or substitutions. A *synonym* is a word with the same meaning as another. "Physician" is a synonym for "doctor." "Courage," "boldness," "fearlessness," and even "valor" are synonyms for "bravery." A *substitute word or phrase,* while not a synonym, clearly represents an earlier idea. For example, in the following paragraph, synonyms and substitutions (shown in italic) refer to many key terms (shown in bold type):

> **George Washington** was an extremely precise man, and his **handwritten will**—*composed* without legal assistance—demonstrated this trait with an almost maddening neatness. *The former first president penned* it on 15 sheets of personal watermarked **parchment.** He filled both sides, numbered and signed each one, and with an apparent concern for the *document's* artistic appeal, **engineered** every line to be of precisely the same length. He *employed* dashes to extend short lines, and hyphens to break a long line's last word irrespective of proper syllabication. *The text* looks computer set, with perfectly aligned margins.

A *thesaurus* (a dictionary of synonyms) is an excellent reference work for finding word substitutions. Many computer word processing programs include on-line thesauruses as well. But choose synonyms wisely; be sure you fully understand their meanings. A misused synonym causes confusion, not coherence—and may even provoke laughter from readers at your expense.

6   Achieving Coherence Through Use of Synonyms and Substitutions

Increase the coherence of the following passage by filling in appropriate synonyms or substitutions for the italicized words.

The Man Behind the Legends of George Washington

❏   (1) Everyone knows that *George Washington* chopped down a cherry tree when _____the young man_____ was only 6 years old. (2) But most Americans don't know that this story of ____the future president's____ honesty is the product of the lively imagination of Mason Locke "Parson" Weems (1760–1825).

(3) The cherry tree *tale* is only one of the _____ in Weems's biography, *Life of George Washington; with Curious Anecdotes, Equally Honorable to Himself; and Exemplary to His Young Countrymen.*

(4) This _____ is a largely fictional—or at least largely exaggerated—account of Washington's life and times. (5) *Weems* had a talent for exaggeration, for _____ knew what the reading public loved and would buy. (6) Weems wasn't necessarily a liar; he just got naturally carried away with his own *enthusiasm.* (7) As an ordained minister in Maryland, for eight years he exhibited that strong _____ in his sermons. (8) But Weems was dissatisfied with his life, so he took up a new *occupation* as a traveling bookseller for Matthew Carey, a publisher of religious books in Philadelphia. (9) Weems loved his _____ and soon also began to write a number of "improvement *books*" such as the _____ about George Washington. (10) His customers were often shocked by his *outrageous stunts and racy remarks.* (11) His employer, Mr. Carey, never liked such _____, and the two men had constant *feuds* for 30 years. (12) But despite these

_____, Carey would not fire Weems because

_____ was too valuable as a salesperson.

Revising for Coherence

Direct your attention to pronouns and nouns as you revise. If any are unclear or monotonous, replace them with appropriate pronouns, repeated key terms, or synonyms and substitutions. Look again, for example, at part of the model paragraph.

> *The girls were there, gathering in groups or driving their parents' cars. The girls were the main reason that boys hung around. Eventually, at least some of the girls would pair up with boys, and by 2:00 A.M. the square would be almost empty.*

Which *boys* does the passage mean? None have been specifically mentioned earlier—but *punks, cruisers, and preppies* have—so perhaps those terms could be repeated. Furthermore, the word *girls* appears too often, and the phrase "the square would be almost empty" might raise a question of who, in fact, would still be there. Additional pronouns and substitutions would strengthen the passage.

> *The girls were there, gathering in groups or driving their parents' cars. The girls were the main reason that the **punks, the cruisers, and the preppies** hung around. Eventually, at least some of **the members of one sex would pair up with members of the other**, and by 2:00 A.M. the square would be empty of all but **the most dedicated girl- or boy-seekers.***

Thus, consider following this procedure as you revise:

◆ Identify the pronouns and nouns, perhaps by circling or underlining them.
◆ Check the antecedent of each pronoun and, if you find possible confusion, rewrite the sentence, perhaps replacing the pronoun with a repeated key term.
◆ Check for nouns repeated too often and replace one or more with pronouns, synonyms, or substitutions. If you revise by hand instead of on the computer, make your changes above the lines; you needn't rewrite this draft of the paragraph unless it becomes too messy.

✍ 7   Revising Your First Draft

Return to the first draft of the paragraph you wrote in Exercise 3 and revise it so all pronouns clearly refer to their antecedents and nouns are not repeated too often.

ESTABLISHING COHERENCE THROUGH TRANSITIONS

The final method for achieving coherence is supply *transitions,* which establish logical connections among ideas—such as adding ideas together, contrasting ideas, locating ideas in a time or space sequence, or showing one as the cause or result of another. Transitions can be single words, such as *therefore, also, however, later,* or *finally,* or they can be short expressions, such as *in the center, at the top,* or *as a result.* In either of these cases, they cement relationships among ideas. Notice in the following paragraph how transitional expressions (in italics) enumerate the reasons mentioned in the topic sentence and help you identify each one.

The Career of Paul Revere

topic sentence ❏ *Paul Revere is notable for a number of reasons. First,* of course, he is best known from Longfellow's poem about his midnight ride—during which, in 1775, he alerted the American colonists that the British were coming. *Second,* he is well known as a silversmith, the man who founded the company that today makes Revereware pots and pans. *Third,* he is perhaps less well known as a manufacturer of teeth, a manufacturer of munitions, and an artist and en-

transitional expressions graver. *Fourth,* and what is least known about him and most surprising, is that as an artist, he forged other artists' pictures.

In this next passage, you can easily follow the movement of the action because of the transitional expressions of time and location (in italics):

The Origins of Our Nation's Capital

❏ Congress had an important reason for meeting *in June 1783* to decide to relocate the nation's capital from Philadelphia to Washington, D.C. With the War of Independence having just been concluded *in February,* the new nation was flat broke. It had no credit, still lacked a president, and was heavily in debt to soldiers for back pay. As a result, a large and angry mob of unpaid soldiers invaded *Philadelphia on June 20* to demand that they be paid by Congress. It was not the first such violent confrontation. *That day,* though, a number of angry or frightened members of Congress expressed their frustration with such direct threats. *At their meeting in the Old City Hall,* they launched a movement to establish a federal city in an isolated, inconvenient area where lawmakers could conduct the business of government without being bothered by citizens.

The location for the new capital arose as a compromise. New Englanders, led by Alexander Hamilton of New York, wanted a capital in the North. Southerners, represented by Thomas Jefferson of Virginia, argued for a location in the South. *In 1790,* the recently elected president, George Washington, attempted to satisfy both sides by choosing *a site 18 miles up the Potomac River from his home in Mount Vernon—an area then midway between North and South.* No one denied, however, that the 10-mile-square site was a swamp.

These two sample passages employ particular types of transitional expressions— enumerating expressions (in the first passage) and time and place expressions (in the second). However, many paragraphs express a greater variety of relationships among ideas and thus require a broader variety of transitions. Each of the chapters in Unit Two includes a list of transitions appropriate to the method of paragraph development discussed. Meanwhile, the following list of common transitional expressions, arranged according to meaning, may provide a useful reference as you draft and revise.

Transitions Expressing Enumeration (or Counting)

first, second, third, next, then, after that, finally

Transitions Expressing Space Relationships

above, around, behind, below, beneath, beyond, close by, farther away, in front of, in the front (back, rear), in the middle (center), inside, on the inside (outside), nearby, next to, to the left (right), to the north (south), on the right (left, bottom, top), outside, over, under, underneath

Transitions Expressing Time Relationships

In sequence: after, after a while, afterward, and then, an hour (a day, a week) later, eventually, finally, first (second, third), later (on), next, soon, still later, the next day (week, year), tomorrow
Simultaneous or close in time: as, as soon as, at that moment, during, immediately, meanwhile, suddenly, when, while
Previous time: before, earlier, last night (month, year), yesterday
At a stated time: in March, in 1983, on July 8

Transitions Expressing Addition

additionally, also, and, furthermore, in addition, moreover, too

Transitions Expressing a Comparison

in the same way (manner), likewise, similarly

Transitions Expressing a Concession

as you probably know, certainly, naturally, no doubt, of course

Transitions Expressing a Contrast

although, but, even though, however, nevertheless, on the contrary, on the other hand, yet

Transitions Expressing Emphasis

above all, especially, indeed, in fact, in particular, most importantly

Transitions Expressing Illustrations

as an example (illustration), for example (for another example), for instance, in particular, such as

Transitions Expressing Qualification

maybe, perhaps, possibly

Transitions Expressing Reasons

a reason for this is, as, because, because of, for, since

Transitions Expressing a Summary

and so, in other words, in short, in summary, to summarize, to sum up

✍ **8   Adding Transitions**

Read each passage and then list four or five transitions you would expect to find in the remainder of each passage.

Passage A.   The steps involved in registering for classes are rather complicated. First, you must request a packet of materials from the Office of Admissions.

Second, Third, Fourth, Finally

_____

Passage B.   The new auditorium is beautiful and spacious. On the first floor, the seats nearest the stage are covered with a plush red velvet material, and the wide spaces between rows allow ample leg room. The seats farther from the stage are equally plush, but the rows are closer, leaving less room for the legs. _____

_____

_____

Passage C.   Friday was extremely busy for Mrs. Johnson. In the morning, she had
to prepare breakfast for the whole family and get the kids off to school. _____

_____

_____

_____

Passage D.   After playing on the muddy ground and in the wet leaves, the 6-year-
old boy was a mess. First, his shoes were caked with mud. Second, his pants were

ripped and grass stained at the knees. _____

_____

_____

Passage E.   (Write your own topic sentence about the picture here. Then list the
transitions you would most likely need.) _____

_____

_____

_____

_____

✍ **9   Composing a First Draft**

Compose a first draft of a paragraph based on the material from one of the passages from the previous exercise. Be sure to include all (or most) of the transitional expressions you have listed.

Revising for Transitions

Too many transitions in a paragraph may be unnecessary and even annoying, so don't overuse them. If you have composed in a confident, natural voice and carefully organized your early drafts, the relationships between most ideas will be clear. Nevertheless, closely examine those relationships when you revise. You may need to add a few transitions, change some that don't express relationships you intended, and substitute for some transitions you have repeated. Let's return once more to a final revision of the model paragraph, whose word choice has been strengthened (especially its verbs), and whose coherence has been strengthened by adding some short transitional expressions (underlined):

> There wasn't much to do on Saturday night in my hometown, so almost everyone ended up in the town square. The bikers were there in their black leather jackets, looking tough and menacing as they circled around the fountain in the center of the square. The punks were there, _too_, cruising the square in their convertibles with radios blaring and horns blasting at the people who lazed on the steps of town hall, lounged on the grass around the fountain, or congregated on the sidewalks in groups of three, four, or more. The preppies were there _as well_, discussing Friday night's high school basketball or football game, who was dating whom, or where everyone would meet for hamburgers or pizza and beer later in the evening. _And_ the girls were there, congregating in groups or driving their dads' cars. _Naturally_, the girls were the main reason that the punks, the cruisers, and the preppies hung around. At least some members of one sex would _eventually_ pair up with members of the other, and by 2:00 A.M. the square would be empty of all but the most dedicated girl- or boy-seekers.

Revising may appear to be a tedious process of returning to your paper again and again, each time looking for a different problem, but, while you must revise a paper more than once, you don't have to approach revisions mechanically. Address the major issues first: the topic sentence, organization, unity, and development. Then turn your attention to all the matters discussed in this (and in later) chapters. With practice, such checking for multiple concerns will become second nature to you.

IN SUMMARY

> **Coherence can be achieved by**
>
> 1. parallelism, or repeated sentence structures;
> 2. pronouns;
> 3. repeated key terms;
> 4. synonyms and substitutions for key words; and
> 5. transitional expressions.

10   Editing for Transition Use

Insert transitions in the following paragraph so the relationships among ideas are clear.

Betsy Ross: The Designer of the American Flag?

☐   (1) We know that the American flag did not have a single dramatic moment of birth. (2) _____ *In fact* _____ , the star-spangled banner's origin evolved slowly and was shaped by many hands. (3) This evolution _____ raises the question of the involvement of a Philadelphia tailor named Betsy Ross in designing and creating it. (4) According-ing to legend, General Washington came to her shop in June of 1776. (5) They discussed various flag designs until they settled on one she suggested: seven red and six white stripes, and 13 five-pointed white stars arranged in a circle.

(6) _____ the general departed, the seamstress began stitching the American flag.

(7) _____ many historians have several problems with this explanation. (8) First of all, not a single one of the many flags that flew at different times during the Revolutionary War carried the design pro-posed by Betsy Ross. (9) _____ the tale was told by Betsy Ross herself—on her deathbed in 1836, and to an 11-year-old boy,

William J. Canby, who was her grandson. (10) _____ he did not publicly relate this account until 1870 at a meeting of the Pennsylvania Historical Society. (11) It was 34 years after he had heard the story as a boy, and almost 100 years after the events had supposedly occurred.

(12) Historical records verify that George Washington was in Philadelphia in June of 1776. (13) _____ his written records don't mention a meeting with a local seamstress; _____ his diary doesn't reveal any concern about designing an official American flag. (14) In fact, Congress had not yet named a committee to tackle any flag de-sign, nor did Congress even discuss the need to replace the flag in use at that

time. (15) _____ many historians believe that the Betsy Ross story is no more than a legend: an unproved tale handed down from gen-eration to generation.

(16) History and legend, _____ , have a way of blending as time passes. (17) Betsy Ross's deathbed tale has rooted itself in the heart of American folklore. (18) Whether her story is ever definitely proved or disproved, Americans will almost assuredly tell and retell it.

✍ **11   Analyzing and Revising Your Draft**

Respond to the questions on the form here to guide you in revising either (1) the paragraph you drafted in Exercise 3 and revised once in Exercise 7, or (2) the paragraph you drafted in Exercise 9. (This exercise could be done collaboratively, with each person reading his or her paper aloud twice and the group responding to the questions.)

Revision Guidelines

1. What was the goal of the paragraph? _____
   _____
   _____
   Was the goal accomplished? _____ If not, what must be done?
   _____
   _____
   _____

2. Is the topic sentence clear? _____ If not, how should it be
   changed? _____
   _____

3. Is the paragraph developed adequately? _____ If not,
   where could examples or details be added? _____
   _____

4. Is the paragraph fully coherent? _____ If not, what
   changes could be made in pronoun use, repeated key terms, substitutions for key
   terms, parallelism, and transitions? _____
   _____
   _____

✍ **12   Proofreading and Polishing Your Paragraph**

After revising the paragraph based on the Revision Guidelines, proofread the paper for errors and write a clean final copy.

Composing Based on Outside Sources

Assume you are composing part of an informative paper about the early history of the Capitol in Washington, D.C. Using the information supplied, write a coherent paragraph that develops the topic sentence. Organize the material logically before you begin to write. Then draft and revise the paragraph so each sentence relates logically to the ones preceding it.

Information:

1. office buildings quickly erected in capital
2. September 1793, President Washington lays cornerstone for the first U.S. Capitol building
3. planning the Capitol takes many years after Washington announces the site in 1790

4. 1800, government moves headquarters from Philadelphia to Washington
5. Senators and members of Congress call the city a "capital of miserable huts" and a "mud hole"
6. President Washington calls it "city of magnificent distances"
7. August 1814, British invade the city, burning president's mansion, the Capitol, and the Navy arsenal
8. change in attitude toward the new capital results from a national tragedy
9. 1814, Jefferson donates his large book collection to replace contents of the Library of Congress
10. the badly charred wooden planks of the president's mansion are painted bright white, and building called the White House
11. furious, Americans decide to rebuild the nation's capital in more glorious ways

Topic Sentence: The city of Washington, D.C., had a difficult birth and infancy.

SUGGESTED TOPICS FOR WRITING

Assume you are a correspondent for a travel magazine whose audience is interested in learning about unusual places. Write a paragraph on the subjects listed here, including a topic sentence and supporting details. Try to achieve coherence through the repetition of sentence structures, the use of pronouns, the repetition or substitution of key words, and the use of transitional expressions.

1. a description of the scene portrayed in one of the photographs (start the process by composing an initial reaction as the preliminary topic sentence; then brainstorm or cluster details that support your reaction)
2. a description of an unusual exhibit in a museum

3. a description of an unusual place you have seen
4. a description of a town square or local gathering place
5. a description of an important place on campus

Composing Types of Paragraphs

Composing Descriptive Paragraphs

One of the most fundamental ways to develop a paragraph is through *description*, the arrangement of physical details so readers can visualize a thing, place, or person. In this chapter we examine the process of composing a description, as follows:

- gathering information for a description;
- unifying the description around a topic idea;
- organizing the materials using *spatial* organization; and
- drafting and revising the description.

DESCRIPTION DESCRIBED

Good description paints a verbal picture of a person, place, or object so readers may visualize the subject described. However, the picture often extends beyond mere sights to include sounds, smells, and the texture of surfaces. And even when only visual, a description should be in Technicolor, not a black-and-white outline of sizes and shapes. Try to work from firsthand experience, actually observing your subject and taking notes on what you see, hear, feel, smell, or even taste. If you write about something or someone from the past, spend a few moments recalling important details. (Sometimes, closing your eyes helps you concentrate on your memories.) In either case, keep these suggestions in mind during the invention stage of gathering and arranging information:

- Examine your subject with all or most of the five senses and note important details. Write down these details as reminders of your observations.
- Draft a preliminary topic sentence based on your strongest reaction to the subject ("impressive, ugly, exciting, handsome, complex").
- Decide which details will make your description clear as well as support the topic sentence.
- Think about comparisons that might help your readers visualize the subject you are describing.
- Decide on a logical arrangement of the details. (For example, first give the general size and shape of an object and then specifically describe it from top to bottom.)

1 Examining a Descriptive Paragraph

Read the following description of Abraham Lincoln's face, and then answer the questions. (This exercise could be done collaboratively.)

❑   (1) Abraham Lincoln may not have been our most handsome president, but his face was certainly among the most memorable. (2) His dark hair and beard formed a frame around his long, angular face. (3) The wavy hair shot up like lava from a volcano, exposing his deeply lined high forehead, but it did not cover his enormous jutting ears. (4) Lincoln's bushy eyebrows that arched in quarter moons shielded his deep-set, almond-shaped eyes. (5) But his most prominent feature may have been his long, straight nose that widened at the tip and nostrils. (6) To the sides were his high bony cheeks, and midway down the right side was a large bump—probably a birthmark, though not discolored or hairy. (7) The lips of his broad mouth were badly matched: a narrow upper lip and fleshy lower one. (8) Finally, his short and neatly trimmed beard covered his chin but did not extend to a mustache. (9) To many Americans, the face of our sixteenth president is instantly recognizable.

1. What is the topic sentence of the paragraph?
2. What is the purpose of sentence 2?
3. What is the organizing principle of the paragraph?
4. What words or phrases in these sentences help you locate the parts of the face?
5. Are there any comparisons in the description? If so, where do they occur?

COMPOSING A DESCRIPTIVE PARAGRAPH

As with any type of writing, you have choices in how to assemble, draft, revise, and edit the materials for your paragraph. We examine some of those choices next.

Invention: Moving from Topic Sentence to Details

Your first reaction to a place, an object, or a person may suggest a preliminary topic sentence to guide you in selecting supporting details. Suppose, for example, that you have been lucky enough to visit the Grand Canyon on a vacation and, overwhelmed by its size and beauty, you want to describe the canyon in a feature article for the campus newspaper. Begin by drafting a topic sentence that summarizes your strongest impression:

> *On my visit to Arizona, I saw one of the earth's greatest natural wonders, the Grand Canyon.*

Then explore specific details (some of which come from brochures on the canyon) and possible comparisons, perhaps in a brainstorming list:

> *incredible beauty—many colors of rock all along its sides*
> *a massive hole in the ground*
> *brochure: over 270 miles long, width varies from 4 to 18 miles,*
> *   and over a mile deep in places (over 100 miles of canyon*
> *   inside Grand Canyon National Park)*

comparison

Colorado River runs along the bottom, **looks like a snake from above,** *but sounds noisy*

from brochure: the powerful currents of river carved out much of the canyon

canyon located in northwestern Arizona

from brochure: canyon 2,000 million years old, with fossils in the rock of prehistoric man, dinosaurs, and earliest forms of plant and animal life

trip down some of the trails of canyon on mules

sides of the canyon have cliffs, ridges, hills, and even valleys

at the bottom, huge towers of rock carved out by the river, **look**

comparison **like Aztec temples**

from the top, the layers of rock are sand colored, then red, then lavender, then blue-brown, then bright red, then black

colors change in the light—very red at noon, but dark red and brown at sunset

That is quite a list, and it doesn't include information about your muleback ride down into the canyon. But you need to narrow the topic, so you probably shouldn't expand the list further.

Organize the details next, including only those that develop the point of the topic sentence. The first ones should offer general information, including dimensions of the canyon; the later ones should focus more narrowly on the colors and shapes of the canyon and on the Colorado River, perhaps arranged from top to bottom. An informal outline might look like this:

I. *General Information*
   Canyon located in northwestern Arizona
   a massive hole in the ground
   brochure: over 270 miles long, width varies from 4 to 18 miles, and over a mile deep in places (over 100 miles of canyon inside Grand Canyon National Park)
   from brochure: canyon 2,000 million years old, with fossils in the rock of prehistoric man, dinosaurs, and the earliest forms of plant and animal life

II. *Specific Details*
   incredible beauty—many colors of rock all along its sides
   from the top, *the layers of rock are sand colored, then red, then lavender, then blue-brown, then bright red, then black*
   colors change in the light—very red at noon, but dark red, purple, and blue at sunset
   sides of the canyon have cliffs, ridges, hills, and even valleys
   at the bottom, *huge towers of rock carved out by the river, look like Aztec temples*
   Colorado River runs along the bottom, looks like a snake from above, but sounds noisy
   from brochure: the powerful currents of river carved out much of the canyon

Now compose your first draft, which needn't follow the outline exactly if new details and arrangements occur to you. As you draft (and revise later), be sure to include words and phrases that unify the paragraph, emphasizing the impressiveness of the Grand Canyon: *incredible* beauty, *massive* hole, *powerful* currents, *huge* towers, *over 270 miles long, over a mile deep in places.*

IN SUMMARY

Descriptive detail

1. supports the topic idea (for example, that something is unusual, massive, exciting, or beautiful);
2. usually begins with the general dimensions of a thing, place, or person—the size, the shape, or any other details that establish the framework;
3. follows with more specific details arranged in some logical order; and
4. includes sounds, smells, and feelings in addition to sights—and describes the sights in color.

Gin Lane, *by William Hogarth (1697–1764). The Metropolitan Museum of Art, Harris Brisbane Dick Fund, 1932.*

2   Drafting a Preliminary topic Sentence

Assume the instructor of a world history class has asked you to compose a paragraph on poverty in eighteenth-century England, based on the picture above. Draft a preliminary topic sentence that states your reaction to the picture, probably—but not necessarily—following this pattern:

The _____ is _____ .

Here are some examples of topic sentences about other subjects:

> The new Cleveland Stadium is a beautiful, modern ballpark with
>   many wonderful features.
> The Central Library is a quiet, dignified structure that is per-
>   fect for reading or studying.
> Wilson Hall is the ugliest building I have ever seen.

_____

_____

3   Selecting Supporting Details

With another student, look at both your preliminary topic sentence from Exercise 2 and the picture on which it is based. What details would establish the general outlines of the picture? What details might a reader expect to see develop the topic idea? Using your predictions as a guide, cluster or brainstorm the supporting details. Record what you see, but also try to imagine the sounds and even the smells you might notice if you were on the scene.

Organizing Through Spatial Order

The most logical way to organize descriptive details is in *spatial order*, that is, arranged in space from top to bottom, left to right, nearest to farthest, or the like. Readers can best visualize an object, a place, or a person when they first see its general outline and then the smaller details arranged according to some plan. Composing a description is like drawing a picture; you start by sketching a general outline, and then you fit in the most important details. For example, the following paragraph first supplies a short history of the dodo and then describes the bird's general appearance, size, and shape:

An Odd Bird

topic sentence ❏ (1) *Of all the extinct species of birds, the most incredible was the ridiculous dodo.* (2) It was discovered on an island in the Indian Ocean but died out by the end of the seventeenth century. (3) The bird resembled a fat and strangely shaped dove (and it was, in fact, a member of the dove family), the size of a large turkey. (4) It was about 3 feet tall, fat, and heavy-footed, with a belly that scraped the ground when it waddled, but it could not fly.

Then come the specific details arranged from top to bottom—from the head, to the neck, to the body, and then down to the feet.

(5) Its head was odd looking, with tiny round eyes near the top, and beneath them a long, lumpy upper beak that hooked over the much smaller lower beak. (6) The dodo's neck formed an *s*, ending at its body, which looked like a large egg that had short feathers glued on it. (7) In the center were the tiny useless wings, and at its rear was the tail, a tuft of feathers that curled over backward like a question mark. (8) Under its body were clawed feet that seemed barely able to support the weight of the body.

The details are organized clearly and support the topic idea: *strangely shaped, fat, a belly that scraped the ground when it waddled, odd looking, lumpy upper beak, tiny useless wings, clawed feet that seemed barely able to support the weight of the body.*

Here is a picture of the dodo. Does it coincide with the mental image you drew from the description you just read? If not, what additional details or comparisons would clarify the description?

Clarifying Through Comparisons

The unfamiliar is easiest to visualize when described in terms of the familiar. At various points during the description of the dodo, for example, the bird is compared to other animals or shapes—a dove, a turkey, the letter *s*, an egg, and a question mark. These comparisons create a shorthand way for us to see what the bird looked like.

✍ **4   Organizing Descriptive Details**

Number the scrambled sentences in each of the following groups to create coherent paragraphs. Be prepared to explain the reasoning behind your choices.

Paragraph A.

_____   The griffin was a combination of an eagle and a lion.

___1___   The mythical griffin was an odd-looking creature often shown in paintings and carvings from ancient times.

_____   Its head, wings, and front legs were those of an eagle.

_____   In addition, the back legs and tail were covered with dragonlike scales.

_____   However, during the Middle Ages, it was thought to be a guardian of gold and hidden treasure.

_____   Its body, back legs, and tail resembled those of a lion.

_____   In ancient times it was believed to be related to the sun god.

Paragraph B.

_____   According to the Greek philosopher Plato, the mythological island of Atlantis was a rich land, full of vegetation and mines of valuable minerals.

_____   At the center of the island was a plain, supposedly the most beautiful and fertile of all plains, and near the middle of the plain was a small hill.

_____   Two springs, hot and cold, provided unlimited water supplies to the temple, and there were indoor heated baths for kings and commoners, for women, and for horses.

_____   Three rings of sea and two rings of land alternated to surround the hill, sort of like a corkscrew.

_____   Next to the shrine was also a temple to Poseidon, which was covered all over in silver, except for the statues, which were of gold.

_____   On the outer rings of land there were docks and harbors, surrounded by a wall with many houses on it.

_____   From this crowded area around the shrine there was constant shouting and noise throughout the day and night.

_____   In the center of the hill was a shrine to the gods Poseidon and Cleito, surrounded by a golden wall that people were forbidden to enter.

_____   The island produced all these in marvelous beauty and endless quantities.

Inserting Transitional Expressions for Description

Transitional words and phrases used in a descriptive paragraph help readers follow the placement of details. For example, in the paragraph about the dodo, these expressions guide the eye along the bird's body from head to toe:

Its head was grotesque, with tiny round eyes *near the top,* and *beneath them....* The dodo's neck formed an *s, ending at its body.... In the center* were the tiny useless wings, and *at its rear* was the tail.... *Under its body* were clawed feet...

In early drafts, you usually include transitional expressions without consciously thinking about them, but during revisions you should add transitions whenever necessary. These are the most common expressions:

> *Transitions to Show Spatial Relationships:* over, above, at the top, in the middle, in the center, at the bottom, below, beneath, under(neath), on the left, on the right, to the left, to the right, on the side, on one side, around, behind, in the rear, in front of, in the front, in the back, next to, beside, nearby, close by, far away, farther away, beyond, inside, on the inside, farther inside, within, outside, on the outside, to the north (south, east, west)

One version of a paragraph on the Grand Canyon, roughly following the outline devised earlier, demonstrates how careful spatial organization and transitions (shown in bold) cement coherence. The paragraph begins with the topic sentence, which is followed by general information and then the smaller details arranged from top to bottom.

> On my visit to Arizona, I saw one of the earth's greatest natural wonders, the Grand Canyon. It is a massive hole in the ground covering much of the northwestern part of the state. In all, the canyon is over 270 miles **in length** (although Grand Canyon National Park includes only 100 miles) and between 4 and 18 miles **in width.** It is also monstrously **deep,** over a mile **in spots,** but a visitor can see all the way to the bottom. The walls are far from flat; they are filled with cliffs, ridges, hills, and even valleys. The multicolored rocks ring the canyon walls in layers, **beginning at the top** with a sand color, **then** red, **then** lavender, **then** blue-brown, **then** bright red, and **then** black **at the very bottom.** These colors change according to shifts in light; at noon they blend into a bright red, but at sunset they turn dark red and brown. **Finally, at the bottom** is the Colorado River, which looks like a tiny snake winding **through the canyon,** although the roar of its current can be heard **in places even at the top.** In fact, that powerful current has carved out much of the canyon over a 2,000-million-year period, and it has left huge towers of rock, like Aztec temples, that rise **from the middle of the canyon floor.** This massive natural excavation project has also exposed fossils of prehistoric man, dinosaurs, and the earliest forms of plant and animal life that lie **within the canyon's walls.** *

* If you want to compose a more formal description, remove any references to yourself from the paragraph. Thus, the topic sentence might read as follows:
     The Grand Canyon in Arizona is one of the earth's greatest natural wonders.
On the other hand, if you want to make a more informal description, include more references to yourself:
     It is also monstrously deep, over a mile in spots, but I could see all the way to the bottom. Standing
     at the top, I saw the multicolored rocks that ring the canyon walls in layers....
These choices depend on the effect you wish to create. The formal paragraph sounds more objective; the paragraph with the pronoun *I* sounds more intimate.

✍ 5   **Supporting a Topic Idea**

Read the paragraph and then rewrite it to develop the new topic sentence supplied. Change the wording and the details, and add more details if necessary.

❑   *My room at home is cramped and messy.* Its dimensions are small, 9 feet by 10 feet, and furniture is crowded into almost every available space. Next to the door is a long chest of drawers, all of which are crammed full. The top of the chest is covered with more clothes, letters, magazines, and personal effects that I cannot put anywhere else. A small mirror is attached to the wall over the dresser, but photographs, invitations, and pictures from magazines are taped over much of its surface. In fact, all of the walls are filled with posters, photos torn from magazines, and unframed pictures. On the left side of the room is a small old desk, covered with papers, books, magazines, pens and pencils. A short, four-shelf bookcase occupies the space just to the right of the desk, and it, too, is overflowing with books, some of them stacked sideways in piles on top of the other books. A wicker wastepaper basket filled with papers, tissues, and candy wrappers lies under the desk, and I often kick it when sitting in the desk chair. My bed occupies almost the entire wall opposite the door, partially blocking the only window in the room. The sheets, blanket, and bedspread hang over the right side of the bed in disarray. On the left of the bed is a night-stand I picked up at a garage sale, and on it are placed my telephone, answering machine, clock radio, jewelry case, keys, wallet, and balled up pieces of paper. On the wall to the right of the bed is a small bench, on which I have placed a 9-year-old 14-inch TV and a cheap stereo system. There isn't enough room on the bench for both speakers, so I have placed one of them on the floor, next to the tiny closet that never has enough room or hangers for my clothes.

My room at home is spacious and neat. _____

_____

_____

_____

_____

_____

_____

_____

_____

_____

_____

_____

_____

_____

✍ 6   **Drafting a Paragraph of Description**

Compose a first draft of a paragraph based on the material from Exercises 2 and 3. Include only the details that develop the topic sentence and arrange them in spatial order. Revise the paragraph at least once, adding transitional expressions where necessary.

COMPUTER TIPS

FOR DRAFTING AND REVISING

1. If you brainstorm a list of details, you can reorganize the list by using the *cut* and *paste* commands in your word processing program. (These commands may have different names in different programs.) Continue to shift around, add to, or remove details until you arrive at coherent organization.

2. While drafting or revising, continue to shift, add, and remove whole sentences or parts of sentences.

3. Insert transitions during the revising process. Simply move the cursor to the spot where you wish to add a transition and then keyboard it in. Experiment with different placements of transitional phrases—at the beginning or end or even in the middle of a sentence—to emphasize ideas, create more graceful sentences, or achieve greater variety in sentences.

✍ **7   Analyzing and Revising Your Draft**

Read the paragraph you drafted in Exercise 6 and respond to each of the following questions. Consider the responses while revising the paragraph, and complete the revision. (This exercise could be done collaboratively, with each person reading his or her paper aloud twice and the group responding to the questions.)

Revision Guidelines

1. Is the point of the topic sentence clear? _____ If it is not clear, how should it be revised? _____

   _____

2. Does the beginning of the paragraph provide a clear general outline of the scene? _____ If not, what should be added or changed? _____

   _____

3. Do the details all support the topic sentence? _____ If not, what should be eliminated, revised, or added? _____

   _____

4. What principle of spatial organization does the paragraph use in arranging the details (for example, top to bottom, center to outside, or nearest to farthest)?

   _____

   Does the paragraph depart from that organizing principle at any point? _____ If so, how should the details be reorganized or rewritten? _____

   _____

   _____

5. Is the description unclear at any point? _____ If so, how should it be revised?

   _____

   _____

6. Are transitions lacking or too vague at any point in the paragraph? _____ If

so, what should be added or revised? _____

_____

_____

7. What was the greatest problem in composing this paragraph? (Ignore this ques-

tion if the writer experienced no significant problems.) _____

_____

If this problem was not resolved, what should be done? _____

_____

_____

✍ 8 Proofreading and Polishing Your Paragraph

After the revision is complete, edit the paragraph, checking for correct spelling and punctuation, complete sentences, and clarity of ideas. Then make a clean copy of the paragraph and proofread it carefully for errors.

Composing Based on Outside Sources

Assume you are composing part of an article on the Loch Ness monster (or "Nessie") for *Nature* magazine. Use the following information to support the topic sentence.

Skin: like a snail's
Size of body: at least 30 feet long and 12 feet wide
Skin color: gray, silver, or black
Tail: rather flat; blunt at the end
Neck: about 4 to 7 feet long, gracefully curved, about as thick as an elephant's trunk
Flippers: two small ones in front; two large ones in back
Length from head to tail: more than 50 feet
Head: like a snail's and very small compared to body

Topic Sentence: Although no conclusive proof of Scotland's Loch Ness monster's exis-tence has ever been established, eyewitness reports have built up a clear picture of "Nessie."

✍ 9 Revising, Proofreading, and Polishing Your Paragraph

Revise, proofread, and polish the paragraph you just drafted, following the advice and guidelines from Exercises 7 and 8.

READINGS

The Beauty of My Town

Max Rodriguez-Reyes

*Max Rodriguez composed this essay in a composition class for
foreign students at Truman College in the summer of 1995.
He is a native of Guatemala and has a wife and child.*

(1) I come from a small town called Coban, far from the city of Guatemala, with a population of about 2,000 people, mostly of Mayan Indian descent. The beauty of green villages and mountains and the spiritual culture of the Mayan Indians are preserved almost intact from the region of their birth.

contrast
good-smelling

(2) In the morning when I am there, I enjoy the cool mountain breezes and the pure golden sunlight as a refreshing **counterpoint** to the endless ticking of the clock. When I leave my house the first things that strike my senses are the smell of **fragrant** wildflowers and the sight of Mayan Indians riding their horses up the mountain on the way to work. In the afternoon I walk along the woodland trails amid the tall trees

countless

and the singing of **innumerable** birds, exchanging endless greetings with the Mayans passing by. Then I wander along the river, where the clear blue water run-

peacefully

ning **serenely** down the mountains never fails to make me yearn for an evening swim.

objects
occurrence

(3) On Saturdays, I visit the local plaza and drink in the sight and sounds of Indians wearing and selling their traditional costumes and **artifacts** made with clay by hand, a **phenomenon** almost unique to the town. On Sunday mornings the plaza looks quiet and almost deserted because virtually the entire population is in church. But by noon of the same day the village square is alive with flocks of brightly costumed children at play under the tolerant eyes of their parents and elder siblings, while on the main stage of the *zocalo* (the town square), the marimbas (the national instrument of Guatemala) are casting their magical spell while people of all ages

good-tasting

dance and sing around them, and I enjoy such **savory** appetizers as Guatemalan tamales and *atole de elote* (the delicious corn soup for which the Mayan are

famous

renowned through the World).

(4) As the magnificent evening sunset filters slowly down through the magically changing blues and greens of the mountain rivers, I reflect once more on the

priceless

inestimable treasures of spiritual beauty with which our humble people have been blessed.

Questions for Investigation and Discussion

1. What is the main point that Max Rodriguez makes?
2. Rodriguez includes several Spanish words, which he then defines or describes in parentheses. Would the description be less effective with the Spanish words removed?
3. Describe the organizational strategy that Rodriguez follows. What governs his choice and arrangement of details in individual paragraphs and in the whole essay?

I Remember . . . My Little *White* Schoolhouse
K. W. Carter

K. W. Carter began writing at the age of 60 after a series of careers as a salesman, a welder, and even a cook. He spent his childhood on his family's farm in Maine.

(1) The little red schoolhouse in my community was white. In fact, I do not recall ever seeing red schoolhouses in rural Maine in the old days; usually they were white or, more commonly, the color of weather beaten shingles. It must be remembered

unwillingness

that the reputation of town officials was measured by their **reluctance** to spend money on education.

(2) I have before me a copy of the 1935 Town Report for Montville. Three grade schools operated there at the time, and the entire budget for schools, including

distributed

money from state funds, was $6,170. Of this amount $2,736.26 was **allotted** to other towns for high school tuition, Montville having no high school of its own. There was an unexpected balance of $408.51 at the end of that year. From this it can be seen that the town operated three grammar schools for a total of $3,025.23.

expressing pain-filled

(3) The outlay for textbooks was $23.95, and for other supplies, $6.08. And this in an era when rural taxpayers were **emitting anguished** cries about the high cost of education! The total budget for teachers was $1,572.50. Out of these handsome salaries, teachers who didn't live within commuting distance of the school paid their board to a local resident.

always

(4) Since the low salaries in rural schools kept the profession from being attractive to men, the teacher was **invariably** a woman. Prior to the 1920s, when teachers were paid even less, they boarded "around," living a week or two at a time with one family and then moving on to the nearest or most desirable place they could find. If some of the living conditions were less than satisfactory, at least they were free, for it was then a public duty for townspeople to take turns "boarding the teacher." After

wandering

two or three years of this rather **nomadic** way of life, most school mistresses were ready to marry anyone who asked their hand, in order to escape. If a teacher was fortunate enough to live near the school, she might make a lifetime career of instructing the young, thereby becoming what was always called "an old maid schoolteacher."

(5) The schoolhouse I attended consisted of one room, roughly 30 feet square, with a large entryway where outdoor clothing, rubbers, and dinner pails could be left during the day. There was a woodshed large enough to store a supply of kindling and five or six split cords of wood, cut in 2½-foot lengths. At the back of the wood-

outhouses; strong; strictly

shed were two **three-holers,** a **stout** board between them **rigorously** segregating the sexes.

(6) The interior of the schoolroom was finished in matched softwood boards which may have been painted a generation before. The floor was of unpainted softwood and so worn that every knot was a good half-inch higher than the rest of the board. Since the building had no basement, winter winds whistled under it and up through cracks in the floor; chill breezes also invaded the room through the walls and around windows and doors; and sometimes fine snow, driven by a northeast wind, filtered in. The room was heated by a potbellied, black-iron barrel stove, stoked with

high-spirited

dry hardwood billets from the woodshed. Sometimes a bit of **exuberant** horseplay at

out of line

recess or lunchtime might lead to one of the stove's three legs being kicked **askew,** tipping the whole thing, fire and all, onto the floor. To keep the small building from going up in smoke required swift, heroic work on the part of the larger boys, and they always managed to avoid disaster.

(7) Some 20 young scholars attended this school, although there were desks for 30. Books, stored in old, glass-fronted bookcases, were used until they were so

the edges of page
turned down

dogeared and defaced as to be almost unreadable. On the rare occasions when new books were available, they were distributed reluctantly, usually, it was believed, to the teacher's favorites. On a table at the back of the room was a well-worn dictionary, a flyspecked globe (word had crept into the community that the world was round), paper, pencils, erasers, and chalk.

(8) Of course, there was no piano nor any musical instruction. The teacher would open "morning exercises" by having us sing a hymn, but more often any ceremony

rituals or procedures

was limited to a recital of the Lord's Prayer and a salute to the flag, mumbling **rites** now outlawed by the wisdom of the Supreme Court.

(9) The curriculum included the three Rs, geography, and American history. Penmanship was taught by the Palmer Method, standard procedure in all Maine schools. Whether there was something wrong with the system of the immortal Palmer or

handwriting

whether I had no talent for **calligraphy** must remain a moot question, since I never learned to write well enough to read my own handwriting an hour after it was put on paper.

(10) Social affairs and extracurricular activities at the little "red" schoolhouse were almost nonexistent. The town fathers felt it unnecessary to spend money on

trivial activity

such **frivolity,** and the poorly paid teachers could not generate enough enthusiasm for any fun and games. Yes, at Christmas time we would have a tree and the children would exchange presents of fudge, little notebooks, or small bags of candy tied up with ribbon. To wind up the festivities we would sing "Jingle Bells" or "Come All Ye Faithful." Then, liberated for two weeks, we would go home for sliding, and for flu and runny noses.

Questions for Investigation and Discussion

1. According to the author, why wasn't the schoolhouse red? What function do the second and third paragraphs serve in explaining the reason?
2. What is the main idea of this essay? That is, what does it tell us about education in K. W. Carter's community?
3. Two paragraphs describe the schoolhouse. What parts of the schoolhouse does paragraph 5 describe? What about paragraph 6?
4. What impression does the description convey about the schoolhouse, and how does this impression support the main idea of the essay?

SUGGESTED TOPICS FOR WRITING

The following list presents some broad topics for descriptive paragraphs. Be sure your paragraph includes a topic sentence, provides adequate detail, and has clear transitions. Be sure, also, that you arrange the details in the paragraph according to spatial order.

1. Assume you are composing a letter to an out-of-town friend. Describe one interesting place, as Max Rodriguez does, depicting the activities there at different times of the day, week, or season and conveying a main point about the place.

2. Assume you have witnessed a crime and need to identify the criminal to the police. Compose a one-paragraph description of the suspect in the photograph.
3. Again for an out-of-town friend, describe a place of great natural beauty.
4. Describe the school or schoolhouse of your childhood—or describe another place of great importance in your childhood. Shape your description to convey a main impression as do both K. W. Carter and Max Rodriguez.

Composing Narrative Paragraphs

A narrative paragraph tells a story that makes a point—and often in dramatic fashion. Therefore, the detail must contribute to developing that point, as well as creating a sense of realism and tension. This chapter examines the process of composing a narrative, as follows:

- ✏ gathering materials for the narrative;
- ✏ unifying the materials around a topic idea;
- ✏ using chronological and climax organization; and
- ✏ adding transitional expressions to express chronology.

NARRATION DEFINED

Narration is storytelling. Unlike physical description, which organizes details in space, narration organizes them *chronologically*—in a time sequence. The best narratives not only tell a story but shape the details to develop a point.

 1   Examining a Narrative

A story that covers a long time period and shifts from location to location usually requires more than one paragraph to explore the content fully. Read the following three-paragraph narrative and then answer the questions about it. (This exercise could be done collaboratively.)

The Legend of Sir Gawain and the Green Knight

❑   (1) At Camelot on a New Year's Day in sixth-century England, there rode into King Arthur's hall a gigantic green warrior on a towering horse, holding a holly branch in one hand and an enormous battle-ax in the other. (2) His skin was green, his hair was green, and even his horse was green. (3) He had come to play what he called a game. (4) Any champion who dared could strike him one blow with the ax, if a year later the champion would submit to a return blow from the green knight. (5) Gawain immediately accepted the challenge and struck the green knight a blow that cut his head clean off his shoulders and sent it rolling on the floor. (6) The green knight then calmly picked up his head by the hair and turned the face toward Gawain. (7) The eyelids opened and the mouth spoke, telling Gawain to meet him for the return blow a year later at the Green Chapel.

(8) The year passed quickly, and Arthur's court grieved for Gawain, sure he was going to his death. (9) Gawain set out, however, on his famous warhorse, Gringolet, saying a man must face his fate, whatever it might be. (10) After a long journey, he came to a castle, where he was welcomed by the

good-natured Sir Bercilak and his lovely young wife. (11) He stayed until New Year's Day, royally entertained by Bercilak and, though greatly tempted, resisting the attempts by Bercilak's wife to seduce him.

(12) Then Gawain went to the Green Chapel, which was nearby. (13) The green knight appeared and Gawain bravely bared his neck for the stroke of the ax. (14) The green knight raised the ax high, but struck Gawain only a glancing blow, which nicked his skin. (15) He then explained that he was Sir Bercilak, transformed into the green knight by the magic of Morgan le Fay, who had planned the whole adventure in hopes of destroying the reputation of the Round Table. (16) Gawain had been spared because he had honorably refrained from making love to Bercilak's wife and had shown himself to be the most faultless knight in the world.

1. What is the setting of the action?
2. Which words and phrases indicate the passage of time? Are all of these expressions located at the beginning of sentences?
3. Why is the narrative divided into three paragraphs?
4. What is the climax of the story? Where does it occur?
5. Where is the topic sentence? What point does it make?

COMPOSING AND REVISING A NARRATIVE

Let's examine the choices available to you as you take your paragraph through the various stages of drafting, revising, editing, and proofreading.

Invention: Moving from Topic Sentence to Details

The stories you tell others are memorable because they involve frightening, exciting, sad, challenging, or happy events. Often, therefore, you can state their significance in a preliminary topic sentence. Here, for example, is the topic sentence from a professionally written narrative, which also provides information about the setting—who, what, when, and where:

A Race to Eternity

> The day that "marathon man" James Worson accepted a challenge to race was the day the proud, athletic English shoemaker screamed once and then mysteriously vanished from the earth.

What is the point of the topic sentence? _____

What information do you learn about the setting?_____

_____

The preliminary topic sentence can then guide you in gathering specific details that develop the story. For example, the details that support the preceding topic sentence might focus on who challenged Worson, when the challenge occurred, how far the race was to be, and what circumstances were involved in Worson's mysterious disappearance. Here is the remainder of the paragraph, which even includes a bit of dialogue to create a sense of immediacy. Notice that the story integrates further information about the setting with details which carry the action forward:

❑ On September 3, 1873, Worson bragged to two friends that he had often raced from one town to another in record time. His friends challenged him to prove his ability, and Worson happily accepted. He would show them, he said, with a 20-mile run from the city of Leamington to Coventry. Worson put on his running clothes and set out. His friends, Hammerson Burns and Barham Wise, carried a camera and trailed close behind him in a horse-drawn buggy. A quarter of the way through the race, Worson was running effortlessly and turning occasionally to exchange words with his friends. But then Worson suddenly stumbled in the middle of a dirt road, pitched forward, and emitted a piercing scream. Wise said later, "It was the most ghastly sound either of us had ever heard." That terrible cry was their last memory of him. Worson's body never struck the ground, for he vanished in the middle of his fall. The road itself provided evidence of what they had witnessed. Burns's pictures of the long-distance runner's tracks show clear footprints suddenly ending as if Worson had crashed into a stone wall. When the men returned to Leamington, a massive hunt began. Searchers combed every inch of the trail without success. Bloodhounds were strangely unwilling to approach the spot where Worson's footprints ended. And for years after his disappearance, there were reports of a ghostly green runner at night on the road from Leamington to Coventry.

Invention: Moving from Details to Topic Sentence

If you aren't sure what point your story will make, you can begin the invention process by brainstorming interesting or amusing details and drafting a topic sentence later. Then you can return to the details, omitting those that don't support the topic sentence and perhaps adding others that do. The story of Worson might have evolved from a brainstorming list that evolved into an informal outline like this:

I. Worson's challenge from friends
    20-mile run from Leamington to Coventry
        beginning the run
            friends in buggy
            carrying a camera
        first one-fourth
            effortless running
            talking to friends
        dramatic moment
        stumble, fall, scream
        disappearance of Worson
II. search for Worson
        photos showing end of footprints
        massive search
        bloodhounds not willing to go to spot of disappearance
III. ghostly reappearance of Worson

✍ 2 **Planning and Drafting a Narrative**

Assume you are composing an entertaining narrative for a young audience, perhaps children in sixth or seventh grade. Compose the first draft of a paragraph on either of the topics that follow. Include a preliminary topic sentence either before or after brainstorming, clustering, or free writing.

1. Discuss a legend or frequently repeated story from your community, your family, or your native country if it was not the United States.
2. Discuss a mysterious event that happened to you or someone you know.

Organizing Through Chronological Order or Climax Order

While experienced storytellers can successfully jump around in time—from past to present and then back again—most beginning writers confuse both themselves and their readers when they try. Therefore, you will probably structure narrative details most clearly in *chronological order*—with the actions occurring consecutively in time from beginning to end. That structure often emerges only in the later stages of composing. Halfway through the first or second draft, you may remember a fact or event that belongs earlier in the story. Don't apologize for your poor organization by composing, "Incidentally, something happened earlier that I forgot to mention." Jot down the fact or event on a separate piece of paper and insert it in the right spot later. (Or, if you are using a word processor, insert the fact or event where it belongs.)

Additionally, the details of a story often lead to a *climax,* a point when the tension is strongest and the outcome of events is determined. However, since stating the point at the beginning weakens the climax later, many narratives don't include a topic sentence. Therefore, stories told in chronological order often make their point not at the beginning but at the end, with the final sentence delivering the punch line. Here is an example. Note how the first sentence establishes the setting, and then how repetition of parallel structures creates dramatic tension.

The Legend of Gobind Singh

❑   (1) In India, a religious brotherhood of warriors called the Sikhs tell the story about one of their early leaders, a guru named Gobind Singh, who lived in the seventeenth century. (2) He gathered the Sikhs together during a crisis and said that the times required supreme loyalty. (3) Drawing his sword, he asked for volunteers to give him their heads. (4) There was a long silence. (5) Finally, one man stepped forward and was led into the guru's tent. (6) Singh reappeared soon after—alone and with a bloody sword. (7) He asked for a second volunteer and then a third and a fourth and a fifth. (8) Each time, a man was led away and, each time, the guru returned with blood on his sword. (9) "Now," said the leader to his followers, "you have proven your courage and devotion to our cause, so I will restore the men to life." (10) Singh returned to his tent and brought the five men back, unharmed—the result of either a miracle or a trick, for some say that a goat had been sacrificed in place of the men.

IN SUMMARY

A narrative paragraph

1. should make a point;
2. may begin with a topic sentence that states the point;
3. establishes the setting—when, where, what, and who;
4. includes only details that carry the action forward;
5. organizes the details in chronological order, from beginning to end;
6. generally leads to a climax; and
7. may delay stating the topic idea until after the climax of the story.

3 Organizing Narrative Details in Chronological Order

Number each of the scrambled sentences in the following groups so that each group makes a coherent paragraph. Be prepared to explain the reasoning behind your choices. (This exercise could be done collaboratively.)

Earth Making (a Cherokee Legend)

Paragraph A.

_____ Although living creatures existed, their home was up there, above the rainbow, and it was crowded.

__1__ In the beginning, water covered everything.

_____ "We are all jammed together," the animals said.

_____ Wondering what was under the water, they sent Water Beetle to look around.

_____ "We need more room."

Paragraph B.

_____ Water Beetle skimmed over the surface, but couldn't find any solid footing.

_____ Someone Powerful then fastened it to the sky ceiling with cords.

_____ Magically, the mud spread out in the four directions and became the island we are living on—this earth.

_____ So Water Beetle dived down to the bottom and brought up a little dab of soft mud.

Paragraph C.

_____ At first, the earth was flat, soft, and moist.

_____ But the birds all flew back up and said there was still no spot they could perch on.

_____ Therefore, they kept sending down birds to see if the mud had dried and hardened enough to take their weight.

_____ All the animals were eager to live on the earth.

Paragraph D.

_____ Then the animals sent Grandfather Buzzard down.

_____ When he swept up his wings, they made a mountain.

_____ But when he glided low over what would become Cherokee country, he found that the mud was getting harder.

_____ It's because of Grandfather Buzzard that we have so many mountains in Cherokee land.

_____ By that time, Buzzard was tired and dragging.

_____ So when he flapped his wings down, they made a valley where they touched the earth.

_____ The animals watching him from above the rainbow said, "If he keeps on, there will be only mountains," and they made him come back.

_____ He flew very close and saw that the earth was very soft.

Paragraph E.

_____ The crawfish had his back sticking out of a stream, and Sun burned it red.

_____ The animals couldn't see very well because they had no sun or moon.

_____ Now they had light, but it was much too hot because Sun was too close to earth.

_____ Then someone said, "Let's grab Sun from up there behind the rainbow! Let's get him down, too!"

_____ At last the earth was hard and dry enough, and the animals descended.

_____ His meat was spoiled forever, and the people still won't eat crawfish.

_____ Pulling Sun down, they told him, "Here's a road for you," and they showed him the way to go—from east to west.

Paragraph F.

_____ They pushed him up as high as a man, but it was still too hot.

_____ They tried four times and then, when they had Sun up to the height of four men, he was just hot enough.

_____ So they pushed him farther, but it wasn't far enough.

_____ Everyone asked the sorcerers, the shamans, to go put Sun higher.

_____ Everyone was satisfied, so they left him there.

Inserting Transitional Expressions for Narration

As you have seen, transitional expressions add coherence to a narrative paragraph by helping readers note the relationship of events in time. This list shows the most common transitional expressions:

> _Movement in time:_ after, after a while, afterward, and then, an hour (a day, a week) later, finally, first (second, third), later (on), next, soon, still later, the next day (week, year)
>
> _Same time:_ as, as soon as, at that moment, during, immediately, meanwhile, suddenly, when, while
>
> _Specific time:_ in October, in 1975, on January 9, at noon, at 8:30

 **4   Drafting and Revising a Narrative**

Returning to the materials you gathered in Exercise 2, draft and revise a draft of your story. Try to avoid establishing the setting too mechanically; that is, introduce the *who, what, where, when* information in sentences that also carry the narrative forward. Arrange the details chronologically to arrive at a climax. Indicate the movement in time through appropriate transitional expressions. You may choose to state the point of the story either at the beginning or end of the narrative.

COMPUTER TIPS

FOR DRAFTING AND REVISING YOUR NARRATIVE

1. The purpose of most stories is to entertain, so, of course, you will be attempting to incorporate strong detail and create lively sentences. However, you shouldn't try to revise and polish every sentence while composing the first draft. Record your ideas and do some quick revisions, but plan on making further revisions later. Print a double-spaced, wide-margined copy of your first draft, and make changes on the page before returning to the computer.

2. Strong verbs propel the action of a story forward. If your word processing program includes an on-line thesaurus, let it suggest alternatives to commonplace and lifeless verbs such as *go, do, make, run, get, put,* and *take.* Be careful, though. Choose only words that you understand and feel confident using.

3. Look at the nouns in each sentence during revisions. If an object has a name, use it. "We threw the suitcases into the back seat of our old Pontiac" creates a greater sense of realism than "We put our suitcases into the back of the car." Enter these changes.

 **5   Analyzing and Revising Your Draft**

Now reread your story and respond to each of the following questions. Consider the responses while revising the paragraph, and complete the revision. (This exercise could be done collaboratively, with each person reading his or her paper aloud twice and the group responding to the questions.)

Revision Guidelines

1. Is the point of the story clear? _____ If not, what would make the point

   clearer? _____

   _____

2. Does the beginning of the paragraph establish all the important information

   about the setting? _____ If not, what should be added or changed? _____

   _____

   _____

3. Do all the details develop the point? _____ If not, what should be eliminated, revised, or added? _____

_____

_____

4. Is the paragraph organized chronologically? _____ If not, what should be moved, added, or eliminated? _____

_____

_____

5. Is the narration unclear in any spots? _____ If so, how should it be revised?

_____

_____

6. Are transitions lacking or too vague at any point in the paragraph? _____ If so, what should be added or revised? _____

_____

_____

7. What was the greatest problem in composing this paragraph? (Ignore this question if the writer experienced no significant problems.) _____

_____

If this problem was not resolved, what should be done? _____

_____

_____

_____

6   Revising, Proofreading, and Polishing Your Paragraph

After the revision is complete, edit the paragraph, checking for correct spelling and punctuation, complete sentences, and clarity of ideas. Then make a clean copy of the paragraph and proofread it carefully for errors.

READINGS

The Footsteps in the House

Bunny Dewar

Bunny Dewar was a student at Truman College in 1994.
She worked as an acupuncturist and was returning
to school for additional training.

(1) The first time I walked through the door of the old house I could feel its presence. The house had five floors with 12-foot ceilings. It was built in 1890 and, like most old houses, it was drafty. But unmistakable warmth hovered over me as I did some exploring.

(2) The first night I slept there a strange thing happened. At around one o'clock I

woke up to some noise. I'm a very light sleeper, so it could have been anything. I lay there in the dark listening to all the creaks and moans that an old house can make. It was then that I heard the footsteps. They were slowly coming up the stairs, not heavy steps but rather light and steady. They turned right at the top of the stairs and hesitated outside of the bedrooms at that end of the hall. As I listened I heard them start toward my door. I felt my heart pounding as I waited to see the doorknob turn. After a moment of silence the footsteps continued down to the other end of the hall. I don't know how long I listened but I must have fallen back to sleep because the next thing I knew it was morning.

(3) I knew Bob hadn't heard a thing because like all men he sleeps like a baby, so I decided not to say anything. The next night I awoke to the sound of steps again. I wish I could have been brave enough to open the door, but I'm no dummy. I've seen all the horror movies where the audience knows the heroine shouldn't open the door and she does anyway and pays for her stupidity by running right into the monster. Again, I lay there in the dark listening and waiting, but nothing happened.

(4) The third time was the strangest. I heard the footsteps as usual, but this time I knew to whom they belonged. I have always been a little psychic. Sometimes I just know things. I don't have any control over it; it just happens. As the footsteps walked by my door, I knew who this person was—or I should say who she was when she was alive. She and her family had built this house. I didn't know her name and couldn't see her face, but I knew she was wearing a long robe and carrying a candle. She was making her nightly check on the children before she retired to her bedroom at the other end of the hall. This explained the pauses I had heard in front of each doorway and why the footsteps never returned once they reached the end of the hall.

(5) Actually, her presence made me feel quite safe. You might think such noises in an old house would be a little spooky, but they seemed to bathe my house in a warm glow. Even other people would comment on the comfort during their visits. The darkest recesses held no threat, and I was at ease with my nightly visitor.

(6) Bob had gone out of town, and this was the first time I would be alone in the house. That night as I went upstairs to bed, I had an overwhelming urge to talk to her. I stood in the hallway and told her I knew she was there and that I loved this house as much as she did. I was glad no one could see me now or they would have thought I had gone off the deep end. Suddenly I was surrounded by a warm breeze. The hair on my arms and neck stood on end. She was there! I could smell a touch of lavender, and her warmth swept over me like a cloud. I regained my composure and continued my conversation with her. I'm not sure how long I went on because the encounter became so intense. As I went to bed that night, I knew I really belonged in this house.

(7) We are doing construction on our second floor right now, so I'm not hearing her on her nightly rounds. But I can still feel her in every corner of the house, and maybe if you come to visit sometime you'll be able to feel her too!

Questions for Investigation and Discussion

1. Why does the first sentence of the first paragraph refer to "its presence" rather than naming the object that was present?
2. Which paragraphs begin with topic sentences? Why doesn't every paragraph contain a topic sentence?
3. Transitional expressions of chronological order are very explicit in this story. Why?
4. What is Bunny Dewar's attitude toward the strange being who occupies her house? What statements and details reveal that attitude?
5. At what points in the story are the details most specific and dramatic? How do these details contribute to the central idea and mood of the story?

The Mystery of Bridey Murphy

Roger Boar and Nigel Blundell

This article appeared in Mystery, Intrigue, and the
Supernatural *(New York: Dorset Press, 1991.)*

(1) There was nothing about Mrs. Virginia Tighe, a trim, smart young American housewife who lived in Pueblo, Colorado, to suggest she held a key to the past. She and her husband, Rex, were part of the bright, contemporary social scene and filled their lives with bridge parties, cocktails, and club dances. Under hypnosis, however, Mrs. Tighe became someone quite different—a little girl who lived in nineteenth century Ireland and whose name was Bridey Murphy.

famous
backward looking
(2) The story of Bridey Murphy is one of the most **celebrated** in the records of **regression** hypnosis, a technique which, it is claimed, can sometimes take the subject so far back in time that previous lives are revealed.

(3) It all began on the night of November 29, 1952.

(4) Colorado businessman and amateur hypnotist Morey Bernstein had discovered that Virginia Tighe was a remarkably good subject. She had the ability to slip easily into a very deep trance. He asked if she would cooperate in an experiment in which he would take her back to **infancy,** then perhaps beyond. He had not attempted this before.

early childhood

restrained
lying down
(5) There was a feeling of **suppressed** excitement when she arrived at his home that night. He made her comfortable in a **reclining** position on a couch, lit a candle and turned off all the lights, with the exception of one lamp.

(6) She drifted easily back through the years, reliving the memory of childhood scenes, until she was only one year old. Bernstein told her that her mind could go even further back to different scenes, in some other time. "What do you see?" he asked her gently.

(7) He leaned forward, holding his breath, as a child's voice with a soft Irish accent said: "I scratched the paint off all my bed. Jus' painted it, 'n' made it pretty. It was a metal bed, and I scratched the paint off it. Dug my nails on every post and just ruined it. Was jus' terrible."

(8) "Why did you do that?"

(9) "Don't know. I was just mad. Got an awful spanking."

(10) Her name, she told him, was Bridget or Bridey Murphy and she was four years old, had red hair and lived in a house in Cork . . . she had a brother called Duncan . . . and her father's name was Duncan too.

(11) Bridey Murphy's story slowly came together in a number of sessions in which 29-year-old Virginia Tighe slipped back into a life and character so different from her own. She had been born, she said, in Cork on December 20, 1798. She was the daughter of Duncan and Kathleen Murphy, both Protestants. Her father was a
lawyer **barrister** in Cork and they lived in a white wooden house called The Meadows on the outskirts of town. She had a brother, Duncan, who was two years older than herself.

(12) When she was 15 she went to a day school run by a lady called Mrs. Strayne. Asked what she had been taught at school, Bridey answered, "Oh, to be a lady . . . just house things . . . and proper things." Her brother married Mrs. Strayne's daughter, Aime. In 1818 Bridey met a lawyer from Belfast called Sean Brian MacCarthy. His father was also a barrister and the families appeared pleased with the match, though she did not like him when she accepted his proposal. "I just went with him . . . 'twas taken for granted, I think."

(13) There were certain difficulties from the outset. "Brian," as she preferred to call him, was a Catholic, so after being married in Cork (to please her family) she had to go through another ceremony in Belfast, to please her husband. They made the journey north in a horse and carriage, and Bridey described the places they passed through.

a Christian sacrament;
supplies
slips

(14) She did not enjoy living in Belfast as much as in Cork, but seemed happy enough with Brian, and proud of the fact that he taught at Queen's University. They attended St. Theresa's Church, where the priest was Father John Gorman, but she was not allowed to take **communion** or confession. Bridey shopped for **provisions** with a grocer named Farr, bought fruit and vegetables at Carrington's and blouses and **camisoles** at Caden House. She never had children, though she enjoyed visits to friends' houses and occasional trips to the sea. She was interested in Irish mythology, knew some Irish songs and was a neat dancer of Irish jigs. At the end of one sitting Mrs. Tighe, not quite fully conscious, danced round the room.

bagpipes

(15) Toward the end of her life she had a fall. Her death came quietly and without pain while her husband was at church one Sunday. She remembered that they had played the **uillean pipes** at her funeral. She also told how she watched her burial, describing the state of being after death. Somehow she was reborn in America, but could not explain how that had happened.

false name

(16) Corey Bernstein finished his sessions with Bridey Murphy in October 1953 and three years later published his best-selling book of the case, *The Search for Bridey Murphy.* In it his subject was given the **pseudonym** Ruth Simmons.

(17) From the moment Bridey's story appeared in print there was a scramble to see who could be first to check the facts. Investigators and reporters swarmed over to Ireland, burrowing through records, talking to aged inhabitants and checking maps.

(18) Some facts could not be checked. There was no possibility, for instance, of confirming the dates of marriages and deaths in Cork, as no records were kept there until 1864. On the negative side, no information could be unearthed about the wooden house called The Meadows, St. Theresa's Church, or Father Gorman. On the positive side, she gave an accurate description of the Antrim coastline and of the journey from Cork to Belfast. It was discovered that the shops she mentioned had all existed and the coins she mentioned in her shopping transactions had all belonged to that period. Bridey had said that uillean pipes had been played at her funeral, and it was indeed found to have been the custom because of their soft tone.

inconsistencies

unimportant

(19) Despite certain **discrepancies** there was no doubt that Bridey's story gave a remarkably detailed account of the life of a fairly privileged member of the professional class in nineteenth century Ireland. It was full of the sort of **trivial**, intimate information that is seldom recorded in books but has to be experienced.

(20) Mrs. Tighe emphatically denied that she had ever visited Ireland or had much to do with Irish people. But one interesting fact emerged after the publication of Bernstein's book. She had been born in Madison, Wisconsin, where she lived with her mother and father until she was three years old and both parents were part Irish. After that she was brought up in Chicago by a Norwegian uncle and his wife who claimed Irish blood somewhere in the family. Could she have stored knowledge she heard as such a small child? Even that does not seem enough to explain how she came to have been Bridey Murphy or how without any dramatic talent she could so enter her personality as to make her seem a real person.

Questions for Investigation and Discussion

1. What is the function of the first paragraph? Where is the topic idea of the story stated?
2. Examine the places where dialogue is introduced. How is the dialogue treated mechanically—that is, in terms of punctuation, paragraphing, and capitalization? How are the speakers identified mechanically?
3. Locate important transitional expressions throughout the story. How do they differ from the transitional expressions found in Bunny Dewar's story?
4. Does the narrative imply either that Mrs. Tighe's recollections of Bridey Murphy were true or untrue? Cite evidence to support your answer.

SUGGESTED TOPICS FOR WRITING

1. Assume you are composing a narrative for the college literary magazine and your primary purpose is to entertain. Like Bunny Dewar or Roger Boar and Nigel Blundell, tell the story of a mysterious experience that you or someone you know has encountered. Gather material for and compose the first draft of a story, organizing the paragraph in climax order. Be sure to save the most important or dramatic detail for last. Then edit and revise the story.

2. Again assume you are composing a narrative for the college literary magazine and your primary purpose is to entertain. Gather material for and compose the first draft of a story about a time when you or someone else was a hero. (Acts of heroism can be large or small.) Again, organize the paragraph using climax order. Then edit and revise the story.

3. Assume you are composing an inspirational story for *Reader's Digest.* Tell about a time when something exciting happened to you, a friend, or a family member.

4. Again for *Reader's Digest,* narrate a story that one of your parents or grandparents told you about life in an earlier time.

5. Narrate the experience of gaining a new brother, a new sister, a new son, a new daughter, or a new friend.

6. Tell the story of a dangerous or embarrassing experience.

Composing Process Paragraphs

Previous chapters have examined paragraph unity and coherence, and the composing of descriptive and narrative paragraphs. This chapter explores another method of paragraph development—*process analysis*—in which you explain how to do something or how something works. It discusses the following matters:

- ✏ how to plan and organize a process-analysis paragraph, working from a topic sentence and rough outline;
- ✏ how to compose the first draft, including a step-by-step description of the process; and
- ✏ how to revise for clarity and coherence while adding appropriate transitions.

PROCESS ANALYSIS DEFINED

Giving and receiving directions plays a large role in communication as you and others learn skills, acquire education, or perform daily tasks. Teachers and students, managers and workers, parents and children must explain how to complete a task, assemble or run a machine, go from one place to another, or understand the workings of our universe. These are all instances of *process analysis*—the explanation of how to do something or how something works. Its purpose is always to inform.

A process analysis can be a simple manual for assembling or operating a new appliance or toy. It can also be a recipe in a cookbook or an orientation booklet for new students or new workers, showing the layout of the college or business and the responsibilities of each department. It can be an explanation of photosynthesis, Newton's third law, or creating a computer database. Thus, process analysis can be classified into three types:

1. *Explanations of how to do something* provide directions for making something or performing an operation (for example, baking a flourless chocolate cake, using a fax modem, entering income and expenses in a ledger book, or traveling by car from St. Louis to Minneapolis). Most often, these directions are written in the second person, addressing the audience directly as *you*.
2. *Explanations of how something works* discuss the operation of a machine, a scientific experiment, or a natural phenomenon (for example, a printing press stamping out copies of a newspaper, a mixture of chemicals producing a powerful drug, or a tadpole developing into a frog). Drawings or photographs often accompany such explanations, which are usually written in the third person (*it* or *they*).
3. *Explanations of how something is organized* analyze a complex organization by breaking it down into smaller parts (for example, the divisions within

a large corporation, the departments in a university, the roles of the bees in a beehive). These explanations are usually written in the third person.

The more complicated the process is, the more you must explain, and some explanations require whole compositions or even book-size manuals. Therefore, in a one-paragraph composition, you must limit the topic to a simple process that can be developed in a short amount of space.

ORGANIZING A PROCESS-ANALYSIS PARAGRAPH

An effective process analysis must provide readers with clear enough directions so they may understand or perform a task or activity. Thus, you should plan and organize your paragraph with extreme care, keeping your audience's needs in mind; explain the process in easy-to-follow steps; define unfamiliar terms; and compare unfamiliar, complex operations to familiar, simpler ones. In short, try to accomplish the following goals:

◆ Make clear what the process is and, if necessary, why it is important.
◆ Make clear whether you want your audience to *perform* or merely *understand* the process. Performing a process usually requires more explanation than does simply understanding the process.
◆ List the materials (tools, parts, or ingredients) involved in the process and explain unfamiliar terms. You can include them at the beginning—especially in explanations of how to perform a task* —or introduce some of them at relevant points throughout the explanation.
◆ Analyze the process, breaking it down into separate steps that readers can visualize or perform.
◆ Explain the process clearly and systematically.

Arranging the Explanation in Chronological Order

Like narrative paragraphs, process-analysis paragraphs are usually organized chronologically. They examine each step in sequence, explaining what happens first, second, third, and so on. The steps, however, are more explicit than those in narration paragraphs.

The following paragraph, which is arranged in chronological order, gives a description of an unusual type of surgical device. Although more humorous than informative (the writer obviously doesn't expect you to perform operations), the description is, nevertheless, tightly structured. The first three sentences attract your interest, describe the tools involved in the surgery (the ants' jaws), and state the topic of the paragraph.

The Surgeon Ants

❑ (1) Next time you are stocking your first-aid kit or medicine cabinet, don't forget to throw in a jar of ants—doctor ants, that is. (2) These tiny six-legged medicine men from the forests of South America have sharp, viselike jaws that allow a swarm of ants to strip an entire citrus grove overnight. (3) *However, the Brazilian Indians have found a use for the ants to stitch up incisions during surgery.*

After a transitional sentence, the paragraph goes on to describe four steps in the process, signaled by the transitional expressions *first, then, after,* and *later.*

* For example, the assembly instructions for toys, furniture, and appliances always begin with a parts and tools list so you don't discover that something is missing halfway through the assembly.

(4) Here is how the Brazilians do it. (5) They *first* press the edges of the wound together. (6) *Then* they apply the doctor ants along the seam. (7) *After* the ants have bitten the wound closed, they snap off the ants' bodies, leaving the jaws in place. (8) *Later,* after a suitable healing period, the Brazilians remove the heads, leaving the patient with a cleanly stitched incision—and probably a low medical insurance bill.

Notice that this how-to paragraph is written in the *third-person plural.* If it were really giving advice to its audience, it would address them directly through the second-person pronoun *you:* "*You* first press the edges of the wound together. Then *you* apply the doctor ants along the seam." Or it could address the audience directly through another form of the second person, the *imperative,* which gives commands while omitting the pronoun *you:* "First press the edges of the wound together. Then apply the doctor ants along the seam." Either second-person form is appropriate, provided you use it consistently throughout the paragraph. Therefore, carefully check your paragraph for unintended shifts between second person and imperative when you revise.*

Here's another example of a process paragraph, this time intended to help readers understand a natural process. Sentence 1 attracts your interest and introduces the topic; sentence 2 states the point.

A Matter of Gravity

❏ (1) If you travel to the moon someday, be prepared for some surprises, for the moon's gravity is only one-sixth as strong as the earth's. (2) *This reduced gravitational pull affects not only a person's weight and strength but also atmospheric conditions on the moon.*

In the explanation that follows, the transitional expressions (shown in italic) label the three main points and the examples that illustrate them.

(3) *First of all,* a person's weight is greatly reduced. (4) On their moon walks, the American astronauts, *for example,* were five-sixths lighter than they were on earth. (5) *To put it another way,* a 180-pound person on the mother planet would weigh only 30 pounds on the moon. (6) *Furthermore,* because of this weak gravitational pull, a person's strength is increased proportionately. (7) *For instance,* an Olympic high jumper who clears 8 feet on earth would leap 48 feet on the moon. (8) *Finally,* because the moon's gravity is too weak to capture and hold an atmosphere, there is no weather at all on the moon—in fact, no wind, sound, or life. (9) Without an atmosphere to regulate climate, the moon's surface experiences great swings in temperature from day to night. (10) *During the day* the surface is hot enough to boil water, *but at night* the temperature drops to 260 degrees below zero.

✍ 1 **Examining a Process-Analysis Paragraph**

Read the following paragraph and then answer the questions. (This exercise could be done collaboratively.)

❏ (1) When we have a cold, doctors advise us to drink plenty of liquids for a simple reason: to prevent dehydration, which can be dangerous. (2) Three processes are at work during the cold, emptying our body of water. (3) The first and most obvious is that we don't want to eat or drink very much when we don't feel well, so our bodies lose moisture. (4) The second process results

---

* For more explanation and practice in consistency, see Chapter 12.

from fevers speeding up the metabolism. (5) When this happens, we blow off more carbon dioxide and need more oxygen to run our bodies, so we breathe faster. (6) Every time we breathe, we give off moisture. (7) We are literally blowing off water as well as hot air, just as a whale's spout shoots out water. (8) The final process occurs because our bodies try to fight off a high fever by evaporating moisture off and through the skin. (9) Sometimes the moisture is imperceptible; sometimes it's a spritz (which is why we are usually sweaty from a high fever); and other times, when a fever is finally breaking, it can be drenching. (10) Drinking plenty of liquids, then, is a way of replenishing the water lost by poor eating habits, evaporation, sweating, and breathing.

1. What is the topic sentence of the paragraph?
2. Which transitional sentence introduces the discussion of the processes involved?
3. Which sentences begin each discussion of a process? How do you know?
4. What does the transitional expression "When this happens" refer to in sentence 5?
5. What is the function of sentence 10?
6. The paragraph is written in the first-person plural (using *we*). How would your reaction to it change if it were written in the third person?

COMPOSING A PROCESS-ANALYSIS PARAGRAPH

Because the success of a process-analysis paragraph depends on a clear, well-organized presentation, you should plan the paragraph with special care. During the invention stage, you can arrive at a structure in whatever way works best for you—clustering, free writing, or brainstorming, and then drafting and revising. But you may want to spend more time than usual on the plan, either during invention or the early drafting stages.

Beginning with Discovery, Planning, and Outlining

After exploring your ideas through free writing, clustering, or brainstorming, shape them into an informal outline. The outline helps you determine the goal of the process analysis, the steps in the process, the terms to define, and the tools or materials to mention. Think of the outline as a starting point, for you will modify the paragraph several times as you draft and revise. Suppose, for example, that you were composing a short article for *Outdoor Photographer* magazine on how to take pictures of animals in a forest. Here is one type of simple outline:

Goal: *readers to perform the task*
Terms to define: *none*
Tools or materials needed
  1. *a good camera*
  2. *clothing that blends into the background of the woods*

Steps in the process:
  1. *preparation: loading the camera*
  2. *finding spot where animals are likely to frequent: place where there is water or food*
  3. *waiting quietly with camera ready*
  4. *aiming quickly and taking several pictures in rapid succession*

When drafting a paragraph based on this outline, you might realize that many people won't understand what you mean by a "good" camera and, if you try to explain it, they won't understand such terms as *lens opening* and *shutter speed.* Therefore, add this information to your outline—or to the paragraph itself. These are the relevant changes in the outline:

Terms to define
1. *lens opening (for amount of light exposure)*
2. *shutter speed*

Tools or materials needed: *a good camera that can be adjusted for the amount of light and that can be adjusted to take clear pictures of moving objects*

Steps in the process
1. *preparation: loading the camera and setting the lens opening and shutter speed*

COMPUTER TIP

FOR GENERATING AND ORGANIZING MATERIALS

Create the outline of the paragraph in the outline mode of your word processing program (or simply generate ideas in a brainstorming list). Doing so will allow you to add or delete items and reorganize the outline without having to copy it over. Use the cut and paste commands for moving items, and insert the cursor in the spot where you wish to insert new material.

Drafting the Topic Sentence

At some point in the planning and drafting stages, draft the topic sentence. Since the purpose of process analysis is to inform, your topic sentence needn't be clever or catchy, but should state your point as clearly as possible. The following are a few examples of preliminary topic sentences, written in third person or second person:

> *Anyone can take good pictures of wildlife in the woods if he or she observes these steps.*
> *You can become a good wildlife photographer if you follow this advice.*
> *Four steps are involved in taking good pictures of wildlife in the woods.*
> *Taking good pictures of wildlife in the woods involves four steps.*

✍ **2 Planning a Process-Analysis Paragraph**

For each of the following paragraph plans, make an outline and draft a preliminary topic sentence. Supply the information you would include to meet the predictions of

an audience of people unfamiliar with the process. Write in pencil, for you will probably change your mind more than once as you go along. Part of each outline has been
completed for you.

Paragraph A.

Topic: how to prepare for a job interview

Goal: _____

Terms to define: _____

Tools or materials needed: brochures and pamphlets about the company, and a
personal résumé

Steps in the process:

1. analyzing the type of company and job you will interview for

2. _____

3. _____

4. _____

5. _____

Topic sentence: _____

_____

Paragraph B.

Topic: ways to pay for a college education

Goal: _____

Terms to define: scholarship, grant, student loan (all or any of these)

Tools or materials needed: _____

Steps in the process:

1. _____

2. _____

3. _____

4. _____

5. _____

Topic sentence: _____

_____

Paragraph C.

Topic: how to make a _____

Goal: _____

Terms to define: _____

Tools or materials needed: _____

Steps in the process:

1. *gathering the tools and materials* _____

2. _____

3. _____

4. _____

5. _____

Topic sentence: _____

_____

3 Gathering and Organizing Materials for a Process-Analysis Paragraph

Choose a process you know how to do well: for example, changing a car's spark plugs, reconciling a checkbook with a bank statement, changing a child's diaper, traveling with small children, or performing some task at work. Assume you are composing either a short manual or a letter to a friend in which you explain the process. Explore your ideas by free writing, clustering, or brainstorming, and then prepare an informal outline and preliminary topic sentence as in Exercise 2.

4 Organizing Process-Analysis Paragraphs

Each of the following groups of sentences can be organized into a paragraph that develops the topic sentence. Number the sentences in each group in a logical order, and be prepared to explain your choices. (This exercise could be done collaboratively.)

Paragraph A.

Topic Sentence: Look at any middle-class neighborhood and you will see a great many mistakes in one of the simplest and most straightforward rules of grammar—the formation of plurals of proper names.

_____ All you need do is add *s* to the name or *es* if the name already ends in *s* or an *-s* - like sound, and you never use an apostrophe before or after this final *s* or *es*.

_____ Yet few grammatical processes in English are easier than making proper nouns plural.

_____ Therefore, the proper plurals ought to be *the Robinsons, the Smiths, the Joneses,* and *the Marxes.*

_____ On many mailboxes or wrought-iron signs, you will find such misspellings as *the Robinson's, the Smith's,* or even *the Jone's's.*

Paragraph B.

Topic Sentence: The blood is composed of three different elements—red corpuscles, white corpuscles, and plasma—each of which has a different function.

_____ White corpuscles fight disease in the body by crowding around bacteria and digesting them.

_____ These red, disk-like objects are very small, and there may be several million of them in a single drop of blood.

_____ However, the disks wear out quite quickly—within a few weeks—and must be remade in the bone marrow.

_____ The red corpuscles carry oxygen through the blood.

_____ White corpuscles are much larger and are rather shapeless, and there are far fewer of them than red corpuscles, which usually outnumber them 500 to 1.

_____ The plasma, in which both the red and white corpuscles float, carries food and chemicals throughout the body while collecting carbon dioxide that will be passed out through the lungs.

_____ Therefore, when necessary, the body makes more of them to combat attacks from germs.

5   Drafting Your Paragraph

Compose the first draft of a paragraph based on one of the informal outlines and preliminary topic sentences you prepared in Exercises 2 or 3. Depart from the plan if new ideas occur to you. Include a topic sentence.

Inserting Transitions Within a Process Paragraph

You can help readers identify each step in the process you are describing by adding appropriate transitions to the beginnings of sentences. The following list includes the most common transitions for process analysis:

For steps in consecutive order:	first, second, third, after that, next, then, later, as soon as, until, when, once
For steps occurring simultaneously:	at the same time, during, meanwhile, while
For steps ending the process:	finally, last (of all), most importantly, to finish

Here is the final version of the paragraph on taking pictures of wildlife. Notice that after making the plan, revising it, composing the first draft, and then revising and editing the draft, the writer discovered other ideas and made further changes. For example, the steps in the process have been increased to five. (The topic sentence and the transitional expressions introducing the steps are in bold type.)

(1) _If you are interested in animals and photography, you can put the two together by photographing wild animals—not in a zoo but out in their natural environment, the woods._ (2) **Six steps are involved in taking pictures of wildlife in the woods.** (3) **First,** _you will need clothing that blends into the background_

> *of the woods. (Combat fatigues from an army surplus store are good.) (4) **Second,** you need a good camera that allows you to bypass its automatic features. (5) You want to be able to zoom in or out on your subject, as well as to adjust both the time that the lens is open (called the F-stop) and the width of the lens (called the aperture). (6) A lens that is open too long will produce a blurred image of a quickly moving animal, and a lens that is not open wide enough will produce muddy images caused by the darkness of the woods. (7) **Third,** you need to find a spot in the woods where animals are likely to come—probably around water or food (fruit, leaves, and the like). (8) Experienced hunters or nature photographers can offer you advice on where to go. (9) **Fourth,** after arriving at the spot, you will need to make final preparations: choosing a place to conceal yourself and adjusting your camera's lens opening and shutter speed for the conditions. (10) **Fifth,** you must wait patiently. (11) You may have to sit for many hours—and be willing to accept the possibility that no animals will come at all. (12) **Finally,** if one does appear, you will need to act quickly. (13) You must aim your camera and take as many pictures as you can, for under these conditions only a few shots will be interesting or even clear.*

6   Editing a Paragraph for Missing Transitions

Supply the missing transitions in the following paragraph. The first transition has been inserted for you as an example. Be careful: Not every transition introduces a step in the process.

☐ (1) Although white light is composed of many colors—each with its own separate wavelength—you can't see the colors until the light strikes or passes through objects. (2) One of the most popular experiments for observing the colors in light is passing it through a glass prism—an object with many sides, such as a diamond. (3) _____*When this happens,*_____ the light waves are bent, and the colors are separated. (4) The process works in the following way.

(5) _____ white light enters the prism. (6) _____ _____ the light is slowed down by the glass, and it bends or is "refracted." (7) _____ it reenters the air, and it bends again.

(8) _____ each of the different wavelengths bends at a slightly different angle from the others, the colors can be seen. (9) Those with shorter wavelengths are bent more than those with longer wavelengths.

(10) _____ violet has the shortest wavelength, and thus it is bent the most. (11) _____ red, at the opposite end of the color spectrum, has the longest wavelength and is bent the least.

✍ **7   Analyzing and Revising Your Draft**

Read the paragraph you drafted in Exercise 5 and respond to each of the following questions. Consider the responses while revising the paragraph, and then complete the revision. (This exercise could be done collaboratively, with each person reading his or her paper aloud twice and the group responding to the questions.)

Revision Guidelines

1. Does the topic sentence make clear what process is being described? _____

   If not, how should it be revised? _____

   _____

2. Does the paragraph include all the tools and materials needed? _____

   Does it mention them in appropriate places? _____ If not, what should

   be added or changed? _____

3. Are all important steps in the process explained? _____ Are the steps

   explained chronologically? _____ If not, what should be added or shifted?

   _____

4. Do any terms need to be defined? _____ If so, which ones, and where

   should they be defined? _____

5. Is the explanation unclear at any point? _____ If so, how should it be

   revised? _____

6. Are transitions lacking or too vague at any point in the paragraph? _____

   If so, what should be added or revised? _____

   _____

7. What was the greatest problem in composing this paragraph? (Ignore this ques-

   tion if the writer experienced no significant problems.) _____

   _____

   If this problem was not resolved, what should be done? _____

   _____

   _____

✍ **8   Proofreading and Polishing Your Paragraph**

After completing the revision, edit the paragraph, checking for correct spelling and punctuation, complete sentences, and clarity of ideas. Then make a clean copy of the paragraph and proofread it carefully for errors.

Composing Based on Outside Sources

Assume you are an instructor writing a newsletter to parents who do not understand *tenure.* Draft and then revise a paragraph based on the information provided. The topic sentence has been supplied for you.

Topic Sentence: Although *tenure* is widely misunderstood as guaranteeing the jobs of teachers for life, to be "on tenure" simply means that someone cannot be dismissed without a good cause.

1. protection against firing for unimportant or unfair reasons
2. a formal hearing to present charges and supporting evidence
3. at the hearing, evidence weighed and decision made
4. tenure procedure similar to a trial with due process
5. many grounds for dismissing tenured teachers, including incompetence
6. after the hearing, dismissed person generally can appeal
7. the person charged allowed to defend himself or herself

I N   S U M M A R Y

Process analysis

1. explains how to do something, how something works, or how something is organized;
2. first establishes what the process is and (if necessary) why it is important;
3. establishes whether its goal is that readers understand the process or perform it;
4. mentions the tools or materials involved in the process;
5. breaks the process down into separate steps and explains each one; and
6. is most often organized chronologically.

READINGS

Replacing a Broken Window Pane

This advice appeared in America's Handyman Book *in 1970.*

(1) Sooner or later, any handyman is going to be faced with the problem of replacing a broken or cracked pane of glass, no matter what type of window. Putting in the new glass is relatively simple. The importance of a good glass cutter cannot be overemphasized. Buy one that is individually packaged. Cutters stocked loosely in bins are likely to have nicks in the cutting wheel or they may be rusty. Test the cutter on a piece of glass before purchase. If the scored line shows a series of dots and dashes or skips, don't buy the cutter—it's worthless. Find one that makes a steady sound as it scores a line on the glass. Keep your cutter in good condition by storing it in a glass jar with a piece of cloth or felt in the bottom and about 1" of kerosene over this pad. The pad protects the wheel from nicks and the kerosene prevents rust.

(2) The glass to be cut should be clean, for dust or grit will interfere with the cutting wheel. Cover your working surface with a single layer of not too thick blanket, rug, or layers of newspaper. A China marking crayon or a piece of sharpened soapstone is ideal for marking the line on the *reverse* side of the glass where the cut is to be made. A good method to anchor your straight-edged cutting guide is to drive two **brads** into the table and set the guide against them. Metal makes the better guide. Hold the glass cutter firmly, in a more **perpendicular** position than you would hold a pencil. Keep the cutting wheel away from the body. The cutting line starts just inside the farther edge of the glass. Use an even pressure and draw the cutter toward your body and past the nearer edge. Only through experience and practice can you learn how much pressure is necessary. The slow, deliberate speed of the cutter will make an

small nails
upright

even sound which indicates the quality and depth of the cut. You will gradually learn to cut by "ear" as well as by hand.

(3) After the line is scored, gently tap the underside of the cut near the edge of the glass with the reverse end of the cutter. This will start the cleavage, or split. The split will continue through the entire length of the glass if the break is forced by pressure. Another way to complete the break is to place a pencil or guide on the table under the scored line on the glass and press down on each side of the scored line. Cut only one line at a time. That is, don't score two lines crossing each other without breaking. (The cutting procedure is the same with heavier types of glass such as mirrors and plate glass—with this exception: apply a thin film of lubricating oil on the line to be cut. In the case of mirrors, do *not* apply oil to the backing side, as it may damage the mirror.)

(4) The replacement of a broken window pane is similar for most styles of wood frames. The first step often proves to be the hardest, removal of the remaining shreds of glass and the old putty from the frame. The glass can usually be lifted out by hand (protected with heavy gloves), but only very old putty will come away easily. A **soldering iron** or electrical paint remover will often provide enough heat to soften the putty; and if you work fast, you can scrape it away before it cools and resets. Take out the old **glazier's points** along with the putty. The job then proceeds as [follows].*

a device used to melt solder that joins metal

glass-setter's

1. Remove broken bits of glass with glove-protected hands. Remove old putty by softening with heat and then scraping off.
2. Paint groove of frame with linseed oil, and then lay in a bed of putty or glazier's compound about 1/8-inch thick all around. Layer of putty cushions glass and seals out air.
3. Putty should have consistency of thick, dry dough. To soften old putty, add linseed oil and knead on a piece of glass.
4. Run small ribbon of putty inside opening all around and press glass into putty. Insert two glazier's points at each side to hold glass in position and tap them halfway into wood.
5. Insert glazier's points about every 4 inches. Start points with finger pressure, and then drive them in about halfway with chisel. Slide chisel along surface of pane.
6. Roll putty into a l/2-inch-thick rope and lay it along all four sides. The easiest way to apply putty is with the fingers, pressing it against wood and glass.
7. Your putty knife now takes over and smooths out fingerprints, stripping off excess putty. Putty surface should be smooth, unbroken, and firmly sealed.
8. Any exterior grade, oil-base paint can be applied over the putty immediately.

Questions for Investigation and Discussion

1. What is the purpose of this article? How does the purpose affect the organization and choice of information?
2. Who is the audience for this article? Would the readers find the article "boring"? Why or why not?
3. What tools and materials are needed to change a window pane? Where are these tools and materials mentioned, and why?
4. The article essentially divides the process into three main sections. What are these sections, and what transitions introduce the steps?
5. What is the purpose of the eight numbers at the end of the article?
6. What advice does the article give for the safety of the person performing the task?

---

* Each of the numbered steps appears as a caption underneath a photograph in the original article.

How to Write a Personal Letter

Garrison Keillor

Garrison Keillor is a well-known humorist, radio personality,
and author of Lake Woebegone Days.

(1) We shy persons need to write a letter now and then, or else we'll dry up and blow away. It's true. And I speak as one who loves to reach for the phone and talk. The telephone is to shyness what Hawaii is to February, it's a way out of the woods. *And yet:* a letter is better.

(2) Such a sweet gift—a piece of handmade writing, in an envelope that is not a bill, sitting in our friend's path when she **trudges** home from a long day spent among wahoos and savages, a day our words will help repair. They don't need to be immortal, just sincere. She can read them twice and again tomorrow: *You're someone I care about, Corinne, and think of often, and every time I do, you make me smile.*

walks slowly

(3) We need to write, otherwise nobody will know who we are. They will have only a vague impression of us as A Nice Person, because, frankly, we don't shine at conversation, we lack the confidence to **thrust** our faces forward and say, "Hi, I'm Heather Hooten, let me tell you about my week." Mostly we say "Uh-huh" and "Oh really." People smile and look over our shoulder, looking for someone else to talk to.

shove

(4) So a shy person sits down and writes a letter. To be known by another person—to meet and talk freely on the page to be close despite distance. To escape from **anonymity** and be our own sweet selves and express the music of our souls.

being unknown

(5) We want our dear Aunt Eleanor to know that we have fallen in love, that we quit our job, that we're moving to New York, and we want to say a few things that might not get said in casual conversation: *Thank you for what you've meant to me. I am very happy right now.*

(6) The first step in writing letters is to get over the guilt of *not* writing. You don't "owe" anybody a letter. Letters are a gift. The burning shame you feel when you see unanswered mail makes it harder to pick up a pen and makes for a cheerless letter when you finally do. *I feel bad about not writing, but I've been so busy,* etc. Skip this. Few letters are **obligatory,** and they are *Thanks for the wonderful gift* and *I am terribly sorry to hear about George's death.* Write these promptly if you want to keep your friends. Don't worry about the others, except love letters, of course. When your true love writes *Dear Light of My Life, Joy of My Heart,* some response is called for.

required

(7) Some of the best letters are tossed off in a burst of inspiration, so keep your writing stuff in one place where you can sit down for a few minutes and—*Dear Roy, I am in the middle of an essay but thought I'd drop you a line. Hi to your sweetie too*—dash off a note to a pal. Envelopes, stamps, address book, everything in a drawer so you can write fast when the pen is hot.

(8) A blank white 8" x 11" sheet can look as big as Montana if the pen's not so hot—try a smaller page and write boldly. Get a pen that makes a **sensuous** line, get a comfortable typewriter, a friendly word processor—whichever feels easy to the hand.

stimulating

(9) Sit for a few minutes with the blank sheet of paper in front of you, and let your friend come to mind. Remember the last time you saw each other and how your friend looked and what you said and what perhaps was unsaid between you; when your friend becomes real to you, start to write.

(10) Write the **salutation**—*Dear You*—and take a deep breath and plunge in. A simple **declarative sentence** will do, followed by another and another. As if you were talking to us. Don't think about grammar, don't think about style, just give us your news. Where did you go, who did you see, what did they say, what do you think?

greeting
statement

(11) If you don't know where to begin, start with the present: *I'm sitting at the kitchen table on a rainy Saturday morning. Everyone is gone and the house is quiet.* Let the letter drift along. The toughest letter to crank out is one that is meant to impress, as we all know from writing job applications; if it's hard work to slip off a letter to a

friend, maybe you're trying too hard to be terrific. A letter is only a report to someone who already likes you for reasons other than your brilliance. Take it easy.

(12) Don't worry about form. It's not a term paper. When you come to the end
of one episode, just start a new paragraph. You can go from a few lines about the sad
state of rock 'n' roll to the fight with your mother to your fond memories of Mexico
to the kitchen sink and what's in it. The more you write, the easier it gets, and when

brother or sister   you have a True True Friend to write to, a soul **sibling,** then it's like driving a car; you
just press on the gas.

(13) Don't tear up the page and start over when you write a bad line—try to
write your way out of it. Make mistakes and plunge on. Let the letter cook along and
let yourself be bold. Outrage, confusion, love—whatever is in your mind, let it find a
way to the page. Writing is a means of discovery, always, and when you come to the
end and write *Yours ever* or *Hugs and Kisses,* you'll know something you didn't when
you wrote *Dear Pal.*

(14) Probably your friend will put your letter away, and it'll be read again a few
years from now—and it will improve with age.

(15) And 40 years from now, your friend's grandkids will dig it out of the attic
and read it, a sweet and precious relic of the ancient Eighties that gives them a sudden clear glimpse of the world we old-timers knew. You will have then created an object of art. Your simple lines about where you went, who you saw, what they said, will
speak to those children and they will feel in their hearts the humanity of our times.

(16) You can't pick up a phone and call the future and tell them about our times.
You have to pick up a piece of paper.

Questions for Investigation and Discussion

1. Keillor is known primarily as a humorist. Is the purpose of his essay to entertain?
   How would you characterize his attitude toward his subject? Why does he take
   that attitude?
2. Who is the audience for the essay? Why does he feel that writing letters is important for them?
3. Keillor doesn't explicitly label most of the steps involved in writing the letter, but
   what are those steps?
4. Keillor tends to break the "rules" concerning punctuation and sentence fragments. How does his rule-breaking affect your reaction to the essay? Are any of
   his rule-breaking sentences unclear?
5. Is any of Keillor's advice useful to people attempting other kinds of writing?

SUGGESTED TOPICS FOR WRITING

For each suggested subject provided, include a topic sentence and a step-by-step
chronological explanation of the process. Include whatever transitions are necessary to show the logical relationship between ideas.

1. Assume that, like the authors of *America's Handyman Book,* you are explaining a process to people who need to fix or assemble some machine.
   Write clear, step-by-step directions, beginning with a list of the materials
   and tools needed.
2. Assume that, like Garrison Keillor, you are writing advice to others about
   performing a simple, familiar task in a way that would make it very special:
   how to make a dinner party a wonderful experience for your guests, how to
   have a truly romantic date, how to bring a story to life for children as you
   read it out loud, how to plan an exciting birthday party, or any other com-

monplace task. Write about it with practical, specific, and imaginative suggestions, and illustrate your advice as does Keillor.

3. Assume you are writing for a humor magazine like *Mad* or *National Lampoon*. Compose a caption to be placed under this cartoon, in which you explain the process.

Self-Watering Palm Tree

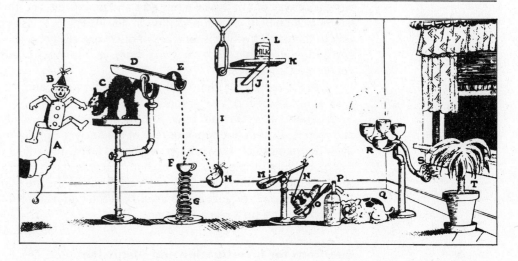

Rube Goldberg: Self-watering palm tree. *Reprinted with special permission of King Features Syndicate, Inc.*

4. Like Rube Goldberg, design your own complex and crazy machine for performing a simple task: opening a door, turning on a light, fanning yourself, pouring dog chow into a bowl, and so on. Then explain how the contraption works, including your own crude drawing of the apparatus.

5. Assume again that you are writing for a humor magazine; compose an explanation of how to wake up slowly in the morning.

6. Again for a humor magazine, compose an explanation of how to write an F paper.

7. Compose a letter to a friend who is planning a visit. Advise him or her on how to do any of the following tasks:
   a. locate your home or dormitory;
   b. be safe from street criminals (or from local drivers); or
   c. dress for the climate (or according to the styles in your circle of friends and acquaintances).

8. Assume you are a coach of an athletic team and are writing a short instruction manual on any of the following subjects: how to steal a base, swim a certain stroke, serve in tennis, shoot a jump shot, or warm up before exercising.

Composing Comparison-Contrast Paragraphs

This chapter discusses comparing and contrasting—that is, methods of exploring the similarities and differences among ideas. We examine two ways of structuring comparison-contrast paragraphs:

✏ through whole-to-whole organization; and
✏ through part-to-part organization.

Then we examine the process of composing comparison-contrast paragraphs:

✏ planning and organizing ideas;
✏ drafting the paragraphs; and
✏ revising the paragraphs while supplying appropriate transitions.

COMPARISON AND CONTRAST DEFINED

You constantly make choices: what to buy, where to live or work, what to study, for whom to vote, and even what to eat for dinner. Virtually every choice requires that you evaluate ideas, things, or people by comparing and contrasting them.

◆ A *comparison* (also sometimes called an *analogy*) is an examination of similarities.
◆ A *contrast* is an examination of differences.
◆ A *comparison and contrast* is an examination of both similarities and differences.

You also constantly encounter new ideas and concepts: new subjects in school, new discoveries and beliefs, new fashions or fads, new practices in the business world, and new products and inventions. You can best understand something unfamiliar when you see it compared through *analogy* to something familiar—when you approach the unknown through something you know.

Thus, you generally compare and contrast to evaluate or clarify. If you write an advertisement for a new car (or write to recommend the car to a friend), you can compare and contrast the car to others, showing why your choice is easier to drive, more comfortable, and more economical. Likewise, if you describe the duties of the manager and co-workers in your company, you can compare and contrast those duties, showing where they overlap and differ. If you explain how radar works, you can use the analogy of a ball bouncing off a wall, showing how the speed and travel time of the ball allow you to measure its location at any point. Whatever you decide to compare and contrast, keep this advice in mind:

1. *Make a point* in your comparison. Don't just say that two things are similar or different. Evaluate them, arguing that one is better than the other, or be informative, relating something new to something familiar through analogy.

2. *Don't oversimplify.* Few subjects are entirely identical or different. It's fine to say that sailing a boat is like steering a bicycle, but show the differences—unless you want your readers to drown. It's fine to say a Panther EX-LE automobile is better than a Slugmobile, but don't claim that a Slugmobile is a waste of money. It may be a perfectly good car, but not as good as a Panther EX-LE.

3. *Whenever possible, supply examples and explanations to support your comparisons.* Don't say merely that the Panther EX-LE is comfortable; describe its ample leg room, contoured seats, and soft upholstery.

ORGANIZING A COMPARISON-CONTRAST PARAGRAPH

Comparisons and contrasts within paragraphs are most understandable when organized in a clear and consistent way. Two possible methods of structuring such paragraphs are whole-to-whole or part-to-part organizations. Let's examine both.

Employing Whole-to-Whole Organization

Whole-to-whole organization means just what its name implies: a complete discussion of one subject followed by a complete discussion of another. Whole-to-whole organization works best with simple and easily understood material. For example, a paragraph on the Slugmobile and the Panther EX-LE can begin by describing the important features of the first car—its price, style, power, seating capacity, special features, ease of handling—and then repeat the process with the second car while drawing comparisons and contrasts. Here is the general outline of the Slugmobile-Panther EX-LE comparison:

Slugmobile

1. price: $27,000
2. style: two-door coupe
3. power: 180 litre, V-4 engine
4. gasoline consumption: 18 miles per gallon
5. seating capacity: four people (two in front bench seats, two in back)
6. safety features: dual air bags, antilock braking
7. special features: power windows, power door locks, cruise control, remote-controlled door opener, four-speaker radio and cassette music system

Panther EX-LE

1. price: $31,000 (more than Slugmobile's)
2. style: four-door sedan (more stylish than Slugmobile's)
3. power: 250 litre, V-6 engine (better than Slugmobile's)
4. gasoline consumption: 25 miles per gallon (better than Slugmobile's)
5. seating capacity: five people, two in front bucket seats, three in back (better than Slugmobile's)
6. safety features: dual air bags, antilock braking, steel-beam reinforced doors (safer than Slugmobile's)
7. special features: power windows, power door locks, cruise control, remote-controlled door opener, leather seats, automatic climate control, six-speaker radio, cassette, and compact disc music system (better than Slugmobile's)

Arranged in climax order, this comparison makes a persuasive case for the Panther EX-LE. It argues that the Panther EX-LE is superior in style, power, economy of gasoline consumption, seating capacity, safety features, special features consumption—although it costs more.

The following paragraph employs a whole-to-whole structure to compare and contrast two men. Sentences 1 and 2 establish the reason for the comparison, which is then introduced in sentence 3—a topic sentence for the first part of the comparison. (There is no topic sentence for the entire paragraph.)

Rivals in Love as Well as Politics

❏ (1) Abraham Lincoln and Stephen Douglas were famous political rivals, and they were romantic rivals as well. (2) Both men wanted to marry a flirtatious young lady named Mary Todd after she moved to Springfield, Illinois, in 1839. (3) *To her family, the differences between the two couldn't have been more pronounced.*

It continues by describing the traits of Douglas.

(4) Mary Todd's parents much preferred Douglas, a lawyer who, like Mary, had money, social status, and ambition. (5) Some people said the young man might even be president one day. (6) Douglas was handsome and well dressed, with a powerful voice, and was called the "Little Giant" because he stood just over 5 feet tall.

Sentence 7 serves as the transitional and topic sentence for the remainder of the paragraph, which turns to a discussion of Lincoln's traits, but refers back to Douglas's along the way.

(7) For some reason, however, Mary was attracted to Lincoln, *another lawyer, who Mary's family felt lacked wealth, class, and a desire to get ahead.* (8) Although he was four years older than Douglas, he had been a state legislator since 1834 and seemed to be going nowhere. (9) Unlike Douglas, Lincoln was hardly a physical prize, with his unpolished manners, high-pitched voice, and poorly fitting clothes draped over his lanky 6-feet-4-inch frame. (10) Nevertheless, Mary got her wish and became Mrs. Lincoln in 1842.

The paragraph ends with this evaluation and summing up, spoken by Mary Todd:

(11) She was indeed a better judge of the man than her parents were, for, in 1861, Lincoln defeated Douglas in another contest—for the presidency of the United States. (12) As Mary commented during a debate between the two in 1858, "Mr. Douglas is a very little, little giant by the side of my tall Kentuckian, and intellectually my husband towers over Douglas just as he does physically."

The Lincoln-Douglas Debate, *by Robert M. Root. Illinois State Capitol, Springfield.*

Although the paragraph mentions or implies a few similarities between the men (both were lawyers and politicians; both were intelligent and ambitious), it primarily stresses their differences. These contrasts are sharp because the details are presented in the same order.

Douglas	*Lincoln*
"had money, social standing, and ambition" "handsome and well dressed, with a powerful voice, and was called 'Little Giant' because he stood just over 5 feet tall"	"lacked wealth, class, and a desire to get ahead" "hardly a physical prize, with his unpolished manners, high-pitched voice, and poorly fitting clothes draped over his lanky 6-feet-4-inch frame"

Employing Part-to-Part Organization

Suppose you are composing a one-paragraph advertisement for a revolutionary automobile, the Omicron, and need to emphasize the differences between the car and a familiar, conventional automobile such as a Chevrolet. Because much of the information about the Omicron is new and complex, readers of the ad might not remember, understand, or appreciate all of the car's features if they are presented at the same time. A part-by-part organization, therefore, sharpens the focus. It alternates between Chevrolet and Omicron while discussing each feature, perhaps by examining the similarities first and the differences later. A preliminary outline of the paragraph might look like this:

Similarities Between the Chevrolet and the Omicron

1. appearance
2. seating

Differences Between the Chevrolet and the Omicron

3. motor (gas in the Chevrolet; electric in the Omicron)
4. placement of motor (in the front for the Chevrolet; in the rear for the Omicron)
5. economy of operation (25 miles per gallon in the Chevrolet; the equivalent of 75 miles per gallon in the Omicron)
6. speed (100 miles per hour in the Chevrolet; 140 miles per hour in the Omicron)
7. maintenance (tune-ups and oil changes in the Chevrolet; neither in the Omicron)
8. brake system (disc in the Chevrolet; magnetic in the Omicron)
9. frame and panels (steel in the Chevrolet; hardened plastic alloy in the Omicron)

Here is the final draft of the paragraph as it emerged from the initial outline:

❏ The car of the future is available today: the revolutionary Omicron. While in appearance and seating capacity it resembles a conventional car like the

Chevrolet, the Omicron differs dramatically in every other aspect. Unlike the front-mounted gasoline motor in a conventional car, the Omicron's powerful rear-mounted electric motor emits no pollution and runs far more economically. Its cost in electricity translates to an amazing 75 miles per gallon of gasoline—three times the mileage of the Chevrolet. Yet despite this economy, the Omicron is a powerful driving machine, achieving a top speed of 140 miles per hour, compared to 100 mph in the Chevrolet. Other advances in technology make the Omicron virtually maintenance free; it never requires a tune-up or an oil change. And, perhaps most important of all, the Omicron is the safest car you can drive. The reliability and stability of its magnetic braking system far exceed those of disc-brake systems in conventional cars. The Omicron's patented reinforced plastic alloy frame and panels—four times stronger than the steel found in conventional cars—provide unsurpassed protection against injury in collisions. Don't wait until the next century to ride in the comfort, safety, and economy of the Omicron. See your local Omicron dealer and test-drive the car of the future today.

The next paragraph also employs a part-to-part structure to clarify (and make interesting) a complex matter: the separate functions of the nose. The paragraph draws an analogy between the workings of a heating and air-conditioning system and the workings of the nose. The opening sentence establishes the basic comparison; the topic sentence outlines the discussion that follows:

❑ (1) Your nose is like a complex heating and air-conditioning system. (2) *It controls the temperature and humidity of the air you take into your lungs, and it filters out unwanted materials such as bacteria and dust.*

The remaining sentences of the paragraph follow the outline stated in the topic sentence, switching back and forth between the heating and air-conditioning system and the nose. (The italicized transitional expressions introduce each point of comparison.)

(3) *First,* because the lungs need air at a constant temperature, your nose must regulate that temperature in much the same way as a heating or air-conditioning system does. (4) In a heating and air-conditioning system, the air passes over coils for warming or cooling. (5) In your nose, air passes over thousands of tiny veins filled with blood that, at a constant temperature of 98.6 degrees, warm or cool the air as well. (6) *Second,* because the lungs need air with a 75 percent moisture content, the nose resembles a humidifier in a heating system. (7) Just like the wet liner in a humidifier, the wet tissue inside the nose adds moisture to the dry air. (8) *Finally,* because your lungs become diseased from bacteria and dust, your nose must act like the filter on a furnace or air conditioner, although the process of filtering air in the nose is more complicated. (9) The nose is lined with a sticky substance called *mucus,* which is constantly draining into your stomach. (10) The mucus traps bacteria entering your nose and kills them with chemicals. (11) The mucus also captures small particles of dust and carries them into your stomach, where they are made harmless by digestive juices. (12) And the final part of the filtering system, the hairs inside your nose, prevent big particles of dust from entering at all.

After this complex explanation, the last sentence—in effect a second topic sentence—restates the main points of the comparison.

(13) Thus, thanks to that efficient heating, cooling, and filtering system called the nose, your lungs receive a constant supply of warm, moist, clean air.

Note that the transitional expressions throughout the paragraph signal the similarities and the one difference.

Similarities

"*in much the same way as* a heating or air-conditioning system does"
"the nose *resembles* a humidifier in a heating system"
"*Just like* the wet liner in a humidifier"
"*like* the filter on a furnace or air conditioner"

Difference

"the process of filtering air in the nose is *more complicated*"

1   Examining Comparison-Contrast Paragraphs

Read the following two paragraphs and then answer the questions that follow. (This exercise could be done collaboratively.)

White Castle's Unorthodox Success Story

(1) In the competitive world of fast-food hamburgers, White Castle is the odd man out. (2) It does everything "wrong" and yet it has been successful since 1921. (3) Here are just a few of the ways in which White Castle differs from the bigger players on the block. (4) While McDonald's, Burger King, and Wendy's earn much of their income from selling franchises to individual owners, all White Castle stores are owned by the parent company. (5) While the Big Three have tried to expand their business quickly and widely through franchising, White Castle has been content to maintain operations in the midwestern states, as well as in Kentucky, New Jersey, and New York. (6) While other fast-food restaurants have expanded their menus, offering breakfast, gourmet sandwiches, and salad bars, White Castle has stuck with the staples. (7) Yes, it does carry french fries, onion rings, and a couple of other sandwiches, but hamburger sales account for a full 60 percent of its gross profit, a much higher figure than any other major hamburger chain's. (8) While the other fast-food outfits emphasize the large size of their patties, White Castle sticks with its tiny, inexpensive burgers. (9) What customers get is a patty that is 2 inches square and very thin. (10) White Castle is like its competitor Wendy's in one respect: serving square burgers (and, in White Castle's case, square buns). (11) Unlike Wendy's, however, which chose the square shape for marketing reasons, White Castle packs 30 square patties onto its square grills for quick, efficient cooking. (12) Another major difference between White Castle and its competitors is the way the burgers taste and feel. (13) There is no delicate way of stating it: White Castle burgers reek of onions and have a soggy texture. (14) Far from an insult, these are the reasons White Castle fans love them. (15) Devotees call the little burgers "sliders," undoubtedly because the bun and patty are soggy enough to slide down the throat without chewing. (16) The final and most striking difference between White Castle and its competitors is that each White Castle patty has five little holes. (17) As usual with White Castle, these holes serve a totally practical function. (18) They allow steam and grease from the grill to rise to the upper bun, which sits on top of each patty. (19) The meat therefore cooks evenly without having to be flipped over. (20) In sum, White Castle doesn't think there is anything fancy about the hamburger business.

(21) It has taken a soggy, smelly burger that MBA types would probably consider impossible to sell and created a mini-empire.

A Doggone Good Question

❏ (1) Dogs apparently love to stick their heads out of the windows of speeding cars, but the same animals hate when someone blows in their ears. (2) Why is one act so pleasurable and the other so distasteful? (3) Of course, nobody has been able to interview canines on the subject, but most experts contend that the circumstances have nothing in common. (4) Apparently, dogs stick their heads out of car windows because they like the view. (5) Most dogs are not tall enough to have an unobstructed view of the outside world from the front seat, and most dogs are too short to look out the front or back windows from the back seat. (6) Poking their heads out of the window is therefore a good way to check out the surroundings and enjoy a nice cool breeze at the same time. (7) However, blowing in a dog's ear, even gently, can be painful to the animal, not because of the softness of the skin or the sensitivity of the nerves, but because of the sound of the blowing. (8) Ben Klein, a veterinarian, explains that one way of testing a dog for deafness is to blow into its ear through a funnel. (9) If the dog doesn't get upset, that indicates possible deafness. (10) So while many people might think that blowing into a dog's ear is a playful act, to the dog it is the canine equivalent of scratching a blackboard with fingernails. (11) The high frequency of the sound drives the animal crazy.

1. What organizational approach does each paragraph take: whole-to-whole or part-to-part comparison? What words or phrases draw the comparisons?
2. How many major points of comparison does each paragraph draw? How do you know?
3. Does a topic sentence explicitly state the comparison in each paragraph, or is the comparison implied? What transitional sentences introduce the major comparisons?
4. Do these paragraphs discuss similarities, differences, or both?
5. Is the style of each paragraph formal or informal? What evidence supports your judgment? Is the purpose of each paragraph to inform, persuade, or entertain? How does the style support that purpose?

IN SUMMARY

Comparison-contrast

1. examines the similarities and differences among people, ideas, or things;
2. can be used to *evaluate*, usually by showing similarities and differences, or can be used to *inform*, usually by comparing the new to the familiar through analogy;
3. can be structured in a *whole-to-whole* organization, with one subject fully discussed and then the second one fully discussed while compared to or contrasted with the first;
4. can be structured in a *part-to-part* organization, with one point about both subjects compared or contrasted, then a second point, and so on;
5. doesn't oversimplify by painting a black-versus-white portrait, but instead shows similarities as well as differences; and

> 6. is developed through explanations and examples, rather than merely
>   listing similarities and differences.

COMPOSING A COMPARISON-CONTRAST PARAGRAPH

The preceding examples have shown that a comparison-contrast paragraph must be carefully structured. Although you should plan, draft, and revise the paragraph in a way most comfortable to you, the following suggestions may prove helpful.

Beginning with Discovery, Planning, and Outlining

After choosing a subject, explore your ideas through brainstorming, clustering, or free writing. Suppose, for example, that in a counseling class you are asked to compare two careers so you and your instructor can evaluate which is best for you. Your initial free writing might look like this:

> Interested in accounting—a lucrative, challenging profession. Need to major in business, a very competitive field; can enter program only as a junior if I have a 3.75 average. Then need to pass the C.P.A. [Certified Public Accountant] exam. Takes more training—more time, work, and money spent on schooling. Probably work for a big firm, be involved in exciting deals as I get promotions and more responsibility. Don't know if I want the nine-to-five life, though. Like working with people, being freer, more creative. Also interested in high school teaching—doesn't pay nearly as much, but certainly challenging. Doesn't have much prestige these days, and involves a lot of paper shuffling. I'd get summers off—a big plus since I won't have to worry about arranging child care for kids during school vacations. And I could teach math, which I'm good at and is much in demand. Program easy to get into, but I understand it has a lot of "Mickey Mouse" courses. Don't know if I can tolerate them. Lots to consider, but I'm leaning toward teaching.

You can return to this free writing again, adding more details as they occur to you and your ideas solidify. Simply draft them on separate sheets of paper or insert them in the original draft in your computer program.

You can make an informal list of the points of comparison next, perhaps arranged into separate categories of similarities and differences, such as this list based largely on the free writing, with some details that were added later.

Similarities
    challenging and exciting
    involve math
    involve attention to detail, filling out forms, following rules

Differences

Accountant	Teacher
high pay	low pay
high prestige	low prestige
nine-to-five or later hours	shorter hours, summers off
competitive program	easier program, with some "Mickey Mouse" courses
high grades required	lower grades required
C.P.A. exam	teaching exam (easier)
help corporations	help youngsters
work with numbers	work with numbers and people

Then decide on an organization to use, reading down the columns of differences for whole-to-whole and across the columns for part-to-part organization. Your decision will probably be based on the following matters:

◆ the audience for the comparison (classmates struggling with similar decisions);
◆ the reason for comparing (probably to inform your readers of their options); and
◆ the complexity of the subject matter (not very complex) and your audience's familiarity with it. (They know it fairly well.)

In this case, the answer seems to be a whole-to-whole approach, but, after attempting to draft the paragraph, you might discover you actually feel more comfortable with a part-to-part organization.

COMPUTER TIP

FOR GENERATING AND ORGANIZING COMPARISONS AND CONTRASTS

Many word processing programs include a feature for arranging materials in columns or in a table, like the grid contrasting the differences between accountant and teacher you just saw. This feature has two advantages:

1. the columns help you generate and examine exact parallels between the traits of the subjects you compare and contrast; and

2. it allows you to rearrange the items simply through the *cut and paste* (or similar) commands.

Drafting the Topic Sentence

Try to draft a preliminary topic sentence that not only states the comparison but also implies the reason for making the comparison. Four examples follow, the first two in the first person and the others in the third person. (In each case, the rest of the paragraph would continue to maintain the voice used in the topic sentence.)

> *As I compare and contrast teaching mathematics with being an accountant, I find I would rather be a teacher.*
>
> *I believe I would be happier as a mathematics teacher than as an accountant for several reasons.*
>
> *Teaching mathematics has more attractions than working as an accountant.*
>
> *Although both accounting and the teaching of mathematics have advantages and disadvantages, teaching seems to be the better choice.*

The first topic sentence states, and the three others imply, that you are comparing the two disciplines to evaluate them.

✎ **2   Exploring Ideas for Comparisons and Contrasts**

Assume that in a sociology class you have been asked to compose a paragraph discussing the different responsibilities and behavior of people in various roles. Complete each of the following lists by supplying additional similarities and differences, and then draft a preliminary topic sentence stating the comparison. Finally, indicate whether you will use a whole-to-whole or part-to-part organization.

Comparison A.

a typical single person	*a typical married person*
1. *lives alone or with roommate*	1. *lives with spouse*
2. _____	2. _____
3. _____	3. _____
4. _____	4. _____
5. _____	5. _____
6. _____	6. _____

Topic Sentence: _____

Organization: _____

Comparison B.

a tourist	*an explorer*
1. *visits popular places*	1. *goes to hard-to-reach places*
2. *stays in hotels or motels*	2. _____

3. _____   3. _____

4. _____   4. _____

5. _____   5. _____

6. *takes many photographs or videos*   6. _____

Topic Sentence: _____

Organization: _____

Comparison C.

a parent   *a pet owner*

1. *responsible for feeding, care, etc.*   1. *responsible for feeding, care, etc.*

2. _____   2. _____

3. _____   3. _____

4. _____   4. _____

5. _____   5. _____

6. _____   6. _____

Topic Sentence: _____

Organization: _____

Comparison D.

a 10-year-old child   *a college freshman*

1. *responsible for feeding, care, etc.*   1. *responsible for feeding, care, etc.*

2. _____   2. _____

3. _____   3. _____

4. _____   4. _____

5. _____   5. _____

6. _____   6. _____

Topic Sentence: _____

Organization: _____

3   Exploring Ideas for Contrasts

Assume you are composing a magazine advertisement for a brand of detergent, an automobile, cereal, artificial sweetener or egg substitute, or any other real or imaginary product. List the superiorities of your product over the competitor, and then supply a topic sentence and method of organization as explained in Exercise 2.

your product   *its competitor(s)*

1. _____   1. _____

2. _____   2. _____

3. _____   3. _____

4. _____   4. _____

5. _____   5. _____

6. _____   6. _____

Topic Sentence:_____

Organization: _____

✍ 4   **Organizing Materials for a Comparison-Contrast Paragraph**

Assume you are composing a one-paragraph essay examination answer based on the points in each of the following lists from outside sources. Decide on a whole-to-whole or part-to-part organization, and write your choice in the space after the topic sentence. Then, on the lines that follow, write the numbers of the supporting points (such as A1, B3) in the most effective order. (This exercise could be done collaboratively.)

Paragraph A.   (for a psychology course)

psychiatrists

A1. are always M.D.s
A2. may treat patients face to face across desk
A3. may not personally have undergone therapy
A4. may use variety of techniques: medication, behavior modification, electric shock, Freudian analysis, or other therapy
A5. may also be psychoanalysts if they have undergone psychoanalysis

psychoanalysts

B1. have personally undergone psychoanalysis
B2. use classical Freudian analysis or other methods of exploring a patient's past life
B3. most often treat patients who lie on a couch
B4. are not necessarily M.D.s
B5. always have formal training as analysts

Organization: _____

Topic Sentence: *Although many people think psychiatrists and psychoanalysts are the same, the two are more different than they are alike.*

_A1_   _B4_

____   ____

____   ____

____   ____

____   ____

Paragraph B.   (for a biology course)

a beehive

A1. houses workers who perform different tasks
A2. is responsible for two activities: making honey and producing more bees
A3. has older workers that bring materials—pollen and nectar—to make honey
A4. has younger bees that receive and transfer pollen and nectar into open cells in the honeycomb

A5. has drone bees to impregnate the queen bee
A6. has queen bee that lays eggs in cells while tended to by worker bees
A7. has worker bees that make major decisions: when to get rid of drones, when to
     increase the number of queen bees, or when to kill the existing ones

a human factory

B1. houses workers who manufacture products
B2. receives materials that are used in manufacturing
B3. is responsible for one activity: making a product
B4. usually has highly organized division of labor
B5. has workers who perform different tasks
B6. has workers who unload and store materials
B7. has managers and supervisors who make decisions

Organization: _____

Topic Sentence: *In many ways, the operation of a beehive is like the operation of a modern factory.*

```
_____    _____

_____    _____

_____    _____

_____    _____

_____    _____

_____    _____

_____    _____
```

5   Composing a Comparison-Contrast Paragraph

Compose a first draft of a paragraph based on the topic you found most interesting in Exercises 2, 3, or 4. Try to use parallel structure in sentences that compare each point. Revise the paragraph at least once.

Inserting Transitions Within a Comparison-Contrast Paragraph

Although you have already seen several transitions in the sample comparison-contrast paragraphs in this chapter, the following list may be a useful guide as you draft your own paragraphs:

> TRANSITIONS FOR SIMILARITIES: also, as well as, both, each of, in the same way,
> (just) like, neither, similarly, the same, too
>
> TRANSITIONS FOR DIFFERENCES: although, by contrast, but, however, in spite of,
> instead of, nevertheless, nor, on the one hand—
> on the other hand, though, unlike, while

The next paragraph is a later draft of the accountant-versus-teacher comparison and contrast, complete with transitions (shown in bold type). It begins with two introductory sentences, followed by the topic sentence (also in bold type), which takes a form somewhat different from any found in earlier versions. Notice that the part-to-part organization first explores the similarities between accountancy and teaching and then the differences between the two. It also discusses both the advantages and the disadvantages of teaching.

Like many students, I have had a hard time deciding on a college major—and by extension, a career. I have been torn between studying to become a high school mathematics teacher or an accountant. **However, after evaluating the advantages and disadvantages of each, I believe I would be happier as a mathematics teacher.** Both professions are challenging and both involve mathematics, which I am good at, **but that is where the similarity ends. Although** the rewards of accounting are high pay and high prestige from working for a big firm, the rewards of teaching outweigh these. I would work **not** to help corporations **but** to help youngsters. I would have the freedom to plan my own lessons; to be my own boss in class; and to travel, take courses, work elsewhere, and be with my children during the summers without worrying about arrangements for child care. **Instead of** working long hours as an accountant, I would finish earlier and have more days off. Of course, I would have papers to grade at home, but I am sure that accountants take their work home **as well.** The biggest disadvantage to becoming a teacher is putting up with the "Mickey Mouse" courses that teacher-training programs are supposed to include. That disadvantage, however, is far more tolerable than those I would encounter as a business major: the extended schooling at high cost and the stiff competition to earn a 3.75 average needed for admission to the program as a junior. I tried to make a choice based on the values most important to me, not those most important to my friends or even my parents. Perhaps every student should do the same.

✏️ **6   Editing a Passage for Transitions**

In the following passage, insert transitions showing similarities or differences among ideas.

What's Up—Or Down—Your Sleeve?

❑   Men's shirts come in sleeve lengths—32 inches, 33 inches, and so on—
_____*but*_____ women's blouses don't have standard sleeve lengths. What accounts for the difference between the wearing apparel of the sexes? Cory Greenspan, of the Federation of Apparel Manufacturers, explains. _*First of*_
_*all,*___ men's and women's sleeves are designed to serve different purposes. Men's long-sleeve shirts are designed to be worn with a jacket so that the sleeve will hang just below the wrist line when the wearer is standing.

_____ women wear long-sleeve blouses with other garments or no

covering at all. _____ the "appropriate" length of a women's sleeve varies depending on the ideas of the fashion designer and the purpose of the outfit.

_____, women have a much wider choice of blouses than men do of dress shirts. If each blouse came with sleeve sizes, retail stores would have to cut down on their selection in order to provide all the different sizes.

_____ men are content with the usual boring solids and stripes, even the dressiest women's blouses are available in a wide range of colors and textures. No store could stock all of them in differing sleeve lengths.

7   Analyzing Your Paragraph

Read the paragraph you drafted in Exercise 5 and respond to each of the following questions. Use the responses as guidelines for revising the paragraph, and then do the revision. (This exercise could be done collaboratively, with each person reading his or her paper aloud twice and the group responding to the questions.)

Revision Guidelines

1. Is the topic sentence clear, and does it suggest the reason for the comparison? _____ If not, how should it be revised? _____

2. Does the paragraph follow a consistent whole-to-whole or part-to-part organization? _____ If not, what should be changed? _____
   _____

3. Do the details all support the topic sentence? _____ If not, what should be eliminated, revised, or added? _____
   _____

4. Are the similarities and differences unclear at any point? _____ If so, how should the paragraph be revised? _____
   _____

5. Are transitions lacking or too vague at any point in the paragraph? _____ If so, what should be added or revised? _____
   _____

6. What was the greatest problem in composing this paragraph? (Ignore this question if the writer experienced no significant problems.) _____
   _____

   If this problem was not resolved, what should be done? _____
   _____
   _____

8   Proofreading and Polishing Your Paragraph

After completing the revision, edit the paragraph, checking for correct spelling and punctuation, complete sentences, and clarity of ideas. Then make a clean copy of the paragraph and proofread it carefully for errors.

✍ **9   Drafting, Revising, and Editing a Paragraph**

Draft another paragraph based on one of the lists you prepared in Exercises 2, 3, or 4. Revise the paragraph, including transitional expressions as needed. Then edit and proofread the paragraph.

READINGS

Testing the New Small-Dish Satellite Systems

From *Consumer Reports,* March 1995

Consumer Reports *is a monthly magazine that tests
and evaluates products for consumers.*

(1) It's long been possible to pluck TV programming from the sky by using a satellite dish. Problem is, until now such dishes have cost more than $2000 and measured 6 to 10 feet in diameter—a poor fit with the budget and backyard of most households.

choice   (2) Enter a smaller, simpler satellite-TV **alternative.** Instead of rotating to pluck programs from 24 different satellites, as do the big dishes, the new systems aim at only one or two satellites that provide a package of up to 150 channels. The home user needs only a fixed dish as small as a garbage-can lid.

(3) Introduced in the U.S. just a year ago, small-dish satellite systems are already in more than 600,000 homes. We tested the two small-dish systems available: The RCA Digital Satellite System, with its 18-inch diameter dish; and the Primestar system, with its 39-inch dish.

skillful   (4) RCA's equipment costs $700 to $900, plus another $200 for professional installation (only **adept** do-it-yourselfers should consider buying the $70 installation kit and installing the system). Primestar requires that its equipment be professionally installed, at a cost of about $300. You rent the Primestar system, rather than buy it; the rental charge (which doesn't include the channels) is about $8 a month.

(5) The cost of programming for a small-dish system is about the same as for cable, and so are many of the channels, including such cable regulars as *CNN* and
extra-cost   *Arts & Entertainment,* the **premium** movie channels, and pay-per-view offerings.
related stations However, you can't get the local network **affiliates;** for that, you'll need an antenna or basic cable service. If you can't pick up those affiliates well by antenna, the satellite programmers will provide network programs, usually from an affiliate in a far-off city—and at extra cost.

in-the-area   (6) Programming you can get with a dish includes audio-only music channels, **regional** sports channels, and a Sunday-afternoon NFL package. Also, on the dish's pay-per-view channels, the same programming is carried on several
varied   channels, with schedules **staggered**—so you could watch "The Firm," say, at 8 or 8:30 P.M.

staff member of   (7) Like cable rates, the cost of Primestar varies by region. A **staffer** in the far
Consumer Reports northern New York City suburbs paid $30 a month for a basic package—30 channels, including at least 8 sports channels and *The Disney Channel* (a basic channel on Primestar). HBO or Cinemax was $10 more.

supplier   (8) With the RCA system, no programming **provider** has it all. For $30 a month, DirecTV offers 40 channels, including six *Encore* movie channels. However, DirecTV
etc.   does not offer the familiar premium channels—*HBO* **and the like.** For those, you must subscribe to USSB. It offers five packages—from an $8, six-channel "basics" package to a $35 "entertainment plus" package that includes five premium channels. However, USSB offers only a handful of basic channels.

match
arrangement

(9) Taping programs can be a hassle with a dish. VCRs lack the ability to tape one channel off a satellite receiver, then change to another channel and tape that one. Primestar at least allows you to set a timer that will change the receiver channel to **synchronize** with the VCR, although that means setting two timers. RCA's system offers no such **provision.**

product
small problems
short

(10) In our tests, we judged the pictures and sound from the satellite systems to be superior to what's typically found on cable—close to laser-disc **output.** However, there are occasional **glitches** in the reception. In some fast-moving scenes such as sporting events, there is **momentary** loss of detail as the picture breaks down into tiny squares. Some channels, particularly the network feeds, aren't quite as clear as others. Also, to connect additional TV sets to a dish, you have to buy additional equipment or pay an extra programming fee, or both.

examination
possible
don't allow

(11) A dish must be installed on property with a clear southern exposure and it must be aimed fairly close to the horizon. Primestar will make a free site **survey** to determine whether a hookup is **feasible.** Check local laws too; some localities **prohibit** dishes.

(12) Compared with Primestar, the RCA system is more compact, and it offers features such as on-screen programming summaries and handy scroll-through programming menus, which allow a channel to be called up with the push of a button.

Questions for Investigation and Discussion

1. What is the purpose of this article?
2. What are the main differences between the older satellite dishes and the new ones (Primestar and RCA)?
3. Does the comparison and contrast between Primestar and RCA follow a whole-to-whole or part-to-part organization? Why?
4. What features of the two satellite systems does the article compare and contrast? In what ways are they different? In what ways are they similar?
5. In what ways are the two satellite systems better than free or cable TV? In what ways are they worse?
6. The article doesn't recommend that you buy either of these systems. Why?

A Tale of Two Gravies

Karen P. Bellitto

Karen P. Bellitto is a social work assistant in a nursing home.
Her interest in and affection for the elderly are evident
in this essay.

(1) "Come on kids! We're going to Grandma's."
(2) "Which one?"
(3) During my childhood, these words were typical in my home almost every Saturday and Sunday afternoon. On Saturday, we'd go a few blocks to Grandma Ruth's, my father's mother; on Sunday, my mother would answer, "Grandma Meatball," her mom, and we'd drive to the suburbs. Each of those visits was enormously different, at least from the eyes of the little girl I was. I always wondered then why Grandma Ruth's "gravy" was thick and brown and poured over mashed potatoes, but Grandma Meatball's was tomato sauce that she ladled over macaroni, sausage, and beef. As I grew up, however, I began to understand that Grandma Ruth and

different

Grandma Meatball, who came from entirely **diverse** worlds, were more alike than I ever imagined.
(4) "Come on kids. We're going to Grandma's."
(5) "Which one?"

(6) It was Saturday. "Grandma Ruth's." She lived only five minutes away, in an apartment building off Allerton Avenue in the Bronx. When she knew we were coming she would poke her head out the window so she could point out the best parking space when we got closer to the apartment. The building was old and there was no elevator. We climbed the five flights of stairs that led to my Grandma's apartment, for some still unknown reason marked "2E."

(7) The doorbell was much higher than my reach and my dad would lift me up so I could ring it. The kitchen was about three feet from the door, so it wasn't long before Grandma Ruth came rushing out. She wasn't that tall, only about five-four, and slender, but she still smothered me and my sister, Tami. Looking at pictures of her when she was younger you'd say she never changed. She had begun to gray *thin* when she was only 16 and the years in between made her **wispy** hair bright white. Grandma Ruth, in my mind's eye, will always be one of those young old people: young in mind and spirit with a body that just couldn't keep up.

(8) Grandma Ruth was born in New York and was a city girl her whole life. She *loud and rowdy* had three **raucous** boys. Grandma Ruth loved to talk and laugh; she was always having "company" over. My father remembers sitting at the kitchen table stuffing fundraising envelopes she'd brought home from work so they could make a little extra money. Grandma Ruth would tell him stories of her family picnics in upstate New *legend* York. These became family **lore** for me, too.

(9) Grandma Ruth's Saturday meals were spectacular. The smells coming from the kitchen made the two hours before dinner almost unbearable. Roast beef with gravy, mashed potatoes, creamed onions, mashed turnips, and string beans were the usuals. The roast beef was sometimes replaced by a roast pork or leg of lamb. Whatever the main course, it was meat, and there was always bread and butter. The weekend after Grandma Ruth died, my mother made this exact meal. It was our way of saying good-bye—and thanks.

(10) Years ago, while we waited for her dinner, we'd get bored with the grown-up conversation. I would sit at my grandmother's desk by the phone and play secretary with her datebook. She had a desk set of those marble pen holders where the pen is attached by a chain. This became my telephone since I wasn't allowed to use the real one. When even this got boring, I would begin to wander around the house looking for the next thing to keep my interest. The dining room had all kinds of cool stuff in it so I would usually end up there. Trinkets and books lined long *covered* shelves that **spanned** one entire wall of the room; there was plenty to explore and keep my imagination busy.

(11) The dining room table was set with white dishes with green flowers on the edges. Even the glasses were frosted white with matching green flowers. The kiddy bridge table was just off to the left, but it was set the same way so we wouldn't feel left out. The adults drank wine; we drank Hoffman's lemon soda. It always amazed me how much the adults could talk while they ate, though my mother told me not *ended* to talk when we chewed. The laughter and chatter never **ceased.** After dinner, my folks would sprawl out on her bed and take a nap. My sister and I would look out the window, just like Grandma.

(12) "Come on kids, we're going to Mass, then we're going to Grandma's."

(13) "Which one?"

(14) Sunday: "Grandma Meatball."

(15) After ten o'clock Mass we'd pile into my father's long, tired Pontiac for the 45-minute trip to Long Island. For as long as I could remember, Grandma Meatball and Grandpa lived in Uncle Vinny's basement apartment. In marked contrast to Grandma Ruth, Grandma Meatball was very Old World Italian. She was a quiet woman who spoke more with the smiling silence of her eyes; her house was filled with religious paintings and statues. When she did talk, she'd amaze us with her stories of Arthur Avenue, a noisy Italian section of town, where she and Grandpa raised a brood of seven children in a three-room apartment. She'd remember life in the Italian

countryside before she came to America. Simply thinking that this wise old woman was once a little girl, like me, who barely knew English was not something I could picture.

(16) When we arrived, stir crazy from the long trip, Tami and I would swing around to the backyard of the house where Grandpa was fussing with his vegetable garden. He knew we were coming and he wanted to have a bag of tomatoes ready to go home with us. Then we'd go down the concrete steps to the basement where Grandma was standing by the stove stirring her "gravy." The minute we'd walk in, she'd say hello with her quiet eyes; we'd literally get lost in her round hugs, stronger than a man's. After the long greeting— she never let go easily, even years later as she lay in her hospital bed—she'd lead us over to the stove where the bowl of meatballs was waiting for us. Grandma would always fry extra meatballs for us to eat when we got there. She had to make a double batch, because half went into the gravy and the rest got eaten one by one by whoever walked into the kitchen.

(17) Macaroni didn't have to get thrown in until the last minute before we ate, so we were basically waiting for the gravy meat to cook. While Grandma put out bread, cheese, wine, and fruit to pick at before dinner, my cousins came down from upstairs and we played. Grandma's basement apartment was perfect for hide and seek: there were nooks and crannies all over the place. The closets were enough to keep us busy until we were called to eat, but the laundry room was off limits ever since my cousin John got thrown in the dryer by his brothers. It was on at the time.

(18) There wasn't enough room for everyone to eat downstairs, so we would carry the meal up to Aunt Mary and Uncle Vinny's kitchen because it was bigger. I had five aunts and uncles all together, so if everyone was on Long Island at once there was absolutely no way we could fit everyone, even in the larger kitchen. The kids would be in the living room sitting at the bridge table. There was no room for us to make our own plate, so each mother would make one up for her kids. We didn't feel left out because we were in the other room. Everyone talked so loudly we were able to contribute from where we were.

(19) The autumn my grandmothers died, I thought often about those big week-end dinners. When I was a kid, all I was able to see were the differences between these women. Looking back, I realize that the cultural, emotional, even personal **disparity** fascinated me at that time. But as I grew and learned more about their lives, I came to understand that Grandma Ruth and Grandma Meatball were much more alike than I had ever imagined.

difference

(20) They loved and protected their children and grandchildren passionately. The good family values that are so often missing from today's world were daily lessons in their homes: they taught my mother and father to keep a family together, to put each other and their children first, and to understand that a family that stuck together no matter what could never be poor. By educating my parents, each of my grandmothers, unique as they were, contributed to my growth as a young woman in these same ways. They each loved me in their own language and expressed that love on their own terms. Their separate worlds merged together to make me the whole that I am. They taught me that where I stand depends on where they stood before me. A little girl sees the old fashioned ways of her grandmothers. The young woman understands the underlying importance, even timeliness, of their commitment to be **matriarchs** to their families. To remember their stories and pass them on to my own family, then, is to honor them. That is their **legacy,** and my responsibility.

female rulers
gift

Questions for Investigation and Discussion

1. What sentences or phrases in the first paragraph introduce the topic ideas of Karen Bellitto's essay? The essay is about far more than the "two gravies" of the title and first paragraph; what larger ideas or themes do the two gravies represent?

2. Does Bellitto employ a whole-to-whole or part-to-part organization in drawing contrasts between her grandmothers? Why? When discussing their similarities late in the essay, which organization does she use? Why?
3. Make your own list of the contrasts between the two grandmothers. Are they introduced in the same order? Is each trait of one grandmother contrasted to a trait of the other grandmother?

SUGGESTED TOPICS FOR WRITING

This list of topics may help you formulate ideas for paragraphs of comparison or contrast. For each paragraph you compose, include a topic sentence (or at least make the topic idea clear), arrange the paragraph according to a whole-to-whole or part-to-part structure, and insert appropriate transitions when necessary. Be sure the purpose of the paragraph (to explain or to evaluate) is clearly stated or implied, and be sure to develop each idea fully.

1. Like Karen Bellitto, compose a story about two relatives whose lives and personalities were quite different but similar in larger ways. Discuss what a typical experience with them was like, but don't limit yourself merely to narration. Like Bellitto, analyze or explain the similarities between the two relatives. Assume you would publish the story in a student literary magazine.
2. Assume you are an explorer who is reporting to the news media the discovery of the animal below. Describe the animal by comparing its features to those of the familiar animals in the picture on the following page.

Warthog.

Domestic pigs.

3. Assume you are a writer who evaluates cars, electronics, or computers for *Consumer Reports, Car and Driver, Audio, Video,* or *PC Magazine.* Compare the main features of two such items, recommending one as the better buy.
4. Assume you are writing for a fashion magazine. Describe a new style in clothes by comparing it with an earlier style.
5. Assume you are composing a paper for a music appreciation class. Describe a new musical performer, a new group, or a new musical style by comparing it with an older, more familiar one.
6. Assume you are composing a paper for an education course in which you must analyze different teaching (or learning) styles. Describe and compare two such styles.

9

Composing Classification Paragraphs

Throughout this unit, you have studied several ways to develop and organize paragraphs, beginning with the simplest methods and progressing to more complex ones. This chapter introduces yet another method of paragraph development: *classification,* which is a way of organizing ideas into categories. As usual, the chapter begins with the following sections:

✏ defining the term *classification;*
✏ observing the organization of classification paragraphs; and
✏ exploring the process of composing such paragraphs.

The last section, on the composing process, offers you practice in the following skills:

✏ drafting a topic sentence (the formal statement of classification); and
✏ drafting paragraphs complete with explanations, illustrations, and transitional expressions.

CLASSIFICATION DEFINED

Look in any office and you will find a filing system (although nowadays it may be on a computer) with records grouped in categories: paid accounts in one folder, unpaid accounts in another, and potential accounts in yet another. Look in any supermarket and you will find the merchandise grouped in categories, with dairy products in the cooler, breakfast food and cereals in one aisle, and soap and detergents in another. Look in any school and you will find even the students grouped in categories: first graders in one room and second graders in another, or English classes in one room and math in another. Such arrangements are a natural part of our thinking and writing. We like to organize things, people, and ideas so we can define, locate, compare, contrast, and understand them.

The term for these arrangements is *classification,** the process of grouping together similar people or things into categories or types. Classification touches on virtually every kind of paragraph development you have encountered in earlier chapters—description, narration, process analysis, and comparison and contrast. When writing about the causes of unemployment, for example, you might classify and then describe them in four categories, such as lack of education, lack of enough jobs, lack of incentives for people to work, and lack of transportation to and from work. When analyzing the process of studying, you might establish three categories: before-class behavior (reading and library work), in-class behavior (note

---

* It is sometimes called *division,* for the process may involve dividing a large group of people or things into separate categories.

taking and question asking), and after-class behavior (reviewing, outlining, and memorizing). You can devote a whole composition to a classification, with each paragraph exploring and explaining a separate category. However, limit yourself for now to a one-paragraph classification, which includes all the categories and a short explanation of each.

ORGANIZING A CLASSIFICATION PAPER

While many categories seem a natural part of the world, in reality they exist only in our minds. People create categories, and one grouping may be as valid as another provided it is based on only one *criterion,* or standard. For example, a natural criterion for classifying the stages of human life is *a person's physical development,* with such categories as infancy, childhood, adolescence, adulthood, middle age, and old age. The criterion, however, can just as easily be *a person's intellectual development.* Based on this criterion, not only will the categories change but so will the placement of people within them. One category, *the reasoning stage,* might include children aged 9 or 10 while excluding some mentally handicapped adults. Therefore, if you want categories to be clear and consistent, follow these guidelines in your paragraph:

- ◆ *Use only one criterion for classifying.* Group people according to their nationality, race, or religion—but not according to nationality and race, or race and religion. Otherwise the groupings will overlap with, for example, the same person fitting into the categories of *whites, Italians,* and *Catholics.*
- ◆ *Allow room in the categories for everyone or everything you classify.* A classification of Americans according to religion should include *Protestants, Catholics, Jews, Muslims,* and *Buddhists,* but it should also include *other religions* (or *religions with less than 10,000 members*) and *no religion.*
- ◆ *Explain or illustrate all the categories.* Don't just list categories; clarify and explain them. For example, explain that the category *no religion* probably includes those who claim no formal relationship with a church or synagogue or who refuse to discuss their religion.
- ◆ *Arrange the categories in some consistent order.* Start, for example, with the largest groups and end with the smallest, or start with the most expensive and end with the cheapest.

The following paragraph, which might be found in the lifestyle section of a newspaper or in a magazine on fitness and sports, is an example of a classification. The first four sentences introduce the reason for the classification: to inform people about the types of swords used in fencing.

(1) In these days of running, cycling, and pumping iron, there is one sport you probably have overlooked: fencing. (2) It demands quickness, endurance, and quick reflexes. (3) And, while actually an updated version of the traditional duel with swords, fencing shouldn't injure you because of the protective masks and thick padding you wear. (4) Before trying it out, though, you had better become familiar with the weapons.

The next sentence is both the formal statement of classification and the topic sentence, which establishes the criterion for classification and the number of categories.

(5) You can arm yourself with three kinds of swords, determined according to the size and shape of their blades.

Then the paragraph presents the categories (shown in italic) and their supporting explanations, arranged from the lightest to the heaviest sword.

(6) The blade of the first sword, the *foil*, is light and flexible. (7) It is slightly thicker than a pencil, flattened on the sides, and tipped at the end to prevent injury. (8) The rules allow you to use it only for thrusts (hits with the tip) to your opponent's body, but not to the arms, legs, or head. (9) The second weapon, the *épée*, has a stiffer shaft and most resembles the old dueling sword. (10) Although it is also long, narrow, and tapered to a dull point, the sides are fluted (like the indentations on a column) and have no cutting edges. (11) According to the rules, you may use it for thrusts anywhere to the body, head, or limbs. (12) The third and heaviest weapon, the *sabre*, is like the old calvary sword. (13) Because its blade has two cutting edges and a sharp-tipped point, you are free to slash, stab, thrust, and cut with it. (14) Thus, if you are interested in a physically and mentally challenging sport, choose a weapon and say "en garde."

✍ 1   Examining a Classification Paragraph

Read the following paragraph and then answer the questions. (This exercise could be done collaboratively.)

❏   (1) Students in colleges or universities are sometimes puzzled about how to address their teachers, for not everyone who gives grades is a professor. (2) Academic titles are, in fact, as rigid in what they represent as ranks in the military. (3) In terms of prestige (and often pay), teachers on American campuses can be classified from highest to lowest as follows. (4) The generals, colonels, and captains are the *full professors, associate professors,* and *assistant professors.* (5) Although the reasons for these rankings are not consistent, most professors have Ph.D.s, and full professors are typically senior faculty members who have taught for many years and published many articles or books. (6) The associate professors are generally less experienced and have published less material. (7) And the assistant professors are usually the least experienced and published. (8) Nevertheless, you can properly address all three as "Professor." (9) Next come the sergeants—*the instructors*—followed by the foot soldiers in the academic wars—the *fellows* and *assistants* (or *teaching assistants, graduate assistants,* or some similar title). (10) Instructors may or may not hold Ph.D.s, and usually they are relative newcomers to the faculty. (11) Fellows and assistants are graduate students in the university who teach while they complete their studies. (12) You should probably address all of them as "Mr.," "Mrs.," "Miss," "Ms.," or, if they prefer, "Dr." (assuming they have Ph.D.s). (13) One final category can be added to this list—*lecturer,* an academic title in some colleges and universities, although its meaning varies. (14) Most often it is the title for a part-time teacher who ranks somewhere around instructor.

1. Although no single sentence states the reason for classifying teachers in colleges and universities, several sentences imply it. What is the reason?
2. Who is the likely audience for this paragraph?
3. What is the topic sentence that introduces the classification?
4. What is the criterion for classifying teachers?
5. Does the classification include room for all teachers? Why is the category of *lecturer* introduced separately at the end of the paragraph?
6. What comparison is used throughout the paragraph to clarify the ranking of teachers?
7. Based on the description of the teachers' educational background and ex-

perience, what other criteria can be used for classifying the teachers? How will the categories then change?

IN SUMMARY

> **Classification**
>
> 1. is the process of grouping together similar people or things into categories or types;
> 2. is based on a single criterion or standard so that categories do not overlap;
> 3. accounts for everyone or everything classified;
> 4. defines, explains, and often illustrates each category; and
> 5. is arranged with categories in some consistent order—for example, tallest to shortest, or closest to farthest.

COMPOSING A CLASSIFICATION PARAGRAPH

While the process of composing a paragraph of classification will follow your own invention, drafting, and revising practices, you need to focus early on classifying the material into categories. The following steps may serve as a useful guide.

Beginning with Discovery, Planning, and Outlining

After exploring your ideas through brainstorming, clustering, or free writing, you should establish categories for classifying the material based on a single criterion. Otherwise, the categories may overlap and your classification won't be clear. Here are some suggestions to help you:

1. *Make one or more lists of your ideas, experimenting with different groupings.* Explore what your ideas have in common. For example, group types of study behavior according to when they occur (before class, in class, and after class), where they occur (at home, in class, or in the library), or how often they occur (daily, weekly, or only before tests).
2. *Consider your purpose and topic,* for they should help determine the categories. For example, if you want to persuade college students about how best to study, you might decide that the process should be arranged according to a time sequence: reading and outlining textbooks at home, note taking in class, and studying all this material before tests.
3. *Arrive at an informal outline based on your criterion for classification.* You can generate an outline in two ways: determine the criterion and then create the groupings, or create the groupings and then determine the criterion. Either approach may require some adjusting and rewording.

COMPUTER   TIP

FOR ARRANGING CATEGORIES

Again, as in Chapter 8, use the *table* or *column* feature to give you flexibility in generating and organizing the categories and supporting details of your classification.

✍ **2   Selecting Criteria for Classifying**

On the line after each of the following classifications, write the criterion used to determine the categories.

Classification A. slow workers, workers of average speed, and fast workers

Criterion: *speed of the workers*

Classification B. bicycles without gear shifts, three-speed bicycles, five-speed bicycles, ten-speed bicycles, and bicycles with more than ten gear ratios

Criterion: _____

Classification C. ostriches and monkeys, cows and cats, and fish and snakes

Criterion: _____

Classification D. doctors and lawyers, nurses and teachers, mechanics and technicians, and factory workers and fast-food workers

Criterion: _____

Classification E. superstition, religion, and science

Criterion: _____

✍ **3   Arranging Categories Logically**

Each of the following classifications is based on more than one criterion, so the categories within the classification overlap. Choose a single criterion for classification, state the criterion, and then rearrange and rewrite the information to fit within a clear outline. (You don't have to use all the information.)

Classification A. types of dressers

Original arrangement	*Revised arrangement*
	Criterion: *degree of concern with popular fashions*
the fancy dresser	I. *The conservative dresser*
the plain dresser	*A. plain*
the fashionable dresser	*B. practical*
the conservative dresser	II. *The fashionable dresser*
the practical dresser	*A. fancy*
the impractical dresser	*B. impractical*
the sexy dresser	*C. sexy*

Classification B. types of students

Original arrangement	*Revised arrangement*
	Criterion: _____
lazy students	_____
hard-working students	_____
intelligent students	_____

unintelligent students   _____

well-organized students   _____

disorganized students   _____

successful students   _____

unsuccessful students   _____

Classification C. types of houses

Original arrangement   *Revised arrangement*

                               *Criterion:*_____

expensive houses   _____

inexpensive houses   _____

moderately priced houses   _____

two-bedroom houses   _____

three-bedroom houses   _____

four-or-more-bedroom houses   _____

new houses   _____

old houses   _____

middle-aged houses   _____

4 Planning a Classification Paragraph

Assume you are the director of an overnight camp that offers a number of water activities: swimming in the pool and lake, canoeing, sailing, and waterskiing. You must
compose a letter to the parents of the campers, aged 9 to 16, explaining who will be
allowed to participate in each of these activities. Classify the campers according to
some criterion, and create an outline based on the classification.

or

Assume you are the manager of a fast-food restaurant who must compose a memo to
employees explaining how pay raises will be determined. List and classify the various
factors involved, and create an outline based on the classification.

Drafting the Formal Statement of Classification (and Topic Sentence)

Your classification paragraph should include a formal statement of classification to
help readers distinguish among categories. Draft the statement early in the composing process to avoid trouble with overlapping categories later on. (Of course, you can
revise this sentence at any point.) Such a formal statement often serves as the topic
sentence of a paragraph and follows a typical pattern. It first names the subject to be
classified and usually mentions the number of categories in the classification.

> *Food (subject) can be classified into five categories (number of
> categories). . . .*
> *You should develop three sets (number of categories) of study
> habits (subject). . . .*

> Teachers use several methods (number of categories) of teaching reading (subject). . . .
> Cars (subject) can be classified (no mention of number of categories, which will be introduced later in the paragraph by transitional expressions such as first, second, and last). . . .

Notice that this first part of the formal statement often includes such categorizing words as *types, categories, methods, kinds, ways,* and *classifications.* The second part of the statement introduces the criterion for classification.

> Foods can be classified into five categories, according to the amount of protein they contain.
> You should develop three sets of study habits, based on when they occur: before class, during class, and after class.
> Teachers use several methods of teaching reading, determined by the ways in which students most easily perceive words.
> Cars can be classified on the basis of their size.

Notice, too, that this second part usually begins with phrases such as *determined by, according to, based on,* and *on the basis of.* The criterion always involves a *range of categories,* which you may introduce two ways:

◆ in a single word that implies a range of choices—for example, *size, speed, height, intelligence,* or *wealth;* or
◆ in a phrase that states a range of choices—for example, *the amount of* protein, *the number of* members, or *the degree of* participation.

IN SUMMARY

A formal statement of classification

1. includes the subject to be classified;
2. usually includes the number of categories in the classification;
3. uses categorizing words such as *categories, types, methods, kinds,* or *ways;*
4. includes the criterion for classification;
5. introduces the criterion with phrases such as *determined by, according to, based on,* or *on the basis of;* and
6. includes a word that implies a range of choices (*height, temperature,* or *speed*) or a phrase that states a range of choices (*the amount of, the number of,* or *the degree of*).

✍ 5   **Predicting the Development of the Paragraph**

After each of the following topic sentences, list at least three categories you expect the paragraph to develop. (This exercise could be done collaboratively.)

A. Animals can be classified according to their intelligence.

 1. *highly intelligent animals*

 2. *moderately intelligent animals*

   3. *somewhat unintelligent animals* _____

   4. *primitively intelligent animals* _____

   5. *animals unable to think* _____

B. Most adults choose their leisure-time activities according to how much mental
and physical effort they wish to expend.

_____

_____

_____

_____

_____

C. On weekends this city offers a variety of activities to do and see in all price
ranges.

_____

_____

_____

_____

_____

6   Drafting a Preliminary Topic Sentence

Draft a formal statement of classification for each of the following subjects and their
categories. Be sure to include the criterion for classification.

A. Subject.   homicide

Categories: murder, manslaughter, government-sponsored killing, and killing of
the enemy in war

Statement: *There are at least four ways of viewing homicide, based on the*

punishment or reward given to the person who commits the killing.

B. Subject.   clocks

Categories: pendulum-operated, battery-powered, powered by household current, and mainspring-operated

Statement: _____

_____

_____

C. Subject.   elementary schools

Categories: public, private religious, and private nonreligious

Statement: _____

_____

_____

D. Subject. thieves

Categories: armed robbers, burglars, con artists, and embezzlers

Statement: _____

_____

_____

Composing the Classification Paragraph

Having established categories and prepared a formal statement of classification, you can now compose the first draft of the paragraph. Try to attract the readers' interest, making clear not only what you are discussing but also why you are discussing the subject. (That is, the classification can inform, persuade, or entertain.) The following paragraph introductions are based on two of the classifications in Exercise 3, each suggesting a different purpose:

> Take a good look at your classmates and you will see them attired in as wide a variety of costumes as you would find in any circus. To help you seek order in this chaos, I have devised the following simple classifications: those who dress conservatively and those who dress fashionably. (purpose: to entertain)
>
> Someone once said that the secret to success in school is to find out what the teachers want and then give it to them. It is good advice, and students can be classified according to how diligent they are in mastering that technique. (purpose: to inform)

Remember that the body of the paragraph should be more than a random list of categories. Explain and illustrate each category, and organize the categories according to some principle: smallest to largest, most to least, and so on.

7 Drafting and Revising the Paragraph

Compose a first draft of a paragraph on the materials you prepared in Exercise 4. Be sure to include a formal statement of classification, and explain and illustrate each category in the classification. Then revise the paragraph at least once.

Inserting Transitions Within a Classification Paragraph

After drafting the formal statement of classification, you will introduce, explain, and illustrate the categories in the rest of the paragraph. Therefore, you may need to use the following familiar transitions:

For listing categories	first, second, third, next, finally, the last
For illustrating categories	as an example (illustration), for example, for instance, to illustrate
For explaining categories	in other words, that means

✍️   **8   Editing for Transitions**

In the following paragraph, insert transitions showing the arrangement of categories, the explanation of categories, and any other logical relationships between ideas.

❑   (1) Most of the eggs sold over the counter in supermarkets are "AA" grade, the highest ranking. (2) The next grade is "A," and _____ grade is "B." ("C," the victim of grade inflation, has been phased out.) (3) According to the United States Dairy Association (USDA), these grades have nothing to do with egg size, but are based on criteria relating to the shell, the air cell at the large end of the egg, the egg whites, and the yolks. (4) _____ the shell of both "A" and "AA" grades must be clean and unbroken with "a practically normal appearance." (5) However, "B" quality eggs may be slightly stained. (6) _____ a solid stain may cover 1/32 of the egg's surface, but a series of scattered stains may occupy 1/16 of the surface. (7) Grade "B" eggs may _____ be abnormally shaped or have a ridge or thin spots. (8) _____ the air cell—the space between the shell membranes usually found at the large end of the egg—cannot be larger than 1/8-inch in grade "AA," 1/16-inch in grade "A," and 3/16-inch in grade "B." (9) _____ egg whites in grade "AA" eggs must be clear and firm. (10) Grade "A" whites must be clear and "reasonably firm" with a "fairly well-defined yolk outline when the egg is twirled." (11) _____ Grade "B" eggs not only can look weak and watery but can contain small blood and meat spots. (12) _____ the yolks in "AA" eggs stand up tall and blend into the surrounding white. (13) Grade "A" yolks are round and have a more noticeable outline. (14) _____ Grade "B" yolks are enlarged, flattened, and somewhat shapeless. (15) While these differences among the grades certainly affect the way the eggs look and feel, they do not greatly affect the way eggs taste.

✍️   **9   Analyzing Your Paragraph**

Read the paragraph you drafted in Exercise 7 and respond to each of the following questions. Use the responses for revising the paragraph, and then do the revision. (This exercise could be done collaboratively, with each person reading his or her paper aloud twice and the group responding to the questions.)

Revision Guidelines

1. Is there a clear formal statement of classification? _____ If the statement is not clear, how should it be revised? _____

_____

2. Are the categories determined by a single criterion? _____ If not, what should the criterion be and how should the categories be changed? _____

_____

3. Are the categories arranged in a logical order? _____ If not, how should they be arranged? _____

_____

4. Are all the categories sufficiently explained and illustrated? _____ If not, what should be changed or added? _____

_____

5. Are transitions lacking or too vague at any point in the paragraph? _____ If so, what should be added or revised? _____

_____

6. What does the paragraph do best? _____

_____

7. What was the greatest problem in composing this paragraph? (Ignore this question if the writer experienced no significant problems.) _____

_____

_____

If this problem was not resolved, what should be done? _____

_____

_____

✍ 10 Proofreading and Polishing Your Paragraph

After completing the revision, edit the paragraph, checking for correct spelling and punctuation, complete sentences, and clarity of ideas. Then make a clean copy of the paragraph and proofread it carefully for errors.

Composing Based on Outside Sources

Assume you are composing a report for a social science class. Complete the following paragraph using the information provided from outside sources. (You don't have to use all the information.) Include a formal statement of classification, transitions between categories of the classification, and explanations of the classifications.

Areas preserved for their beauty or other natural features
1. balance of nature cannot be disturbed
2. fishing permitted, but not hunting, mining, or logging
3. examples: Yellowstone, Grand Canyon, Mammoth Cave, Grand Teton, Everglades, Yosemite, Hot Springs, Badlands, Glacier Bay, Hawaii Volcanoes, Death Valley
4. scientific research encouraged
5. visitors cannot harm the areas

Areas preserved for historical reasons
1. include forts, monuments, historic buildings and bridges
2. the original appearance preserved or restored

3. examples: Lincoln's birthplace, Fort Bowie, Fort Laramie, Vanderbilt Mansion, Washington Monument, Gettysburg Battlefield, Vietnam Veterans Memorial, Arlington National Cemetery, the White House
4. lectures and tours for visitors
5. most free to public

Areas preserved for recreation
1. include parks, beaches, rivers, trails, mountain areas
2. swimming, hiking, horseback riding, sailing, fishing, and snorkeling allowed
3. examples: Lake Mead, Blue Ridge Parkway, Wolf Trap Farm Park for the Performing Arts, Indiana Dunes, Rio Grande Wild and Scenic River, and Cape Cod
4 visitors cannot remove or destroy plants
5. visitors cannot touch or feed wild animals

As one of the largest countries in the world, the United States contains an abundance of natural, historical, and recreational sites for its citizens to visit and enjoy. The government has set aside over 330 of these sites as parts of the national park system to protect and preserve them for the benefit and enjoyment of the public.

READINGS

Darkness at Noon

Harold Krents

Harold Krents, a lawyer, is a graduate of Harvard University and Oxford University. This article appeared in the New York Times *in May 1976.*

(1) Blind from birth, I have never had the opportunity to see myself and I have been completely dependent on the image I create in the eye of the observer. To date it has not been **narcissistic**. self-centered

(2) There are those who assume that since I can't see, I obviously also cannot hear. Very often people will converse with me at the top of their lungs, **enunciating** each word very carefully. Conversely, people will also often whisper, assuming that since my eyes don't work, my ears don't either. pronouncing

(3) For example, when I go to the airport and ask the ticket agent for assistance to the plane, he or she will **invariably** pick up the phone, call a ground hostess and whisper, "Hi, Jane. We've got a 76 here." I have concluded that the word "blind" is not used for one of two reasons: either they fear that if the **dread** word is spoken, the ticket agent's **retina** will immediately detach or they are **reluctant** to inform me of my condition of which I may not have been previously aware. without fail

terrible
a part of the eye;
unwilling

(4) On the other hand, others know that of course I can hear, but believe that I can't talk. Often, therefore, when my wife and I go out to dinner, a waiter or waitress will ask Kit if "*he* would like a drink" to which I respond that "indeed he would."

(5) This point was graphically driven home to me while we were in England. I had been given a year's leave of absence from my Washington law firm to study for a diploma in law degree at Oxford University. During the year I became ill and was hospitalized. Immediately after admission, I was wheeled down to the X-ray room. Just at the door sat an elderly woman—elderly I would judge from the sound of her voice. "What is his name?" the woman asked the orderly who had been wheeling me.

(6) "What's your name?" the orderly repeated to me.

(7) "Harold Krents," I replied.

(8) "When was he born?"

(9) "November 5, 1944," I responded.

recited

(10) "November 5, 1944," the orderly **intoned**.

nature

(11) This procedure continued for approximately five minutes at which point even my saint-like **disposition** deserted me. "Look," I finally blurted out, "this is absolutely ridiculous. Okay, granted I can't see, but it's got to have become pretty clear to both of you that I don't need an interpreter."

(12) "He says he doesn't need an interpreter," the orderly reported to the woman.

misunderstanding

(13) The toughest **misconception** of all is the view that because I can't see, I can't work. I was turned down by over 40 law firms because of my blindness, even

highest honors

though my qualifications included a **cum laude** degree from Harvard College and a good ranking in my Harvard Law School class.

(14) The attempt to find employment, the continuous frustration of being told that it was impossible for a blind person to practice law, the rejection letters, not based on my lack of ability but rather on my disability, will always remain one of the

disappointing

most **disillusioning** experiences of my life.

shorcomings
require

(15) Fortunately, this view of **limitation** and exclusion is beginning to change. On April 16 [1976], the Department of Labor issued regulations that **mandate** equal-employment opportunities for the handicapped. By and large, the business community's response to offering employment to the disabled has been enthusiastic.

(16) I therefore look forward to the day, with the expectation that it is certain to come, when employers will view their handicapped workers as a little child did me years ago when my family still lived in Scarsdale.

(17) I was playing basketball with my father in our backyard according to procedures we had developed. My father would stand beneath the hoop, shout, and I would shoot over his head at the basket, attached to our garage. Our next-door neighbor, aged five, wandered over into our yard with a playmate. "He's blind," our neighbor whispered to her friend in a voice that could be heard distinctly by Dad and me. Dad shot and missed; I did the same. Dad hit the rim; I missed entirely: Dad shot and missed the garage entirely. "Which one is blind?" whispered back the little friend.

(18) I would hope that in the near future when a plant manager is touring the factory with the foreman and comes upon a handicapped and nonhandicapped person working together, his comment after watching them work will be,

(19) "Which one is disabled?"

Questions for Examination and Discussion

1. Harold Krents establishes three categories in his essay. What are they, and what criterion are they based on?
2. How does he illustrate each category?
3. How would you describe Krents's tone in the essay: angry? sarcastic? amused? What evidence supports your response? Is Krents serious when he mentions his "saint-like disposition"?
4. What is Krents's purpose in writing this essay? What is his point, and where does he state or imply it?

Friends, Good Friends—and Such Good Friends

Judith Viorst

Judith Viorst is a contributing editor of Redbook *magazine and the author of a number of books for children.*

(1) Women are friends, I once would have said, when they totally love and support and trust each other, and bare to each other the secrets of their souls, and run—

unpleasant

no questions asked—to help each other, and tell **harsh** truths to each other (no, you can't wear that dress unless you lose 10 pounds first) when harsh truths must be told.

a Swedish filmmaker;
a French writer; passion;
a band leader

(2) Women are friends, I once would have said, when they share the same affection for **Ingmar Bergman,** plus train rides, cats, warm rain, charades, **Camus,** and hate with equal **ardor** Newark and Brussels sprouts and **Lawrence Welk** and camping.

(3) In other words, I once would have said that a friend is a friend all the way, but now I believe that's a narrow point of view. For the friendships I have and the

depth

friendships I see are conducted on many levels of **intensity,** serve many different functions, meet different needs and range from those as all-the-way as the friendship

offhand

of the soul sisters mentioned above to that of the most **nonchalant** and casual playmates.

(4) Consider these varieties of friendship:

1. Convenience friends. These are women with whom, if our paths weren't crossing all the time, we'd have no particular reason to be friends: a next-door neighbor, a woman in our car pool, the mother of one of our children's closest friends or maybe some mommy with whom we serve juice and cookies each week at the Glenwood Co-op Nursery.

(5) Convenience friends are convenient indeed. They'll lend us their cups and silverware for a party. They'll drive our kids to soccer when we're sick. They'll take us to pick up our car when we need a lift to the garage. They'll even take our cats when we go on vacation. As we will for them.

(6) But we don't, with convenience friends, ever come too close or tell too much; we maintain our public face and emotional distance. "Which means," says Elaine, "that I'll talk about being overweight but not about being depressed. Which means I'll admit being mad but not blind with rage. Which means that I might say that we're pinched this month but never that I'm worried sick over money."

enough
shared
close

(7) But which doesn't mean that there isn't **sufficient** value to be found in these friendships of **mutual** aid, in convenience friends.

(8) 2. Special-interest friends. These friendships aren't **intimate,** and they needn't involve kids or silverware or cats. Their value lies in some interest jointly shared. And so we may have an office friend or a yoga friend or a tennis friend or a friend from the Women's Democratic Club.

(9) "I've got one woman friend," says Joyce, "who likes, as I do, to take psychology courses. Which makes it nice for me—and nice for her. It's fun to go with someone you know and it's fun to discuss what you've learned, driving back from the classes." And for the most part, she says, that's all they discuss.

(10) "I'd say that what we're doing *is doing* together, not being together," Suzanne says of her Tuesday-doubles friends. "It's mainly a tennis relationship, but we play together well. And I guess we all need to have a couple of playmates."

(11) I agree.

(12) My playmate is a shopping friend, a woman of marvelous taste, a woman who knows exactly *where* to buy *what,* and furthermore is a woman who always knows beyond a doubt what one ought to be buying. I don't have the time to keep up with what's new in eyeshadow, hemlines and shoes and whether the smock look is in or finished already. But since (oh, shame!) I care a lot about eyeshadow, hemlines and shoes, and since I don't *want to* wear smocks if the smock look is finished, I'm very glad to have a shopping friend.

(13) 3. Historical friends. We all have a friend who knew us when . . . maybe way back in Miss Meltzer's second grade, when our family lived in that three-room flat in Brooklyn, when our dad was out of work for seven months, when our brother Allie got in that fight where they had to call the police, when our sister married the

a type of dentist

endodontist from Yonkers and when, the morning after we lost our virginity, she was the first, the only, friend we told.

(14) The years have gone by and we've gone separate ways and we've little in common now, but we're still an intimate part of each other's past. And so whenever

we go to Detroit we always go to visit this friend of our girlhood. Who knows how we looked before our teeth were straightened. Who knows how we talked before our voice got un-Brooklyned. Who knows what we ate before we learned about artichokes. And who, by her presence, puts us in touch with an earlier part of ourself, a part of ourself it's important never to lose.

brothers and sisters in competition

(15) "What this friend means to me and what I mean to her," says Grace, "is having a sister without **sibling rivalry.** We know the texture of each other's lives. She remembers my grandmother's cabbage soup. I remember the way her uncle played the piano. There's simply no other friend who remembers those things."

(16) 4. Crossroads friends. Like historical friends, our crossroads friends are important for *what was*—for the friendship we shared at a crucial, now past, time of life. A time, perhaps, when we roomed in college together; or worked as eager young singles in the Big City together; or went together, as my friend Elizabeth and I did, through pregnancy, birth and that scary first year of new motherhood.

hammer out; last

(17) Crossroads friends **forge** powerful links, links strong enough to **endure** with not much more contact than once-a-year letters at Christmas. And out of respect for those crossroads years, for those dramas and dreams we once shared, we will always be friends.

asleep or inactive; awakened

(18) 5. Cross-generational friends. Historical friends and crossroads friends seem to maintain a special kind of intimacy—**dormant** but always ready to be **revived**—and though we may rarely meet, whenever we do connect, it's personal and intense. Another kind of intimacy exists in the friendships that form across generations in what one woman calls her daughter-mother and her mother-daughter relationships.

viewpoint

(19) Evelyn's friend is her mother's age—"but I share so much more than I ever could with my mother"—a woman she talks to of music, of books and of life. "What I get from her is the benefit of her experience. What she gets—and enjoys—from me is a youthful **perspective.** It's a pleasure for both of us."

priceless

perfect

(20) I have in my own life a **precious** friend, a woman of 65 who has lived very hard, who is wise, who listens well; who has been where I am and can help me understand it; and who represents not only an **ultimate** ideal mother to me but also the person I'd like to be when I grow up.

confession

searching

(21) In our daughter role we tend to do more than our share of self-**revelation;** in our mother role we tend to receive what's revealed. It's another kind of pleasure—playing wise mother to a **questing** younger person. It's another very lovely kind of friendship.

(22) 6. Part-of-a-couple friends. Some of the women we call our friends we never see alone—we see them as part of a couple at couples' parties. And though we share interests in many things and respect each other's views, we aren't moved to deepen the relationship. Whatever the reason, a lack of time or—and this is more likely—a lack of chemistry, our friendship remains in the context of a group. But the fact that our feeling on seeing each other is always, "I'm *so* glad she's here" and the fact that we spend half the evening talking together says that this too, in its own way, counts as a friendship.

(23) (Other part-of-a-couple friends are the friends that came with the marriage, and some of these are friends we could live without. But sometimes, alas, she married our husband's best friend; and sometimes, alas, she is our husband's best friend. And so we find ourself dealing with her, somewhat against our will, in a spirit of what I'll

unwilling

call *reluctant* friendship.)

(24) 7. Men who are friends. I wanted to write just of women friends, but the women I've talked to won't let me—they say I must mention man-woman friendships too. For these friendships can be just as close and as dear as those that we form with women. Listen to Lucy's description of one such friendship:

(25) "We've found we have things to talk about that are different from what he talks about with my husband and different from what I talk about with his wife. So sometimes we call on the phone or meet for lunch. There are similar intellectual in-

terests—we always pass on to each other the books that we love—but there's also something tender and caring too."

(26) In a couple of crises, Lucy says, "he offered himself for talking and for helping. And when someone died in his family he wanted me there. The sexual, flirty part of our friendship is very small, but *some*—just enough to make it fun and different." She thinks—and I agree—that the sexual part, though small, is always *some,* is always there when a man and a woman are friends.

(27) It's only in the past few years that I've made friends with men, in the sense of a friendship that's mine, not just part of two couples. And achieving with them the ease and the trust I've found with women friends has value indeed. Under the dryer at home last week, putting on mascara and rouge, I comfortably sat and talked with a fellow named Peter. Peter, I finally decided, could handle the shock of me minus mascara under the dryer. Because we care for each other. Because we're friends.

adjusted (28) 8. There are medium friends, and pretty good friends, and very good friends indeed, and these friendships are defined by their level of intimacy. And what we'll reveal at each of these levels of intimacy is **calibrated** with care. We might tell a medium friend for example, that yesterday eve we had a fight with our husband. And we might tell a pretty good friend that this fight with our husband made us so mad that we slept on the couch. And we might tell a very good friend that the reason we got so mad in that fight that we slept on the couch had something to do with that girl who works in his office. But it's only to our very best friends that we're willing to tell all, to tell what's going on with that girl in his office.

(29) The best of friends, I still believe, totally love and support and trust each other, and bare to each other the secrets of their souls, and run—no questions asked—to help each other, and tell harsh truths to each other when they must be told.

(30) But we needn't agree about everything (only 12-year-old girl friends agree about *everything*) to tolerate each other's point of view. To accept without judgment. To give and to take without ever keeping score. And to *be* there, as I am for them and as they are for me, to comfort our sorrows, to celebrate our joys.

Questions for Examination and Discussion

1. What criterion or criteria does Viorst use in classifying friends? (Locate her formal statement of classification.) Are there any serious problems with overlapping categories—that is, would you be bothered that the categories might overlap?
2. What is Viorst's purpose for writing? What point is she making?
3. Viorst's style is very informal. Identify some traits of her informality.
4. What type of information does Viorst use to support and illustrate her categories?
5. What transitional expressions and other devices does Viorst use to label the categories and introduce explanations and examples?
6. At various points in the essay, Viorst contrasts and compares two categories. Why? In other words, what function do they serve?
7. At the end of the essay, Viorst repeats the language she used to describe the best of friends. What purpose does this repetition serve in making her point?

SUGGESTED TOPICS FOR WRITING

As always, choose a subject you know and feel comfortable with. As you plan, draft, and revise the paper, check it for clarity, development of ideas, and liveliness. The finished product should include a topic sentence and formal statement of classification, a logical ordering of categories, and an explanation and illustration of each one. Use any of the following topics or choose your own.

1. Does the background, appearance, or any other special circumstance make you or someone you know unusual in any way? Like Harold Krents, establish three categories that describe the way people have treated or still treat you or the person you know because of this unusual trait. Illustrate each category with examples. Assume you are writing for a popular men's or women's magazine such as *Esquire* or *Redbook,* or a magazine popular with similar ethnic or lifestyle groups.

2. Assume you are writing for a men's magazine such as *Esquire* or *Gentlemen's Quarterly.* Following Judith Viorst's model about women friends, compose an entertaining classification of the types of friends men have. Illustrate the categories with people you know—but don't use their real names.

3. Assume you are composing a guide for visitors to a local zoo. Place the animals in the photographs into larger categories (such as water animals and great apes) and explain where these groupings can be found in the zoo. If you wish, draw a map of the zoo to accompany your paragraph.

4. Assume you are a music, television, or movie critic for your campus or local newspaper. Compose an informative classification of the newest trends in popular music, television, or movies.
5. Assume you are composing a letter of advice to a friend seeking a job. Compose a paragraph describing several types of bosses your friend might encounter and which types are most preferable.
6. Assume you are writing a letter to a friend who is moving into your community and looking for a family doctor. Describe several types your friend might encounter and which are most preferable.
7. Assume you teach child development courses and are preparing your students for dealing with the typical behavior of 2- to 3-year-old children in a day-care center. Compose a one-paragraph analysis of several types of behavior.
8. For the same audience as in the previous suggestion, compose an analysis of the behavior of the parents of the children.

Composing Definition Paragraphs

Every chapter in this unit has begun by defining important terms to minimize misunderstandings. In your own writing, you should also be careful to define a word or phrase your readers might not know. Although a definition may take only a few words, it can require more extensive explanation in an entire paragraph. This chapter focuses on definition paragraphs in the following way:

- by defining the term *definition;*
- by discussing the five types of words most often defined;
- by working with drafting single-sentence definitions by synonym and by classification;
- by examining the development of definition paragraphs through illustration, negation, and historical process; and
- by exploring the process of composing definition paragraphs, from invention and planning to drafting and revising.

DEFINITION DEFINED

To be effective, communication must be clear. Whenever you draft and revise, therefore, try to anticipate the times your readers will ask, "What do you mean?" Suppose, for example, that in a letter to your local school board suggesting some changes in the curriculum, you use the phrase "good students." The board members might wonder whether you mean quiet students or inquiring students, competitive students or cooperative students, students who can recite what they learn or students who can apply it. Thus, you need to define the phrase, perhaps in a full paragraph.

A *definition* is an explanation of the meaning of a term (a word or phrase). You don't have to define every term, but which ones should you therefore define? Although the answer depends partly on your readers' familiarity with the subject, five types of terms are the most likely candidates for definition:

- *Vague terms.* People have their own personal understandings of abstract and general terms such as *love, faith, happiness, cultured,* or even *well educated.* (Can a person be well educated without learning the classics or a foreign language—or, for that matter, a computer language?) You must specify what these terms mean.
- *Relative terms.* Many terms represent a range of values, so people interpret them differently. *Rich,* for example, may suggest billions of dollars to a Rockefeller but $10,000 to the rest of us. *Tall* may mean 6 feet to you but 7 feet to a basketball coach. You may have to specify where these terms lie within the range.

◆ *Terms with several meanings.* Some terms have more than one definition. For example, *interest* can mean "curiosity," "a share in something," "the amount paid on a loan," or "self-advantage." While the context of the sentence often makes the meanings clear, the context isn't always enough. In such cases, you need to specify the definition you intend.

◆ *Related or commonly confused terms.* The meanings of two closely related terms may differ in small yet important ways, while two commonly confused terms may differ significantly. For example, if you are a lawyer presenting a case to the jurors in a criminal trial, you may need to distinguish between *murder* and *manslaughter* because that distinction can determine the length of a jail sentence. Similarly, since *uninterested* means "without interest" but *disinterested* means "objective" or "without prejudice," you may ask the jury to reach a disinterested and fair verdict.

◆ *Specialized or technical terms.* People interested or employed in technical or specialized fields may know the meanings of terms within those fields, but their readers may not. For example, what is *megabyte* in computer sciences, *enculturation* in sociology, or *basis points* in bond trading? Likewise, many slang terms are "specialized" as well, for their meanings are clear only to the groups that use them.

Some everyday terms may convey entirely different meanings within specialized fields. If you are a psychologist writing to the relatives of a patient, for example, you might need to define the term *affect.* The word normally is a verb meaning "influence," but to a psychologist, it is a noun meaning "any type of emotion."

EXAMINING WAYS OF DEFINING TERMS

Some terms can be defined in a few words, but many require whole paragraphs, especially those needing examples and complex explanations. While specific methods of developing a paragraph of definition vary, most paragraphs include two parts: (1) a single sentence that defines the term (it may also serve as the topic sentence of the paragraph), and (2) several more sentences that explain, illustrate, or contrast the term to other terms. Let's examine both parts.

Composing Single-Sentence Definitions

Single-sentence definitions are of two types: (1) definition by synonym, and (2) definition by classification.

Defining by Synonym.   A *synonym* is a word or phrase with virtually the same meaning as another. The easiest and shortest way to define a term is to supply a familiar synonym.

A CRT is computer terminology for a *monitor* or *television screen.*
The *aardvark*—or *anteater*—is found in southern Africa.
To eschew means *to avoid.*
His *impetuous* (that is, *impulsive*) behavior has gotten him into trouble more than once.

The synonym and the word it defines must be the same part of speech (noun and noun, infinitive and infinitive, adjective and adjective) so that one term can substitute for another.

✍ **1   Defining by Synonym**

Draft sentences that define each of the following words by synonyms. Use your dictionary if necessary, but don't copy.

1. bison _____

2. elated _____

3. to masticate _____

4. infinite _____

5. prevaricator _____

Defining by Classification.   When the meaning of a term is too complex to define by synonym, define it by classification (see Chapter 9). This is the formal method of definition, the method most often used in dictionaries and college compositions. Such definitions begin by placing the term into a larger category, or class.

Word	Category or class
A psychiatrist	is a medical doctor. . . .
Manslaughter	is an unlawful killing. . . .
A billing cycle	is a period of time. . . .

Then the definitions explain what distinguishes the term from all the others in the category.

Word	Category or class	Distinguishing characteristics
A psychiatrist	is a medical doctor	who specializes in the study, diagnosis, treatment, and prevention of mental illnesses.
Manslaughter	is an unlawful killing	without the clear intent to do harm to the victim.
A billing cycle	is a period of time	during which customers receive and pay their bills (typically 30 days).

When you define by classification, choose your words carefully, probably revising the definition several times. Otherwise, your definition may be unclear or imprecise. Avoid the following common errors:

1. *Don't rely too heavily on a dictionary.* If you consult a dictionary, the definition may not fit your purposes or match your writing style. Thus, restate the definition in your own words whenever possible. If you choose to copy the definition exactly, quote it, and mention the name of the dictionary.

2. *Don't make the category too broad.* It is not enough to say that a *psychiatrist* is a "person," or even a "doctor." A psychiatrist is a *medical doctor;* there are many Ph.D.'s practicing psychology, but they aren't psychiatrists.

3. *Don't make the distinguishing information too vague.* It is not enough to say that a psychiatrist *treats* mental illnesses; he or she *studies, diagnoses,* and *prevents* them as well.

4. *Don't make the definition circular.* Don't repeat the term in a slightly different form as part of the definition. It is not enough to say that a *psychiatrist*
practices *psychiatry;* explain what that practice involves.

✍ **2 Composing Formal Definitions**

Define each of the following terms by placing it in a class and specifying its distinguishing characteristics. You may use a dictionary, but restate the definition in your
own words.

Term	Class	Distinguishing characteristics
1. An *impresario*	is a sponsor or a pro-ducer of entertainment	most often, of an opera company
2. A *mantra*		
3. A *satellite*		
4. A *taboo*		

Also define two slang words you use with your friends, or two specialized terms you
use at work or in a class on a technical subject, such as biology, accounting, or computer science.

5. _____	_____	_____
6. _____	_____	_____

DEVELOPING THE DEFINITION

A full paragraph of definition not only defines a term but also illustrates its meaning through examples, contrasts it with closely related ideas, or traces its historical
origins. The following methods of development closely resemble those discussed in
earlier chapters of this book.

Developing by Illustration

Examples make a definition more concrete and lively, especially when you want to
show what a term means to you personally or means within the context of your
composition. You can develop the examples through either description or narration
(discussed in Chapters 5 and 6).

Consider the word *teacher.* A dictionary formally defines the term as a spe-
cially trained person hired by a school to provide instruction. Nonetheless, a man
named Ken Macrorie, who wants more than mere instruction from teachers, defines the term very differently. He says in his book *20 Teachers* (Oxford University
Press, 1984) that the best teachers are *enablers*—people who enable students to

use their own powers fully so that they do good work—good for them and good for the community at large. The 20 teachers he interviews in the book illustrate his definition as they discuss their practices and beliefs or tell stories about classroom experiences. You don't have to write a book to develop a definition, but you can provide descriptions or stories to illustrate one. The illustration needn't be long, but it should be long enough to enable your readers to understand or visualize the idea you are defining.

Developing by Negation

When you suspect that readers misunderstand a term or confuse it with another, you should clear up those misconceptions. A *definition by negation,* therefore, states what the term *is not* as well as saying what it is. Typically, you structure the paragraph in contrast organization (discussed in Chapter 8). Suppose, for example, that you are writing a letter to the administrators of your local community college proposing that free adult education courses be offered to the residents of a nearby nursing home. Your argument involves defining what you mean by *maturity,* which disagrees with the standard formal definition:

> *Maturity* is not, contrary to what most dictionaries say, "a state of development in which all growth has been completed." To my mind, maturity is exactly the opposite: a state of mental development in which people understand the need for much more growth. Mature people realize that they will stop learning only when they die.

Then you can establish point-to-point contrasts between what does not and does characterize maturity:

> Mature people aren't know-it-alls; they admit their ignorance. Mature people don't close their minds; they change their minds often. Mature people don't live only for today; they plan for tomorrow as well. Thus, an elderly person can be mature in the best sense of the word: still inquisitive about, involved in, and interested in learning.

Developing by Historical Process

Sometimes you can best explain a term's meaning by tracing its origin and development over time. A *paragraph of historical definition* typically uses a narrative structure (discussed in Chapter 5). The example that follows shows how a familiar term evolved. The first two sentences of the paragraph attract the reader's interest and state the topic.

❑   (1) The expression "male chauvinism" is now part of everyday American vocabulary. (2) The man who inspired the word *chauvinism,* however, had nothing against women.

Then it tells a story in climax order. The formal definition of the term occurs near the end of the paragraph in sentence 11.

(3) Nicholas Chauvin was a French soldier in Napoleon's army who was wounded badly no less than 17 times. (4) He was eventually too scarred to

continue fighting and had to retire. (5) This poor man received nothing more for his efforts than a medal, a ceremonial sword, and a pension of 200 francs (about $40). (6) Other men might have become bitter, but not Chauvin. (7) Instead, he became obsessed with Napoleon, ranting and raving constantly about the greatness of France. (8) Even after Napoleon's downfall, Chauvin remained his supporter. (9) Chauvin's hero worship grew so intense that he became the laughingstock of his village. (10) Two French playwrights, Jean and Charles Cogniard, heard of the patriotic madman and used him as a character in a comedy. (11) After several other playwrights followed their example, Chauvin's name came to represent extreme devotion to a name or cause. (12) Today, of course, the women's movement uses the term *chauvinism* to describe the excessive defense of men's "privileges." (13) What would the battle-bruised, faithful soldier have thought if he heard the expression "male chauvinist pig"?

You may wish to consult books that specialize in word histories (also called *etymologies*) if you choose to define a word according to its origin and evolution. English instructors often consult the *Oxford English Dictionary,* a multivolume reference book that traces the evolution of virtually every word in the language. Other sources include H. L. Mencken's *The American Language,* Eric Partridge's *Origins,* Joseph T. Shipley's *Dictionary of Word Origins,* and books by other lovers of the language.

3   Analyzing a Paragraph of Definition

Read the following paragraph and then answer the questions. (This exercise could be done collaboratively.)

❑   (1) The words *assault* and *battery* are linked in many people's minds, but they do not mean the same thing at all. (2) *Assault* in legal terms is an attempt or threat to use force or violence and doesn't have to involve actual physical contact. (3) *Battery* is the actual use of force. (4) The distinction is important. (5) Without it, a person who fails in a holdup and doesn't harm his victim might not be charged with a crime. (6) Another example comes from everyday life. (7) Shaking your fist at your neighbor is assault—if he or she wants to press charges. (8) It is not battery unless you follow it up by punching your neighbor in the nose, at which point it becomes assault and battery.

1. What is the topic sentence of the paragraph?
2. How many terms does the paragraph actually define?
3. Are the terms defined by synonym or class?
4. Is the paragraph developed by negation, historical process, or illustration? Which sentences employ the method of development?
5. What words, phrases, or sentences serve as transitions in the paragraph?
6. What sentences serve to illustrate the definitions?

IN SUMMARY

A definition

1. is an explanation of the meaning of a term (a word or phrase);
2. most often is used to explain vague terms, relative terms, terms with several meanings, related or commonly confused terms, and specialized and technical terms;
3. can begin with a *synonym* (a term with nearly the same meaning);
4. can be formally stated by *class*—placing the term in a larger category and showing its differences from other terms within that category;

> 5. doesn't rely heavily on a dictionary, doesn't place a term in too broad a category, isn't vague in distinguishing a term from others in a category, and isn't circular (repeating the term in slightly different form); and
> 6. can be developed in full paragraphs that illustrate the meaning of a term, use *negation* (that is, say what it doesn't mean), or trace its historical origins.

4   Predicting the Development of Definition Paragraphs

After each of the following topic sentences, write the method of development you expect to find in the paragraph—illustration, negation, historical process, or a combination of these—and list two or three examples of each. (This exercise could be done collaboratively.)

1. The meaning of the word *lady* has changed considerably over the last thousand years.

   *Method of development:*_____ *historical process* _____

   *Examples:*____ *its first meaning, any later meaning, its current meaning* ____

2. Although the dolphin lives in the sea, it is unlike most other marine-dwelling creatures.

   *Method of development:*_____

   *Examples:*_____

3. Since the process of conceiving, carrying, and giving birth to a child has become so complicated in recent years, biological motherhood is not easily defined.

   *Method of development:*_____

   *Examples:*_____

4. For me, true heroism goes way beyond merely risking one's life.

   *Method of development:*_____

   *Examples:*_____

COMPOSING A PARAGRAPH OF DEFINITION

Your personal practices, the needs of the audience, and the word to be defined will determine how you compose a paragraph of definition. Here are a variety of options to choose from.

Beginning with Discovery, Planning, and Drafting

Discovering.   The first step in composing an extended definition is exploring your own ideas about the term. Almost every word in English has more than one meaning, and many terms have dozens. If you can't think of a synonym or formal definition that conveys your meaning, look in a dictionary—or in several. You may find a definition that closely expresses your views or you strongly disagree with, which you might therefore include in a definition by negation. If you can't easily define a slang or specialized term, discuss its meaning with friends, parents, or co-workers. Perhaps they can explain the origins of the term and thus help you formulate a historical definition. Then explore and develop your thoughts further through brainstorming, clustering, or free writing. See what explanations, examples, or stories emerge. Once these ideas take form, you are ready for the next step.

Planning. As you plan a paragraph, make choices concerning the following two matters (although you can always change your mind later as you compose):

◆ *whether to define the word formally or by synonym.* If you choose the formal definition, you may need to revise it several times, although you can do this in later drafts of the paper.
◆ *whether to develop the paragraph by illustration, negation, or historical narrative (or a mixture of these).* The term you define and its intended audience will in part determine the choice, but you can experiment with different approaches (or a combination of them) before settling on one.

At some point during this planning process, you might outline your ideas informally as they take shape. Here, for example, is the outline that could have been used for the paragraph defining *chauvinism:*

I. Nicholas Chauvin as war hero
French soldier in Napoleon's army
wounded 17 times
too scarred to continue fighting

II. His retirement
total rewards: a medal, a sword, and small pension

III. His devotion to Napoleon
emotional and unstoppable
eventual subject of ridicule

IV. Chauvin as character in plays
first by Jean and Charles Cogniard
then others

V. Thus definition: Chauvinism = extreme devotion to a name or cause
change of meaning because of women's movement = men who believe in and defend their superiority to women

Drafting. The method of development you choose will affect how the paragraph is structured. For example, because definition by negation uses contrast organization, your composing process should be similar to the one discussed in Chapter 8. After arranging on a grid the contrasts between what the term is and is not, decide on a whole-to-whole or part-to-part organization and compose several drafts, using transitional expressions appropriate to contrast organization. The other methods of paragraph development—illustration or historical process—are basically description or narration, so your composing processes (and the transitional expressions you use) should be similar to those discussed in Chapters 5 and 6. In any case, try not only to define a term but to explore how that definition emerged, how it works, or what results from the term.

✎ **5   Planning a Formal Definition and Examples**

Suppose you are writing a proposal to people in your community or neighborhood, asking them to establish (or modify) a children's summer athletics program that stresses the best qualities of sportsmanship. Define what *sportsmanship* means in this context. (Go beyond the dictionary definition of the term if you can.) Try to arrive at a formal definition, using your dictionary if you wish. Then explore ways of illustrating the definition, either by listing several examples or by telling the story of one person who meets the criteria you establish. Include a preliminary definition below, followed by the list or a rough outline of the story.

Definition: _____

List, description, or story: _____

_____

_____

_____

_____

_____

_____

_____

_____

✎ **6   Planning a Definition by Negation**

Suppose you are serving as one of the parents on a committee to hire a new elementary school principal. Your first task is to compose a job description that includes the most essential traits of a true academic leader. Explain what you mean by the term *academic leadership,* and explore ways of defining the term through negation. (For example, must a leader not dictate policies but consult the people whom the policies most affect? Is the first practice justified at times and, if so, when?)

Draft a preliminary definition, and then list both the negative and positive traits in opposite columns, but don't supply a contrast for each trait if none comes to mind.

Definition: _____

_____

Negative or unnecessary traits	*Positive and necessary traits*
_____	_____
_____	_____
_____	_____
_____	_____
_____	_____
_____	_____
_____	_____

✍ **7 Planning a Definition by Historical Process**

Every family or religious or ethnic group uses nicknames or other words and phrases that have special meanings for members of the family or group. The terms may be formal or playful, but their meanings are generally understood only within the family or group. Assume that a friend of a different nationality or culture has been curious about one such term, so you are writing him a letter to explain that term and how it evolved in your family. Draft an outline of the process by which the word or phrase evolved.

_____

_____

_____

_____

_____

_____

_____

_____

Drafting the Topic Sentence

The topic sentence often states the definition of a term, but this isn't absolutely necessary. More importantly, the topic sentence makes clear to readers why (or at least by what method) you are defining the term. Here are a few examples:

Computer-assisted instruction is any kind of teaching that occurs with the help of a computer, but it must always be a supplement to normal instruction by teachers or tutors, as these examples will demonstrate.

There are probably a number of misconceptions about the term *illegitimate child,* as its history suggests.

In my experience, the traits of *an effective teacher* go far beyond what can be measured objectively on teacher evaluation forms.

My family and old friends call me Rolly instead of Rawley, and there is an interesting story about how I got the nickname.

✍ **8 Drafting Topic Sentences and Supporting Details**

Return to the definitions and material you prepared in Exercises 5, 6, and 7, and draft a preliminary topic sentence for a paragraph on each subject.

Paragraph defining sportsmanship: _____

_____

Paragraph defining an academic leader: _____

_____

Paragraph defining a special term: _____

_____

Now compose a first draft of a paragraph based on your materials for one of the definitions you just wrote.

9   Organizing a Paragraph of Definition

Number each of the following sentences so they make a logical and coherent paragraph of definition. Put a check mark next to the sentence that formally defines the term.

___1___   Few legal concepts are more widely misunderstood than *circumstantial evidence,* which many people believe means suspicion without proof.

_____   Since in our legal tradition a person accused of a crime is considered innocent until proved guilty, he or she must confess or be convicted on the basis of testimony—which is often unreliable—or circumstances.

_____   Mistakes in convictions, however, are much more likely to result from false testimony, since people tend to lie or misinterpret what they have seen.

_____   Without it, no legal system can possibly work.

_____   An example of a murderer who must be convicted on the basis of circumstantial evidence is the one caught while bending with a smoking gun over the dying victim.

_____   No one has actually seen him commit the crime.

_____   As a matter of fact, all evidence except that given by witnesses or victims is circumstantial—that is, based on the conditions, weapons, or facts relating to the crime.

Inserting Transitions Within a Definition Paragraph

A paragraph of definition can be structured through examples, negation, historical process—or any combination of these methods. So the paragraph uses transitions appropriate to those methods of development. Here is a list of common transitions for each:

For examples:	as an example (illustration), for example (for another example), for instance, in particular, such as
For contrasts:	although, but, even though, however, nevertheless, on the other hand, on the contrary, yet
For historical process:	as a result, consequently, a result of this is, another (a second) result of this is, so, soon, later, afterward (or any time expression)

10   Adding Transitions

Insert transitions between ideas in the following paragraph of definition by historical origin.

The Tale Behind the Ax

❑ (1) Many people think that Benjamin Franklin coined the wonderful expression "an ax to grind" (that is, an ax to sharpen). (2) However, it was actually invented by the humorist Charles Miner well after Franklin's death. (3) Miner described how, as a boy, he met an agreeable stranger carrying an ax, who inquired if he could borrow the family grindstone. (4) Young Miner _____ said yes. (5) _____ the man asked him in pleasant tones if he was strong enough to turn the grindstone. (6) Young Miner proudly said that he was and offered to demonstrate. (7) The smiling stranger, holding the ax to the stone, praised the boy's hard work. (8) However, _____ the ax was sharpened, the man walked off without saying a word of thanks. (9) _____ , said Miner, "_____ I see a merchant overpolite to his customers, begging them to taste a little brandy . . . thinks I, that the man has an ax to grind."

(10) _____ , it's a story worth remembering whenever you encounter some overagreeable person who's eager to buy you drinks, but may be motivated by selfishness.

✍ **11 Analyzing Your Paragraph**

Read the paragraph you drafted in Exercise 8 and respond to each of the following questions. Use the responses as guidelines for revising the paragraph and then do the revision. (This exercise could be done collaboratively, with each person reading his or her paper aloud twice and the group responding to the questions.)

Revision Guidelines

1. Is there a clear definition by formal statement? _____ If the definition is not clear, how should it be expanded or revised? _____

_____

_____

2. Is the definition developed sufficiently by illustration, negation, or historical process? _____ If not, what should be added or changed?_____

_____

_____

3. Is all the material in the paragraph relevant to the definition? _____ If not, what should be eliminated, revised, or added? _____

_____

_____

4. Is the paragraph unclear at any point? _____ If so, how should it be revised?

_____

_____

5. Are transitions lacking or too vague at any point in the paragraph? _____ If so, what should be added or revised?_____

_____

_____

6. What was the greatest problem in composing this paragraph? (Ignore this question if the writer experienced no significant problems.) _____

_____

_____

If this problem was not resolved, what should be done? _____

_____

_____

12   Proofreading and Polishing Your Paragraph

After completing the revision, edit the paragraph, checking for correct spelling and punctuation, complete sentences, and clarity of ideas. Then make a clean copy of the paragraph and proofread it carefully for errors.

Composing Based on Outside Sources

Complete the following paragraph by using the material supplied. Begin by completing the sentence that defines the term, and develop the rest of the paragraph through definition by negation.

England	*Great Britain (or Britain)*
1. a country 2. one of three (England, Scotland, and Wales) on same island	1. an island with three countries on it 2. the largest of the British Isles (Britain, Ireland, the Isle of Man, and the Channel Islands) 3. member of the United Kingdom, which includes all countries in the British Isles, with the exception of part of Ireland

Many Americans use the terms Britain and England interchangeably. This is incorrect and sometimes offends the British themselves. Great Britain (or Britain)

_____

_____

_____

_____

_____

_____

_____

_____

READINGS

Play It as It Lays

Bill Cosby

Bill Cosby—comedian, television and movie star, and writer—
also possesses a doctorate in education, which he received
when he was 39 and well established as a celebrity.
This article appeared in his book Fatherhood.

deep insight

(1) It is no **profound revelation** to say that fathering has changed greatly from the days when my own father used me for batting practice. However, the baffling behavior of children is exactly the same today as it was when Joseph's brothers peddled him to the Egyptians. And in the face of such constantly baffling behavior, many men have wondered: Just what *is* a father's role today? As a taskmaster, he's inept. As a referee, he's hopeless. And as a short-order cook, he may have the wrong menu.

unable to cope

(2) The answer, of course, is that no matter how hopeless or **copeless** a father may be, his role is simply to *be* there, sharing all the chores with his wife. Let her *have* the babies; but after that, try to share every job around. Any man today who returns from work, sinks into a chair, and calls for his pipe is a man with an appetite for danger. Actually, changing a diaper takes much less time than waxing a car. A car doesn't spit on your pants, of course, but a baby's book value is considerably higher.

confused

(3) If the new American father feels **bewildered** and even defeated, let him take comfort from the fact that whatever he does in any fathering situation has a fifty percent chance of being right. Having five children has taught me a truth as cosmic as any that you can find on a mountain in Tibet: There are no absolutes in raising children. In any stressful situation, fathering is always a roll of the dice. The game may be messy, but I have never found one with more rewards and joys.

(4) You know the only people who are *always* sure about the proper way to raise children? Those who've never had any.

Questions for Investigation and Discussion

1. What is the purpose of Bill Cosby's article? Who is his likely audience?
2. Cosby in part defines the *new American father* by negation. What does he say a father cannot do? What examples of incorrect behavior does he cite?
3. What, according to Cosby, is the main role of a father? What does Cosby think about setting down rigid rules?
4. Cosby compares diaper changing to waxing a car. Why?
5. What does Cosby say are the pitfalls of fatherhood? What are the rewards?
6. Compose a formal definition of the new American father. What traits must he possess?

Why I Want a Wife

Judy Brady

Judy Brady has been a free-lance writer since she received
a bachelor of fine arts degree from the University of Iowa
in 1962. The following article appeared in
Ms. *magazine in 1971.*

(1) I belong to the classification of people known as wives. I am A Wife. And, not

accidentally

altogether **incidentally**, I am a mother.

(2) Not too long ago a male friend of mine appeared on the scene from the Midwest fresh from a recent divorce. He had one child, who is, of course, with his ex-wife. He is obviously looking for another wife. As I thought about him while I was

ironing one evening, it suddenly occurred to me that I, too, would like to have a wife. Why do I want a wife?

(3) I would like to go back to school so that I can become economically independent, support myself, and, if need be, support those dependent upon me. I want a wife who will work and send me to school. And while I am going to school, I want a wife to take care of my children. I want a wife to keep track of the children's doctor and dentist appointments. And to keep track of mine, too. I want a wife to make sure my children eat properly and are kept clean. I want a wife who will wash the children's clothes and keep them mended. I want a wife who is a good **nurturant attendant** to my children, arranges for their schooling, makes sure that they have an adequate social life with their peers, takes them to the park, the zoo, etc. I want a wife who takes care of the children when they are sick, a wife who arranges to be around when the children need special care, because, of course, I cannot miss classes at school. My wife must arrange to lose time at work and not lose the job. It may mean a small cut in my wife's income from time to time, but I guess I can tolerate that. Needless to say, my wife will arrange and pay for the care of the children while my wife is working.

care-providing servant

(4) I want a wife who will take care of my physical needs. I want a wife who will keep my house clean. A wife who will pick up after my children, a wife who will pick up after me. I want a wife who will keep my clothes clean, ironed, mended, replaced when need be, and who will see to it that my personal things are kept in their proper place so that I can find what I need the minute I need it. I want a wife who cooks the meals, a wife who is *a good* cook. I want a wife who will plan the menus, do the necessary grocery shopping, prepare the meals, serve them pleasantly, and then do the cleaning up while I do my studying. I want a wife who will care for me when I am sick and sympathize with my pain and loss of time from school. I want a wife to go along when our family takes a vacation so that someone can continue to care for me and my children when I need a rest and a change of scene.

long-winded

(5) I want a wife who will not bother me with **rambling** complaints about a wife's duties. But I want a wife who will listen to me when I feel the need to explain a rather difficult point I have come across in my course of studies. And I want a wife who will type my papers for me when I have written them.

(6) I want a wife who will take care of the details of my social life. When my wife and I are invited out by my friends, I want a wife who will take care of the babysitting arrangements. When I meet people at school that I like and want to entertain, I want a wife who will have the house clean, will prepare a special meal, serve it to me and my friends, and not interrupt when I talk about the things that interest me and my friends. I want a wife who will have arranged that the children are fed and ready for bed before my guests arrive so that the children do not bother us. I want a wife who takes care of the needs of my guests so that they feel comfortable, who makes sure that they have an ashtray, that they are passed the hors d'oeuvres, that they are offered a second helping of the food, that their wine glasses are replenished when necessary, that their coffee is served to them as they like it. And I want a wife who knows that sometimes I need a night out by myself.

(7) I want a wife who is sensitive to my sexual needs, a wife who makes love passionately and eagerly when I feel like it, a wife who makes sure that I am satisfied. And, of course, I want a wife who will not demand sexual attention when I am not in the mood for it. I want a wife who assumes the complete responsibility for birth control, because I do not want more children. I want a wife who will remain sexually faithful to me so that I do not have to clutter up my intellectual life with jealousies. And I want a wife who understands that my sexual needs may entail more than strict adherence to monogamy. I must, after all, be able to relate to people as fully as possible.

(8) If, by chance, I find another person more suitable as a wife than the wife I already have, I want the liberty to replace my present wife with another one. Naturally, I will expect a fresh, new life; my wife will take the children and be solely responsible for them so that I am left free.

(9) When I am through with school and have acquired a job, I want my wife to quit working and remain at home so that my wife can more fully and completely take care of a wife's duties.

(10) My God, who *wouldn't* want a wife?

Questions for Investigation and Discussion

1. What is the purpose of Judy Brady's article? Who is her likely audience?
2. List some traits Brady says she would expect in a wife.
3. What devices does Brady use to establish unity and coherence?
4. Compare Bill Cosby's attitude toward the husband-wife roles with Brady's. How are they alike or different?

SUGGESTED TOPICS FOR WRITING

As always, choose topics you know best for paragraphs of definition (that is, terms related to your interests, hobbies, field of study, profession, or family life). The topics in the list that follows are suggestions. No matter what subject you choose, define it by synonym or class and make sure the definition is clear and precise. (The sentence of definition may or may not be part of the paragraph's topic sentence.) Develop the definition through illustration, negation, or historical process. Be sure to revise the paragraph for clarity and coherence.

Development by Illustration (or Other Method)

1. Like Cosby or Brady, define the role of a modern-day college student, grown son or daughter, coach, worker, manager, or any other role you are familiar with. Explain and illustrate several different "duties," behaviors, or attitudes that you associate with the role. Assume you are writing a short article for a magazine that is read by people who have roles similar to the one you describe.
2. Assume you are preparing a one-page handout about the company you work for (or would like to work for) to be distributed at a college or high school career day. Define and describe a term important to potential job applicants.
3. Assume that, as a summer camp administrator or senior counselor, you are preparing an informational brochure for the parents of children who might attend the camp. Choose an important term associated with the camp's programs, rules, or activities to define and illustrate.
4. Assume that, as the manager of a day-care center, you must prepare a fact sheet for parents on the rules and regulations of the center. Define and illustrate an important term.

Development by Contrast

5. Assume you are representing an advertising agency for an automobile manufacturer. Define and describe the all-purpose van pictured on the following page by comparing it with the other vehicles shown.

6. Assume that, because of controversy about student cheating, your college has asked you to serve as a member of the student government, which will consider the issue. Define cheating and contrast it to legitimate student collaboration.

7. Assume that, in a world history class, your instructor has asked you to write a short definition of a dictator. Define the term and contrast it to a leader in a democracy.

Development by Historical Process

8. Assume your English teacher has asked you to write a short paper defining one of the following terms that originated as the names of persons or places. Consult an encyclopedia, an etymological dictionary, or another reference book for information about their origin and development. Do not copy the information; compose the story in your own words.
   a. hero
   b. bedlam
   c. guillotine
   d. Achilles' heel or Achilles' tendon

Composing Causal Paragraphs

This chapter introduces you to another method of paragraph development—*causal analysis,* or the examination of causes or effects. The chapter explores the following matters:

- two types of causal paragraphs: those that analyze causes and those that analyze effects;
- the two most common ways to organize these paragraphs: in chronological or climax order; and
- the process of composing a causal paragraph: (1) by formulating ideas, (2) by organizing and drafting the paragraph, and (3) by revising the paragraph while adding appropriate transitions.

CAUSAL ANALYSIS DEFINED

People are problem solvers. When they encounter a physical or social illness (cancer, unemployment, or pollution), they try to find its causes to help them devise a cure. When they explore a past problem (World War II, the Great Depression, or last year's traffic deaths), they try to find its causes to guide them in the future. When they encounter a change in society (more computerization of services, fewer children, or increasing health-care costs), they try to predict the results of the change to avoid future problems.

Once they have found the causes or results, people become communicators. They want to share their information—sometimes to inform, other times to warn, and still other times to persuade other people to act. If, for example, people become aware that eating too much fat contributes to heart attacks, some people may change their diets.

Since you are also a problem solver and communicator, you should know how to compose a paragraph (and later a composition) using *causal analysis,* an explanation of why something happened, is happening, or could happen. Causal analysis is also called a *cause-effect* organization. It deals with *effects*—the results of some events or actions—and it deals with *causes*—the reasons for the effects. You can approach causal analysis from two angles:

1. *You can trace the causes of an effect,* such as the causes of high unemployment, the reasons for the extinction of dinosaurs, or the reasons Johnny can't read.
2. *You can trace the effects of a cause,* such as the results of widespread drug use in our society, the effects of smoking, or the changes that fax modems are creating in businesses and homes.

ORGANIZING A CAUSAL-ANALYSIS PARAGRAPH

Because few things in life are simple, an effect can have more than one cause and a cause can have more than one effect. Therefore, as you generate and organize your ideas, try to structure them the same way you would in process analysis or narration.

◆ Most often, you can explain the causes or effects *chronologically,* moving from the first to the last. Unlike in a narrative paragraph, however, your causal-analysis paragraph will also include interpretation and examples that explain not only how but why.

◆ Occasionally, when some causes or effects are more important than others, you can explain them in *climax order,* moving from the least important reason or result to the most.

Employing Chronological Organization

Most discussions of causes first state the effect and then trace its causes in chronological order—consecutively in time. The following paragraph, which examines the reasons that a mile equals 5,280 feet, is an example. The first two sentences raise a question about an effect, which the third sentence (the topic sentence) begins to answer by addressing its causes:

How the Mile Came into Being

❏ (1) The Romans invented the mile, a term that comes from the Latin word *mille,* meaning one thousand. (2) So why aren't there 1,000 feet in a mile? (3) *The answer lies in some important changes that occurred when the British adopted the measurement from the Romans.*

The rest of the paragraph then examines chronologically the causes for the change in the measurement. (The transitional expressions for time are italicized.)

(4) *As* Rome set out to conquer the known world *2,000 years ago,* the Romans measured a mile as 100 Roman paces (that is, 2,000 steps) by their marching soldiers. (5) Since the average marching stride was about 5 feet, the Roman mile was almost exactly 5,000 feet. (6) *In about the year 1280,* however, the British favored the *furlong,* a unit of measurement that is now used primarily at horse racetracks. (7) *Even before* written records of land were kept, British farmers built stone walls to enclose fields whose length was standardized—the plowmen dug furrows the equivalent of 220 modern yards. (8) Furlong was the slurred pronunciation of furrow-long, and the furlong remained the designation *for 220 years.* (9) When Britain adopted the mile *at the beginning of the sixteenth century,* farmers insisted that it be tied to their basic unit of measurement, the furlong. (10) The Roman mile consisted of a little more than 7 1/2 furlongs. (11) Because the British so loved the furlong, they decided to change the length of the Roman mile. (12) Instead of 5,000 feet, the British mile became 8 furlongs, or 1,760 yards, the exact measurement we use today—5,280 feet.

Employing Climax Organization

You may occasionally want to emphasize the most important cause or effect, so you state it last, at the end of a paragraph arranged in climax order. The following paragraph discussing the effects of several strikes by doctors is an example. Although the strikes occurred at different times, they aren't introduced chronologically. Instead, the writer discusses them according to the rate of patient deaths during the strikes—that is, the decrease in the rate. The first sentence only hints at the point that will be stated explicitly at the end of the paragraph:

Does Medicine Heal?

❑ (1) According to Dr. Robert S. Mendelsohn's *Confessions of a Medical Heretic,* there are some surprising effects when doctors strike.

The paragraph then examines several examples of such strikes and their results. Notice the transitional expressions (italicized) for both time and cause-effect relationships.

(2) For example, doctors in Los Angeles went on strike *in 1976* to protest the high cost of malpractice insurance. (3) *The result was* that with no doctors around, the death rate dropped by 18 percent. (4) *That same year,* doctors in Bogotá, Colombia, refused to provide any services except for emergency care. (5) *Consequently,* there was a 35 percent drop in the death rate. (6) *Three years earlier,* when Israeli doctors reduced their daily contact, the Jerusalem Burial Society reported that the death rate *during that period* was cut in half. (7) The only similar drop in the death rate occurred *in 1953*—the last time Israeli doctors went on strike.

The final sentence—the topic sentence of the paragraph—offers a rather shocking analysis of these cause-effect relationships. Nonetheless, since the analysis is based on inconclusive evidence, the statement is carefully qualified. (The qualifying words are italicized.)

(8) These statistics *suggest a rather unsettling possibility,* that modern medical treatment may do more harm than good.

✍ **1** **Examining a Cause-Effect Paragraph**

Read the following paragraph and then answer the questions. (This exercise could be done collaboratively.)

Why Is June So Popular for Weddings?

❑ (1) June is the month when most schools break for vacation and when weather is appropriate for most outdoor weddings, but these truths don't explain why June has long been a popular month for weddings. (2) The explanations can be found in ancient mythology. (3) The first reason derives from the Roman goddess for whom the month was named. (4) As the goddess of marriage and young people, Juno supposedly insisted that couples marry during "her" month. (5) Thus an ancient Roman proverb counseled, "Prosperity to the man and happiness to the maid when married in June." (6) However, there is a second, more important reason why so many weddings are performed in June. (7) May has been long considered the unluckiest month for marriage, as shown by the superstitious rhyme "Marry in May, and rue the day." (8) The superstition itself originated in Roman mythology. (9) The month of May honors *Maia,* a Roman earth goddess and the mistress of the fire god Vulcan, who signified danger. (10) Maia was also the goddess of the elderly, and therefore not an appealing symbol for young people who wished to marry. (11) Therefore, the superstitions about May marriages have enabled June to fill its own quota plus some of May's postponed weddings as well.

1. Does the paragraph explain causes of an effect, or effects of a cause?
2. What is the topic sentence of the paragraph?
3. How many main reasons for June weddings does the paragraph provide? Is one more important than the other(s)?
4. Is the organization of the paragraph in chronological or climax order? What transitional expressions show the organization?

2   Predicting Paragraph Development

After each of the following topic sentences, place a check mark next to the most likely development of the paragraph that follows. Will it discuss causes or effects? Will it be arranged in chronological or climax order? (This exercise could be done collaboratively.)

1. Picasso is considered a major artist for three important reasons.

   ___✔___ a. causes   _____ a. chronological order

   _____ b. effects   ___✔___ b. climax order

2. A job in health care—whether as doctor, nurse, technician, or aide—offers several important benefits.

   _____ a. causes   _____ a. chronological order

   _____ b. effects   _____ b. climax order

3. A series of changes in my life led to my decision to return to school.

   _____ a. causes   _____ a. chronological order

   _____ b. effects   _____ b. climax order

4. A child who runs away from home can—and should—expect to encounter some serious and even dangerous problems.

   _____ a. causes   _____ a. chronological order

   _____ b. effects   _____ b. climax order

5. The war of 1898 between Spain and the United States broke out as the result of many foolish and selfish acts, not out of any real threat to our safety or well-being.

   _____ a. causes   _____ a. chronological order

   _____ b. effects   _____ b. climax order

6. The reduction of college tuition scholarships for the poor is causing a number of serious changes in our society.

   _____ a. causes   _____ a. chronological order

   _____ b. effects   _____ b. climax order

COMPOSING A CAUSAL-ANALYSIS PARAGRAPH

Beginning with Discovery, Planning, and Outlining

Because of the complexity of cause-effect relations, composing causal analysis takes careful thought and planning. Choose a subject you know well, either through personal experience or study. For example, suppose that you work in a health club and have been asked to describe the physical and mental benefits of aerobic exercise for people interested in joining the club. You might begin by considering these matters:

◆ *your purpose:* to inform, persuade, or entertain. You will probably be persuading readers to try aerobic exercise by informing them of its benefits.

◆ *your audience:* You will be writing primarily to physically inactive people.

◆ *whether you are analyzing the causes of an effect (the reasons for something) or tracing the effects of a cause (the results of something):* Although you will be discussing the results of aerobic exercise, you could briefly discuss the reasons, too, if you choose first to explain why people feel motivated to begin such a program (perhaps shortness of breath and a general desire to look and feel better). Think of the causes or effects as steps in a ladder leading up or down to your topic:

topic	
↑ *causes* as steps leading up to the event	↓ *effects* as steps leading down from the event
1.	1.
2.	2.
3.	3.
4.	4.

As you plan the paragraph, explore various causes or effects, consider the probability of each, and include the most likely ones. A brainstorming list may work better than clustering or free writing, but use the method you find most comfortable. In any case, you will discover other ideas and reject some of your original ones while continuing through the composing process. Here, for example, is a list of effects you can discuss:

slimmer waist (most people lose one to two inches)

less body fat

much more stamina

sleep better

increased strength in legs, back, and stomach muscles

fewer colds and other common illnesses

increased self-confidence; physical strength leads to mental strength

think more about other habits of good health—eating better or not smoking

time to think, relax, solve problems

fellowship with others engaged in aerobics
negatives: get sweated up, some days must force yourself to do
it, possible injury from improper warm-ups or carelessness

Return to this list later and select the details to include. Challenge each detail: Is it necessary? Is it important? Does it need explanation? For instance, the claim about less body fat might need to be explained:

When the body uses more calories than a person consumes, it
then begins to burn the calories stored as fat.

And do any details need examples? For instance, readers might more clearly understand the statement about increased stamina if you illustrate it:

Physically fit people can play many sports without tiring.
They can lift heavy weights. And they don't get sleepy in the late
afternoon.

Then rearrange the details, explanations, and examples logically—probably in climax order.

COMPUTER TIPS

FOR DRAFTING AND REVISING A CAUSAL-ANALYSIS PARAGRAPH

After generating the list of details or composing the first draft, print out a double-spaced or even triple-spaced copy of your work. Then mark where explanations or examples are needed, and, if possible, draft these additions between the lines. Add transitional expressions in similar fashion. Finally, enter all your additions and alterations in the computer file and print out a copy once again.

3 Generating and Selecting Details for Causal Paragraphs

Assume you are composing a letter for admission to a program in a field that interests you (for example, in computer science, nursing, law, medicine, or business). Name the program, and develop each of the three topic ideas that follows by listing some causes or effects, explaining these causes when necessary, and illustrating them through examples. Then put a check mark (√) next to the material you would most likely include in your letter.

Type of Program: _____

Topic A. why you deserve admission to the program

_____

_____

_____

_____

_____

_____

Topic B. how you would benefit from the program

_____

_____

_____

_____

_____

_____

_____

Topic C. how you would contribute to society after completing the program

_____

_____

_____

_____

_____

_____

_____

4 Generating Material for Another Causal Paragraph

Think about an important decision you have made: quitting a job; returning to school; getting married, beginning a relationship with someone, or ending the marriage or relationship; moving to another neighborhood, city, or country. What events caused you to make the decision, and did one event lead to another?

Assume you are writing about your experience in order to advise people who are contemplating a similar decision. In retrospect, would you recommend that they follow your example? Explore your ideas through brainstorming, free writing, or clustering.

Drafting the Topic Sentence

At some point during the planning or drafting of a paper, formulate a topic sentence that introduces the number of causes or effects the paragraph will discuss. Place that sentence at or near the beginning of the paragraph, perhaps after one or two opening sentences that attract your audience's interest. Here is a preliminary version of a topic sentence for the paragraph on aerobic exercise:

> *A regular program of aerobic exercise three or more times a week may result in a great many physical and mental benefits and has very few drawbacks.*

5 Drafting Topic Sentences

Draft a preliminary topic sentence for each list you prepared in Exercise 3.

Topic A. _____

_____

Topic B. _____

_____

Topic C. _____

_____

Alternatively, draft a topic sentence for the material you prepared in Exercise 4.

_____

_____

6   Drafting Causal Paragraphs

Compose a first draft of a paragraph based on the materials and one of the topic sentences you generated in Exercise 3 or 4 and Exercise 5. Structure the paragraph either in chronological or climax order.

Alternatively, draft a longer paragraph based on *all three topic ideas and their supporting details* from Exercises 4 and 5. Include a new topic sentence that introduces all three reasons, and modify the three original topic sentences to serve as transitional statements introducing the three main reasons that support the larger topic idea.

7   Arranging Causal Paragraphs in Chronological Order

Number the following sentences in each paragraph so they trace the causes of an effect in chronological order. Be prepared to explain your organization. (This exercise could be done collaboratively.)

The Earliest Origins of Football

Paragraph A.

_____   Then, shortly after the Danes were defeated in 1042, an Englishman dug up the skull of a buried Danish soldier and kicked it around his field.

__1__   If it weren't for the forces of civilization, we might call the game "headball" instead of football because the earliest ancestor of football used human skulls as the ball.

_____   The Danes occupied England in the early eleventh century.

_____   Therefore, they looked for other choices of sporting equipment.

_____   Others dug up Danish "headballs" and enjoyed the pastime of kicking them around until they found the object to be rather hard on the foot.

_____   They quickly found the obvious choice: inflated cow bladders, of course.

Paragraph B.

_____   The game began when a bladder was dropped between two neighboring towns.

_____   Finally, however, King Henry II (reigned 1154–1189) outlawed the sport, not only to eliminate uncontrolled vandalism and violence but to eliminate a security threat.

_____   A later version of the game became popular and created large-scale insanity.

_____ A team won if it managed to kick the bladder into the center of the other's town.

_____ The reason was that his soldiers were playing futballe instead of practicing their archery. So, for the next 400 years, futballe was against the law, but continued to be played anyway.

_____ The game became increasingly violent. Although the players never touched the ball with their hands (indeed, they called the game *futballe*), they were quite willing to use their fists to hit each other.

Paragraph C.

_____ And the game became even more polite when round balls replaced cow bladders.

_____ The ban against futballe was lifted by James I (reigned 1603–1625), who honored the wishes of sportsmen.

_____ This game became known as Association Football.

_____ The game developed formal rules by placing it in standard-size playing fields and awarding points for passing the other team's goal.

_____ The shortening of Association to Assoc. led to the slang expression "soccer," which is the sport's modern name.

Paragraph D.

_____ The name of his college was Rugby.

_____ Although his action was not rewarded, his college became notorious for its unsportsmanlike behavior.

_____ The next important historical development in the history of football occurred in 1823.

_____ He scored a touchdown, but it was illegal.

_____ (And now you know why this is the only sport whose name is often capitalized, at least when it refers to English Rugby.)

_____ During a game in England, a college student named William Ellis became frustrated, picked up the ball, and ran with it.

_____ Eventually, the games of soccer and rugby came to American colleges, where they evolved into modern-day football.

8 Arranging Causal Paragraphs In Climax Order

Read the introductory and topic sentences for the following paragraph, and then number the supporting sentences in climax order, with the most important reason coming last. The paragraph should include four reasons for the end of Prohibition, and each reason should be developed specifically by other statements. Add transitional expressions (such as *second, third, finally, therefore,* and *for example*) to the beginnings of sentences. Be prepared to explain your organization. (This exercise could be done collaboratively.)

After a long campaign against alcohol by ministers, the Women's Christian Temperance Union, and others, a constitutional amendment banned the production and sale of all alcohol throughout the country in 1920. *However, the ban, known as Prohibition, lasted only 13 years for several reasons.*

_1_	_First_	Prohibition was unable to prevent people from drinking.
_____	_____	"distilleries" in out-of-the-way factories, in people's basements, and even in bathtubs produced illegal booze.
_____	_____	the illegal use of alcohol was widespread throughout society, from average citizens to politicians, who drank at home or at liquor-serving night clubs, called _speakeasies_.
_____	_____	the desire for even more liquor created a whole new class of gangsters, who became rich from making and selling alcohol.
_____	_____	in 1933 another constitutional amendment was passed, reversing the earlier one and ending the era of Prohibition in the United States.
_____	_____	Prohibition eliminated too many jobs.
_____	_____	at the beginning of the depression in the 1930s, there were many claims that the legal manufacture and sale of alcohol would create badly needed work for honest citizens.
_____	_____	Prohibition was unable to eliminate the manufacture of alcohol.
_____	_____	A great deal of liquor was manufactured in Canada and then smuggled into the United States.

Inserting Transitions Within a Causal-Analysis Paragraph

Most causal paragraphs are structured in chronological or climax order, so they use the transitions appropriate to those methods of development. However, the following transitions may also be helpful:

For items in a series	first, second, third, finally, for one thing, for another
For showing causes	because, because of, since, for, one cause (reason) is, another (a second) reason is
For showing effects	as a result, consequently, later, a (one) result of this is, another (a second) result of this is, so, therefore, thus

Here is the final version of the aerobic exercise paragraph, complete with transitions (shown in bold). Notice that it omits some information from the initial list of benefits, mentions no drawbacks, and slightly changes the topic sentence.

Many people have grown tired of hiding their flabby thighs, sucking in their stomachs at the beach, and trying one fad diet or another. The only solution to weight reduction is a serious program of aerobic exercise. **Such a program of exercise for 20 minutes three times a week provides at least five physical and mental benefits. First,** the body tends to become slimmer. Typically, a person engaged in aerobics loses one or more inches around the waist and sheds a large amount of body fat. **The reason for this loss of body fat** is that the body uses more *calories than the person has consumed up to that moment, so it begins to burn the calories stored in fat cells. **Second,** the exercise strengthens much of the body—arms, shoulders, chest, legs, thighs, back, and stomach. Exercisers **therefore** feel more fit and look it, too. **Third,** aerobic fitness generally re-sults in better health. Most physically fit people probably de-crease their chances of suffering a heart attack or stroke, and, in addition, suffer from fewer colds or cases of influenza. In fact, many people who exercise regularly also find that they sleep better. **Fourth,** aerobic fitness also increases stamina. Physically fit people can play many sports without tiring, can lift heavy weights, and don't get sleepy in the late afternoon. **Finally,** aerobics improves people's mental condition. They feel more relaxed and self-confident, **for** physical strength seems to lead to mental strength. They feel in better control of their lives and **consequently** give up smoking and eat less junk food. All of these benefits are more than enough **reasons** to engage in some form of aerobic activity.*

9   Adding Transitional Expressions to Causal Paragraphs

In the following passage, insert transitions showing causes or effects, the movement from one cause or effect to another, and any other logical relationship between ideas.

A Tale of a Sneaker

❏   (1) The rubber-bottomed athletic shoe whose silent footsteps earned it the name "sneaker" developed only after a breakthrough in technology: the vulcan-ization of rubber by Charles Goodyear in the 1860s. (2) Goodyear proved that the natural gum from a rubber plant did not have to be sticky when warm or brittle when cold. (3) Goodyear mixed rubber with sulfur—a process he called "vulcanizing"—and the rubber turned into a dry, smooth, and flexible sub-stance. (4) _As a result of this breakthrough,_ manufacturers soon employed rubber in making rain galoshes (or "rubbers"), one of its first successful uses in wearing apparel.

(5) Rubber also appeared on the soles of leather shoes at the beginning of the twentieth century. (6) _____ , shoemakers soon glued rubber soles to canvas tops to produce what they advertised as a revolution in athletic footwear. (7) In 1917, the U.S. Rubber Company intro-duced Keds, the first popularly marketed sneaker. (8) The name was chosen

_____ it suggested "kids" and rhymed with *ped,* the Latin word for "foot." (9) Unlike the white sneakers of today, these early models featured black soles and brown canvas tops that resembled the most popular men's leather shoes of the time.

(10) The basic design of sneakers varied little until the early 1960s.

(11) _____ a former college runner and his coach originated a business that ushered in the era of the modern, waffle-soled run-

ning shoe. (12) As a miler at the University of Oregon, Phil Knight preferred to run in European sneakers _____ they were lighter in weight than American models. (13) After competing successfully in races, Knight believed that other track and field athletes would buy similar shoes

_____ improve their performances.

(14) _____ , Knight and coach Bill Bowerman started to import top-notch Japanese models in 1962.

(15) The lightweight shoes attracted customers, but Bowerman wanted to improve the traction, or gripping ability, of the soles. (16) Up to that point, manufacturers had relied on the design that automobile tire manufacturers

used—a jagged tread. (17) _____ that design didn't lend itself well to the movements of the foot while running. (18) When Bower-man looked at his kitchen waffle iron one morning, the device inspired him to

experiment. (19) _____ he stuffed a piece of rub-ber into the iron, heated it, and produced a deeply waffle-shaped sole pattern that soon established itself as the world standard for sneakers. (20) In addition to the sole, the new sneakers featured three other innovations: a wedged heel, a cushioned mid-sole as protection against shock, and nylon tops that reduced the weight of the shoe to provide more "breathing" for the foot.

(21) _____ to promote the waffle-soled nylon shoes, which he named Nikes after the winged Greek goddess of victory, Knight turned to the Olympic trials in Eugene, Oregon, in 1972. (22) Several marathoners raced in the custom-designed shoes, and advertisements hailed the sneakers as having been on the feet of "four of the top seven finishers," although the ads failed to mention that the first-, second-, and third-place

runners competed in Adidas sneakers from Germany. (23) _____

_____ , waffle-soled sneakers, in a variety of brands, so completely dominated the market that, by the end of the decade, the flat-soled canvas shoes virtually disappeared from the feet of runners everywhere.

10 Analyzing and Revising Your Draft

Read the paragraph you drafted in Exercise 6 and respond to each of the following questions. Consider the responses while revising the paragraph, and then complete the revision. (This exercise could be done collaboratively, with each person reading his or her paper aloud twice and the group responding to the questions.)

Revision Guidelines

1. Is the topic sentence clear, and does it make a point? _____ If it is not clear or

    makes no point, how should it be revised? _____

    _____

    _____

2. Do all the details support the topic sentence? _____ If not, what should be

    eliminated, revised, or added? _____

    _____

    _____

3. Is the paragraph well organized, either chronologically or in climax order? _____ If not, what should be eliminated, moved, or changed? _____

_____

_____

4. Are logical connections between causes and effects clear? _____ If not, what sentences should be revised, or where should transitions be added? _____

_____

_____

5. What was the greatest problem in composing this paragraph? (Ignore this question if the writer experienced no significant problems.) _____

_____

_____

If this problem was not resolved, what should be done? _____

_____

_____

11   Proofreading and Polishing Your Paragraph

After completing the revision, edit the paragraph, checking for correct spelling and punctuation, complete sentences, and clarity of ideas. Then make a clean copy of the paragraph and proofread it carefully for errors.

Composing Based on Outside Sources

Assume you are preparing a short brochure for a meeting of members of the American Dairy Association and you wish to tell them an interesting story about the origins of margarine. Compose a cause-effect paragraph based on the following information. Include transitional expressions and qualifying words as necessary. The topic sentence has been provided for you.

Topic Sentence: Margarine was invented and then grew popular for several reasons.

1. after popularity in France, margarine spread throughout Europe
2. butter shortage in United States during World War I (1914–1918); margarine arrived
3. butter spoils in heat
4. during Franco-Prussian War in 1869, butter substitute needed by France; had to be stored on ships
5. Emperor Napoleon III of France sponsor of contest with prize for best substitute
6. butter expensive in second half of nineteenth century
7. winner: the Frenchman Hippolyte Mege-Mouries
8. his formula: combination of beef fat and milk
9. Mege-Mouries called product oleomargarine because mistakenly believed beef fat possessed margaric acid

---

READINGS

Magic's Revelation Transcends Sports

Alison Muscatine

This article appeared in the Washington Post *on November 10, 1991, after Magic Johnson had announced he was infected with the HIV virus.*

(1) Before he died of a rare form of paralysis in 1941, baseball player Lou Gehrig was known as "the Iron Horse." His death at age 37 so moved the entire nation that the disease that killed him was named for him.

shadow

(2) Roberto Clemente, the great Pittsburgh Pirates outfielder, died on New Year's Eve in 1972 in a plane crash while on a humanitarian mission to help earthquake victims in Nicaragua. Only 38 when he died, Clemente's tragedy cast a **pall** far beyond his native Puerto Rico.

sleeping

(3) And then there was the shocking death of University of Maryland basketball player Len Bias, who died in June 1986 of a cocaine overdose two days after the Boston Celtics picked him second overall in the NBA draft. Overnight, his mother, Louise, was transformed into a national spokeswoman about drug abuse. Her son's death at age 22 helped awaken a **slumbering** public about the problems of drugs and young people.

caught
happen to; awareness

(4) Now we are stunned again, this time by news that one of the world's most popular and most visible athletes, basketball superstar Magic Johnson, has **contracted** the AIDS virus. Is there anyone in America who isn't talking about it? Tragedies that **befall** athletes seem to penetrate the American **consciousness** more than any others, unleashing a wave of emotion and shock that crosses class, race, gender and generational lines. Most people, it seems, know and love Magic. Now, it seems, most people are worried about him.

power

(5) "It's their youth, those astonishingly powerful bodies, the sense of youth and immortality that because of television is ever more fixed in our minds," said David Halberstam, a Pulitzer Prize-winning journalist and author of numerous books, including ones about basketball, baseball and rowing. "It's someone who makes his or her living by **dint** of physical activity and achievement, and then we see them struck down in their prime."

demonstrate

(6) Todd Gitlin, a sociologist at the University of California at Berkeley, said Johnson's case has captured the public's imagination because athletes are among the few celebrities universally loved by the public. "There are very few figures in modern society who are famous and don't have enemies," Gitlin said. "And who, at the same time, **embody** some virtue, some talent, some charm, some larger-than-life humanity which many people feel embody their best selves."

honest confession; relief

(7) Celebrities from various walks of life have reminded us over the years that no one, however rich or famous, is immune to tragedy. Former First Lady Betty Ford's **candid disclosure** of her problems with alcoholism provided comfort and **solace** to millions of families who had experienced similar pain and shame. And movie star Rock Hudson's death from AIDS signaled that a disease often associated with those out of the mainstream—gays, minorities, drug users—could also strike down a Hollywood legend.

inner mind

(8) But despite their celebrity status in American society, neither Betty Ford nor Rock Hudson ever touched our collective **psyche** the way Magic Johnson did when he appeared at a news conference in Inglewood, Calif. on Thursday and in typical good humor announced that he had tested positive for HIV, which causes AIDS.

(9) "Even with what we know about athletes and the stories we've read about them, they are still heroes," said Jim Frey, a sports sociologist at the University of Nevada-Las Vegas. "When one falls off the pedestal, it devastates us."

(10) The affection reserved for athletes is part of a national folklore that distinguishes them from other celebrities and makes sports a more binding activity in our culture than any other. We only know actors and actresses through the characters they play, and musicians through the music they create.

(11) We may envy politicians for their power, but we don't necessarily like or trust them. We often admire businessmen for their wealth and success, but we don't see them on television and probably wouldn't recognize their faces on the street.

(12) Athletes, by contrast, are right there in front of us, performing feats that most Americans—young and old—wish they could do too.

(13) "I don't know a person yet who wouldn't change places with some athlete at sometime in their life, whether it's Chris Evert or Michael Jordan," said former tennis star Arthur Ashe.* "They're the objects of fantasy and fantasizing, so when something happens to them, something happens to us too. It makes us more aware of our own mortality."

is the victim of

(14) This is not to say that every athlete who **succumbs** to tragedy captures our hearts. Football player Don Rogers died of a cocaine overdose a few days after Bias, but his death caused only a ripple by comparison. Several athletes, including former Washington Redskins tight end Jerry Smith and race car driver Tim Richmond, died with AIDS and there was little public commotion over their deaths. New York Yankees catcher Thurman Munson lost his life in a plane crash, a sad event that nonetheless

strong impact
greatly outdo

lacked the **resonance** of Clemente's tragedy. Johnson's experience seems likely to **eclipse** them all. With the initial reports of Johnson's illness, many found themselves recalling the impact of the news that John F. Kennedy and Martin Luther King Jr. had been killed.

(15) "I don't even think the hostages in Iran brought out this sort of sentiment," Gitlin said, adding that the nation has been "obsessed" with news about Johnson. As in the case of Gehrig, whose emotional farewell in Yankee Stadium in 1939 has been

tragedy of an idol;
continuing power;
end

replayed on television over the decades, Johnson's experience is of **"iconic enormity,"** Gitlin said. "There is the same sort of **resonance**, the **curtailment** of the apparent immortality of someone great."

enthusiasm

(16) The reason is that, while athletes in general are symbols of energy and vitality, Johnson is even more so. Everything about him is alive. His smile. His **zest** for the game. His fascination with business. His countless good deeds for those less fortu-

unequaled
emphasizes
ability to be harmed;
ideas

nate. And his nearly **unprecedented** acceptance across racial lines. Now, in the face of a frightening and mysterious disease, he awaits an uncertain fate that **underscores** his **vulnerability** and shatters our **notions**.

(17) "This is a tragedy that relates to the physical self," said Allen Guttmann, a professor of American studies at Amherst College who has written several sports books. "Physical feats are what athletes do. That's why they're famous. Here is a 6-foot-9 athlete of tremendous physical ability who is doomed to disintegrate physically. And he's so young."

Questions for Examination and Discussion

1. How do the first three paragraphs contribute to Alison Muscatine's point in the fourth paragraph?
2. Throughout the article, Muscatine quotes various authorities on the causes of our shock and concern upon hearing of Magic Johnson's illness. What, according to these authorities, are the causes?
3. What does Muscatine say separates Johnson's tragedy from those of other athletes?
4. The article is organized in climax order. What transitions show the connections between ideas and the movement toward a climax?

---

* Ashe later died from complications of AIDS, which he contracted from blood transfusions.

Mother Tongue

Amy Tan

Amy Tan is the author of The Joy Luck Club *and*
The Kitchen God's Wife, *two novels that explore the complex*
histories of Chinese immigrants, especially female, and their re-
lationships with their daughters.

academic expert
varieties

(1) I am not a **scholar** of English or literature. I cannot give you much more than personal opinions on the English language and its **variations** in this country or others.

(2) I am a writer. And by that definition, I am someone who has always loved language. I am fascinated by language in daily life. I spend a great deal of my time
bring out thinking about the power of language—the way it can **evoke** an emotion, a visual image, a complex idea, or a simple truth. Language is the tool of my trade. And I use them all—all the Englishes I grew up with.

sharply

(3) Recently, I was made **keenly** aware of the different Englishes I do use. I was giving a talk to a large group of people, the same talk I had already given to half a dozen other groups. The nature of the talk was about my writing, my life, and my book, *The Joy Luck Club*. The talk was going along well enough, until I remembered one major difference that made the whole talk sound wrong. My mother was in the room. And it was perhaps the first time she had heard me give a lengthy speech, using the kind of English I have never used with her. I was saying things like, "The intersection of memory upon imagination" and "There is an aspect of my fiction that
constructed relates to thus and thus"—a speech filled with carefully **wrought** grammatical
weighted down phrases, **burdened,** it suddenly seemed to me, with nominalized forms, past perfect tenses, conditional phrases, all the forms of standard English that I had learned in school and through books, the forms of English I did not use at home with my mother.

(4) Just last week, I was walking down the street with my mother, and I again
aware found myself **conscious** of the English I was using, the English I do use with her. We were talking about the price of new and used furniture and I heard myself saying this: "Not waste money that way." My husband was with us as well, and he didn't notice any switch in my English. And then I realized why. It's because over the 20 years we've been together I've often used that same kind of English with him, and some-
closeness times he even uses it with me. It has become our language of **intimacy,** a different sort of English that relates to family talk, the language I grew up with.

(5) So you'll have some idea of what this family talk I heard sounds like, I'll quote what my mother said during a recent conversation which I videotaped and then transcribed. During this conversation, my mother was talking about a political gangster in Shanghai who had the same last name as her family's, Du, and how the gangster in his early years wanted to be adopted by her family, which was rich by comparison. Later, the gangster became more powerful, far richer than my mother's family, and one day showed up at my mother's wedding to pay his respects. Here's what she said in part:

(6) "Du Yusong having business like fruit stand. Like off the street kind. He is Du like Du Zong—but not Tsung-ming Island people. The local people call putong, the river east side, he belong to that side local people. That man want to ask Du Zong father take him in like become own family. Du Zong father wasn't look down on him, but didn't take seriously, until that man big like become a mafia. Now important person, very hard to inviting him. Chinese way, came only to show respect, don't stay for dinner. Respect for making big celebration, he shows up. Mean gives lots of respect. Chinese custom. Chinese social life that way. If too important won't have to stay too long. He come to my wedding. I didn't see, I heard it. I gone to boy's side, they have YMCA dinner. Chinese age I was 19."

oral; doesn't reveal

(7) You should know that my mother's **expressive** command of English **belies** how much she actually understands. She reads the *Forbes* report, listens to *Wall Street*

Week, converses daily with her stockbroker, reads all of Shirley MacLaine's books with ease—all kinds of things I can't begin to understand. Yet some of my friends tell me they understand 50 percent of what my mother says. Some say they understand 80 to 90 percent. Some say they understand none of it, as if she were speaking pure Chinese. But to me, my mother's English is perfectly clear, perfectly natural. It's my mother tongue. Her language, as I hear it, is vivid, direct, full of observation and imagery. That was the language that helped shape the way I saw things, expressed things, made sense of the world .

flinch

understandings

factual

(8) Lately, I've been giving more thought to the kind of English my mother speaks. Like others, I have described it to people as "broken" or "fractured" English. But I **wince** when I say that. It has always bothered me that I can think of no way to describe it other than "broken," as if it were damaged and needed to be fixed, as if it lacked a certain wholeness and soundness. I've heard other terms used, "limited English," for example. But they seem just as bad, as if everything is limited, including people's **perceptions** of the limited English speaker.

(9) I know this for a fact, because when I was growing up, my mother's "limited" English limited my perception of her. I was ashamed of her English. I believed that her English reflected the quality of what she had to say. That is, because she expressed them imperfectly her thoughts were imperfect. And I had plenty of **empirical** evidence to support me: the fact that people in department stores, at banks, and at restaurants did not take her seriously, did not give her good service, pretended not to understand her, or even acted as if they did not hear her.

collection of stocks

(10) My mother has long realized the limitations of her English as well. When I was 15, she used to have me call people on the phone to pretend I was she. In this guise, I was forced to ask for information or even to complain and yell at people who had been rude to her. One time it was a call to her stockbroker in New York. She had cashed out her small **portfolio** and it just so happened we were going to go to New York the next week, our very first trip outside California. I had to get on the phone and say in an adolescent voice that was not very convincing, "This is Mrs. Tan."

(11) And my mother was standing in the back whispering loudly, "Why he don't send me check, already two weeks late. So mad he lie to me, losing me money."

(12) And then I said in perfect English, "Yes, I'm getting rather concerned. You had agreed to send the check two weeks ago, but it hasn't arrived."

(13) Then she began to talk more loudly. "What he want, I come to New York tell him front of his boss, you cheating me?" And I was trying to calm her down, make her be quiet, while telling the stockbroker, "I can't tolerate any more excuses. If I don't receive the check immediately, I am going to have to speak to your manager when I'm in New York next week." And sure enough, the following week there we were in front of this astonished stockbroker, and I was sitting there red-faced and quiet, and my mother, the real Mrs. Tan, was shouting at his boss in her **impeccable** broken English.

perfect

not cancerous

promises

unfortunate

(14) We used a similar routine just five days ago, for a situation that was far less humorous. My mother had gone to the hospital for an appointment, to find out about a **benign** brain tumor a CAT scan had revealed a month ago. She said she had spoken very good English, her best English, no mistakes. Still, she said, the hospital did not apologize when they said they had lost the CAT scan and she had come for nothing. She said they did not seem to have any sympathy when she told them she was anxious to know the exact diagnosis, since her husband and son had both died of brain tumors. She said they would not give her any more information until the next time and she would have to make another appointment for that. So she said she would not leave until the doctor called her daughter. She wouldn't budge. And when the doctor finally called her daughter, me, who spoke in perfect English—lo and behold—we had **assurances** the CAT scan would be found, promises that a conference call on Monday would be held, and apologies for any suffering my mother had gone through for a most **regrettable** mistake.

experts on language
companions
isolated from others

(15) I think my mother's English almost had an effect on limiting my possibilities in life as well. Sociologists and **linguists** probably will tell you that a person's developing language skills are more influenced by **peers.** But I do think that the language spoken in the family, especially in immigrant families which are more **insular,** plays a large role in shaping the language of the child. And I believe that it affected my results on achievement tests, IQ tests, and the SAT. While my English skills were never judged as poor, compared to math, English could not be considered my strong suit.
In grade school I did moderately well, getting perhaps B's, sometimes B-pluses, in English and scoring perhaps in the 60th or 70th percentile on achievement tests. But

outweigh

those scores were not good enough to **override** the opinion that my true abilities lay in math and science, because in those areas I achieved A's and scored in the 90th percentile or higher.

(16) This was understandable. Math is precise; there is only one correct answer. Whereas, for me at least, the answers on English tests were always a judgment call, a matter of opinion and personal experience. Those tests were constructed around items like fill-in-the-blank sentence completion, such as, "Even though Tom was _____ _____ , Mary thought he was _____ ." And the correct answer always

unimaginative

seemed to be the most **bland** combinations of thoughts, for example, "Even though Tom was shy, Mary thought he was charming," with the grammatical structure "even

meaning

though" limiting the correct answer to some sort of **semantic** opposites, so you wouldn't get answers like, "Even though Tom was foolish, Mary thought he was ridiculous." Well, according to my mother, there were very few limitations as to what Tom could have been and what Mary might have thought of him. So I never did well on tests like that.

(17) The same was true with word analogies, pairs of words in which you were supposed to find some sort of logical, semantic relationship—for example, "*Sunset is to* nightfall as _____ is to _____." And here you would be presented with a list of four possible pairs, one of which showed the same kind of relationship: *red* is to *stoplight, bus* is to *arrival, chills* is to *fever, yawn* is to *boring.* Well, I could never think that way. I knew what the tests were asking, but I could not block out of my mind the images already created by the first pair, "*sunset* is to *nightfall*"—and I would see a burst of colors against a darkening sky, the moon rising, the lowering of a curtain of stars. And all the other pairs of words—red, bus, stoplight, boring—just threw up a mass of confusing images, making it impossible for me to sort out some-

comes before

thing as logical as saying: "A sunset **precedes** nightfall" is the same as "a chill pre-

cause-effect

cedes a fever." The only way I would have gotten that answer right would have been to imagine an **associative** situation, for example, my being disobedient and staying out past sunset, catching a chill at night, which turns into feverish pneumonia as punishment, which indeed did happen to me.

(18) I have been thinking about all this lately, about my mother's English, about achievement tests. Because lately I've been asked, as a writer, why there are not more Asian-Americans represented in American literature. Why are there few Asian-Americans enrolled in creative writing programs? Why do so many Chinese students go into engineering? Well, these are broad sociological questions I can't begin to answer. But I have noticed in surveys—in fact, just last week—that Asian students, as a whole, always do significantly better on math achievement tests than in English. And this makes me think that there are other Asian-American students whose English spoken in the home might also be described as "broken" or "limited." And perhaps they also have teachers who are steering them away from writing and into math and science, which is what happened to me.

(19) Fortunately, I happen to be rebellious in nature and enjoy the challenge of

proving wrong
independent writer

disproving assumptions made about me. I became an English major my first year in college, after being enrolled as pre-med. I started writing nonfiction as a **freelancer** the week after I was told by my former boss that writing was my worst skill and I should hone my talents toward account management.

(20) But it wasn't until 1985 that I finally began to write fiction. And at first I wrote using what I thought to be wittily crafted sentences, sentences that would finally prove I had mastery over the English language. Here's an example from the first draft of a story that later made its way into *The Joy Luck Club*, but without this line: "That was my mental quandary in its nascent state." A terrible line, which I can barely pronounce.

(21) Fortunately, for reasons I won't get into today, I later decided I should envision a reader for the stories I would write. And the reader I decided upon was my mother, because these were stories about mothers. So with this reader in mind—and in fact she did read my early drafts—I began to write stories using all the Englishes I grew up with: the English I spoke to my mother, which for lack of a better term might be described as "simple"; the English she used with me, which for lack of a better term might be described as "broken"; my translation of her Chinese, which could certainly be described as "watered down"; and what I imagined to be her translation of her Chinese if she could speak in perfect English, her internal language, attempted; central / quality — and for that I **sought** to preserve the **essence,** but neither an English nor a Chinese structure. I wanted to capture what language ability tests can never reveal: her intent, her passion, her imagery, the rhythms of her speech and the nature of her thoughts.

(22) Apart from what any critic had to say about my writing, I knew I had succeeded where it counted when my mother finished reading my book and gave me her verdict: "So easy to read."

Questions for Examination and Discussion

1. What, according to Amy Tan, made her self-conscious about the English she "had learned in school or through books?"
2. Tan says her mother's language "is vivid, direct, full of observation and imagery." Did Tan always feel that way? Show evidence.
3. Tan also claims that the English spoken in her home affected her school performance, test scores, and choice of possible careers. How were they affected and why? What does Tan think causes many Chinese to enter engineering programs?
4. Conversely, how did the language of her mother affect Tan's creativity? According to Tan, can this creativity be measured by standardized tests?
5. Tan implies but does not state the point of her essay in the last two paragraphs. What is that point? Does the point apply only to herself and her mother?

SUGGESTED TOPICS FOR WRITING

The best topics for causal paragraphs are based on your own experiences or interests. The subjects that follow may help you gather ideas. For each paragraph, include a topic sentence and arrange the causes or effects in chronological or climax order. Use appropriate transitions as well.

1. Assume you are composing a short autobiography about some part of your life for a student literary magazine. Like Amy Tan, examine how your early experiences (at home, in school, in your community, or in your ethnic background) affected your feelings about yourself or possibly your behavior. Like Tan, explore some incidents that illustrate the experiences.
2. Like Alison Muscatine, consider how the news about a famous person, a friend, or family member greatly upset you. Try to analyze the reasons for your reaction. Describe each reason and, if possible, illustrate it through an example. Assume again you are writing for a student literary magazine.

3. Assume you are composing a paper for a psychology course. Describe what you think to be the most important reasons that adolescents smoke, drink, or take drugs.

4. For the same class, discuss the influences—good or bad—that professional athletes have on teenagers.

5. Assume you are composing an article for *TV Guide*. Discuss the effects that television has on elections.

6. Assume you are composing an editorial for your campus newspaper. Discuss the problems that unprepared or unmotivated students cause for themselves and their classmates.

UNIT THREE

Revising to Strengthen Your Writing

Achieving Consistency

The three chapters in this unit explain strategies for revising your papers for clarity, strength, and gracefulness. We begin with strategies for achieving consistency—a major goal in improving the clarity of your writing. Remember that your readers aren't passive; they are actively attempting to understand your ideas. They make predictions as they see patterns developing, so illogical shifts in word forms or tense can confuse or annoy them. In the early stages of composing, you may not notice these inconsistencies, but you should spot and change them in later drafts. This chapter provides you with practice in eliminating four such inconsistencies:

- ➭ illogical shifts in person and number;
- ➭ shifts in parallel construction;
- ➭ shifts in tense; and
- ➭ shifts in quotations and reported speech.

ESTABLISHING CONSISTENCY IN PERSON AND NUMBER

You probably know that each noun or pronoun represents a *person* (first, second, or third) and *number* (singular or plural).

	Singular	*Plural*
First person	I	we
Second person	you	you
Third person	he	they
	she	
	it	
	singular nouns	plural nouns

You probably also know that a pronoun should agree in person and number with its *antecedent,* a word or phrase that precedes the pronoun:

Antecedent	*Pronoun*
a man	he/him/his
a woman	she/her/her
a car, the committee	it/its
people wages the rain and snow	they/them/their

Establishing Consistency in Person

Illogical shifts in person can be confusing, as in the following sentence:

> *I* won't eat Papa Mangiano's spicy meatballs because they make *you* sick.

Are you wondering how the meatballs transfer from the writer's body to yours? Revising the second half of the sentence to "they make *me* sick" eliminates the confusion.

Shifts in person can not only be confusing but even insulting.

> Security is so poor in Goodman's Department store that *you* could steal just about anything.

Although the writer probably intends *you* to mean *a person,* the sentence implies that the readers are thieves. The sentence needs to be revised, with an appropriate noun replacing the pronoun.

> Security is so poor in Goodman's Department Store that *a thief* could steal just about anything.

Establishing Consistency in Number

Many people insist that formal writing use only the *third person* (*he* or *she*) while avoiding the pronoun *you.* But third-person pronouns create problems with consistency. Look at this muddled sentence:

> *A person* on vacation should carry *their* money in traveler's checks.*

Does the writer intend to discuss *a person* or *more than one*? Here is a revised version, written in the third-person plural throughout:

> *People* on vacation should carry *their* money in traveler's checks.

Revise the next sentence yourself.

> These days, *a mother has* to be careful about all the violence and sex that television exposes *their* children to.

_____

_____

_____

Your revision could have taken either of these forms:

> These days, **a mother** has to be careful about all the violence and sex that television exposes **her** children to.
> These days, **mothers have** to be careful about all the violence and sex that television exposes **their** children to.

* See Chapter 23 for a fuller treatment of pronoun use, as well as a discussion of ways to avoid gender bias (sexism) with pronouns.

The main point, therefore, is that clarity requires consistency. Choose one pronoun and number—*we, you,* or *people*—and stick with it unless you have a logical reason to switch.

IN SUMMARY

> **To avoid confusing shifts in person or number,**
>
> decide which person and number is most appropriate for your audience and purpose, and then consistently use that person and number unless you have a logical reason to change.

1 Maintaining Consistency in Pronoun Use

Write appropriate pronouns in the blank spaces. When the antecedent is third-person singular, use either *he* or *she* (or *his* or *her*).

Just Who Is the Mother Fish?

1. Some fish in India called the mouth-breeding bettas mate and create offspring in unusual ways. Each of the parents plays _____*its*_____ own strange role in the process.
2. When the female lays her eggs, the male catches _____ in _____ rear fin and fertilizes _____ .
3. The female then gathers the eggs in _____ mouth and spits each one at the male, who catches _____ in _____ mouth.
4. He will occasionally return an egg to _____ mate, and the "ball game" between the two might continue for several throws.
5. The female expects the male to take care of all the eggs, however, so eventually _____ stuffs them all in _____ mouth, where _____ will incubate for the next four or five days.
6. During this time, nothing else can make _____ way into the male's mouth, including food.
7. Even after the eggs hatch, the entire group of offspring will seek protection in the parents' mouths when anything threatens _____ .

2 Composing with Consistency in Person and Number

Complete each of the following sentences, maintaining the same person and number in pronouns and nouns.

1. A dog is the most popular pet in America because *the animal gives unconditional love to its masters.*

2. We should attempt to save endangered species if _____

   _____

3. The average owner of 17 cats _____

   _____ when _____

4. Alligator breeders and snake lovers _____

   _____

5. One should avoid placing _____ inside the mouth of a

hungry python unless _____

_____

3   Editing to Correct Errors in Person and Number

Several sentences in the following passage contain illogical shifts in person or number. Eliminate these shifts by making changes above the lines.

Wake Me When Winter Is Over

☐   (1) Hibernation is one of nature's most baffling tricks. (2) A wild bear, for

instance, can sleep for up to five months, and all during that time ∧*it doesn't* ~~they don't~~

eat, drink, urinate, or defecate. (3) For about a month before a bear goes into

winter sleep, they are incredibly hungry. (4) It eats 20 hours a day and gains

more than 100 pounds. (5) A bear's temperature during hibernation drops by

only 4 degrees, which is why they sleep quite lightly and it is liable to attack

people if you disturb it.

(6) Woodchucks, ground squirrels, and many reptiles also hibernate, and it

can experience a drop in temperature of more than 60 degrees. (7) They sleep

so soundly that a person can pick it up and toss them around and you won't

awaken it. (8) Hibernation is therefore more than mere sleep, but we don't

fully understand how it occurs.

ESTABLISHING CONSISTENCY IN PARALLELISM

The following sentences sound odd:

> He is very tall, weight 185 pounds, and brown eyes.
> They enjoyed swimming, to fish, and the beach.

These sentences sound odd because they are unbalanced. They join similar ideas but don't employ similar grammatical structures. This repetition of sentence structures, called *parallelism* or *parallel construction,* signals to readers that ideas not only are related but are equally important. Notice the improvement in clarity and grace when their ideas are made parallel. Notice, too, that *and* typically introduces the final element in a series of parallel structures.

> He *is* very tall, *weighs* 185 pounds, and *has* brown eyes.
> They enjoyed *swimming, fishing,* and *lying* on the beach.

Use parallelism to balance subjects with subjects, verbs with verbs, phrases with phrases, and clauses with clauses. Here are more examples:

> The cat *arched* its back, *bared* its teeth, and *hissed* loudly. (past tense verbs)
>
> Our dog is *gentle, affectionate,* and incredibly *dumb*. (adjectives)
>
> The wind blew the papers *off the desk, onto the floor,* and *out the back window*. (prepositional phrases)

Composing such balanced structures will become second nature to you as you continue to develop confidence in your ideas and writing voice. Meanwhile, concentrate on sharpening and polishing these structures during revisions. Look for groups of equally important ideas and make them parallel.

IN SUMMARY

To join similar ideas by using parallel construction,

repeat the same grammatical structure (for example, noun and noun, present tense verb and present tense verb, -ing word and -ing word, and so forth).

✍ **4   Identifying Parallel Structures**

Circle the structure that is not parallel in each group. (This exercise could be done collaboratively.)

1. lying on the beach
   (a relaxing day)
   getting a suntan
   swimming in the ocean
2. a man of few words
   a man with strong character
   a man without fear
   a man who knows what to do
3. take a vacation
   get a rest
   calm your nerves
   to be refreshed and ready to go
4. taken their time
   known the procedures
   see solutions
   understood the directions
5. a popular girl
   smart
   witty
   friendly
6. writes with pen
   adds with pencil
   copies with carbon paper
   satisfied with an old-fashioned approach

✎ **5 Composing in Parallel Structures**

Complete each of the following sentences, using parallel construction.

1. Tom is handsome, athletic, *and extremely conceited*.

2. During the spring break, I intend to _____, _____, and _____.

3. Senator Foghorn was greeting the crowd, _____, and _____.

4. Have fun and _____, but _____.

5. She's tall, _____, and _____.

6. Mr. Williams _____ the door, _____ his wife, and _____ the dog.

✎ **6 Editing for Parallelism**

Rewrite italicized parts in each of the following paragraphs to use parallel construction.

The Truth About Some Animals

Paragraph A. (1) An opossum doesn't "play possum"—that is, play dead when endangered. (2) If cornered, it will hiss and snap. (3) If chased, it will run away. (4) *It will bite if you handle it.* (5) Occasionally, an opossum may collapse and appear motionless, but scientists don't think the reaction is deliberate. (6) Instead, *it is thought to be like the shock a human accident victim suffers.*

Rewritten: (4) *If handled, it will bite.*

(6) *Instead, they think it is like the shock a human accident victim suffers.*

Paragraph B. (1) Poets—and most other people—have always assumed that birds sing to attract the opposite sex, to show off, *or simply expressing joy.* (2) But all of these theories are probably wrong. (3) The more likely reason that birds sing is to stake out their territories *and announcing their domains.* (4) Apparently, no one has determined why birds sing more in some seasons than in others, and at some times of the day than in others. (5) One naturalist observed a bird that seemed to be staking out territory in the morning instead of the evening—perhaps because the bird was less tired and more ambitious in the morning.

Rewritten: (1) _____

(3) _____

Paragraph C. (1) The behavior of wolves is greatly misunderstood. (2) Wolves do not customarily form large packs when they hunt. (3) They do not howl when they hunt. (4) *And other animals are not frightened by them when they howl.* (5) Like most animals, wolves get their food the easiest way they can, and with the least risk. (6) They prey on mice, squirrels, rabbits, *and they also kill lambs and calves.* (7) Only in winter do wolves form packs to hunt larger game. (8) These packs are usually small, often merely a family group consisting of an old couple and their adult offspring.

Rewritten: (4) _____

(6) _____

Paragraph D. (1) Few creatures create such a mixture of awe, fear, and *are as fascinating as snakes.* (2) And few are the subject of so many myths and folk beliefs. (3) One of the oldest is that a "snake" tempted Adam and Eve in the Garden of Eden. (4) In truth, the book of Genesis calls the tempter a "serpent." (5) In ancient times, the word serpent could refer to any creeping animal, especially if poisonous or deadly. (6) *And in the fifteenth and sixteenth centuries, a variety of creatures could be referred to as a serpent, including both salamanders and crocodiles.*

Rewritten: (1) _____

(6) _____

ESTABLISHING CONSISTENCY IN TENSE

As you become absorbed in composing first drafts, you may unconsciously shift from one tense to another, especially when telling a story or discussing literature, movies, or plays in the present tense:

> The book **includes** a shocking scene in which several dolphins **are** caught in the nets of a tuna fishing boat. When the sailors **raise** the nets and **dump** their contents onto the deck, many of the dolphins **died** from strangulation in the ropes.

You should make the verb tenses consistent when you revise:

> *includes . . . are . . . raise . . . dump . . . die*

In this next example, an illogical use of *would* creates a problem.

> The ancient Egyptians **worshipped** cats, **protected** them from harm, **would embalm** them, and **buried** them in elaborate caskets when the animals **died.**

The shift is annoying, for the sentence establishes a pattern of past tense verbs that readers expect to continue:

> *. . . worshipped . . . protected . . . embalmed . . . buried . . . died*

The longer the paragraph (or composition) you compose, the more likely you are to shift tenses accidentally. Therefore, look carefully at your verb tenses as you revise and correct any inconsistencies. Reading your paper aloud may help you identify illogical tense shifts.

IN   SUMMARY

To correct illogical shifts in tense,

1. read over your early drafts (and read them aloud), looking specifically at the tenses of the verbs;
2. identify illogical tense shifts; and
3. correct the tense shifts as you revise.

✍ **7   Revising the Tenses of Verbs**

Each of the following sentences contains an illogical shift in tense. First read each sentence carefully, and then clarify its meaning by correcting the verb tense error.

A Dark History of Black Cats

1. Fear of cats, especially black ones, began in Europe in the Middle Ages, where
   the cities ∧ ~~would become~~ *became* overpopulated with the animals.

2. The cats were independent, stubborn, and quiet, so they make people uneasy.

3. People in the cities became increasingly superstitious and distrust anything they don't understand.

4. Fear of witches spread throughout Europe, and people say that the homeless old ladies who fed alley cats are practicing black magic.

5. Naturally, the cat companions (especially black ones) are guilty of witchery by association.

6. The witch scare turns into a frenzy, and many innocent women and their harmless pets were burned at the stake.

7. A massive campaign to exterminate cats begins in France, and thousands of the animals were put to flames monthly until King Louis XIII stops the practice in the 1630s.

8. Amazingly, even though black cats were slaughtered throughout Europe for centuries, the color does not disappear from the species.

✍ **8   Composing to Maintain Consistent Verb Tense**

Complete the following sentences, using verbs in the appropriate tenses.

1. Because I overslept this morning, I had to skip breakfast and <u>rush to school.</u>

2. Every day when class begins, our instructor _____

   _____

3. We'll meet you at 8:30, and we _____

   _____

4. Did you know that _____

   _____

5. He has been absent from school this week because _____

   _____

6. The repairman said that _____

   _____

✍ **9   Transforming Verb Tenses in a Passage**

The following passage contains illogical shifts in tense. Correct any errors by rewriting the verbs above the lines. (This exercise could be done collaboratively.)

It's No Sweat off Their Tongues

believe

❑   (1) A dog does not "sweat with its tongue," as many people ∧b̶e̶l̶i̶e̶v̶e̶d̶. (2) A
dog has some sweat glands, but the only significant glands will be on the soles
of its feet. (3) There are no sweat glands anywhere in or around a dog's mouth.
(4) The animal cools itself primarily by breathing rapidly, which is why it
panted after running. (5) But when it sticks out its tongue, the canine does so
because the tongue was moist and evaporation helped to cool it—not because
the dog needed to sweat.

ESTABLISHING CONSISTENCY IN QUOTATIONS OR REPORTED SPEECH

You can relate what someone else said in two ways:

◆ by directly quoting the person's words; or

◆ by reporting what the person said.

A **direct quotation** reproduces *exactly* what the speaker says or said—in the
same words and in the same verb tense. Quotation marks enclose the quotation;
and commas, periods, and question marks usually precede the end quotation mark.
The words that identify the speaker are *never* quoted.*

Direct Quotation

Susan asked Tom, "Does your dog have a pedigree?"
Tom replied, "No, it's a mutt that came from the city animal pound."
"Can you tell me where the pound is?" she inquired.

Reported speech, as its name suggests, *reports but does not quote* what the
speaker says or said. It *never* uses quotation marks but often employs *that* before
statements and *if* before questions:

Reported Speech

Susan asked Tom *if* his dog had a pedigree.
Tom told her *that* it was a mutt that came from the city animal pound.
She asked Tom to tell her the location of the pound.

Let's examine one of the examples more closely to see the differences between
quoted and reported speech:

Verb tenses identifying the speaker

Quotation:	Susan *asked* . . .	(She spoke in the past.)
Reported Speech:	Susan *inquired* if . . .	(She spoke in the past.)

---

* See Chapter 26 for a full discussion of quotations and their punctuation.

Verb tenses of the speaker's words

Quotation:	"Does . . . dog *have* . . ."	(She was referring to the present.)
Reported Speech:	if . . . dog *had* . . .	(She spoke in the past.)

Pronouns

Quotation:	". . . *your* dog . . ."	(She addressed Tom directly.)
Reported Speech:	. . . *his* dog . . .	(The sentences reports whom she asked.)

Word order

Quotation:	"Does your dog have . . ."	(This is a direct question and uses question word order.)
Reported Speech:	. . . Tom's dog had . . .	(This is a statement and uses statement word order.)

Whether you quote or report on a speaker's words, you must be consistent.

Inconsistent:	Susan said that "it was the cutest dog I've ever seen."
Consistent:	Susan said, "It's the cutest dog I've ever seen."
Consistent:	Susan said that it was the cutest dog she had ever seen.

Inconsistent:	Susan asked could I tell her where I got it?
Consistent:	Susan asked, "Can you tell me where you got it?"
Consistent:	Susan asked if I could tell her where I got it.

IN SUMMARY

To correct inconsistencies in quotations,

1. quote the exact words of a speaker—using the same tense, word order, and pronouns that the speaker employs or employed; and
2. do not include the identification of the speaker in the quote.

To correct inconsistencies in reported speech,

1. introduce the reported speech with *that* for statements or *if* for questions;
2. do not use quotation marks;
3. adjust the verb tense, pronouns, and word order to fit the sentence that reports what the speaker says or said.

✐ **10**   **Composing Quotations and Reported Speech**

Rewrite the direct quotations as reported speech or vice versa, changing tense, person, and word order as necessary.

Direct quote	*Reported speech*
1. Juan said, "I'm sure you are correct."	1. *Juan said that he was sure I was correct.*
2. Every weekend, my brother asks me, "Can I borrow your car?"	2. _____
3. _____	3. Dr. Smith told Bill that he could turn in the paper on Tuesday.
4. The new student asked, "Where is the counseling office?"	4. _____
5. The doctor warned me, "Don't go to work until tomorrow."	5. _____

✐ **11**   **Using Quotations or Reported Speech**

Suppose you are telling the story of a disagreement between your friends Maria and William, who are fraternal twins. Use your imagination and, based on the information supplied, compose sentences that quote or report what each of them said.

1. Tom to Maria: can't find dictionary/ thinks she has taken it
   Tom told Maria, "I can't find my dictionary. Did you take it?"

   or

   Tom told Maria that he couldn't find his dictionary. He asked her if she had taken it.

2. Maria to Tom: denies she took it/ says he's always blaming her

   _____

   _____

3. Tom to Maria: accuses her of always taking pens, paper, stapler, and tape

   _____

   _____

4. Maria to Tom: denies the accusation/ says he always swipes her compact disks

   _____

   _____

5. Mother to both: stop arguing and learn to share

   _____

   _____

12 Editing for Consistency in Quotations or Reported Speech

Correct any errors in quotations or reported speech by writing your changes after each paragraph.

Cats on the Post Office Payroll

❑ Cats have been on the official payroll of the British Post Office for more than a century. They're not hired to sort or deliver mail, of course, but to keep it from being eaten by mice. The problem was especially bad in London in the mid-1800s, when mice invaded the sorting rooms to gnaw at mail, money orders, and employees' sandwiches. Traps and poisons proved ineffective, and in 1868 the secretary of the post office approved the hiring of three female cats at a weekly allowance of four pence each. But he cautioned, "If the mice are not reduced in number in six months, he would have to stop a further portion of the allowance."

Rewritten:_____

_____

Within months, the rodent population had shrunk dramatically, and post offices received the go-ahead to hire more cats. Many did, and as the felines became more prominent in the work force, their pay improved. In 1953, the assistant postmaster general assured the House of Commons "that female mouse-hunters received very adequate maternity benefits and he gives them the same wages and employment opportunities as male cats."

Rewritten:_____

_____

As of the mid-1980s, cats were on the payroll at three postal sites in London. A terror named Kojak at London's Nine Elms postal garage was, at £1.80, among the top-paid mousers in the land. Bill Woodford, the officer in charge, said that most weeks, he leaves a couple of rats on my desk as well as an array of mice.

Rewritten:_____

_____

13 Editing a Passage for Consistency

The following passage contains illogical shifts in person and number, shifts in quotations or reported speech, illogical shifts in tense, and errors in parallelism. Above each line, make any changes necessary to eliminate these shifts and errors.

Charles Waterton: A Most Daring Naturalist

❑ (1) An Englishman named Charles Waterton (1782—1865) was among the

strangest naturalists who ever lived. (2) He was constantly involved in strange

stemmed
and wild adventures, all of which∧ stem from his love of nature. (3) After com-

pleting school in 1800, where he has displayed a talent in natural history, he

decided to live in South America. (4) Then, in 1812, he made his first trek into

regions of the Brazilian jungle where no one had ever gone. (5) His goal is to search for a form of poison that was supposed to cure an illness. (6) On this and three later trips to the region, he will perform many truly eccentric feats.

(7) For example, after he heard a report that someone had spotted a large python in the vicinity, he dashed off barefoot to capture it. (8) (He never wears shoes or putting on boots in the jungle.) (9) After the natives had pinned the snake's head to the ground, Waterton threw himself onto the python's body and tying the creature's mouth with his suspenders. (10) The safari made their way back to Waterton's hut, where the natives deposited the python in a large sack, closed the opening with a knotted rope, and would place the sack in a corner of the hut to pass the night. (11) You could hear the snake thrash around violently in the sack all night long, but Waterton apparently does not object to sharing his sleeping quarters with a python.

(12) On another occasion, he was trying to capture a crocodile, but his helpers can't pull the creature from the river. (13) "I saw he was in a state of fear," said Waterton. (14) Finally, when they got the crocodile within a few yards of the bank, Waterton sprang from the boat and jumping on the animal's back. (15) "I seized his forelegs," he said, "and, by main force, twisted them on the animal's back, where he could use them for a bridle." (16) With Waterton riding the crocodile, his helpers dragged it onto the bank. (17) He remarked that it was the first and last time I was ever on a crocodile's back.

(18) On another of his trips into the jungle, Waterton learned of the vampire bat's habit of sucking human blood and decided to let them drink some of his. (19) He brought one of the creatures into his quarters and purposely was sleeping with one foot exposed. (20) Yet despite his best efforts, Waterton is frustrated. (21) The vampire bat ignored him and instead sank its teeth into the big toe of an Indian who slept nearby.

✍ 14   Editing Your Own Work

Look at a paragraph or composition you are now writing or return to one you have written previously, and check it carefully for illogical shifts in person and number, shifts in tense, and errors in parallelism. Then rewrite the paper to correct these errors.

Writing Directly and Vividly

Strong writing goes beyond mere structure and grammar. It demands good style—concrete, exact, direct, and lively. It comes from composing with confidence as you listen to your writing voice and then revise to strengthen that voice. This chapter helps you develop and polish your style by adopting the following practices:

- ✏ choosing strong verbs and adjectives;
- ✏ eliminating wordiness and unnecessary repetition;
- ✏ avoiding clichés; and
- ✏ employing metaphors and similes.

STRONG WRITING DEFINED

Strong writing says the most in the fewest words. It is specific and fresh, graceful and economical. Bad writing is vague and stale, repetitious and wordy. Compare these sentences:

1. In my opinion, a good place to get good food which is not too expensive is a restaurant named the New Café, which is located on the corner of Franklin Street and Second Avenue.
2. The New Café, on the corner of Franklin Street and Second Avenue, serves delicious food at reasonable prices.

You probably prefer the second version. It states the point directly in just 18 words, while the first version squanders many of its 34 words. Let's analyze the waste.

In my opinion . . . (If you are recommending a restaurant, that is an opinion, so why state the obvious? And why state it in a *cliché*—a lifeless expression that everyone uses?)

a good place to get good food . . . (This carelessly repeats the vague adjective *good* and needlessly mentions the word *place*, since a restaurant is obviously a place. The second version's adjectives, *delicious* and *reasonable,* are more lively and exact.)

which is not too expensive . . . (If you are recommending the restaurant, why do it negatively by using the phrase *not too expensive?* Compare this expression to the second version's *at reasonable prices,* an affirmative phrase that avoids the weak verb *is.*)

is a restaurant named the New Café . . . (This repeats *is* and wastes two more words: *restaurant named.* The New Café is obviously the name of a restaurant.)

which is located on the corner of Franklin Street and Second Avenue. (Here is more weak repetition: a third *is,* a second *which,* and the wasted word *located,* since *on the corner of Franklin Street and Second Avenue* is obviously its location.)

In short, the first version is filled with *deadwood:* lifeless and useless language. It states the obvious, repeats dull words unnecessarily and carelessly, and overrelies on the linking verb *is* (instead of the single action verb *serves* in the second version).

Strong writing, therefore, puts every word to work. It is direct, colorful, concrete, and action filled. But achieving it requires keen attention to the sounds and rhythms of your sentences in first drafts, and then close attention to word choice during revisions. Begin by composing in a strong and confident voice; then revise to prune the deadwood and strengthen what remains. With practice, of course, these revising skills will shift to first-drafting skills.

REVISING TO ELIMINATE WEAK VERBS

Don't fret over each word while composing first drafts. Let your ideas and words flow comfortably. During revisions, however, pay special attention to verbs. The most common (and therefore the most overused) ones such as *is/are/am, go, get, have, make, do, run, put, take, see, use,* and *talk* are boring, colorless, and vague. The verb *get,* for example, expresses countless meanings.

get an idea, get a present for someone, get a present from someone, get a job, get home, get an A, get sick, get married, get a raise, get angry, get up, get off, get on, get in, get out, get over, get around, get down, get through, get to work, get to sleep, get finished, get lost, get ahead, get away with, get together, get even with, . . . and so on.

You cannot avoid these common verbs entirely, but don't overuse them. During revisions, circle weak verbs and try to replace them with verbs or phrases that more precisely express your meaning. Such substitutions needn't be fancy, just more exact.

got to sleep	I	*fell asleep* / *nodded off* / *drowsed off*	at midnight.
got angry	The coach	*exploded* / *roared* / *fumed*	at the players.
got home	He	*arrived home* / *staggered in the door* / *burst into the house*	at 9:30.

Similarly, the verb *have* to show possession often leads to a wasted sentence, for a single word such as *my* can express its idea.

Poor:	I have a good friend named Bill. We are together all the time.
Better:	My good friend Bill and I are together all the time.

A Tip

If you cannot think of a stronger word, whether a verb or any part of speech, you may wish to consult a *thesaurus*—a dictionary of synonyms—for suggestions. In fact, many word processing programs include an on-line thesaurus that is available with a keystroke or click of a mouse. *But let the thesaurus remind you of synonyms you already know.* Don't substitute a word whose meaning and usage you aren't sure of, or you may say something foolish.

IN SUMMARY

To write with strong verbs,

1. during revisions, circle weak verbs such as *is/are/am, go, get, have, make, do, run, put, take, see, use,* and *talk;* and
2. then, whenever possible, substitute a verb or phrase that more exactly and vividly expresses your meaning. Use a thesaurus if you wish, but only to remind you of words you already know and can use correctly.

✍ **1   Composing with Strong Verbs**

Write three to five different verbs that express the idea in parentheses, and be prepared to discuss the differences in meaning among the verbs.

1. (slow movement)   Black Bart _ambled_ into the saloon.

    strolled

    swaggered

    staggered

    crawled

2. (fast movement)   The runner _____ past the cheering crowd.

    _____

    _____

    _____

3. (removal)   The thief _____ the woman's purse.

    _____

    _____

    _____

    _____

4. (see)   I _____ the document for several minutes.

    _____

    _____

    _____

    _____

5. (make)   She _____ a wonderful dessert.

_____

_____

_____

_____

2   Revising to Tighten Sentences

Combine each of the following pairs of sentences or clauses, eliminating the verb *have.*

1. Bill has a crazy friend. He is always getting into trouble.

   *Bill's crazy friend is always getting into trouble.*_____

2. She has a used car. It barely runs during the winter.

   _____

3. When I was a child, I had a cat. She slept on my bed every night.

   _____

4. We have some homework. We must finish it by Friday.

   _____

5. My father has a favorite chair that he sits in every night.

   _____

6. William has a blue coat that he wears to church on Sunday.

   _____

3   Revising to Eliminate Overly Used Verbs

The following passage overuses the verbs *go* and *get.* Rewrite the passage, substituting more exact and interesting word choices.

> I leave the house around 7:30 and go to pick up my friend, and then we go to school. At 2:00 I get out of school and go home. Then I get started on my homework. I usually eat dinner about 5:00, and after I get finished with dinner, I go out with my friends. We usually go to someone's house or go to a game room nearby for an hour. But I try to get home by 11:00 so that I can get my clothes ready for the next day, and then I go to bed.

*I leave the house around 7:30 to pick up my friend on the way to school.*_____

_____

_____

_____

_____

_____

_____

_____

✍ **4 Revising Your Own Sentences**

Write five sentences, each of which includes a verb from the following list: *put, do, make, have, take, run, move, say, talk, give, look, use,* and *go.* Then revise each sentence, substituting a stronger, more precise verb.

1. <u>My counselor gave me some advice on scheduling my classes for next</u>
   <u>semester.</u>
   Revision: <u>My counselor advised me about scheduling my classes for next</u>
   <u>semester.</u>

2. _____
   Revision: _____
   _____

3. _____
   Revision: _____
   _____

4. _____
   Revision: _____
   _____

5. _____
   Revision: _____
   _____

6. _____
   Revision: _____
   _____

REVISING TO ELIMINATE VAGUE ADJECTIVES AND EXPRESSIONS

Like common verbs, the most common adjectives are often sickly and bland. (Here is the same sentence written with common adjectives: "Like common verbs, the most common adjectives are often bad and uninteresting." Which version do you prefer?) Thus, as you revise, circle overused adjectives such as *good, bad, nice, different, interesting,* and *pretty,* and try to substitute more vivid adjectives and expressions.

Weak	Better
One scene in the movie was *very interesting*.	One scene in the movie was { astonishing. / fascinating. / horrifying.
	One scene in the movie made me want to dive under my seat and hide.

Furthermore, vague expressions such as *what they did, the things he does, what he said,* and *we saw a lot of things* communicate almost nothing. Try to substitute more specific phrases during revisions.

Weak	Better
What the man did next scared me to death.	I closed my eyes when the man in the mask swung his ax at the knight's head.
I don't like Jim because of the things he does.	I don't like Jim because he constantly insults people, mooches money from me, and bullies little children.

IN SUMMARY

To write using strong adjectives and expressions,

1. during revisions, circle weak adjectives such as *good, bad, nice, different, interesting, funny,* and *pretty,* and weak expressions such as *what he does* or *the things he does;* and
2. then substitute expressions that more vividly and exactly express your meaning.

5   Revising Weak Sentences

Rewrite each of the following sentences in more vivid and exact language.

1. The things my brother does at the dinner table are disgusting. *When my brother eats with his hands, talks with his mouth full, and belches, I would like to break a plate over his head.*

2. On my last vacation, I did some interesting things. _____

   _____

   _____

3. What the man did wasn't too nice. _____

   _____

   _____

4. A strange cat was doing weird things in my yard. _____

   _____

   _____

5. I saw a dude today who really looked bad. _____

   _____

   _____

REVISING TO ELIMINATE WORDINESS

Weak writing wastes words, saying in five what can be said in one or two. You might replace a phrase with a single word:

Phrase	Replacement
in this day and age	*now*
due to the fact that	*because*
She dances *with a great deal of grace.*	She dances *gracefully.*

You might replace a weak verb and its modifier or object with a single strong verb:

Weak verb and modifier	*Replacement*
He *looked* at her *in an angry manner.*	He *scowled* at her.

Weak verb and object	*Replacement*
He *has the ability* to swim well.	He *can* swim well.

Weak writing also insults the intelligence of readers, explaining what needn't be explained or placing ideas in empty or obvious categories:

Poor:	*As far as intelligence is concerned,* Bill is very smart. (What else could *smart* refer to but *intelligence*?)
Better:	Bill is very intelligent.

Poor:	My father is *the type of man who* never misses work. (Why say that your father is a *man*? What else could he be? And why mention that he is *a type*?)
Better:	My father never misses work.

Poor:	August *was a month that* caused several *different kinds of* problems for me. (Why say that August was *a month*? And why mention both *different* and *kinds,* since one implies the other?)
Better:	August caused several kinds of problems for me.

Poor:	*The reason why* he failed was *because* he didn't study. (*The reason, why,* and *because* all express the same meaning.)
Better:	He failed because he didn't study.

Poor:	The box was very large in size. (Why mention *in size,* since *large* includes that idea? And why say *very large* when a single word expresses that idea?)
Better:	The box was huge.

IN SUMMARY

> **To avoid wordiness,**
>
> 1. during revisions, shorten clauses to phrases or phrases to single words whenever possible;
> 2. eliminate words whose meanings are already included in other words;
> 3. eliminate empty categorizing words such as *type of, kind of, way, area ,* and *method;* but
> 4. violate this advice when the revision is unclear or awkward.

6   Revising for Conciseness

Replace each of the following phrases with a single word or two.

1. in this day and age _____*now*_____

2. talked in an extremely loud voice _____

3. has the ability to write _____

4. the reason why _____

5. a blue color _____

6. 9 P.M. at night _____

7. true facts _____

8. during the same time that _____

7   Revising to Tighten Sentences

Rewrite each of the following sentences, eliminating unnecessary words and empty phrases.

1. When my teacher returned my test back this morning, I saw that I had made a lot of careless mistakes that came from not being careful. *When my teacher returned my test this morning, I saw that I had made a lot of careless mistakes.*

2. In today's modern world, there are always new innovations in home electronics. _____

   _____

3. The kinds of imported cars that come into the country from Japan and Europe have a reputation of being better than the types of American cars made in the United States. _____

   _____

   _____

4. The reason why I like the Black Tie club is because I see people who are dressed in the wildest kinds of clothes I have ever seen people wear._____

   _____

   _____

5. In my opinion, I feel that today's athletes are overpaid and making too much

money for the kind of jobs they do._____

_____

_____

6. The story had a lot of specific details that created a feeling of true-to-life real-

ity. _____

_____

_____

REVISING TO ELIMINATE UNNECESSARY REPETITION

While intentional repetition can greatly strengthen writing, unintentional repetition of a word (even in a different form or with a different meaning) usually weakens writing. Repeat a word or phrase only for emphasis or clarity. The following sentences can be pruned of deadwood:

Poor	Better
A good athlete is a hard-working athlete.	A good athlete works hard.
I had problems solving the math problems.	I struggled to solve the math problems.
When the magician pulled the rabbit out of the hat, it was the only trick that tricked me.	I was tricked only when the magician pulled the rabbit out of the hat.
He had a reasonably good reason for his tardiness.	His tardiness was understandable.

IN SUMMARY

To avoid weak repetition,

1. during revisions, circle repeated words, including those used in different forms or with different meanings;
2. decide whether their repetition strengthens or weakens the passage; and
3. rewrite the passage, substituting for or eliminating the weak repetition.

✍ 8   **Revising to Remove Weak Repetition**

Rewrite each of the following sentences to eliminate unnecessary repetition.

1. My break time at work really breaks up the monotony. _My break time at work_

relieves the monotony.

2. My boss, Mr. Carson, is the best boss I could ever want. _____

_____

_____

3. Not too many of my co-workers work hard at work. _____

_____

_____

4. Our center, Stretch Everest, is always the center of attention when he walks

onto the basketball court. _____

_____

_____

5. A large truck crashed into the rear of the automobile. This truck caused consid-

erable damage. _____

_____

_____

6. I usually have a bite to eat in the afternoon. After I finish eating, I then start my

homework. _____

_____

_____

9   Editing to Tighten a Passage

Rewrite the following passage to eliminate unnecessary repetition of words and ideas.
Your revision should be about half as long as the original.

❑   As we arrived at the amusement park, I was very excited to ride the most exciting and scariest ride, which was called the Whirl Around. It was the only ride
I really wanted to ride, for I had heard so many things about how scary it was. I
stood in line and waited anxiously. After I had waited for 20 or 30 minutes, I
reached the entrance, and it was my turn to get strapped into one of the cars. I
got into a little red-colored car. Then the attendant strapped me in. After
everyone was strapped into the cars, we began our ride. First the cars began
slowly, and then they began to pick up speed. It was beginning to become scary
to me. The cars went around and around in a circle. They even went upside
down, and they even went sideways. They finally went at a very fast speed. But
after a while, the speed began to decrease, and the cars pulled back into the
platform. Finally the ride was over, and it had been very exciting and scary.

As we arrived at the amusement park, I was excited to try the most

thrilling and frightening ride, the Whirl Around.

_____

_____

_____

_____

_____

_____
_____
_____

✍ **10 Tightening Your Own Writing**

Compose a six- to ten-sentence paragraph describing a typical activity you perform. Then circle words and ideas you have repeated and consider each one. Is the repetition necessary? Could it be eliminated, perhaps by combining ideas or sentences? Make your changes on the original draft and then revise the paragraph.

Original

_____
_____
_____
_____
_____
_____
_____
_____
_____

Revision

_____
_____
_____
_____
_____
_____
_____
_____
_____
_____

REVISING TO ELIMINATE CLICHÉS

A *cliché* is a lifeless, overused expression that strikes readers with the force of a half-empty balloon. But clichés are a natural part of speech, so you may write several in drafts. Look for them during revisions, and try to substitute either your own words or a fresher expression.

Cliché	Better
I like to do my own thing.	I am independent.
last but not least	finally
He is as strong as an ox.	He is as strong as year-old cheese.

The following list of clichés should serve as examples:

a chip off the old block
after all was said and done
as cold as ice
at this point in time
avoid it like the plague
barely scratches the surface
bite the bullet
bored to tears
easier said than done
few and far between
have a ball
in one ear and out the other
in this day and age
it goes without saying
more fun than a barrel of monkeys

one in a million
over and done with
selling like hotcakes
sleep like a log
stick like glue
stick to our guns
the time of my life
tried and true
up at the crack of dawn
waiting in the wings
water over the dam
water under the bridge
where it's at
where you're coming from

IN SUMMARY   To avoid clichés, circle them during revisions and rewrite the passage in your own words.

11   Revising to Substitute Fresh Expressions

Rewrite each of the following sentences to eliminate clichés.

1. I had the time of my life visiting friends in Austin, Texas. *I loved my visit with friends in Austin, Texas.*

2. He was as happy as a lark. _____

3. Every day my father is up at the crack of dawn to go to work. _____

4. True blue friends are few and far between. _____

5. Once in a blue moon, something happens that makes my blood boil. _____

6. After Ralph blows his top, it is over and done with, and he lets bygones be bygones. _____

7. I worked like a horse outside today from sunup to sundown. _____

_____

8. Last but not least, this exercise should teach you to avoid clichés like the

plague. _____

_____

EMPLOYING SIMILES AND METAPHORS

The opposite of a cliché is a simile or metaphor. A *simile* is a comparison of one thing to another using *like* or *as*. The comparison not only draws a sharp and surprising image for readers but often adds richness of meaning to a passage.

> *Similes*
>
> His temper is *like popcorn in hot oil.* (What does this simile suggest about the man's actions when he is angry?)
> She is as angry *as an arsonist without a match.* (What does this simile suggest about the writer's attitude toward the woman?)

A *metaphor* is a comparison without the words *like* or *as*.

> *Metaphors*
>
> The top of his desk was *a swamp of papers and books.* (What does this metaphor suggest about the desk?)
> He *slithered* into the room and *coiled up* next to me. (What is the man's action being compared to? What does the metaphor suggest about the writer's attitude toward the man?)

Similes and metaphors surprise and delight readers and therefore enliven writing—provided you don't overuse them. You may most effectively substitute them for clichés.

✍ 12   **Drafting Similes and Metaphors**

Complete each of the following sentences with an appropriate simile or metaphor.

1. Gloria's laugh is _contagious;_ it _infects even the most serious people around_
   her.

2. Life in my neighborhood is as exciting as _____

_____.

3. When Fred hears about a sale on CD-ROM disks, he arrives at the store as fast

   as _____

   _____ .

4. He _____ his food like a _____ .

5. Life is a _____ .

6. Television is a _____ .

13   Editing Your Own Work

Look at a paper you are writing now or return to one you have written previously, and revise it to eliminate weak verbs, adjectives, and other expressions, wordiness, unnecessary repetition, and clichés. Add a few similes and metaphors if you can.

Achieving Sentence Variety

Chapter 13 focused on strengthening your writing through use of concise and lively phrasing. This chapter offers further advice on making your writing more interesting, dramatic, and mature. Specifically, you will be examining and practicing the following techniques, which occur most often during revisions:

- ✏ varying the length of sentences;
- ✏ varying the beginnings of sentences;
- ✏ varying the types of sentences: questions, commands, and explanations;
- ✏ varying the ways of joining sentences; and
- ✏ varying other descriptive structures in sentences.

SENTENCE VARIETY EXAMINED

Sentence variety adds maturity to your writing; it provides opportunities for drama, tension, and surprise. It also brings music to your message, through rhythm, repetition, and release. Think for a moment about a musical beat: *dum-da-dum bop! dum-da-dum bop! dum-da-da-dum bop bop!* The power of the *bops* derives from the *dums* and *das* that precede them. Writing that lacks variety is therefore monotonous and flat, as in the following passage where all the sentences are approximately the same length:

❑ (1) In ancient Rome, the upper classes and lower classes ate with their fingers. (2) All the Europeans did the same thing. (3) The practice changed in the fourteenth century. (4) This period is called the Renaissance. (5) It was the dawning of concern for "genteel" behavior. (6) There was a right way and a wrong way to pick up food. (7) There was a refined and vulgar way to pick up food. (8) A commoner grabbed his food with five fingers. (9) A person of breeding politely lifted it with *three* fingers. (10) He didn't want to soil his ring finger or pinkie.

The style is childishly simple, lacking the graceful flow of one idea into the next. Here's a revision:

Finger Food for Everyone

❑ (1) The upper and lower classes of ancient Rome ate with their fingers, as did all the Europeans until the dawning of concern for "genteel" behavior during the Renaissance in the fourteenth century. (2) There was a right and a wrong, a refined and a vulgar, way to pick up food. (3) A commoner grabbed at his food with five fingers, while a person of breeding politely lifted it with *three*. (4) He would never soil his ring finger or pinkie!

This version is faster paced, more lively, and rhythmic—and it sets up the punch line at the end.

Let's take a look at ways to achieve sentence variety as you draft and revise your work. The more options that are available to you, the more interesting and powerful your writing can be.

REVISING TO VARY SENTENCE LENGTH

Varying the length of sentences often serves to emphasize ideas. Notice how short and long sentences alternate in the following paragraph:

From Pitchfork to Table

❑   (1) The word *fork,* which comes from the Latin term for a farmer's pitchfork, is an ancient tool. (2) Miniature pitchforks dating back to 4000 B.C.E. were unearthed during an archeological dig in Turkey. (3) Although no one knows what function these implements served, it probably wasn't as tableware. (4) What we do know is that the first forks as eating utensils appeared in eleventh-century Tuscany, Italy. (5) We also know that they were unpopular. (6) In fact, the priests condemned them outright. (7) Only human fingers created by God, the clergy argued, were worthy of touching the food bestowed on us by God. (8) Nevertheless, two-pronged forks of gold and silver continued to be custom made for wealthy Tuscans. (9) Somebody must have liked the things.

The long sentences set up to punch lines delivered in the short sentences at the middle and end of the passage:

> We also know that they were unpopular.
> In fact, the clergy condemned them outright.
> Somebody must have liked the things.

Experiment with differing sentence lengths and word order as you compose—and especially as you revise—until you arrive at a graceful and emphatic presentation of ideas.

IN   SUMMARY

To achieve sentence variety and emphasize important ideas,

1. **experiment with differing sentence lengths and word order, especially during revisions; and**
2. **place the most important ideas in short sentences or at the end of longer ones.**

✍   **1   Revising Short Sentences**

Rewrite the short sentences in the following passage, experimenting with different sentence lengths and word order. Combine and reword sentences as you wish, but be sure to maintain the same meaning of the passage.

❑   The fork was a shocking novelty. That shock lasted at least 100 years. For example, an Italian historian wrote about a dinner. A Venetian noblewoman ate with a fork at it. She had designed the fork. Several priests condemned her "excessive sign of refinement." The woman died a few days after the meal. It was supposedly from the plague. Clergymen claimed that her death was divine punishment. The punishment warned other people. They shouldn't show off by using a fork.

For at least 100 years, the fork remained a shocking novelty.

_____

_____

_____

_____

_____

_____

_____

_____

REVISING TO VARY SENTENCE BEGINNINGS

Varying Time Expressions

The most common word order at the beginning of a sentence is *subject-verb*:

Subject	Verb	
Thomas à Becket	*was*	the archbishop of Canterbury during the mid-twelfth century.
He	*left*	England in 1164 to escape a trial for treason.
He	*returned*	six years later with some Italian two-pronged forks.
Noblemen	*may have used*	them for dueling soon afterward.

But most sentences contain other information that can be shifted to the beginning for variety and emphasis, such as the time expressions in the examples:

Time Expression	Subject	Verb
During the mid-twelfth century,	Thomas à Becket	was . . .
In 1164,	he	left . . .
Six years later,	he	returned . . .
Soon afterward,	noblemen	may have used . . .

Many time expressions are *prepositional phrases*—a combination of a preposition and an object, usually a noun. You will see other kinds of time expressions later in the chapter. Here are some further examples:

Preposition	Object
After	a few days,
About	8:15,
Around	midnight,
At	noon,
Before	the start of the show,
By	eight o'clock,
During	the week,
In	1985,
On	November 22,
Since	last year,
Until	the end of the decade,
Within	a short time,

As with other introductory phrases, a comma follows most time expressions that begin sentences. However, many one- or two-word time expressions such as *now, then, soon, sometimes, next, today, yesterday, last week,* and *next year* don't need a comma.* Use a comma with these short expressions only when you want your readers to pause.

IN SUMMARY

To punctuate introductory time expressions,

1. follow most expressions with a comma;
2. with one- or two-word expressions such as *now, then, today, soon, sometimes,* and *next month,* use the comma only when you wish to signal a pause.

2 Beginning Sentences with Time Expressions

Shift the time expression to the beginning of each sentence that follows. Use commas as needed.

1. The fork was still nothing more than an expensive and mostly decorative device in England by the fourteenth century. *By the fourteenth century, the fork was still nothing more than an expensive and mostly decorative device in England.*

2. King Edward I had thousands of royal knives and hundreds of spoons but only seven forks: six silver, one gold, in 1307. _____

   _____

3. King Charles V of France owned only 12 forks, most of them "decorated with precious stones," later in the century. _____

   _____

4. None of these forks were used for eating even at that point. _____

   _____

* See Chapter 25 for a full discussion of punctuating introductory elements.

5. Customs ever so slowly began to change then. _____

_____

6. A fork would appear at the table of a lord or lady sometimes. _____

_____

✍ 3   Composing Sentences That Begin with Time Expressions

Compose a short narrative about an experience that happened to you over a period of time. Begin the first sentence by stating when the experience started ("Three years ago," "Last Thursday evening," "When I was 16," etc.). Then indicate the sequence of events by beginning each sentence that follows with a time expression. Here, for reference, is a short list of time expressions: *a few minutes (hours, days, months) later, soon, eventually, then, meanwhile, at the same time, later on, after a short (long) time, after a while, awhile later, at that moment, in April, in 1973, on Tuesday, by the week-end, during the next few hours (days, months).*

1. _____

_____

2. _____

_____

3. _____

_____

4. _____

_____

5. _____

_____

6. _____

_____

Varying the Use of Adverbs and Other Prepositional Phrases

Instead of an introductory time expression, you may employ an adverb or another kind of prepositional phrase. *Adverbs,* which often end in *-ly,* usually come between the subject and verb or between the first two words of a verb phrase:

Subject	Adverb	Verb	
People	*continually*	shunned	forks until the eighteenth century.

Subject	Verb	Adverb	Verb
The implements	were	*typically*	regarded as effeminate and unworthy of men.
Fork users	were	*often*	ridiculed and insulted.

Notice how these adverbs take on greater emphasis if you shift them to the beginning of sentences:

> *Continually, people shunned forks until the eighteenth century.*
> *Typically, the implements were regarded as effeminate and*
> *unworthy of men.*
> *Often, fork users were ridiculed and insulted.*

In addition to establishing time relationships, *prepositional phrases* can express other meanings and can appear almost anywhere in a sentence:

> *In Italy,* the country *of the fork's origin,* the implement could still be a
> source *of ridicule* all the way *into the seventeenth century.*

Here for reference is a list of the most common prepositions:

> *One-word Prepositions*
>
> above, across, against, among, behind, below, beneath, beside, between, beyond, by, despite, down, except, for, from, in, inside, into, like, near, of, off, on, onto, out, over, through, throughout, to, toward, under(neath), up, upon, with, within, without
>
> *Two-or-more-word Prepositions*
>
> as for, aside from, because of, contrary to, due to, except for, in addition to, in case of, in spite of, next to, regardless of

However, you cannot move every prepositional phrase, as in this sentence:

> *People speared their food with one of a pair of eating knives,*
> *cupped it in a spoon, or pinched it with the correct three fingers.*

Shifting a prepositional phrase would destroy the parallelism in the sentence,* and the last two prepositional phrases must follow the words that precede them. ("In a spoon, people speared" makes no sense.)

✐ 4   Revising the Beginnings of Sentences

Rewrite each of the following sentences at least twice to begin with an adverb or prepositional phrase. (You may wish to underline the adverbs and prepositional phrases before beginning.) Add commas where necessary.

---

* See Chapter 12 for a full discussion of parallelism.

1. Women who used forks before the eighteenth century were also often ridiculed as well.

   a. _Often, women who used forks before the eighteenth century were also ridiculed._

   b. _Before the eighteenth century, women who used forks were also often ridiculed._

2. A publication disgustedly tells a story of the wife of the chief official of Venice in 1626.

   a. _____

   b. _____

3. She stupidly ordered a servant to "cut her food into little pieces" and ate with "a two-pronged fork" instead of eating the proper way with knife and fingers.

   a. _____

   _____

   b. _____

   _____

4. A popular etiquette book thoughtfully gave advice on something that was not yet self-evident a quarter century later: "Do not try to eat soup with a fork."

   a. _____

   _____

   b. _____

   _____

5 Drafting Your Own Sentences

Compose five of your own sentences that begin with expressions from the following list: *cautiously, angrily, cleverly, stupidly, happily, without thinking, last year, after a long time, in the next few weeks, before the end of the decade, except for a few lucky people, on a perfect spring day.* Add commas as necessary.

1. _____

_____

2. _____

_____

3. _____

_____

4. _____

_____

5. _____

_____

EMPLOYING OTHER TYPES OF SENTENCES

Employing Rhetorical Questions

Not every sentence you write must be a statement. Why not ask a question from time to time? The question actively engages readers in the subject matter, asking them to consider it for a moment rather than merely telling them what to think. A *rhetorical question* often serves as a topic sentence; the paragraph raises the question and then answers it, as in this example:

> *When did forks become the fashion—and why?* The change occurred in eighteenth-century France, and then, in part, to emphasize class distinctions. With the French Revolution brewing, and with revolutionaries stressing the ideals of "liberty, equality, and fraternity," the nobles increased their use of forks—especially the four-tined variety. The fork became a symbol of luxury, refinement, and status. Suddenly, touching food with even three bare fingers was uncouth and vulgar.

✍ **6 Drafting a Paragraph Beginning with a Question**

Choose one of the following topics and compose a question as the topic sentence of a paragraph, such as this example:

Topic: the benefits of avoiding a too fast-paced life

Topic Sentence Question: *Will Americans ever learn to slow down and enjoy themselves?*

Then compose a first draft of a paragraph that answers (that is, develops) the question.

topics

1. the wasteful use of packaging
2. the benefits (or insanity) of eating (or not eating) certain foods
3. a problem with professional sports (or one professional sport)
4. a problem with (or benefit of) video games
5. the ideal job

Employing Commands, or Imperatives

Mix an occasional command into your writing for variety, or when giving advice or instructions to readers.* A *command* (or *imperative sentence)* addresses your readers directly but omits the implied subject *you,* as in these examples:

> *Affirmative Command*
> *Pick up* your food with three fingers. (The subject, *you,* is understood.)
>
> *Negative Command*
> *Do not try* to eat soup with a fork. (Again, the unstated subject is *you.)*

* See Chapter 7, which discusses process analysis, for further examples of commands in direction giving.

Notice that these commands (and the sentence you are reading right now) give suggestions, directions, or warnings.

7   Drafting a Paragraph of Instructions

Compose a first draft of a paragraph that gives advice or instructions. Use commands in as many sentences as possible. When you finish, revise the paragraph (making corrections above the lines) to eliminate any sentence fragments or inconsistencies in command forms.

Example: Blend the ingredients in a blender or mixer until the batter is smooth but not watery.

Employing Exclamations

Power! That's what an exclamation can bring to a passage. The *exclamation*—a short expression ending in the exclamation point—may not be a full sentence, but it does dramatize a point, as in this example from earlier in the chapter:

> A commoner grabbed at his food with five fingers, while a person of breeding politely lifted it with *three*. He would never soil his ring finger or pinkie!

Thus, don't be afraid to experiment with questions, commands, and exclamations as you draft and revise. They add variety and emphasis to your writing, provided you don't overuse them.

8   Composing Exclamations

Follow each sentence provided with an exclamation.

1. People say that Americans don't work as hard as they used to. *What nonsense!*

2. One week medical researchers tell us not to eat red meat; the next week they tell us the opposite. _____

3. Is camping in Yellowstone or Yosemite National Park really worth the effort?

   _____

4. A developer wants to tear down another 100-year-old house and replace it with a high-rise steel and glass building._____

   _____

5. Tom lost his temper and told off his boss. _____

   _____

IN SUMMARY   **Mix these sentence types into your writing for emphasis and variety:**

1. rhetorical questions, which often serve as topic sentences that the paragraph will develop;
2. commands, which usually give directions, advice, or warnings; and
3. exclamations, which emphasize a point.

Be careful not to overuse them, however.

9   **Varying Sentence Types**

Draft a passage based on the following information. Pose a question at or near the beginning, and include at least one exclamation and one command. Don't change the meanings of the material, but arrange and reword it in any way you wish.

Taking a Place at the Table

1. beginning of eighteenth century: upper class in Europe used individual place settings
2. each aristocrat had full set of cutlery, plates, and glasses
3. fork now part of that set
4. today each member of even the poorest families uses separate dining utensils
5. in eighteenth century most people still shared communal bowls, plates, and even drinking glasses
6. from etiquette book of that period: "When everyone is eating from the same dish, you should take care not to put your hand into it before those of higher rank have done so."
7. almost everyone owned and used two table implements: the knife and the spoon
8. spoon commonly used for thousands of years
9. readers should think about these changes in dining habits

_____

_____

_____

_____

_____

_____

_____

_____

_____

_____

_____

_____

_____

_____

VARYING WAYS OF JOINING SENTENCES*

Employing Compound Subjects

One way to achieve variety and sophistication as you revise is through combining sentences. Consider these examples:

> Spoons have a long history. They were never ridiculed. Their users were never ridiculed, either.

Obviously, these sentences are monotonous and repetitious, but how could they be revised? Here's one possibility. The verb *were ridiculed* appears twice, each time with a separate subject. If you join the subjects with *and,* creating *a compound subject,* you needn't repeat the verb:

> *Compound subject*
> _____
>
> ... they **and** their users   were never ridiculed.

And if you add an introductory prepositional phrase, this mature sentence emerges in the final revision:

> *Over their long history, spoons and their users were never ridiculed.*

Notice that you needn't repeat the exact language of the original sentences as you revise and combine.

Thus, compound subjects are a good option for combining short sentences when two or more subjects perform the same actions:

> *Original*
> _____
>
> Upper-class Greeks used bronze and silver spoons. Upper-class Romans used bronze and silver spoons, too.
>
> *Revision*
> _____
>
> *Upper-class Greeks and Romans* used bronze and silver spoons.

✍ **10   Revising Sentences to Form Compound Subjects**

Combine each of the following groups of sentences to form a single sentence with a compound subject.

---

* See Chapters 19 and 20 for a full discussion of joining sentences through coordination and subordination—including adverb *(when, where, why)* clauses and relative *(who, what, which)* clauses.

The Origins of the Spoon: 20,000 Years Ago

1. The earliest known spoons were found in Asia during archeological digs. Evidence of their use was found at the same time. *The earliest known spoons and evidence of their use were found in Asia during archeological digs.*

2. These spoons date back at least 20,000 years. Primitive bowls also date back that far. _____

   _____

   _____

3. Thick porridge that could not be sipped from a bowl was eaten with a spoon. Thick soupy foods were also eaten with a spoon. _____

   _____

   _____

4. Wooden spoons have been recovered from ancient Egyptian tombs. Stone spoons have been found in these tombs. Ivory spoons have been recovered from them as well. Moreover, gold spoons have been retrieved from these ancient burial sites. _____

   _____

   _____

11   Composing Sentences with Compound Subjects

Complete each of the following sentences, supplying a compound subject.

1. *High intelligence* and ___*good looks*___ are my two most obvious traits.
2. ___*Hard work*___ and _____ will pay off in the end.
3. _____ and _____ enjoy each other's company.
4. _____ and _____ always arrive ten minutes late for class.

Employing Compound Predicates

Like compound subjects that share the same verb, a *compound predicate* combines several verbs that share the same subject. Here's an example:

> *Original*
>
> In ancient times, poor folks carved spoons from wood. Then they used the spoons for eating.
>
> *Revision*
>
> In ancient times, poor folks *carved spoons from wood and then used them* for eating.

You can form compound predicates with other joining words:

◆ *But:* Knives *date back* to the cave dwellers era *but have changed* very little since that time.

◆ *Yet:* For many centuries, men *carved* a roast *yet slit* a man's throat with the same knife.

And you can compose a compound predicate that includes even more than two verbs:

◆ Early people *killed, sliced, and raised* their food to their mouths with the same knives.

12   Revising Sentences to Create Compound Predicates

Combine each of the following groups of sentences to form a single sentence with a compound predicate. Join the verbs with *and*—or with *but* or *yet*—in one of the sentences.

1. Spoons from the Middle Ages were carved from wood. They were also fashioned from bone. And some were hammered from tin. *Spoons from the Middle Ages were carved from wood, fashioned from bone, or hammered from tin.*

2. In Italy during the fifteenth century, wealthy people bought silver "apostle spoons." They gave the spoons to children as baptismal gifts. _____
   _____
   _____

3. The spoons cost a great deal. They were highly popular. _____
   _____
   _____

4. The handle of a typical spoon was shaped like the child's patron saint. It would supposedly protect the child from harm._____
   _____
   _____

5. The expression "born with a silver spoon in his mouth" came from this custom. It meant that a family could afford to have such a spoon made as a gift.
   _____
   _____
   _____

IN SUMMARY

> **To combine sentences,**
>
> 1. create a *compound subject* in which two or more subjects share the same verb;
> 2. create a *compound predicate* in which two or more verbs share the same subject; and
> 3. use *and, but,* or *yet* to join the subjects or verbs.

13   Composing Sentences with Compound Predicates

Complete each of the following sentences, supplying a compound predicate. Be sure to include two verbs (three in sentence 5)—and don't repeat the subject.

1. The spaghetti slipped off the plate and *slid inside Mr. Gottbuck's money belt.*

2. The cat crept up to the large round bowl and _____

_____

3. Ralph tried to pick up the egg rolls with chopsticks but _____

_____

4. Sally washed her hair thoroughly, yet _____

_____

5. Chef Roland whipped the batter in a large bowl, _____

_____ , and _____

Employing Appositives

Here are two sentences that might be combined:

1. Perhaps 1.5 million years ago, *Homo erectus* made the first standardized stone knives for killing prey.
2. *Homo erectus* was an early ancestor of modern humans.

Perhaps you could combine the two sentences in a compound predicate, but in this case there is a better alternative. An *appositive* is a word or phrase that renames or defines a noun which precedes it. Thus, the defining words in sentence 2 can be joined to the term they define in sentence 1:

> Perhaps 1.5 million years ago, *Homo erectus,* an early ancestor of modern humans, made the first standardized stone knives for killing prey.

The appositive can even be reversed:

> . . . an early ancestor of modern humans, *Homo erectus,* . . .

Notice that, in either case,

> ◆ the appositive always comes directly after the term it renames or defines; and
>
> ◆ two commas enclose the appositive like parentheses.

Most short appositives ending with a proper noun don't require commas, but often do when the proper noun comes first:

No commas	*Commas*
my older brother Bill	Bill, my older brother,
their good friend Raoul	Raoul, their good friend,

Of course, an appositive at the end of sentence requires only a single comma:

> The first standardized knives for killing prey were made by *Homo erectus*, an early ancestor of modern humans.

IN SUMMARY

To use an appositive to define or rename a noun that precedes it,

1. place the appositive directly after the noun;
2. enclose the appositive in two commas (or one comma at the end of a sentence); or
3. omit commas with short appositives in which a proper noun comes second.

14 Combining Sentences with Appositives

Join each pair of sentences by creating an appositive, and punctuate each with two or one comma.

1. *Apostle spoons* were all the rage in fifteenth-century Italy.

   They were spoons with handles in the shape of patron saints.

   Apostle spoons, spoons with handles in the shape of patron saints, were all the rage in fifteenth-century Italy.

2. Thomas à Becket brought the two-pronged fork to England in the thirteenth century. He was the archbishop of Canterbury. _____

3. Our word "fork" comes from the Latin term *furca*.
   The Latin term means a farmer's pitchfork.

   _____

   _____

4. Dining customs changed during the Renaissance.
   The Renaissance was a period of cultural growth beginning in the fourteenth century.

   _____

   _____

5. According to legend, Duc de Richelieu greatly reformed table manners.
   He was cardinal and chief minister to the king in seventeenth-century France.

   _____

   _____

15   Completing Sentences with Appositives

Complete each of the following sentences, including an appositive and any necessary commas.

1. You'll be competing *in the pie-eating contest* against Polly Saturated, *the heavyweight champion of the world.*

2. Tommy Teacup _____ has _____

   _____

3. I'll _____ the largest amusement park in the region

   _____

4. My _____ owns _____

   _____

5. The Vietnam War Memorial _____

   _____

Employing *-ing* Modifiers

Another option for achieving sentence variety is to join ideas by creating an *-ing* modifier. For example, look at these two sentences:

1. For centuries, a single knife was an all-purpose tool.
2. It hung from a man's waist.

Sentence 2 describes or provides additional information about the *knife* in sentence 1. You could include the information in a modifying phrase that begins with *-ing* and place it directly after the word *knife:*

For centuries, a single <u>knife</u> **hanging from a man's waist** was an all-purpose tool.

How would you combine the two sets of sentences that follow? Write your versions in the space provided.

    3. During meals, noblemen used the point of their knives to pick their teeth.
    4. This behavior disgusted the Duc de Richelieu.

    _____

    _____

    5. Richelieu attempted to stop this crude practice.

    _____

    _____

    6. He changed the shape of dinner knives.

    _____

    _____

Did your sentences resemble these? Note that the *-ing* modifier can follow or precede the word(s) it relates to.

> During meals, noblemen used the point of their knives <u>to pick their teeth</u>, **disgusting the Duc de Richelieu.**
>
> **Attempting to stop this crude practice,** <u>he</u> changed the shape of dinner knives.

And note these additional traits of *-ing* modifiers:

> ◆ A comma sets off an *-ing* modifier at the beginning of a sentence:
>
>   *Sitting by the pond,* I watched a mother duck and six little ducklings.
>
> ◆ An *-ing* modifier placed directly after the word(s) it describes may not require a comma:
>
>   I saw a mother duck and six little ducklings *swimming by.* (*Swimming by* relates to the duck and ducklings.)
>
> ◆ An *-ing* modifier separated from the word(s) it describes requires a comma:
>
>   I sat by the pond, *watching a mother duck and six little ducklings.* (*Watching . . .* relates to the word *I,* not to *the pond.*)
>
> ◆ An *-ing* modifier can also be placed after some prepositions of time:
>
>   *While*
>   *Before*   watching the ducks . . .
>   *When*
>   *After*

> **A Tip**
>
> Be careful in placing *-ing* modifiers. If they do not directly precede or follow the word(s) they relate to, the result can be unclear or misleading:
>
> *Incorrect:*   I watched a duck and six little ducklings *sitting by the pond.*
>   (The duck and ducklings weren't sitting—you were!)
> *Correct:*   *Sitting by the pond,* I watched . . .

16   Combining Sentences by Forming *-ing* Modifiers

Join each of the following pairs of sentences by changing one into an *-ing* modifier. Place the modifier either before or after the word(s) it relates to, and add commas as needed.

Duc de Richelieu's Crusade for Rounded Knives

1. The round-tip dinner knife supposedly originated in France in the 1630s.

   It followed one man's attempt to end a common but impolite practice.

   The round-tip dinner knife supposedly originated in France in the 1630s,

   following one man's attempt to end a common but impolite practice.

   or   *Following one man's attempt to end a common but impolite practice,*

   the round-tip dinner knife supposedly originated in France in the 1630s.

2. Armand Jean du Plessis was known as the Duc de Richelieu.

   He served King Louis XIII as cardinal and chief minister.

   _____

   _____

3. Richelieu was disgusted by men of high rank at the dinner table.

   They picked their teeth with the pointed end of a knife.

   _____

   _____

4. He was able to stop the practice.

   He ordered his chefs to file the points off his table knives.

   _____

   _____

5. Soon French women began to follow his lead.

   They placed orders for knives with rounded ends.

   _____

   _____

✍ 17   Completing Sentences with -*ing* Modifiers

Add a phrase beginning with an -*ing* modifier (and, if you wish, a preposition of time) to each of the following sentences. Supply commas as needed.

1. *After finishing his seventh helping of banana cream pie,* Albert burped contentedly and wiped his mouth on his sleeve.

2. _____ Chef Louis served the apricot-flavored sushi.

3. Tom tossed the salad in a large wooden bowl _____

_____

4. Several knives and forks fell to the floor _____

_____

5. _____ the dinner guests left after midnight.

✍ 18   Composing Sentences with -*ing* Modifiers

Write five sentences of your own that include -*ing* modifiers (and add prepositions of time if you wish). Be careful to place and punctuate the modifiers correctly.

1. _____

_____

2. _____

_____

3. _____

_____

4. _____

_____

5. _____

_____

Employing Past Participle Modifiers

These two sentences can also be combined:

1. The knife *was invented* in cave dweller times.
2. It joined the spoon as an eating implement 20,000 years ago.

Sentence 1 contains a form of *to be* and a past participle.* You can drop the *to be* verb to form a *past participle modifier*, which you insert and punctuate in another sentence just like an -*ing* modifier:

---

* See Chapter 22 for a full discussion of past participle forms.

> 3. **Invented in cave dweller times,** > <u>the knife</u> joined the
> spoon as an eating implement 20,000 years ago.
>
> 4. <u>The knife</u>, < **invented in cave dweller times,** joined the
> spoon as an eating implement 20,000 years ago.

Note that the modifier in sentence 3 immediately precedes the word it relates to and is set off with a comma. In sentence 4, the modifier follows the word it relates to and is enclosed in two commas (although not all modifiers in this position require commas).

Many past participles following some form of the verb *to be (is, are, was, were)* can be changed to modifiers and included within another sentence. The rules for their use are essentially the same as for *-ing* modifiers.

A Tip

Like *-ing* modifiers, misplaced past participle modifiers can cause problems with clarity:

<u>Unclear:</u>   *Grilled over hot coals,* most people enjoy almost any kind of meat. (The meat—not the people—is grilled.)

<u>Clear:</u>   Most people enjoy almost any kind of meat *grilled over hot coals.*

IN SUMMARY

To join sentences with a past participle modifier,

1. place the modifier directly before or after the word(s) it relates to;
2. follow an introductory modifier with a comma;
3. use two commas (or none) to enclose a modifier following the word(s) it relates to; and
4. be careful not to misplace the modifier and cause a problem with clarity.

✍ 19 **Joining Ideas Through Past Participle Modifiers**

Combine each of the following groups of sentences. Eliminate the verb *to be* to create a past participle modifier, and include commas as needed.

The Origins of the Napkin

1. Small napkins are used today to dab our lips and protect our laps. They would never have sufficed centuries ago. *Small napkins used today to dab our lips and protect our laps would never have sufficed centuries ago.*

2. A multicourse meal was eaten entirely with the fingers. That custom made a napkin the size of a towel essential. _____

_____

3. They were later called "serviettes." Towel-like napkins were used by the ancient Egyptians, the Greeks, and the Romans to wipe food from their hands.

_____

_____

4. And to further cleanse the hands during a meal, all three cultures used finger bowls. They were filled with water. It was scented by flowers and herbs._____

_____

_____

5. In Egypt, the scents—almond, cinnamon, or orange blossom—were tailored to the courses. They were eaten by the people at the table._____

_____

_____

✍ **20 Completing Sentences with Past Participle Modifiers**

Add a phrase beginning with a past participle modifier to each of the following sentences. Supply commas as needed.

1. *Known for its excellent roasted ants and fried caterpillars,* the Petite Crawler is a popular place for dining and passing out.

2. _____ coffee bars are appearing throughout the city.

3. We enjoy a flourless chocolate cake_____

_____

4. Rare roast beef _____ is the specialty of the house.

5. _____ the guests thanked their host for the wonderful meal.

✍ **21 Composing Sentences with Past Participle Modifiers**

Write five sentences that include past participle modifiers of your own or from the following list. Be careful to place and punctuate the modifiers correctly.

amazed	prepared	exhausted	angered	interested
excited	confused	peeled	captured	taken
driven	seen	illuminated	decorated	bored

1. _____

_____

2. _____

_____

3. _____

_____

4. _____

_____

5. _____

_____

IN SUMMARY

Achieve sentence variety in any or all of the following ways:

1. by employing long and short sentences;
2. by beginning sentences with time expressions;
3. by beginning sentences with adverbs or prepositional phrases;
4. by using occasional rhetorical questions, especially as topic sentences;
5. by using occasional commands, or imperative sentences;
6. by using occasional exclamations;
7. by creating compound subjects;
8. by creating compound predicates;
9. by employing appositives;
10. by employing -*ing* modifiers (including some that follow prepositions of time); and
11. by employing past participle modifiers.

✏ **22   Revising a Passage for Sentence Variety**

Complete rewrite the following passage, including long and short sentences, compound subjects and predicates, rhetorical questions, commands, and exclamations. Begin some sentences with time expressions, adverbs, or prepositional phrases. And combine sentences with appositives, -*ing* modifiers, or past participle modifiers.

The Rise and Fall of the Napkin

❑   It was the sixth-century B.C.E. Roman nobles who found a second use for the napkin. It was as a sort of doggie bag. Guests at a banquet were expected to use serviettes. They used them to wrap up goodies from the table. Then they were expected to take them home. It was not good manners to leave empty-handed.

Documents have been preserved. They reveal the splendor of the serviette. It was in Italy in the 1680s. There were 26 favorite shapes for folding dinner napkins. These depended on the guests. They also depended on the occasion. The shapes included Noah's Ark (for clergymen). They also included a hen (for the noblewoman of highest rank present). Other shapes were chicks (for the other women), plus carp, tortoises, bulls, bears, and rabbits.

A book of etiquette discusses the large serviette. The book was published in 1729. The serviette had many uses: "For wiping the mouth, lips, and fingers when they are greasy. For wiping the knife before cutting bread. For cleaning the spoon and fork after using them." The same book then makes an important point. "When the fingers are very greasy, wipe them first on a piece of bread, in order not to spoil the serviette too much."

The towel-size serviette was finally undermined by the fork. It also undermined the finger bowl. Forks handled food. They left fingers spotless. The large napkin became unnecessary. Napkins were still used. They were smaller. They were used to wipe the mouth.

The size of the serviette is shown in the origin of the word "napkin." The function is also shown. The word comes from the Old French *naperon.* The word means "little tablecloth." The English borrowed the word *naperon.* They used it to name a large cloth. It was tied around the waist. It protected the front of the body. The hands were also wiped on it. They called it *a napron.* A punctuation shift occurred. A single letter was dropped. A *napron* became "an apron." Thus, a napkin at one time or another has been a towel. It has also been a tablecloth. It has also been an apron. It survived from a colorful history. The history was also complicated. The napkin was once regarded as noble. It has fallen to the lowly status of a throwaway today.

23   Editing Your Own Work

Return to a paper you are writing now or to one you have written previously. Revise to achieve greater sentence variety, employing any of the sentence structures you have practiced in this chapter.

Strengthening Modifiers

One of the most important ways to develop a sophisticated style is through the use of *modifying phrases*, which describe various structures in sentences. Using such phrases effectively should help you develop a graceful, direct, and mature style. In this chapter, we look at ways to form a variety of modifying phrases within two general categories:

- ➣ adjective phrases; and
- ➣ adverb phrases.

Then we take a look at ways to avoid two common errors with such phrases:

- ➣ misplaced modifiers; and
- ➣ dangling modifiers.

MODIFIERS DEFINED

A *modifier* is a word, phrase, or clause that describes something in a sentence and therefore modifies (that is, changes) the meaning of that structure. Modifiers can describe almost any part of a sentence.

> ◆ If they describe nouns, they function as adjectives.
> ◆ If they describe verbs or other parts of speech, they function as adverbs.

Moreover, adjectives and adverbs take many forms, as you will soon see.

Examining Adjective Modifiers. Suppose you want to describe the noun *apartment*. You can choose from a variety of structures. You can place single-word adjectives before the noun:

> *a large* apartment
> *a large modern* apartment

You can place *adjective phrases* after the noun:

> an apartment *with all the latest conveniences*
> an apartment *facing the lake*
> an apartment *built by Henderson and Company*
> an apartment *to live in*

Or you can place *adjective clauses* after it:

> an apartment *that a famous movie star once owned*
> an apartment *where the Thompsons live*

Examining Adverb Modifiers. Adverbs tell *when, how, where, why,* or *how often* an action occurred. So, for example, you can explain *when* the action of a past-tense verb happened by adding a word, a phrase, or a clause:

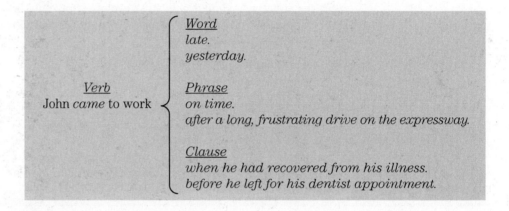

> *Word*
> late.
> yesterday.
>
> *Verb*
> John *came* to work
>
> *Phrase*
> on time.
> after a long, frustrating drive on the expressway.
>
> *Clause*
> when he had recovered from his illness.
> before he left for his dentist appointment.

Each modifying structure—whether a word, a phrase, or a clause—serves a purpose, or it wouldn't exist in the language. However, as Chapters 13 and 14 demonstrated, experienced writers try not to waste words, so they revise and edit with these questions in mind: Can a phrase replace a clause? Can a short phrase replace a longer one? Let's examine ways of shortening modifying structures to achieve a more mature and varied style.

Strengthening Adjective Phrases

You probably already know how to compose *who-which-that* clauses, also called *adjective clauses* or *relative clauses,* and Chapter 20 discusses their use in much greater detail. Meanwhile, let's look at alternative ways of expressing the ideas contained in adjective clauses. For example, look at the following sentences:

> The oil painting *that is hanging over the mantelpiece* was a wedding present.
> The teacher *who is with those students* is Professor Harrison.

You could remove the subjects and verbs—*that is* and *who is*—from the clauses in both sentences, creating phrases that are more emphatic and direct:

> The oil painting *hanging over the mantelpiece* was a wedding present.
> The teacher *with those students* is Professor Harrison.

Here is another example of a clause changed to a phrase:

> My favorite professor, *who is Ms. Johnson,* teaches English literature.
> My favorite professor, *Ms. Johnson,* teaches English literature.

The modifying phrases you have just seen include five types.

1. phrases beginning with *-ing words* (*facing* the lake, *talking* to those students);
2. phrases beginning with *prepositions* (*of* all the latest conveniences, *with* those students);
3. phrases beginning with *past participles* (*built* by Henderson and Company);
4. phrases beginning with *infinitives* (*to live in*); and
5. phrases beginning with *nouns* (*Ms. Johnson*).*

In each case, the phrase is formed by eliminating *who, which,* or *that + be* (*am, is, are, was,* or *were*) from a clause. But you cannot always convert a clause into a phrase that is just as clear and graceful as the clause. For example, the last part of the previous sentence: " . . . into a phrase that is just as clear and graceful as the clause" would sound awkward with *that is* removed. Nevertheless, as a general rule, if you can write a phrase instead of a clause, do it.

1   Forming Phrases from Relative Clauses

Whenever possible, draw a line through *who, which,* or *that* and any form of *to be* in the following sentences. Do not change the sentence if the result sounds awkward.

1. Phineas Taylor (P. T.) Barnum (1810–1891), ~~who was~~ the world's most successful creator of sideshows and exhibitions, made a fortune from manipulating and fooling the public.
2. According to Barnum, there was no difference between exhibiting a monkey to the public and presenting an opera to a prince, for all show business is "trade," which is the practice of buying cheap and selling at a profit.
3. He got his start in show business by exhibiting a black woman named Joice Heath, who was supposedly the oldest living person at 161 years of age.
4. Upon examining Ms. Heath after her death, however, a doctor said that she was far younger, which was a claim Barnum insisted could never be proven.
5. Barnum, who was touring with a circus in 1836, encountered several ministers who were denouncing his activities as immoral.
6. Then, in 1841, the American Museum, which was purchased after a series of intrigues and maneuvers, became Barnum's permanent exhibition hall in New York.

2   Combining Sentences Through Phrases or Clauses

Combine each of the following groups of sentences by changing one sentence into a descriptive phrase or a *who-which-that* clause. Insert commas as needed in the combined sentences.

1. At the end of August 1843, the New York newspapers announced a " Grand Buffalo Hunt, Free of Charge." It was to take place in Hoboken, New Jersey, on a Thursday afternoon.

   At the end of August 1843, the New York newspapers announced a " Grand
   Buffalo Hunt, Free of Charge," to take place in Hoboken, New Jersey, on a
   Thursday afternoon.

* This noun, which renames the noun preceding it, is called an *appositive.*

2. The savage beasts would be lassoed and hunted as part of the entertainment. They would be enclosed in strong fences to protect the public. (Hint: Place the phrase before *The savage beasts,* and begin it with *enclosed.*)

_____

_____

_____

3. What the newspapers did not say was that the buffalo were old and weak animals. They were hardly capable of movement, much less of violence.

_____

_____

_____

P. T. Barnum

4. Barnum had purchased the herd earlier for $700. He bought them to exhibit at a later date.

_____

_____

_____

5. Barnum wisely decided to make admission free. He knew that the spectacle might not be all the audience anticipated. (Hint: Change *knew* to an *-ing* word.)

_____

_____

_____

6. He didn't say that he had made a deal with the ferryboat owners. The owners agreed to take the public from Manhattan to New Jersey and give Barnum a percentage of the fares.

_____

_____

_____

7. All through the day, boatloads of spectators crossed to New Jersey. They came in anticipation of seeing shows scheduled for different times.

_____

_____

_____

8. When the second batch of spectators arrived, they passed the boats filled with the first batch of spectators. The returnees called out that the hunt was the biggest humbug imaginable.

_____

_____

_____

9. However, the eager audience showed no disappointment. They gave three cheers for "the author of the humbug, whoever he might be." (Hint: Change *gave* to an *-ing* word.)

_____

_____

_____

Strengthening Adverb Phrases

Chapter 20 discusses adverb dependent clauses in much more detail. Meanwhile, however, note here that such clauses begin with such words as *after, if, although,* and *because,* as in the following example:

> *Because he understood that American audiences enjoyed cleverly conceived tricks,* Barnum was constantly able to entertain them with other spectacular but phony stunts.

You can convert the clause to a phrase simply by removing the subject from the clause and changing the verb *understood* into an *-ing* word:

> *Understanding that American audiences enjoyed cleverly conceived tricks,* Barnum was constantly able to entertain them with other spectacular but phony stunts.

Most dependent clauses beginning with time expressions such as *when, while, as, after, before,* or *whenever* can be shortened to phrases in this way. However, you may have to shift the subject of the dependent clause to the independent clause, as in this example:

Dependent clause:	*After Barnum had acquired an odd or spectacular exhibit,* he couldn't resist the chance to make it a bit more unusual than the actual truth allowed.
Phrase:	*Having acquired an odd or spectacular exhibit, Barnum* couldn't resist the chance to make it a bit more unusual than the actual truth allowed.

Make a dependent clause into a phrase only if the subject of both the dependent clause and the independent clause are the same. *Do not change* the dependent clause into a phrase if the two subjects are different. Here's what can happen if you do:

Dependent clause:	*Although Barnum never completely analyzed the reasons for his success,* other people considered him a genius at promoting events and exhibitions.
Phrase:	*Although never completely analyzing the reasons for his success,* other people considered . . .

The second version seems to state that *other people*—not Barnum—never analyzed the reasons for his success.

✍ 3 Converting Clauses into Phrases

Whenever possible, change the dependent clause to a phrase in the sentences that follow. Cross out the subject in the dependent clause, and write your changes above the line. Some of the dependent clauses cannot be changed.

        Hearing of   *Barnum*

1. ∧~~When Barnum heard~~ of a dead mermaid from the Fiji Islands, ∧~~he~~ decided to buy it as an exhibit.

2. After a man named Moses Kimball had gotten the mermaid from a sailor, he offered to share profits (and costs) of the exhibition with Barnum. (Hint: Begin with *Having.*)

3. Because Barnum refused to part with any money so quickly, he consulted with a naturalist, who said that the object was a fake.

4. When the naturalist was asked why he gave this verdict, he replied, " Because I don't believe in mermaids."

5. Since the naturalist didn't offer definite proof of a fraud, Barnum decided to ignore this opinion.

6. Because Barnum wanted to protect himself from the attacks of scientists, he exhibited the mermaid but would not buy it.

7. When Barnum sent letters to newspapers across the country, he claimed that a British naturalist named Dr. Griffin had found the mermaid in the " Feejee Islands."

8. Although Dr. Griffin was an impostor whose real name was Levi Lyman, no one knew that at first.

Forming Phrases in Other Ways

There are other ways of replacing dependent clauses with phrases. Look, for example, at this sentence:

When people looked at the mermaid, they realized it wasn't an object of beauty.

The idea of the dependent clause can be expressed in different words and forms:

Looking at the mermaid,
When viewing the mermaid, ⎫ people realized it wasn't an object of beauty.
After a glance at the mermaid, ⎭

Compare the dependent clause and its phrase substitute in this next example:

Barnum wrote so many letters to newspapers *because he wanted to convince people of the mermaid's authenticity.*

Barnum wrote so many letters to newspapers *to convince people of the mermaid's authenticity.*

Notice the similarity between adjective phrases and adverb phrases. In both cases, many of the phrases begin with a preposition, an *-ing* word, a past participle, or an infinitive, such as *to convince* in the last example.

IN SUMMARY

A modifying phrase can begin with

1. a *preposition*, such as *on, from, with, after,* or *in;*
2. an *-ing word*, such as *walking, talking,* or *smiling;*
3. a *past participle,* such as *seen, torn,* or *liked;*
4. an *infinitive,* such as *to complete, to see,* or *to get;* or
5. a *noun* that renames the noun preceding it.

4 Rewriting Clauses as Phrases

Rewrite each of the following sentences, changing the dependent clause into a phrase that uses the words in parentheses.

1. Because the Feejee mermaid consisted of the body of a fish connected to the head and hands of a monkey, it was quite a sight. (With . . .)

   With the body of a fish connected to the head and hands of a monkey, the

   Feejee mermaid was quite a sight.

2. Since the black dried-up animal had an open mouth, a tail twisted at an odd angle, and arms thrown up in air, it appeared to have died in great agony. (with its . . .)

   _____

   _____

3. Because Barnum wanted to emphasize the mermaid's natural origins, he put up "Dr. Griffin" in a New York hotel and then arranged for reporters to call and examine the mermaid. (In order to . . .) _____

   _____

   _____

4. Although the reporters were suspicious at first, they soon became convinced the mermaid was genuine. (Despite . . .)_____

   _____

   _____

5. Barnum then delivered a picture of the mermaid to all the newspaper publishers, because he wanted to explain that Dr. Griffin would not let the mermaid be exhibited. (in order to . . .) _____

   _____

   _____

6. After the public demanded to see the mermaid, Dr Griffin "reluctantly" allowed Barnum to exhibit it at the American Museum. (As a result of . . .)

   _____

   _____

7. When evidence surfaced that the mermaid was a fraud, Barnum emphatically denied any responsibility for the hoax. (In the face of . . .)

_____

_____

✍ 5 **Combining Sentences to Form Modifying Phrases**

Combine each of the following groups of sentences into one sentence. Use modifying phrases whenever possible. (One combined sentence cannot use a modifying phrase.)

1. Barnum hoped to acquire a sacred white elephant from Burma. He bribed the king of that country to send him one. _Hoping to acquire a sacred white elephant from Burma, Barnum bribed the king of that country to send him one._

2. Barnum's men boarded the ship from Burma. They found the holy elephant, but it was gray._____

_____

_____

3. Barnum insisted "that there is no such thing as a pure white elephant." He put the Burmese beast on exhibition. _____

_____

_____

4. The public was disappointed in Barnum's elephant. They flocked to see a competitor's white elephant called "The Light of Asia."_____

_____

_____

5. The elephant certainly was white. The color was painted on—the exhibition was a fraud. _____

_____

_____

PLACING MODIFIERS EFFECTIVELY

Revising to Eliminate Misplaced Modifiers

The location of a modifier can greatly affect the meaning of a sentence. For example, notice how moving the word *just* affects the meaning of this sentence:

Just Bill gave his wife a kiss on the cheek.
Bill *just* gave his wife a kiss on the cheek.
Bill gave *just* his wife a kiss on the cheek.
Bill gave his *just* wife a kiss on the cheek.
Bill gave his wife *just* a kiss on the cheek.
Bill gave his wife a kiss *just* on the cheek.

Shifting the position of a modifying phrase can create similar effects:

Hanging by the tail, I laughed as the monkey made faces at my wife.
I laughed as the monkey made faces at my wife *hanging by the tail.*

Remember that one goal in writing and revising is clarity. Try not to confuse readers or to say things you don't mean. One way to avoid confusion is to position the modifier directly before or after the word it describes:

I laughed as the monkey, *hanging by the tail,* made faces at my wife.

Another way is to rewrite the modifier:

I laughed as the monkey made faces at my wife *as it hung by the tail.*

Remember how you changed dependent clauses into phrases earlier in this chapter. The phrase's meaning was clear only when you placed it next to the subject you removed from the clause. Therefore, when examining a modifying phrase during revisions, ask yourself this question: Would the word nearest the phrase be included in a complete dependent clause?

Correct placement: the monkey [as it was] hanging by the tail
Incorrect placement: made faces at my wife [as it was] hanging by the tail.

Spotting and correcting misplaced modifiers isn't easy, but your skill will improve with practice.

IN SUMMARY

To correct misplaced modifiers,

1. each time during revisions that you see a modifying phrase, ask yourself if the phrase clearly describes the word it is closest to;
2. then move any misplaced phrases to another place in the sentence where its meaning is clear; or
3. rewrite the sentence to clarify the meaning.

6   Editing for Misplaced Modifiers

Each of the following sentences contains a misplaced modifier. Underline the modifier, and then draw a caret (∧) in the spot where it belongs.

1. Barnum cared ∧ about gathering crowds for his shows <u>only</u>, and he didn't mind fooling the public to do it.
2. For example, a man entered his office to beg for a job, and Barnum hired him one time for a dollar and a half a day.
3. Each day, the man would attract crowds by placing five bricks without saying a word on the street, then walking from one to the other, and exchanging them.
4. Within 30 minutes to figure out what was happening, hundreds of people would gather.
5. Every hour the "brick man" would go into Barnum's museum, followed, of course, by citizens who paid the admission fee to find out what the man was doing out of curiosity.
6. This kind of stunt was ideal for Barnum, showing great ingenuity and costing almost nothing.

Revising to Eliminate Dangling Modifiers

Sometimes a modifier doesn't describe anything. It dangles unattached because the word it should describe isn't in the sentence.

> *Sitting on the beach in July,* the sun was very hot. (*Who* was sitting on the beach? It certainly wasn't the sun.)
>
> *Visiting New York,* there are many sights to see. (*Who* is visiting New York? The sentence doesn't say.)

You cannot eliminate a dangling modifier simply by shifting it around, because the sentence lacks the word it modifies. Instead, you must rewrite the sentence, adding the word the modifier actually describes.

> *Sitting on the beach in July, I* felt the hot sun on my face.
>
> There are many sights for $\left. \begin{array}{c} you \\ one \end{array} \right\}$ to see on a visit to New York.

✍ 7 Editing to Eliminate Dangling Modifiers

Underline the dangling modifier in each sentence that follows, and then rewrite the sentence to eliminate the problem. If necessary, change a phrase into a dependent clause.

1. <u>With such large crowds</u>, Barnum confronted some difficulties at the Great American Museum. *Barnum confronted some difficulties at the Great American Museum because it attracted such large crowds.*

2. Unable to get the crowds to leave the museum, new customers had to be turned away. _____

_____

_____

3. After despairing over this dilemma, the perfect solution presented itself.

_____

_____

_____

4. Seeing the scene painter at work on the stage, the man was told by Barnum to immediately paint a huge sign that said "To the Egress." _____

_____

_____

5. Seizing the brush, the sign was painted in 15 minutes and then nailed over the door leading to the alleyway. _____

_____

_____

6. Unaware that *egress* meant *exit,* the alleyway was soon filled, leaving room for new customers. _____

_____

_____

✎ **8   Editing to Correct Misplaced or Dangling Modifiers**

The following passage contains misplaced or dangling modifiers and some dependent clauses that could be phrases. Write your corrections on the lines following each sentence. Some sentences need no changes. The first sentence—which has two corrections—has been completed for you.

1 George Hull, who was a tobacco farmer and cigar maker from a small town in New York, created one of the greatest hoaxes ever perpetrated on the American public in 1869. *In 1869, George Hull, a tobacco farmer and cigar maker from a small town in New York, created one of the greatest hoaxes ever perpetrated on the American public.*

2. A year earlier, after arguing with a preacher about references to giants in the Bible, the idea occurred to Hull of making a giant manlike figure out of stone and promoting it as a petrified man. _____

_____

_____

3. Hull and a partner acquired a five-ton block of gypsum and hired two sculptors with Hull serving as the model to carve a statue 10 1/2 feet tall. _____

_____

_____

4. The giant was then shipped to his cousin William Newell's farm, where it was buried in a five-foot-deep grave behind the barn outside Cardiff, New York.

_____

_____

_____

5. A year later on October 16, 1869, two unsuspecting workmen were hired to dig a well behind the barn, where they unearthed the giant. _____

_____

_____

6. A furor was created in the neighborhood that soon spread throughout the nation. _____

_____

_____

7. Newell immediately erected a tent and began charging 50 cents for a look at the object, which was soon called the "Cardiff Giant." _____

_____

_____

8. But while people rushed to see the giant, suspicions that it was a phony intensified. _____

_____

_____

9. As all the evidence pointed toward a hoax in December, George Hull confessed to the fraud. _____

_____

_____

10. Nevertheless, the public came to see it in growing numbers and the giant for exhibition was moved to Albany and then to New York City. _____

_____

_____

11. Unable to buy the giant, an imitation was made and displayed in New York City by P. T. Barnum that soon outdrew the original one. _____

_____

_____

12. Finally in 1948 the Cardiff Giant was brought to the Farmers' Museum, which is one of the museums administered by the New York State Historical Association of Cooperstown, where it is on display today. _____

_____

_____

9 Editing Your Own Work

Look at a paragraph or composition you are now writing or have previously written, and correct any problems with misplaced modifiers, dangling modifiers, or dependent clauses that could be phrases.

UNIT FOUR

Composing Compositions

Composing Expository Compositions

Now that you have had extensive practice in composing paragraphs, the chapters in Unit Four introduce you to the process of composing compositions: longer unified pieces of writing containing many paragraphs. This chapter explores the first type, the *expository composition,* also called the *expository theme.* After examining the three parts of the composition—the *introduction,* the *body,* and the *conclusion*—the chapter takes you through the process of composing the composition itself. The process involves these familiar steps:

✏ getting started;
✏ organizing; and
✏ composing, revising, and editing a coherent and polished final draft.

THE COMPOSITION DEFINED

The first three units focused primarily on composing individual paragraphs, but now let's turn our attention to the most common role of the paragraph—as part of larger, more complex, pieces of writing consisting of many paragraphs. In college assignments, these longer pieces are typically called *compositions* (or *theme*s or *essays*), which we also examine further in Chapters 17 and 18. Think of a composition as a complete intellectual meal. You wouldn't swallow all the courses at once, but should eat them in smaller, more digestible parts. Therefore, each paragraph serves as one course of the meal (and each sentence as a single bite). A paragraph discusses a smaller part of the main idea—in effect, giving your readers a chance to digest some information and then rest for a moment before moving on to the next part.

Furthermore, a composition must be arranged in an order that makes sense to your readers. The soup shouldn't come after the dessert. Thus, like the paragraph, a typical composition includes an *introduction,* a *body,* and a *conclusion.*

◆ The introduction usually occupies a full paragraph. It attracts the readers' interest, states the point of the composition in a *thesis* statement, and helps readers predict what will follow.
◆ The body fulfills the readers' predictions by breaking down the thesis statement into smaller ideas, each of which may require one or more paragraphs to explain and illustrate. Each of these paragraphs may contain a topic sentence, body sentences, and a concluding sentence that establishes a transition to the next paragraph.
◆ The conclusion, the last paragraph (or two) of the composition, ties all the ideas together and gracefully ends the paper.

Examining the Role of Paragraphs Within a Composition

The writer of the following composition did some research on a subject that interested him and thought, therefore, it would interest the readers of this book. Read it and then answer the questions that follow.

The Origins of Dr. Jekyll and Mr. Hyde

Paragraph A.   (1) Everyone who has read the novel by Robert Louis Stevenson or has seen a version of the movie knows about the fictional Dr. Jekyll and Mr. Hyde. (2) Dr. Jekyll was a respectable physician in the daytime, but at night he swallowed a potion that transformed him into the brutal, evil Mr. Hyde. (3) Although the story sounds impossible, it isn't. (4) There really was a model for Dr. Jekyll and Mr. Hyde: Deacon William Brodie, who led a double life of criminal and respectable citizen in the mid-eighteenth century.

Paragraph B.   (1) Just like the fictional character, William Brodie changed identities in the nighttime. (2) By day, he was a virtuous member of the community in Edinburgh, Scotland. (3) He owned a successful cabinet making business, served as a town councilman, and was the deacon of the local cabinetmaker's union (that is, he assisted the minister of the church in dealings with the union). (4) From appearances, he was a sober bachelor who usually wore white, and he lived quietly with his father and sister. (5) However, Brodie's dark side emerged when the sun set. (6) Wearing a black suit and a black mask, the deacon transformed himself into a gambler, a drunkard, and a thief who kept two mistresses and supported his five illegitimate children with a portion of his loot.

Paragraph C.   (1) Until Brodie let his ego overcome his caution, his numerous crimes went undetected for almost two decades. (2) In 1786, at the age of 27, he committed his first burglary when he stole £800 from a bank. (3) During the next 18 years, his after-hours activities presented few problems. (4) Then Brodie got ambitious—and careless. (5) He dreamed of leading a gang of cutthroats, but his dream turned into a nightmare after he employed three robbers to assist him. (6) The gang botched a robbery of the Scottish General Tax Office, and one of Brodie's cohorts confessed and named names.

Paragraph D.   (1) With the police on his tail, Brodie tried to escape but didn't succeed. (2) He made it to Amsterdam, Holland, and was about to embark for America when he was captured by local authorities, who found him hiding in a cupboard. (3) They took him back to Edinburgh and, in the same courtroom where he had served as a respectable juror six months earlier, he was sentenced to be hanged.

Paragraph E.   (1) Although this man of two lives plotted for a third, his attempt to cheat the hangman failed. (2) Brodie took elaborate actions to soften the noose's impact, including consulting a doctor for assistance and wiring his body so it couldn't be jerked. (3) An hour before he was to face the executioner on October 1, 1788, he even concealed a steel collar under his neckerchief to prevent strangulation. (4) Nevertheless, the gallows were not to be denied, and Brodie died of a broken neck—an unpleasant end for the real Dr. Jekyll and Mr. Hyde.

1. What is the purpose (or purposes) of paragraph A? Does the writer of this composition assume you already know something about the subject? Which sentence introduces you to the main idea of the whole composition?
2. Which sentence in paragraph B introduces the main idea (which is divided into two parts)? Later in the paragraph, which sentence serves as a transition to introduce the second part?
3. In each of paragraphs C, D, and E, which sentence introduces the main idea, and where do these sentences appear?

> 4.   Which sentence in paragraph E ties the ideas of the whole composition to-
>   gether? Does it introduce any new ideas?

The answers to these questions should demonstrate the similarities between the composition and the paragraph—as well as their relationship to each other. The *composition* discusses a single, general idea stated in the introduction, while the paragraphs in the body examine smaller parts of that idea. The *thesis statement* presents the main point of the composition. The *topic sentence* of each body paragraph presents its main point that supports and develops the thesis. We further examine these similarities in a moment.

In a sense, the paragraph could be viewed as a composition in miniature. Look at the paragraph that results from combining the thesis statement and topic sentences of the composition you just read. The paragraph summarizes its main ideas in a structure that makes logical sense—but is far less specific and less detailed than the full composition.

thesis statement   ❑   (1) *There really was a model for Dr. Jekyll and Mr. Hyde: Deacon William Brodie, who led a double life of criminal and respectable citizen in the mid-eighteenth century.* (2) Just like the fictional character, William Brodie changed identities in the nighttime. (3) Until Brodie let his ego overcome his caution, his numerous crimes went undetected for almost two decades. (4) With the police on his tail, Brodie tried to escape but didn't succeed. (5) Although the man of two lives plotted for a third, his attempt to cheat the hangman failed.

Is this an effective paragraph? Only as a summary, for its topic is too large to be developed in so short a space. Thus, a complex, general topic requires a multiparagraph composition to explain and illustrate its ideas; a simpler and more specific topic may require only a single paragraph. Although a paragraph can stand alone as a complete unit, it is usually part of the longer composition or theme: a group of related paragraphs that together discuss a larger main idea. Whether you compose a paragraph or a composition, your goals are the same:

- ◆ to address the needs and interests of your audience;
- ◆ to accomplish a purpose (to inform, persuade, or entertain);
- ◆ to unify ideas around a central topic; and
- ◆ to organize ideas coherently through a logical method of development.

THE EXPOSITORY COMPOSITION DEFINED

We are now in the midst of an information and technological explosion, which requires us to know and learn more than at any time in history. New inventions, new discoveries, new facts, new events bombard us every day. Much of that information is transmitted in written form via a variety of media. Moreover, we not only receive written information but send it to others as well. Students write papers for instructors, and employees write to clients, customers, colleagues, and other employees. As lawyers, accountants, doctors, nurses, psychologists, computer programmers, managers, executives, secretaries, and engineers, we communicate via letters, memos, electronic mail, and even articles in professional journals. Furthermore, in our roles as consumers, parents, and citizens, we write letters (and faxes) to store managers, notes to teachers, letters to government agencies, and letters to friends. For these reasons, mastering the skill of writing exposition is essential.

Remember that when something is exposed, it is opened up to reveal its contents. Thus an *expository composition* (often called an *expository theme*) is an attempt to reveal something to your audience; in other words, its purpose is to inform. For example, it can analyze the causes of the Civil War for your history teacher or explain the operation of a company for potential clients or customers. It can also discuss your qualifications for a job opening or report the outcome of the previous night's football game for readers of a school newspaper. In short, it can share any information that a person or group of people needs or ought to know.

Examining the Parts of an Expository Composition

Let's take a closer look at the three main sections of the composition, as illustrated by a rather lighthearted and informative example.

Looking at the Introduction. In the world outside of school (cynics often call it the "real" world), most people don't have to read your compositions; they do so only if the writing is clear—and clearly interests them. But even in school, your instructor and classmates shouldn't be forced to perish from confusion and boredom. Therefore, the first paragraph of a composition—the *introduction*—performs two critical tasks.

◆ It attracts the readers' interest.
◆ It establishes the central idea in a *thesis statement*, which may also outline (or suggest the outline of) the ideas to follow in the body of the composition.

Here is an example:

The Clean Truth About Pigs

Paragraph A. (1) What is the dirtiest animal? (2) You would probably say the pig, which is known for wallowing in the mud, eating garbage, and observing other practices of a less-than-genteel nature. (3) However, this reputation for slovenly behavior is, pardon the expression, a lot of hogwash. (4) The pig isn't to blame for any unsanitary practices and, in fact, is rather tidy in virtually every way—from living quarters, to toilet habits, to bathing, to eating.

Notice that the first two sentences are attention-getters, attracting interest through a question and answer. Sentence 3 states the thesis, and sentence 4 helps you predict that the body of the composition will discuss four matters—the pig's living quarters, toilet habits, bathing practices, and eating behavior.

Looking at the Body. The middle (and longest) part of the composition—the *body*—specifically develops the main supporting ideas. Four paragraphs in the sample composition examine these ideas in the same order they were presented earlier in sentence 4.

◆ Note that each topic sentence (in italics) supports the thesis statement.
◆ Note also that the remaining sentences in each paragraph explain or illustrate the topic sentence.

Paragraph B. (1) First of all, domestic pigs are supposed to "like" filthy living quarters: dusty pens, muddy areas, and smelly pigsties. (2) *Nevertheless, the* *charge that pigs enjoy such surroundings is not only undeserved but untrue.* (3) In their natural state, wild pigs and boars roam the forests, never staying in one place long enough to create, let alone enjoy, such a mess. (4) In captivity, however, the poor creatures are forced into slums against their wills. (5) This practice can be traced back to early New England, where pigs were usually kept in the worst place on the farm—namely, the sty under the barn, which was a small, dark, and dirty hole.

Paragraph C.   (1) *Second, even in close confinement, the pigs' toilet habits are among the best of domestic animals.* (2) Pigs are actually rather tidy individuals, who defecate in only one spot. (3) This behavior is far more civilized and refined than the practices of horses, cows, and other barnyard creatures. (4) Indeed, pigs are much more selective in their choices of where to relieve themselves than are most pet dogs, as many a frustrated owner of man's best friend can confirm.

Paragraph D.   (1) However, a third charge against pigs is true: They don't bathe but instead wallow in the mud on hot days. (2) *But the animals choose this activity out of necessity, not out of some defect in character.* (3) They cannot perspire, and the cool mud lowers their temperature. (4) Perhaps if swimming pools were readily available, pigs would avoid mud entirely. (5) For, rumor to the contrary, their heavy hooves do not prevent them from swimming. (6) Given the opportunity, they will dive into water and paddle about with perfect ease.

Paragraph E.   (1) *Fourth and finally, pigs can be justifiably accused of eating garbage, since they often do.* (2) However, pigs can't choose their menus; they must eat what they are served. (3) These four-legged gourmets actually prefer diets closest to that of human beings, but farmers take advantage of this desire by feeding pigs scraps from the dinner table. (4) Perhaps this preference for such "garbage" is more a criticism of humans than the animals they call "hogs."

Looking at the Conclusion.   The final paragraph, or *conclusion*, typically performs two roles.

- ◆ It summarizes or ties together the ideas in the composition.
- ◆ It ends the composition with a forceful or clever statement.

The concluding paragraph of the sample composition begins with a summary in the first two sentences, followed by a joke in sentences 3 and 4.

Paragraph F.   (1) In short, pigs have taken a lot of undeserved ribbing. (2) They want to be neat housekeepers, observe proper sanitary and bathing practices, and eat well-balanced meals, but they don't always receive courteous treatment from their hosts and keepers. (3) Be careful, therefore, about calling someone "a filthy pig." (4) You shouldn't slander a guiltless party by associating it with human beings.

This sample composition contains an introductory paragraph, four paragraphs in the body, and a concluding paragraph. Other sample compositions throughout the chapter are even longer. However, as you begin the process of composing a composition, the exercises in this chapter limit you to slightly more modest goals, namely, composing a three-paragraph and then a five-paragraph composition.

✐ **1   Revising and Expanding a One-paragraph Composition**

As a transition between composing single paragraphs and full compositions, return to a long paragraph you have written and expand it into a three- or four-paragraph theme. The first paragraph should contain at least two sentences that attract the readers' interest and state the thesis of the composition. (This thesis statement can be the topic sentence of your original composition.) The middle paragraphs should specifically develop the thesis idea. And the final paragraph should contain at least two sentences that briefly restate the thesis and bring the composition to a close. (These sentences can closely resemble the conclusion of the original composition.) Don't worry if the result is less than perfect; this is only a starting point.

EXAMINING INDIVIDUAL PARAGRAPH DEVELOPMENT

An expository composition may employ one primary form of organization throughout. For instance, the sample composition about the pigs uses contrast organization. Look again at part of the introductory paragraph and the first sentences of each paragraph in the body. Notice that each paragraph explores only one contrast, and note the transitional expressions (shown in italics) that enumerate them.

Paragraph A.   (4) The pig isn't to blame for any unsanitary practices and, in fact, is rather tidy in virtually every way—from living quarters, to toilet habits, to bathing, to eating.

Paragraph B.   (1) *First of all,* domestic pigs are supposed to "like" filthy living quarters: dusty pens, muddy areas, and smelly pigsties. (2) Nevertheless, the charge that pigs enjoy such environs is not only undeserved but untrue.

Paragraph C.   (1) *Second,* even in close confinement, the pigs' toilet habits are among the best of domestic animals.

Paragraph D.   (1) However, a *third* charge against pigs is true: They don't bathe but instead wallow in the mud on hot days. (2) But the animals choose this activity out of necessity, not out of some defect in character.

Paragraph E.   (1) *Fourth and finally,* pigs can be justifiably accused of eating garbage, since they often do. (2) However, pigs can't choose their menus; they must eat what they are served.

The organization of this composition is straightforward and tidy, but not all compositions can be developed so neatly. Complex relationships among ideas require several methods of paragraph development. One paragraph may define a term, another draw a comparison or analogy, another explain the causes of an event, and yet another illustrate a point through a story. In such compositions, a straightforward preview and listing of ideas by number (first, second, third) isn't possible. Instead, transitions must spell out the relationships between paragraphs and achieve coherence, a matter addressed later in this chapter.

2   Analyzing a Complex Composition

The next composition traces the origins of language, and its primary method of development is cause-effect. However, each paragraph employs a different method of development. Read the composition carefully and then answer the questions.

The Search for the First Language

Paragraph A.   (1) It is generally well established that the words people speak and write reflect the lifestyles and needs of their societies. (2) If we study the earliest language, therefore, we can learn a great deal about the earliest civilizations. (3) We have been able to do just that, although everything we have learned about the earliest language is the result of shrewd guesswork rather than hard evidence.

thesis statement   (4) *Nevertheless, the results of our investigations tell us that early people were not too different from ourselves.*

Paragraph B.   (1) Although we don't know how the earliest humans communicated, somewhere between the last ice age and the beginning of recorded history, people certainly used words. (2) Moreover, this event seems to have happened at a specific place and time. (3) Many of the world's languages, from Tibetan to Swahili, are now thought to have evolved from small tribes wandering central Europe about 12,000 years ago.

Paragraph C.   (1) The evidence for this doesn't lie in documents, since the first language was spoken, not written. (2) The evidence comes instead from common words that occur in every tongue, words so similar that they are beyond coincidence. (3) *Father,* for instance, is *athir* in Irish, *pater* in Latin, *pidar* in Persian, and *pitr* in Sanskrit. (4) Water, which today is *voda* in Russian (*vodka* means "little water") or *wasser* in German, resembles the word *water* in the biblical language of a group called the Hittites.

Paragraph D.   (1) Many scholars, beginning with Jacob Grimm, co-author of *Grimm's Fairy Tales,* have conducted the detective work that leads back to the first prehistoric language, which we now call Indo-European. (2) They have guessed at the forms of many key words, which give us a picture of the lives of the Indo-Europeans. (3) We have learned that they emerged at around the time agriculture was being developed. (4) They had domesticated sheep or *owa* (ewes) and *gwou* (cows), which gave them *melg* (milk) to drink. (5) They planted *gran* (grain), which was then ground into *mel* (meal). (6) In due course they mixed it with *wodor* (water) and *yes* (yeast) to make *dheigh* (dough) for *pa* (bread, as in the Latin word *panis).*

Paragraph E.   (1) We have learned other important information about these people, too. (2) On the spiritual side, for example, they believed in *ghutom* (the first word for God, "the being that is worshipped"), who was *sac* (sacred). (3) On the more worldly side, they counted in numbers from one to ten as *oinos, duo, treies, qetwer, pende, sweks, septn, okto, newm,* and *dekm.*

Paragraph F.   (1) So thanks to the work of some clever researchers, we know that civilizations just about everywhere—from those in modern times to those who planted the first seeds—share many traits. (2) While we can only guess at the language of the Indo-Europeans, the probable ancestors of us all, we can see that they, like us, raised animals, made bread, worshipped a god, and counted.

1.   What does the writer of this composition assume the audience knows about the subject?
2.   What is the function of paragraph B in the whole composition?
3.   Identify the topic sentence of each paragraph. Also, identify the sentences that support the topic sentences with examples. What transitional words and phrases introduce examples?
4.   What phrases show the connections between ideas in paragraph E?
5.   In the concluding paragraph, which sentence gives the most specific information? Why is this information mentioned here, but not in paragraph A?

IN SUMMARY

An expository composition or theme

1.   explains an idea or a process;
2.   begins with an introduction—a paragraph that attracts the readers' interest, states the central idea (or thesis) of the composition, and often outlines (or suggests the outline of) the main supporting ideas;

> 3. follows with a much longer section called the body—several paragraphs that explain and illustrate each supporting idea separately and may be developed in a variety of ways; and
> 4. ends with a conclusion—a paragraph that ties together the main ideas of the composition and ends with a forceful statement.

COMPOSING AN EXPOSITORY COMPOSITION

In previous chapters, you have developed your own habits and practices for composing paragraphs. The process of composing a composition involves developing similar habits and practices, usually based on the following matters. Don't view them as steps in the process, though, for many occur simultaneously.

> ◆ Consider the occasion, audience, subject, and purpose.
> ◆ Discover ideas (through clustering, free writing, or brainstorming).
> ◆ Limit or narrow the topic.
> ◆ Draft the thesis statement and topic sentences.
> ◆ Draft the introduction.
> ◆ Draft the body.
> ◆ Draft the conclusion.
> ◆ Revise for coherence and clarity.

Analyzing Occasion, Audience, Subject, and Purpose

As you think about the occasion for writing and the subject you will discuss (as usual, it should be one you know well and feel comfortable with), consider your audience and their knowledge of the subject matter.

Because your purpose is to inform, you must include what your readers need to know, structured in an order that makes sense for them. For example, you might ask yourself any or all of the following questions:

> ◆ Are there terms that should be defined first?
> ◆ Are there unfamiliar processes that should be described next?
> ◆ Would some history of the subject be useful and, if so, where should it be presented?
> ◆ Would comparisons help?
> ◆ Should the information be classified in some way?

You cannot plan a composition without taking the needs of your audience into account. Even when you write a school composition that only your instructor will read, you must keep in mind his or her interests and knowledge of your subject matter.

✍ 3 **Planning a Composition**

Suppose you are describing the most important features of your college to two different audiences: (1) incoming freshmen who have never been to a college anywhere, and (2) transfer students who have completed at least a year at another college. Make separate lists of the matters you can include in your description for each audience.

Incoming freshmen   Transfer students

1. description of class schedule   1. comparison of class course

   and explanation of course   numbers to those found at most

   numbers   colleges

2. a list of required courses   2. _____

   _____   _____

   _____   _____

   _____   _____

   _____   _____

   _____   _____

Discovering and Developing Ideas

Although you can plan, draft, and revise a short paragraph in one night, the composing process is much more complex with a composition. Whenever possible, allow yourself time to experiment, to walk away for a while, to return when you are inspired (and even when you aren't). Give your mind a chance to discover, play with, and organize ideas. Inspiration may strike as you are walking the dog, taking a shower, or tossing sleeplessly in bed. Indeed, whole sentences may occur to you, so force yourself to write them down immediately. Many a brilliant insight at midnight has disappeared by morning because a writer turned over and went back to sleep.

In this longer discovery stage, consider both the information to include and how it relates to the point you want to make. You can generally approach these tasks in two ways: (1) by deciding first on the thesis and topic sentences and then exploring the specific support, or (2) by examining the specifics and then arriving at the thesis and topic sentences of each paragraph.

Starting with the Thesis and Topic Sentences.   When your ideas are clear at the beginning, you can draft a preliminary thesis statement, which you will probably narrow down and modify later as the composition takes its final shape. Then you can prepare a rough outline of the main ideas, which you will later state in the topic sentences.

The sample composition you read earlier in the chapter evolved in this manner. The writer began by quickly jotting down his thesis:

> *Pigs actually have a lot of good traits.*

However, he soon realized that the phrases "a lot" and "good traits" are vague and abstract, so he revised and narrowed the focus of the thesis. What, he asked himself, is the point he wished to make? What traits did he wish to discuss, and why? His answers resulted in this revised thesis:

> *The reputation of pig as a dirty animal unfair; it is really very clean in many of its habits.*

This revision suggested that the composition ought to be developed through contrast organization, so he listed some main points of contrast.

> *Main points:* lives in filth, but actually clean in wild state
> doesn't defecate randomly as other animals do
> wallows in mud but does so to keep cool
> eats garbage, but prefers food we eat

Following these initial decisions, the writer considered his ideas even more carefully, further revised his thesis statement, drafted preliminary topic sentences for each paragraph, and listed some possible support for the topic sentences.

> *Thesis:* The pig can't be blamed for being dirty because in reality it is a rather clean animal.
>
> 1. *Topic sentence:* Farmers put pigs in filthy quarters.
>   *Possible development:* discussion of reasons for pigsty
> 2. *Topic sentence:* Pig's toilet habits are good.
>   *Possible development:* contrast to habits in the wild
> 3. *Topic sentence:* Pig does wallow in mud, but not out of a desire to be dirty.
>   *Possible development:* inability to perspire
> 4. *Topic sentence:* Pig can swim and clean off the mud.
>   *Possible development:* myth about inability to swim
> 5. *Topic sentence:* Pigs do eat garbage, but only because they have no choice.
>   *Possible development:* diet closest to diet of humans

The final version of the composition emerged in an even much tidier form—as it should—because listing and then outlining ideas only start the composing process. From the original plan, the writer produced specific information for each paragraph while discarding or changing some of the original information. Furthermore (after composing a first or second draft of the whole theme), the writer added a preview of the theme's main ideas to the thesis statement. Compare the early and final versions of the thesis statement.

> *Preliminary thesis statement:*   The pig can't be blamed for being dirty because in reality it is a rather clean animal.
>
> *Final version of thesis statement:*   The pig isn't to blame for any unsanitary practices and, in fact, is rather tidy in virtually every way—from living quarters, to toilet habits, to bathing, to eating.

Starting with the Specifics, and Then Adding Thesis and Topic Sentences.
Perhaps you don't feel comfortable with drafting and organizing topic sentences in
the early stages; you prefer instead to formulate ideas in less structured ways,
through brainstorming, clustering, or free writing. Maybe you even wish to delay
the informal outlining until later in the process. Whatever the case, be flexible; no
method works well all of the time. Here is another way the sample theme could
have evolved—from a brainstorming approach. After listing specific details, the
writer arranged them in possible categories for paragraphs.

Living habits:

sty—under the barn
dark, dirty
practice began in New England
farmers probably too cruel, but pigs didn't object
wild pigs in natural state roam forests

Toilet habits:

uses same spot for defecating
cats similar
possible reason: instincts tell pigs to leave no trail for predators
other animals go just about anywhere

Mud bathing:

hot-day practice
pig has no perspiration glands
cool mud lowers temperature
false rumor: that pig cannot swim because would harm itself with
   hooves so pigs can clean themselves

Eating habits:

humans choose the food for them
diet closest to that of humans

Then the writer composed several drafts of the theme, with thesis statement
and topic sentences added at some point.

✍ 4   Considering Organization and Development

Based on each of the following thesis statements, predict the main supporting ideas
you would expect to find discussed in the full composition—and the order in which
they might be introduced.

1.   The methods of choosing the president and vice president have undergone
     three major changes throughout our country's history.

     Paragraph 1. *a discussion of the original method of choosing the president*

     and vice president

     Paragraph 2. *a discussion of the first change and the reasons for it*

     Paragraph 3. *a discussion of the second change and the reasons for it*

     Paragraph 4. *a discussion of the third change and the reasons for it*

2. The Japanese elementary and secondary educational system differs from the American system not only in the length of the school year but also in the subjects emphasized in the curriculum, in the expectations placed on the students both by teachers and parents, and—most importantly—in the quality of the education itself.

_____

_____

_____

_____

_____

3. Despite what many people think, I believe pets are a waste of time, money, and affection that would be better directed toward our children and family.

_____

_____

_____

_____

_____

5   Drafting a Thesis Statement and Topic Sentences

Choose your favorite subject from the following list and compose a preliminary thesis statement (without the preview of main ideas) for a composition. Then draft a preliminary topic sentence for each of three supporting paragraphs in the body of the composition. Revise any of these sentences if they are vague or unclear.

1. In an article for a magazine published by an international airline, explain to people from another country: three reasons for (a) the popularity of an American sport, (b) the appeal of American popular music, or (c) the appeal of a particular sports star or entertainer.
2. In an article for a magazine like *Reader's Digest,* describe the three most important traits or behaviors of a group you know well: your parents; people in your neighborhood or community; people of your ethnic group; people of your faith or in your church, temple, or synagogue; or people in your field of study.
3. In a brochure for entering freshmen at your college, explain three subjects they should study to get a good job after graduation.
4. In an article for a magazine that addresses a specific group of hobbyists (such as people interested in gourmet cooking, personal computers, photography, music, stamp collecting, running, travel—or any other hobby), explain three things that people need to know or do in order to enjoy themselves.

Preliminary thesis statement:

_____

_____

Preliminary topic sentences:

1. _____

_____

_____

2. _____

   _____

   _____

3. _____

   _____

   _____

✎   **6   Examining and Organizing Supporting Materials**

Now further explore your ideas on the topic you chose in Exercise 5. Do some free writing, brainstorming, or clustering. Then arrange the ideas into three major groups, each of which could be developed in a paragraph within the body of a composition.

Choosing Methods of Attracting Your Readers' Interest

Getting started is difficult, so you may wish to delay composing the introductory paragraph until you have drafted the body and even revised the paper once or twice. No matter when you decide to draft the introductory paragraph, however, you can choose from a number of attention-getting openings.

Beginning with a Question.   An opening question actively involves readers in a composition, forcing them to consider an issue, as in the following paragraph. (Notice that a thesis statement and preview of the theme's main ideas immediately follow the question.)

> *Is the biblical story of Jonah being swallowed by a whale just an ancient myth?* Don't be so sure. At the end of the last century, a human being was swallowed by a whale—yet he was rescued, and he survived.

Beginning with Details or Examples.   Specifics are almost always more interesting than generalizations. A surprising fact or example can stimulate the audience to read on, as in the following paragraph in which the opening details lead again into the thesis statement and preview:

> *The 1908 Sears, Roebuck and Company catalog included an unusual feature—a section on mail-order houses shipped by rail in large crates. The build-it-yourself house kits included shingles, windows, precut lumber, and all the other necessary building materials, along with blueprints and assembly instructions.* As this example shows, Sears, one of the world's largest retailers, can and will market almost anything. Today it can not only supply your household goods, but can fix your house, repair your car, and even provide you with eye and medical service.

Beginning with a Story.   A story creates interest by putting abstract ideas into human terms, as in this example:

> *Former President Herbert Hoover recalled that when a small boy asked him for his autograph during a public gathering in Los Angeles, the lad requested and received three copies "because it takes two of yours to trade for one of Babe Ruth's."* Such was the fame and popularity of George Herman "Babe" Ruth, probably the greatest and certainly among the best loved baseball players of all time.

Beginning with a Misunderstood Fact or Belief.   Another way to attract interest is by contradicting a popularly held belief, which leads into the thesis of the composition. The following paragraph employs such a contrast:

> *Most people assume that Ping-Pong and table tennis are the same thing—but they are wrong.* Ping-Pong is a registered trademark, and this accounts for the use of table tennis instead of the other term in publications. Trademarks such as Ping-Pong are official names or symbols registered with the government. Unlike copyrights or patents, trademarks last forever, and there are strict rules on how they may be used.

Beginning with a Direct Statement of the Thesis.   An unusual or surprising thesis alone will attract the readers' interest. The next paragraph begins with a direct statement of the thesis, followed by some supporting details and a preview of the composition's main ideas:

> *Missouri once boasted the world's smallest town that human beings could walk through.* This miniature community, founded in 1925, was known as Tiny Town, for every structure was one-half the size of a normal building. The town occupied 6 acres of a public park in Springfield, Missouri. And it was designed, built, and run by students.

IN SUMMARY

> **An effective attention-getting opening sentence includes**
>
> 1. a question that readers want answered;
> 2. details or examples that illustrate the thesis;
> 3. a story introducing the thesis;
> 4. a misunderstood fact or belief that the thesis contradicts; or
> 5. a direct statement of an unusual thesis.

7   Composing the Opening Paragraph

Compose an introduction to the preliminary thesis statement you drafted in Exercise 5. Use any attention-getting device you wish. (You can experiment with more than one device, too.) Then complete the opening paragraph, including a preview of the main ideas of the composition. The preview can be added onto the thesis statement through linking words such as *because, since,* or *by,* or after a colon (:); or it can be an entirely separate sentence.

_____

_____

_____

_____

_____

_____

_____

_____

Composing the Body

In the body of a composition, you must consider two issues: (1) arranging paragraphs in a logical order, and (2) choosing a method of development for each paragraph. If you have already arrived at an arrangement of paragraphs by formulating topic sentences, think about an appropriate method of development for each paragraph—namely, narration, description, process analysis, cause-effect, comparison-contrast, definition, or classification. Then you can draft and revise the body paragraphs—no doubt changing your plan several times as you proceed. However, if your planning has been less structured, you can now decide on the arrangement of ideas (probably making notes before beginning to write). Then you can draft and revise the paper. This method is a bit chaotic, but many people find it comfortable some or most of the time. In either case, try to present ideas in a sequence that makes the most sense to your audience, with each paragraph logically related to the others.

IN SUMMARY

When composing the body of a composition,

1. follow the organization of your earlier list of topic sentences, choose the method of development appropriate to each paragraph, and compose the first draft; or
2. prepare an organization based on your earlier brainstorming, clustering, or free writing and then compose the first draft; and, finally,
3. revise the first draft several times for clarity of paragraph development and orderly presentation of ideas, based on the needs of your audience.

8 Analyzing Methods of Development in Paragraphs

After each paragraph of the following composition, write the number of the topic sentence and identify the primary method or methods of paragraph development (explanation, narration, definition, comparison or contrast, classification, process analysis, cause to effect, or effect to cause). Then, after paragraph F, write the primary method of development used in the whole composition.

Paragraph A.   (1) Movie theaters are missing out on a great opportunity for concession sales. (2) The theaters could profit from selling facial tissue to all of us who cry at the happy endings of movies like *Pretty Woman, Fried Green Tomatoes,* or *The Bridges of Madison County.* (3) We know that tissue will soak up the tears, but a more interesting question is what causes the waterworks to begin with. (4) Do "tears of happiness" really exist? (5) Psychologists all say no, that there is no such thing. (6) According to them, we cry not because we are happy but because a happy ending stirs up some unpleasant feelings in us.

Topic sentence: _____3_____

Method(s) of development: _____*effect to cause and contrast*_____

Paragraph B.   (1) Actually, we shed our tears at the end of the process of holding them back. (2) Most of us can suppress the urge to cry, but not without spending some emotional energy. (3) When a happy ending shows that our grief is no longer justified, we release the energy used to control our emotions. (4) Sometimes it takes the form of laughter, but more often as tears.

Topic sentence: _____

Method(s) of development: _____

Paragraph C. (1) Curiously, many adults can sit quietly through a tear-jerking documentary on the Holocaust or Vietnam and then sob at a "heartwarming" 30-second long-distance commercial or a reunion on a TV soap opera. (2) But this sobbing is almost completely limited to grown-ups. (3) Happy endings often remind us of an ideal world of kindness and love that we once, as children, believed possible to reach in our own lives. (4) Unlike adults, however, children rarely cry at happy endings, because they have not yet become disappointed about their own future possibilities. (5) For adults, the happy ending is a temporary return to the innocence of childhood; the tears come from recognizing that we must live in the tougher "real" world. (6) For children, the happy ending merely confirms their view that life is filled with possibilities.

Topic sentence: _____

Method(s) of development: _____

Paragraph D. (1) The tendency to cry at happy endings is not limited to movie- or television-viewing. (2) In real life, the relatives of a critically ill patient may not cry before or during a delicate surgery, but they will cry after the operation is successful. (3) Once the relatives feel safe, they can let the tears flow, unleashing all the sadness and anxiety they have held back.

Topic sentence: _____

Method(s) of development: _____

Paragraph E. (1) Psychologists even question whether tears that fall at weddings, graduations, and bar mitzvahs are expressions of joy. (2) These events are *rites of passage,* symbolizing important changes in young people's lives. (3) We cry because these rites stir up our unhappiness about the past ("Why wasn't my wedding as joyous?"), insecurities about the present ("Why haven't I found my true love like the bride and groom have?"), and fear about the future ("How will I survive when my children leave the nest?").

Topic sentence: _____

Method(s) of development: _____

Paragraph F. (1) In our emotional world, we are needy, selfish, and demanding. (2) We cry for *ourselves* at happy endings, not for others. (3) But our tears do not mean we cannot feel joy in others' happiness. (4) Crying at a happy ending reveals our idealistic side—the part of us that longs for the simplicity and love we once thought possible—as well as the part of us that sadly realizes their impossibility.

Topic sentence: _____

Method(s) of development: _____

Primary method of development in the whole composition: _____

_____

✍ **9** **Drafting the Composition**

Compose the first draft of a three-paragraph body of the composition you began in Exercises 5 and 7. Include a topic sentence in each paragraph.

Composing the Conclusion

Because compositions are often complex, the concluding paragraph should remind readers of the thesis, summarize the main ideas, and end with a punch. The easiest way to draft the conclusion is to return to the opening paragraph, restating the thesis and preview in different words. Let's look again, for a moment, at the theme about pigs. The thesis states that pigs are unsanitary through no fault of their own, and the preview lists four aspects of a pig's cleanliness—its choice of living quarters, toilet habits, bathing habits, and eating habits. The conclusion restates these ideas in one sentence.

> They want to be neat housekeepers, observe proper sanitary and bathing practices, and eat well-balanced meals, but they don't always receive courteous treatment from their hosts and keepers.

✍ **10** **Drafting the Final Paragraph**

Return to the introductory paragraph you composed in Exercise 6 and write a first draft of a concluding paragraph based on it. Try to include a forceful or clever final sentence.

_____

_____

_____

_____

_____

_____

_____

_____

IN SUMMARY

The process of composing an expository composition

1. can begin with either
   a. a thesis statement and a list of specifics in a preliminary outline, or
   b. free writing, clustering, or brainstorming, followed by the listing of ideas in some order or the composing of a first draft;
2. can continue with the composing of the introductory paragraph first or later in the process;
3. can be shaped through either
   a. a topic sentence outline, which includes a preliminary thesis statement and primary method of development for the composition, along with a topic sentence and method of development for each paragraph, or

> b. trial and error—that is, examining and then reshaping main ideas after they have been written;
> 4. can end with the composing of a concluding summary of the main ideas based on the thesis statement (and preview) from the first paragraph.

ESTABLISHING COHERENCE AMONG PARAGRAPHS

You will recall that in an effective paragraph, the ideas *cohere*—or hold together. The first sentence leads logically into the second, the second leads logically into the third, and so on. An effective composition requires similar coherence: The links between paragraphs must be logical and clear.

You have already seen that coherence often arises from formulating a logical plan and then outlining it in the preview. However, you can also establish the connections among paragraphs through devices similar to the ones discussed in Chapter 4—that is, coherence within paragraphs:

> ◆ repeated words or phrases (or substitutes for them) from the thesis statement;
> ◆ repeated key words or phrases from the previous paragraph; and
> ◆ transitional words, phrases, or even whole sentences.

Repeating Words or Phrases from the Thesis Statement

The preview in the thesis statement is like a road map that guides readers on their journey through the composition. Then the beginning of each paragraph in the body serves as a signpost identifying the stops along the way. Take a look at the composition on pigs, this time to see how the opening sentences of later paragraphs reuse or rephrase terms from the preview.

Preview.   In fact, the pig is rather tidy in virtually every way—*from living quarters, to toilet habits, to bathing, to eating.*

Paragraph B.   First of all, domestic pigs are supposed to "like" filthy *living quarters.* . . .

Paragraph C.   Second, even in close confinement, the pigs' *toilet habits* are among the best of domestic animals.

Paragraph D.   However, a third charge against pigs is true: They don't *bathe* but instead wallow in the mud on hot days.

Paragraph E.   Fourth and finally, pigs can be justifiably accused of *eating* garbage. . . .

Repeating Words or Phrases from the Previous Paragraph

When a composition employs different methods of development in each paragraph, you can achieve coherence in another way. Let the first sentence of a new paragraph repeat a term or idea from the last sentence of the previous paragraph. Note the repeated expressions (shown in italics) that follow.

Paragraph A.   There is an old joke that the camel looks as if it had been made by committee. And it certainly is odd looking, with its big hump, matted fur, and twisted face. Despite its appearance, though, the animal is very efficiently designed to cope with *its environment*.

Paragraph B. *That environment, of course, is the desert.* As most people know, the camel can exist there for long periods without drinking, and then can take in enormous quantities of water at one time. In fact, this humpbacked creature can do without liquids for as long as eight days in summer and eight weeks in winter. After such a long dry spell, it can *consume as much as 100 quarts in ten minutes*.

Paragraph C. *This ability to absorb so much water* has led many people to believe, incorrectly, that the camel carries a special storage area like a water tank in its body. Some think that the camel has a separate water-carrying stomach or that it keeps water in the hump. There is no such separate water tank or stomach, however, and the hump contains fat that is converted to energy when needed. The water the camel drinks goes directly into its system, and this remarkable system enables the camel to get along with so little fluid.

Adding Transitional Words, Phrases, and Sentences

Another way to express complex relationships among paragraphs is through transitional words or phrases such as *therefore, on the other hand,* or *for example*—or even entire sentences of transition. Here is the remainder of the composition on the camel, with the transitional expressions and sentences at the beginning of each paragraph in italics.

Paragraph C. . . .The water the camel drinks goes directly into its system, and this remarkable system enables the camel to get along with so little fluid.

Paragraph D. *A comparison to our system will illustrate the point.* A human being perspires in hot weather to keep body temperature near the normal 98.6 degrees as water evaporates from the skin. A camel, on the other hand, hardly perspires at all. Its body temperature can rise to 105 degrees before the creature even breaks a sweat. Furthermore, the camel urinates very little. While a human passes off waste water frequently, the camel reuses it—in effect recycling it, as if the camel had an almost closed air-conditioning system.

Paragraph E. *In summary, therefore,* because of its ability to store and reuse water and to perspire only under the most extreme conditions, the camel is ideally suited to the hot desert environment. It is a perfect example of the biological principles of adaptation and of survival of the fittest.

11 Editing for Transitional Expressions

Supply transitional words, phrases, or whole sentences between paragraphs in the following composition. Then compose a concluding paragraph, complete with a short summary.

Throwing Like a Boy: Genetics or Training?

Paragraph A. Not only are some girls (and later, women) unable to throw balls as far as boys, but their form is noticeably different. If you ask an average boy to throw a baseball as far as he can, he will lift his elbow and extend his arm all the way back. A girl may tend to keep her elbow stiff and push the ball forward with her hand like a shot-putter. Why is it that boys and some girls throw so differently?

Paragraph B. _____

One theory is that females have an extra bone that prevents them from throwing like boys. Another theory is that females are missing a bone. However, physiologists say that boys and girls have the same number of bones in their arms.

Paragraph C. _____

In their textbook, *Training for Sport and Activity: The Physiological Basis of the Conditioning Process,* Jack H. Wilmore and David L. Costill, two specialists in exercise physiology, cite studies indicating that boys and girls below the ages of 10 to 12 have remarkably similar scores in athletic ability. In virtually every test, boys just barely beat the girls. With the beginning of puberty, however, males become much stronger and outperform girls in virtually all motor skills. In only one athletic test before and after puberty did the boys far exceed the girls: the softball throw. From the ages of 5 to 16, the average boy can throw a ball about twice as far as the average girl.

Paragraph D. _____

In another study cited by Wilmore and Costill, 200 males and females from ages 3 to 20 threw softballs for science. The result was that males beat females two-to-one when throwing with their dominant hand, but females threw almost as far as males with their nondominant hand. Up until the ages of 10 to 12, girls threw just as far with their nondominant hand as boys did.

Paragraph E. _____

Exercise physiologist Ralph Wickstrom believes most children go through several developmental stages of throwing. Boys simply continue to improve, while girls are not encouraged to throw softballs or baseballs and therefore stop in the learning curve. As an example, Wickstrom notes that most right-handed girls throw with their right foot forward. Simply shifting their left foot forward would increase their throwing distance. Most boys have similar difficulties when they are forced to throw with their nondominant hand. They lose the ability to throw great distances, partly because the muscles of the nondominant side are less developed, but also because the boys haven't practiced throwing from that side.

Paragraph F.

_____

_____

_____

_____

_____

_____

_____

_____

_____

12   Analyzing Your Composition

Read the composition you composed in Exercises 5, 7, and 10, and respond to each of the following questions (or have another person do so). Use the responses as guidelines for revising the composition, and then do the revision.

Revision Guidelines

1. Does the first paragraph include a clear thesis statement and preview of the composition's main ideas? _____ If either is missing or unclear, how should the paragraph be revised? _____

    _____

    _____

2. Does the first paragraph include an effective attention-getting introduction? _____ If not, how should the beginning of the paragraph be revised?_____

    _____

    _____

3. Is the point of each paragraph in the body clear? _____ Is each point stated in a topic sentence? _____ If not, how should these paragraphs be revised? _____

    _____

    _____

4. Do the details in each paragraph support the topic sentences? _____ If not, what should be eliminated, revised, or added? _____

    _____

    _____

5. Are transitions lacking or too vague at any point within or between paragraphs? _____ If so, what should be added or revised?_____

    _____

    _____

6. Does the final paragraph summarize the main ideas and end with a punch? _____ If not, how should it be revised? _____

    _____

    _____

7. What was the greatest problem in composing this composition? (Ignore this question if the writer experienced no significant problems.) _____

    _____

    _____

    If this problem was not resolved, what should be done?_____

    _____

    _____

✍ **13   Proofreading and Polishing Your Composition**

After completing the revision, edit the composition, checking for correct spelling and punctuation, complete sentences, and clarity of ideas. Then make a clean copy of the paragraph and proofread it carefully for errors.

Composing Based on Outside Sources

Read the following information about Monopoly several times and then compose a composition based on the information. Assume your composition will be a feature article in the "Contemporary Living" section of a newspaper. Make sure that the final draft of the composition includes (1) a thesis statement that accounts for most of the information; (2) a topic sentence in each paragraph within the body of the composition; (3) clear transitions between ideas and between paragraphs; and (4) a concluding paragraph that summarizes the main ideas. Arrange the information in any way you wish; you don't have to use all of it.

Monopoly

Best-selling copyrighted game ever
Sales of 90 million sets in 1985
Game first marketed: 1935
Inventor Charles Darrow, an unemployed heating engineer from Philadelphia
Darrow eventually sold idea to Parker Brothers
Company had initially rejected idea in 1933, claiming it contained "52 fundamental playing errors"
At age 46, Darrow retired a millionaire
Spent time traveling and growing exotic orchids
Street names from Atlantic City, New Jersey
In 1974, attempt by Atlantic City council to change two street names of city provoked massive protest
Hundreds of letters from all over the United States and Canada
Group of Princeton University students in committee called "Students to Save Baltic and Mediterranean Avenues"
Threat by students to cover city with Monopoly money if the ordinance passed
300 protesters at committee meeting
Testimony from executives of Parker Brothers
Failure of ordinance
In 1975, amount of real money printed by United States Bureau of Engraving: $22 billion
In 1975, amount of Monopoly money printed by Parker Brothers: $40 billion
Most expensive Monopoly set: $5000, made by Alfred Dunhill
Cost of edible version of game, "the Christmas present with a difference," made of milk chocolate or butterscotch: $600

ADDITIONAL READING

Baby Birds

Gale Lawrence

Gale Lawrence wrote this article in The Beginning Naturalist, *a collection of 52 essays on her encounters with nature.*

offspring

(1) Every spring the "baby bird crisis" occurs. By May many birds have hatched their first **broods** and are feeding them in the nest while they grow their feathers and learn to fly. Baby birds have a way of tumbling out of their nests, and children have a way of finding them and bringing them home. What should a family do if faced with this "crisis"?

(2) First, take the baby bird back to the exact spot where it was found. Look carefully for a nest nearby. If you find the nest and it is accessible, put the bird gently

baby deer

back into the nest. Contrary to popular belief, the mother bird will not reject a baby that has been handled by human beings. A deer, which has a keen sense of smell and fears the human scent, will reject a **fawn** that has been handled, but birds are different. If you find the nest and return the baby, you have done the best you can do.

(3) As a next-best measure, tie a small box onto a branch of a tree or shrub near where the bird was found, and put the baby bird in the box. The bird will thus be off the ground and out of the reach of neighborhood cats and dogs.

(4) The third best thing you can do is simply to leave the bird in the exact spot where it was found. Parent birds are accustomed to having their young fall out of the nest, and they will feed them on the ground. Of course, the baby bird is more vulnerable on the ground than it is in the nest or in a box, but it still stands a better chance of surviving under its own parents' care than under human care. If the baby bird is found near a house, it is better to keep pet dogs and cats indoors than to bring the baby bird indoors in an attempt to protect it.

large

(5) If the baby is truly abandoned or orphaned—something you can learn only by watching it from a distance for an hour or more—you have a decision to make. You can leave it there to die a natural death—which might in fact be the most humane thing to do. Or you can take it in indoors. If you decide to care for it yourself, you are making a **substantial** commitment. And, even if you live up to your commitment, there is no guarantee that the bird will survive.

birdhouse

(6) Two major problems are involved in trying to parent a baby bird. One is feeding it, and the other is preparing it for life in the wild. Parent birds do it all as a matter of course, but a human parent will have to drop other activities for a period of weeks and perhaps install a screened porch or **aviary** to do the job right.

(7) Before you can even address yourself to the problem of feeding, however, you have the more immediate problem of the bird's shock and fright to contend with. Perhaps this is the time to send one member of the family for a book on the care of wild animal young, while another rigs up a heating pad or hot water bottle to warm the baby bird. One good book is *Care of the Wild Feathered and Furred: A Guide to Wildlife Handling and Care* (Santa Cruz: Unity Press, 1973) by Mae Hickman and Maxine Guy. Another is Ronald Rood's *The Care and Feeding of Wild Pets* (New York: Pocket Books, 1976). A third book that is specifically about birds is *Bird Ambulance* (New York: Charles Scribner's Sons, 1971) by Arline Thomas.

(8) Now comes the problem of feeding. The warm milk in an eye dropper that seems to be everyone's immediate impulse when it comes to feeding animal young may be appropriate for baby mammals, but it will come as a complete surprise to the baby bird. Its parents were probably feeding it mashed worms, caterpillars, insects, and other delicious odds and ends. Therefore, you'll need to do the same. At first you should supply the baby bird with protein-rich foods. Eventually you're going to have to identify the species and learn something about its food habits in the wild if you want the bird to grow up properly. Whether the bird is a seed eater, an insect eater, or a predator will make a difference.

(9) Parent birds feed their babies about every 10 or 15 minutes from sunrise to sunset. They also feed them exactly what they need to keep their bowels regulated and their bodies growing properly. They also keep the nest clean by removing the babies' excrement, which usually appears shortly after each feeding. In brief, between finding and preparing appropriate food, feeding, and cleaning up after meals, you're not going to have much time for anything else for a while if you decide to parent a baby bird.

(10) If you do manage to keep the young bird fed properly and growing, your next problem is providing it with enough space for it to practice flying. You cannot expect a bird to go from your kitchen to the wild with one swoop of its wings. You will need to continue feeding and protecting the bird while it is adjusting to the outdoors. If it had stayed with its parents, it would have had adult birds to follow and imitate, but, with nothing but human beings to encourage it, it will have to make

chick

sense out of its environment alone. The young bird that has been raised by humans is at a disadvantage when it comes to competing for food and avoiding the attacks of predators. So even if you do manage to raise a **fledgling** to adulthood, you have not guaranteed its survival in the wild.

(11) If you think I'm trying to sound discouraging, I am. The adoption of a baby bird will probably result in failure. You might even cause a death that would not have occurred had you left the baby bird where it was. Your intentions might be good; the

moral **ethical** impulse that motivates your actions might be of the best kind. But you should know that even experienced veterinarians have a low success rate in caring for wild animals.

(12) Perhaps the most important thing a child or adult can learn from an encounter with a baby bird is the difference between wild animals and domestic pets. Whereas puppies and kittens warm to human attention and become very much a part of the family, a wild bird never will. Attempting to make a pet out of a wild animal is a serious disservice to that animal—so serious, in fact, that there are laws against it. Life in the wild does not consist of friendly humans, readily available meals, and a protected environment. Wild animals must remain wild to survive.

(13) Rather than adopt a baby bird, why not "adopt" a whole bird family—from a distance? Chances are there is a bird's nest somewhere near your home. Or you can build birdhouses to attract birds to your yard. Learn to watch the bird family from a distance. If human beings get too close, the parent birds won't come to the nest. So practice sitting quietly, perhaps with a pair of binoculars, far enough away from the nest that the adult bird won't feel threatened.

(14) Watching birds in the wild is a much healthier and more realistic activity than fantasizing that a bird will become your special friend because you raised it. Unfortunately, movies, television, and children's books have created a "Bambi syndrome" in us. The young of most species are precious and adorable, but the desire to fondle and caress and make pets out of wildlings is dangerously romantic. It should not be encouraged. We'd be much wiser if we were content to be observers of wildlife. If we truly care about wild animals, we should be protectors of their wildness, which enables the best of them to survive.

Questions for Investigation and Discussion

1. Is the purpose of this essay merely to inform? If not, what other purpose does it have?
2. The essay makes a number of points. What is its main point?
3. Who is the audience for this essay? What does Gale Lawrence expect the readers to do with the information and advice she provides?
4. What is the primary method of the development Lawrence uses?
5. There are several major divisions in the essay. Locate the sentences that introduce each of the divisions. What words or phrases relate the ideas to come with the ideas that have preceded?

SUGGESTED TOPICS FOR WRITING

The following suggestions may stimulate your thinking as you choose subjects for expository compositions of five or more paragraphs. Remember that any composition should be logically arranged, based on what your audience needs to know. Be sure that the final draft of your composition includes (1) an introductory paragraph, complete with an attention-getting opening and a thesis statement that outlines the composition; (2) a body that is several paragraphs long and is organized in some logical way; (3) clear links between paragraphs; and (4) a concluding paragraph complete with a summary of the composition's main ideas.

1. Like Gale Lawrence, write an essay in which you advise people about some practical matter. Assume, for example, that you are a high school counselor who advises seniors about how to adjust to college life. Write a multiparagraph pamphlet in which you advise them on how to make the adjustment. Consider any (but not necessarily all) of these issues: living with roommates, budgeting time, budgeting money, taking and organizing notes,

2. Assume you are a social worker who counsels parents of adolescent children. Write a multiparagraph pamphlet in which you describe three or four major problems that adolescents face.

3. Assume you are an executive of a large manufacturer of personal computers. Write a multiparagraph memo to your marketing department suggesting several reasons why a typical American household needs a personal computer.

4. Assume you have completed your education and are applying for a job. Write a letter to a prospective employer in which you describe the education and training, skills, and experience that qualify you for the position.

Composing Persuasive Compositions

Now comes the most challenging but most fascinating composing task: the persuasive composition, in which you attempt to change the minds or behavior of your audience. Persuasion is no easy task, but this chapter offers you advice on how to achieve some success. After defining and discussing the traits of effective persuasion, the chapter explores the steps in composing a persuasive composition:

- ✎ preparing a strategy that addresses your subject, your audience's attitudes, and your reason for persuasion;
- ✎ choosing methods of supporting your arguments; and
- ✎ structuring the introduction, body, and conclusion of the composition.

PERSUASION DEFINED

Persuasion is a central part of everyday life. Each day you see and hear thousands of ads and commercials enticing you to buy goods and services.

"Try Sparkle toothpaste and improve your love life."
"Whiter than white, brighter than bright—that's how your clothes will look when you wash them in Supersuds!"
"To get a good job in the computer field, enroll in the MicroMax Programming School."

Each day in conversation, you make requests, pleas, demands, or even threats—for example, that a friend lend you some money; that your professor allow you more time to complete an assignment; or that your son, roommate, or spouse put the dirty dishes in the sink. And less often—but far more importantly—you make written requests or demands that employers consider you for a job, clients buy your products, senators and representatives support or oppose a law, or the automobile dealer fix your car properly if he ever wants your business again.

What, then, is *persuasion?* It is an attempt to convince others that they should accept your point of view or do your bidding. Persuasion is based on *reasons* and *explanations* (also called *arguments*), *proof* (through facts, figures, and examples), and *emotional appeals.* Sometimes it requires an attack on other viewpoints, but it often requires a defense of your own viewpoint as well. People believe they are rational animals—and they are. Nevertheless, they also hold irrational opinions based on fear, anger, prejudice, and ignorance. They don't easily change their minds—especially about long-held beliefs—so, to be convincing, you must answer their counterarguments, questions, and doubts.

Persuasion is the most difficult communicative skill. Your presentation must be clear, well reasoned, and carefully fitted to the audience. You can be informal and animated with a friend, loud and angry with a teenage son, polite but firm with a repair person, or humble and soft-spoken with a professor. In short, your appeal must actually be a *persuasive strategy* based on the subject, the reason for persuading, and the audience's attitude toward you and the subject.

Considering the Subject

You certainly can't be persuasive about a subject you neither know nor believe in. Discuss something you understand (or can learn) thoroughly. Read about it; talk to people about it. You will not only discover information to support your viewpoint but also encounter the opposing arguments to which you must respond. Furthermore, be confident (but not arrogant) in your position. If you don't sound convinced by your arguments, no one else will be either. Notice, for example, the writer's confident tone in the following opening paragraph of a composition:

> Lost in debate about how our government leaders can survive a nuclear war is the more basic question of whether they *ought* to. A good argument can be made that citizens stumbling aglow with radiation through the ashes of total destruction would have no further use for the same folks who got them into such a fix. . . .

Whether or not you agree with this argument, you probably do want to read further, for the writer's tone is both self-assured and humorous.

Finally, think about what the subject requires you to say. If it is complex or unfamiliar, your first step is to define terms and explain processes. If it is controversial, you should answer the counterarguments in one of two ways:

◆ *Attack the arguments.* Explain the problems with the arguments of opponents, supporting your attack with evidence.
◆ *Acknowledge them.* Admit their validity, but show why your own arguments outweigh them.

✍ 1   **Predicting the Organization of Persuasive Compositions**

After each of the following thesis statements for persuasive compositions, list the matters you, as the audience, expect the writer to address—or the questions you want the writer to answer.

Thesis Statement A: Let's replace the current public educational system with a voucher system so that parents may freely choose the type of private school their children will attend.

1. explanation of a voucher system 2. problems with the current educational system 3. ways that the voucher system would solve these problems 4. What do we do with the currently employed teachers and administrators? 5. How do we make sure that all children are educated in the basics? 6. Should we pay for education in a religious school?

Thesis Statement B: All college athletes, no matter how great their skills or impoverished their background, should be subject to the same college admission requirements as any other student.

_____

_____

_____

_____

_____

_____

Thesis Statement C: I propose that every homeless person be provided with free housing.

_____

_____

_____

_____

_____

_____

Thesis Statement D: Seat-belt use should be mandatory, and anyone who does not wear one should be required to pay a fine.

_____

_____

_____

_____

_____

_____

Thesis Statement E: The legal age for obtaining a driver's license should be raised from 16 to 18.

_____

_____

_____

_____

_____

_____

_____

Considering the Reason for Persuading

A persuasive goal can be modest (for example, a request that people reconsider an opinion) or it can be radical (for example, a demand that people boycott a store, vote for a candidate they oppose, repair your car for free, or quit their jobs). Of course, the more you ask of an audience, the more difficult the task of persuasion becomes. For example, Abraham Lincoln, one of America's greatest speakers and writers, had to ask people to risk or give their lives during the Civil War. In 1863, when he issued the Emancipation Proclamation, many Northerners objected, including James C. Conkling, who said in a letter that he was fighting to unify the nation and that freeing the slaves would only complicate future attempts at peace with the South.

Knowing that any argument that emancipation was "morally" correct would be useless with Conkling, the president appealed to Conkling's own selfish interests. Lincoln replied that slaves fighting for the North would be better soldiers knowing that victory meant their freedom. He asked, "Why should they do anything for us if we will do nothing for them?"

Considering the Audience's Attitude Toward You and the Subject

Some readers can be easily persuaded; others can't. Audiences can generally be classified into three types according to their attitudes toward you and your arguments.

Addressing a Friendly Audience.   People in a friendly audience are the easiest to convince because they already agree with your arguments and trust (or at least don't distrust) you. You can effectively compose an expository composition for them by stating the thesis in the first paragraph and straightforwardly developing each supporting point in the body of the composition.

Addressing a Neutral Audience.   People in a neutral audience approach your arguments with an open mind, neither strongly favoring nor opposing them. You can make a straightforward presentation to them also, but try to anticipate and answer their questions or objections. For example, the following early paragraph from a composition against drinking clears up a common misunderstanding:

> If you think a few cups of black coffee will sober you up, you are badly mistaken. Police and others who must deal with drunken drivers call this "the great coffee myth," for it is actually a dangerous bit of folklore. Many drunks with a half-dozen cups of coffee in them have gone out to die on the highway. Only time can eliminate too much alcohol in the bloodstream. The human body burns alcohol at the rate of about one half ounce an hour. And there is no way to speed up this rate.

Addressing an Unfriendly Audience.   People in an unfriendly audience are hostile to your point of view and perhaps don't trust you. Therefore, show them you are on their side, softening that hostility and mistrust before moving into your main argument. For example, examine the opening of an argument by Ellen Goodman in a nationally syndicated column. Goodman knows she is about to criticize the behavior of Madonna, at that time a heroine of many people under the age of 30, and who is childless but married to actor Sean Penn. So she begins by pledging her "support" for the popular singer in a good-natured and humorous tone. (Paragraphs in newspapers are usually only one or two sentences.)

A Deal with Pop Stars

❏   BOSTON: Let me say right up front that anytime Madonna decides to have a baby, she can count on a pair of booties from me. I'll even throw in a year's supply of Pampers and a "Baby on Board" sticker just for kicks.

I have no problem with a real-life pregnancy for the pop-star . . .

But Madonna is after all, 27 years old, not to mention married. Furthermore, as your basic two-career couple, she and Sean Penn pull in enough of a weekly paycheck to keep any kid in strained peaches and diamond studded diaper pins.

After this tongue-in-cheek description of the "realistic" issues of a pregnancy for Madonna, Goodman can raise her objection to one of the singer's videos:

What gives me a touch of morning sickness is the stereo and video maternity of Madonna. Every time her new hit single passes through my car radio or my cable-television screen, I find myself wishing her an advanced case of varicose veins, or perhaps two months taking care of triplets on a welfare check.

The song, as you may have guessed or heard, features an unwed pregnant adolescent begging her father to bless her decision to keep her baby and marry her daddy. . . .

"Papa don't preach, I'm in trouble deep, Papa don't preach, I've been losing sleep, But I made up my mind, I'm keeping my baby, I'm gonna keep my baby, mmm . . ."

skits

an actor from the 1950s

host of children's show

The video is one of those emotional slice-of-life **vignettes** that work brilliantly in commercials. The problem is that this is a commercial for teenage pregnancy. Madonna not only has a lover as sexy as **James Dean**—"the one you warned me about"—but a father ultimately as understanding as **Mr. Rogers.** By the video's end, she has won the love of both in the family way.

The happily-ever-after image has about as much to do with the reality of adolescent motherhood as Madonna's figure has to do with pregnancy. It's artificially inseminated with romance.

Goodman acknowledges the opposition to her argument, again in a light and humorous tone, before beginning to refute that opposition:

By now, I should know better than to get worked up over rock. Blame it on the beat if you will. Madonna herself predicted that this is a "message song that everyone is going to take the wrong way. Immediately they're going to say I am advising every young girl to go out and get pregnant. . . . This song is really about a girl who is making a decision in her life."

All of last year's Madonna Wannabees are not, I know, gonna wanna be pregnant this year. But if you think that rock stars have no influence on teenage behavior, I can tell you where to find a whole lot of used lace gloves. If this is a song about "a girl making a decision in her life," part of her decision making comes from the endless romantic messages like this one.

Goodman then returns to the fantasy-versus-reality theme of her argument, this time describing her "own personal fantasy," before directly stating her point:

[I'd like] to see just one movie in which the passionate male lead looks deeply into the eyes of the exquisite female lead as they sit before the fire in the lonely cabin, kissing soulfully, and asks whether they should use his contraceptive or hers. Just once I would like to hear a rock-and-roll song in which the lead pants huskily, "No, no, no."

I don't, however, expect to ever hear an upbeat ode to the diaphragm. Or a lyric on midnight feeding. Indeed, if you want an **antonym** for romance in our multimedia show, try "realistic" or "responsible." Responsible romance is an **oxymoron.** True lovers are not planners; they are carried away. Just ask pregnant teenagers, almost a million a year.

opposite word

contradiction

Adolescents are fed the pop image of love that is zipless and parenthood that comes without bills or diapers. But even Madonna, 27 and a lady in control of her life, knows better. Asked what she imagines as postscript to the happy ending of her first-trimester video, she says, "Of course, who knows how it will end?" The realists among us do have a pretty good or, should I say, pretty bleak, statistical idea. In poverty.

Does that sound like a sermon? The song says, "Papa don't preach." Let's make a deal, instead. Papa and Momma will call off all the preaching, if pop stars call off the propaganda.

No matter what their attitude is, be sure to respect your audience. Never underestimate their intelligence, and make your argument logical and fair. Appeal to emotions, but don't attempt to manipulate them. Don't reduce an argument to personal attacks on opponents. And don't distort the truth, for you will lose the trust of your readers.

IN SUMMARY

Persuasion

1. is the attempt to urge others to accept your point of view or do your bidding;
2. is based on reasons and explanations, proof, and emotional appeals;
3. must be based on a strategy that accommodates the subject, the reason for persuading, and the audience's attitude toward you and the subject; and
4. attacks or acknowledges the arguments against your point of view.

2 Examining a Persuasive Composition

Read the following letter written by a suburban homemaker to the readers of *The People's Almanac*. Then answer the questions.

Paragraph A. (1) It may seem strange to suggest that a drug as evil as heroin be legalized, but please hear me out. (2) If I had my way, no one would take heroin. (3) But, in reality, lots and lots of people use it and many of them become addicts. (4) And these addicts need large amounts of money, every day, to support their habits. (5) To get this money, many heroin addicts become thieves, preying on innocent people so the addicts can afford the outrageous prices that pushers are able to charge since they deal in an illegal, underground substance which they sell to customers who have to have it.

Paragraph B. (1) If heroin were legal, the price would go way down, addicts wouldn't have to steal to support their habit, and the rest of us wouldn't be victimized. (2) Who would lose if heroin were legal? (3) Only the pushers and the crime syndicates. (4) It makes you wonder why politicians have allowed the heroin trade to go on as long as they have. (5) If heroin were legal, the police would have more time to deal with other crimes. (6) I have heard that over 50 percent of the crime in New York City is committed by heroin addicts.

Paragraph C. (1) The victims of heroin addiction are both rich and poor. (2) Last summer, three blocks from my suburban home, two darling teenagers were shot to death when they came home from school and surprised a burglar. (3) That burglar turned out to be a heroin addict with a $300-a-day habit. (4) Four days later my housekeeper came to work crying because her brother was in critical condition in the hospital, having been stabbed by an intruder. (5) Fortunately, he survived, but this intruder, too, was a heroin addict.

Paragraph D. (1) Perhaps it is true that legalizing heroin would cause there to be more addicts, but those addicts would commit far fewer crimes than the ones in the system we now have. (2) When I told my friends about my idea to make heroin legal, one of them said that she had heard the idea before on the radio. (3) And she said that some well-known lawyers and even judges supported it. (4) If this is so, then why is heroin still illegal? (5) Are the politicians afraid that if they support legal heroin, people will think they are pro-drugs? (6) Or is organized crime so strong that it can buy off the politicians or otherwise convince them not to act?

—(Mrs.) Marsha Phillips, Silver Springs, Maryland

1. What is the purpose of sentences 1 and 2 in paragraph A?
2. Which sentences in paragraph A define the problem?
3. Where does the writer propose a solution to the problem, and what is that solution?
4. What does the writer predict would result if her solution were adopted? Does she predict any negative results and, if so, where?
5. Where does the writer cite statistics to support her argument? Where does she cite respected members of the community?
6. Why does the writer mention in paragraph C that the victims of heroin addiction are both rich and poor?
7. What, according to the writer, seems to prevent her solution from being enacted?
8. Does the writer directly call upon people to act? If not, what actions do you think she would suggest?

COMPOSING A PERSUASIVE COMPOSITION

Developing a Persuasive Strategy

Once you have chosen a subject, established your reason for persuading, and considered the attitudes of your audience, continue the careful planning of a persuasive strategy that addresses the following questions:

> ◆ Based on the attitudes of your audience and their knowledge of the subject, what major arguments will you make and in what order? Where will you define the problem? Where will you propose a solution?
> ◆ What objections from your audience should you answer, how will you answer them, and at what point will you do so (near the beginning, middle, or end)?
> ◆ When will you state the thesis—immediately, or later on after you have dealt with the readers' objections?
> ◆ When will you make the major arguments—before or after you have answered objections?

There are no "right" answers to these questions, but you must take them seriously. In planning and composing a paper, you may need to call on all the resources available to you—free writing, clustering, brainstorming, outlining, topic sentence outlining, drafting, and revising. In fact, don't be surprised if you change strategies and revise your paper many times. Here are some important guidelines to keep in mind when developing a strategy.

Preparing a Preliminary Thesis Statement.   Although you may choose to state the thesis late in the paper, make it clear and direct. Let your readers know exactly what you want them to believe or do. For example, this statement clearly argues against the death penalty:

> The death penalty should be abolished for a simple reason: Although there
> are countless numbers of people who believe that the death penalty is a
> deterrent to crime, the evidence of many studies proves otherwise.

A thesis statement generally makes a recommendation or demand and therefore uses the verbs *should, ought,* or *must,* as the following examples illustrate:

> Anyone interested in American history should visit Boston and its sur-
> rounding areas, where our independent nation was really founded.
>
> You ought to be eating more foods with high fiber content, while cutting
> down on eggs, red meats, and whole-milk dairy products.
>
> If we and our children hope to survive in the next century, we must stop
> the destruction of the ozone layer.

3   Composing Thesis Statements

Assume you write editorials for your college newspaper. Choose a topic that most interests you from those listed here and draft a thesis statement that best reflects your
position on the topic.

1. the grading system
2. required courses
3. college sports
4. tutoring and academic support services
5. smoking or tobacco use

Basing Your Argument Primarily on Facts.   Whenever possible, provide evidence—facts and figures—to support your argument. Furthermore, explain the
significance of the numbers; don't just list them. To bolster his argument that over-
work is literally killing the Japanese, for example, Pete Hamill cites and compares
statistics, then quotes a Japanese friend's reaction to them:

> Japan works harder than any nation on earth. According to 1989 figures
> from the Ministry of International Trade and Industry, the Japanese worker
> put in 2246.8 hours of work the year before—300 more than the average
> American, 600 more than the West Germans and the French.
>   "That's too low," one Japanese editor friend said, making calculations
> with a pencil. "They must be leaving out overtime. If I could work 2,500
> hours a year, I'd feel as if I was on vacation."

Discussing the Issue in Human Terms.   Find detailed and specific examples
from people's lives, or relate the issue to the personal concerns of the audience (as
Lincoln did in his letter to Conkling).

Citing Respected Authorities and Organizations.   Quotes from authorities and
findings from respected organizations give additional weight and prestige to an ar-

gument. Recall Marsha Phillips's claims that many well-known judges and lawyers support the legalization of heroin. In the following example, the writer cites a study by a prestigious organization that shows the public's mixed feelings about abortions "when the primary motive for the procedure is simple inconvenience":

> According to the National Opinion Research Center, a nonprofit group affiliated with the University of Chicago, a large majority of Americans support abortion only when the woman's health is seriously endangered, when the pregnancy is the result of rape or incest, and when the baby is likely to be born with a serious birth defect. But if a woman wants an abortion because she is unmarried or does not want more children or is too poor to support them—the circumstances under which most abortions take place—slightly less than half of Americans think a legal abortion should be available.

Predicting the Results of Actions.   Show the benefits to your readers and to society if your solution is adopted, while warning against the dangers if it is not.

IN SUMMARY

An effective persuasive strategy

1. includes a thesis statement that makes clear what you are recommending or advocating (often using verbs such as *ought, should,* or *must*);
2. defines the problem to which it offers a solution;
3. is based primarily on facts;
4. discusses an issue in human terms;
5. cites respected authorities and organizations as proof; and
6. predicts the results of actions.

4   Examining Support for Thesis Statements

Supply possible backing for each of the following thesis statements based on the type of supporting material indicated. You needn't write complete sentences.

1. The elderly need better care than we are currently providing them. (facts)

   Poor food and sanitary conditions in nursing homes. Not enough services to allow sick elderly to live at home. Not enough useful activities for retired persons to do.

2. The cafeteria in this college needs improvement (or is quite adequate). (facts)

   _____

   _____

   _____

3. You and I need to be treated more as individuals and less as faces in the crowd. (specific example from someone's life)

_____

_____

_____

4. In this era of big government, big business, and computer records available on everyone, Americans must protect their right to privacy. (specific example from someone's life)

_____

_____

_____

5. The air everyone breathes and the water everyone drinks must be protected against polluters. (name of specific authority or type of information authority would give)

_____

_____

_____

6. This country needs to step up the search for cheap, practical sources of solar energy. (prediction of results)

_____

_____

_____

5 Shaping Arguments for the Intended Audiences

Assume you are persuading a neutral or hostile audience to accept each of the following thesis statements. List one or two supporting arguments you would make, as well as one or two opposing arguments you would have to answer.

1. **Thesis:** Academic freedom, the right of every teacher to speak out on any subject without censorship, should be unlimited.

   Audience: teachers

   Supporting argument(s): 1. Since no one knows what the "truth" is, students should be exposed to all viewpoints and be allowed to make up their own minds. 2. Teachers, like all other citizens, have the right to free speech.

   Opposing argument(s): 1. Schools should teach the values of the communities they serve; especially in elementary and high schools, teachers should reinforce the views of the children's parents. 2. Adults easily influence children, who are not sophisticated enough to make up their own minds.

2. **Thesis:** Students should grade instructors on their performance, just as instructors grade students.

   Audience: college administrators

   Supporting argument(s):

   _____

   _____

   _____

   Opposing argument(s):

   _____

   _____

   _____

3. **Thesis:** College education should be free.

   Audience: state legislators

   Supporting argument(s):

   _____

   _____

   _____

   Opposing argument(s):

   _____

   _____

   _____

4. **Thesis:** The use of marijuana should be legalized.

   Audience: police officers

   Supporting argument(s):

   _____

   _____

   _____

   Opposing argument(s):

   _____

   _____

   _____

5. **Thesis:** _____ should be abolished or changed.

   Audience: politicians, young urban professionals, African Americans, Latinos, teachers, or any other group who could influence the change

Supporting argument(s):

_____

_____

_____

Opposing argument(s):

_____

_____

_____

✍ **6   Exploring Your Responses to Counterarguments**

Choose a topic from Exercises 3, 4, or 5 that you would like to make the subject of a persuasive composition, and consider how you would deal with the main objections to your arguments. Then outline or compose rough drafts of your responses.

Composing the Introduction, Body, and Conclusion

The introduction, body, and conclusion of a persuasive composition can differ greatly from the structure of an expository composition—depending on the most effective strategy for revealing your thesis, making the main arguments, and refuting counterarguments.

Planning and Drafting the Introduction.   Remember that when the audience is open to you and your argument, the composition can begin with a straightforward thesis statement and a preview of the main ideas. However, when the audience is suspicious or hostile, begin by showing you are on their side and establishing their trust.

With a hostile audience, decide whether to state your thesis and preview in the introduction or gradually build up to the thesis in a climax organization. You don't have to make this decision immediately, of course. You can draft the introductory paragraph after the arguments and persuasive strategy have taken form.

✍ **7   Identifying Effective Persuasive Strategies**

Label each of the following introductory paragraphs as *effective* or *ineffective* for their audience. Be prepared to explain the reasons for your choices.

Paragraph A.

Audience: a group of lower-middle-class people opposed to welfare

There have been, and will continue to be, isolated cases of welfare fraud. Nevertheless, anyone who seriously believes that most people on welfare are cheating the public is either an idiot or a hypocrite. Everybody, everywhere, cheats. People lie on their income tax returns. Clergy steal from collection boxes. Even President Nixon lied all the way through the Watergate scandal.

Label: _____

Paragraph B.

Audience: parents of juvenile delinquents

No one is in favor of juvenile crime, and surely no parent teaches his or her children to be drug dealers, thieves, pimps, prostitutes, or killers. We as a society, however, must take a stand against teenagers who control the streets in our neighborhoods and terrorize so many decent people. We must get these punks and thugs off the streets and into constructive activities so they can become useful members of our communities.

Label: _____

Paragraph C.

Audience: college seniors

Has it ever occurred to you that you have been wasting your time in college? There is plenty of evidence to support that theory. The time, hard work, and money you have spent so far could have been invested in activities that would already have profited you in far more significant ways. Countless studies, in fact, have shown that it is not education that makes success but hard work, the right kind of personality, and the courage to seize opportunities when they arise.

Label: _____

Paragraph D.

Audience: anti-abortion or pro-life groups

No one could quarrel with someone who opposes murder. And I know that you believe that abortion is murder. It is a serious position, a moral position, and I respect it. I ask only that you respect me enough to hear my case: that individuals must have the opportunity to choose for themselves, based on their own circumstances, beliefs, and religious teaching.

Label: _____

8   Composing an Introductory Paragraph

Return once again to the topic you chose in Exercise 6 and draft an introductory paragraph for a persuasive composition. Be sure to address the needs of the audience (for example, omitting the thesis statement with a hostile audience).

Planning and Drafting the Body.   When arranging the support paragraphs, devise a careful strategy. For example, with a friendly or neutral audience, you can begin with your strongest arguments, supporting each with facts and figures, references to authorities, predictions of the consequences, and so on. With a suspicious or hostile audience, however, you may have to begin with a systematic attack of the counterarguments before introducing your arguments and the support for each. Even then, you may have to move from the most easily accepted argument to the most difficult, from the most familiar argument to the least familiar, or from the simplest to the most complicated.

9   Composing the Body of the Composition

Plan the body of the composition based on the material you have prepared from Exercises 6 and 8. Think of a strategic arrangement that incorporates both your main support arguments and your answers to the objections that neutral or hostile readers might raise. Then draft an informal outline of both arrangements, or simply list the ideas in the most effective order. Be prepared to explain your arrangements.

Planning and Drafting the Conclusion.   With a friendly audience, you can conclude with the standard summary of ideas, along with a call to action. With a hostile audience, however, you may conclude by finally stating your thesis. These decisions also depend on your reason for persuading. For example, at the end of an angry letter to an automobile dealership, you might threaten legal action if your new car isn't fixed satisfactorily.

✍ 10 **Composing the Concluding Paragraph**

Using the material you have developed in Exercises 6, 8, and 9, compose the first draft of a concluding paragraph for the composition. Summarize the main points of your argument and end with a strong appeal for the audience to accept your viewpoint or act in some way. Then draft a complete composition based on your plan.

✍ 11 **Analyzing Your Composition**

Read the composition you composed in Exercise 10 and respond to each of the following questions (or have another person do so). Use the responses as guidelines for revising the composition, and then do the revision.

Revision Guidelines

1. Does the composition define the problem to which it offers a solution? _____
   If not, how should the problem be defined? _____
   _____
   _____
   _____

2. Is the thesis of the argument clear? _____ If the thesis has been omitted or
   wrongly placed, where should it appear? _____
   _____
   _____
   _____

   How should the thesis be stated or clarified? _____
   _____
   _____
   _____

3. Is the reason for persuading apparent? _____ If not, where should the reason
   be stated or made more explicit? _____
   _____
   _____
   _____

   What should be said at that point? _____
   _____
   _____
   _____

4. Are the organization and persuasive strategy effective for their intended audience? _____ If not, what should be revised, eliminated, added, or shifted?

_____

_____

_____

5. Are the persuasive appeals effective? _____ If not, what should be eliminated, revised, or added? (Check the paper for its reliance on facts, discussion of the issue in human terms, citing of authorities and organizations, and predicting of the results of actions.) _____

_____

_____

_____

6. Are transitions lacking or too vague at any point in the composition? _____ If so, what should be added or revised? _____

_____

_____

_____

7. What was the greatest problem in composing this composition? (Ignore this question if the writer experienced no significant problems.) _____

_____

_____

If this problem was not resolved, what should be done? _____

_____

_____

✍ **12 Proofreading and Polishing Your Composition**

After completing the revision, edit the composition, checking for correct spelling and punctuation, complete sentences, and clarity of ideas. Then make a clean copy of the composition and proofread it carefully for errors.

Composing Based on Outside Sources

Assume you are writing an article on abortion for a magazine such as *Harper's, Atlantic,* or *The New Republic,* most of whose readers are college educated. Defend or attack the right of a woman to have an abortion, using relevant information from the list provided below and any other information you choose. Assume also that many in your audience will oppose your argument. (Very few people are neutral on the abortion issue.)

1. in 1800, abortion allowed until "quickening," the movement of fetus in womb during fourth or fifth month—at the time the only certain proof of pregnancy

2. by 1860, abortion illegal in most states because of medical dangers, dropping birthrates, or moral opposition
3. 1973 Supreme Court decision in *Roe v. Wade,* allowing abortion based on woman's right to privacy: in first three months, decision left to woman and her doctor; in second three months, states may intervene to protect woman's health; in last three months, states may deny woman an abortion, since fetus could survive outside womb
4. laws prohibit people from abusing their bodies with drugs
5. in most Protestant and Jewish denominations, the fetus (an unborn child) is considered a potential person, not an actual one
6. when childbirth threatens a woman's life, her safety generally more important than preserving the fetus
7. the Catholic church and many Protestant and Orthodox Jewish sects forbid abortion
8. fertilized egg splits into twins 7 to 14 days after conception
9. 96 percent of abortions performed during first three months of pregnancy
10. of remaining 4 percent of abortions, majority performed to save woman's life or when fetus is deformed
11. 94 percent of the women who died from illegal abortions in New York in 1970 were black or Puerto Rican
12. abortion was always available to wealthy women even when illegal—either by their traveling to places where abortion was legal or by their having legal medical procedures that aborted child (such as dilation and curettage)
13. in most states, abortions cost about one-seventeenth the cost of paying welfare for a child for one year
14. women who have two or more abortions are two to three times more likely to have miscarriages in later pregnancies
15. birth control effectiveness: condom and diaphragm have 15 percent failure rate; birth control pills have very small failure rate
16. study by Dr. Robin Badley: in 1976 twice as many women had repeat abortions than did women before Supreme Court decision. Of those, almost half not practicing birth control before second pregnancy
17. prior to 1973, 500 to 1,000 women died from illegal abortions yearly
18. at four to five weeks, baby in womb has heartbeat; at eight weeks, all limbs and organs formed
19. in 1989 Gallup poll, 61 percent of Americans don't want *Roe v. Wade* overturned
20. in 1989 *Los Angeles Times* poll, a majority of Americans think the choice to abort should be left to women
21. in same poll, most Americans think that abortion is murder
22. in 1990, the number of abortions since *Roe v. Wade* had doubled to 1.6 million a year
23. in 1990, the United States had the highest rate of teenage pregnancy of any developed country

---

ADDITIONAL READING

Strike Out Little League

Robin Roberts

Robin Roberts, a member of major league baseball's Hall of Fame, was one of the finest pitchers of his era. The following article, which appeared in Newsweek *magazine, is a classic example of persuasion.*

(1) In 1939, Little League baseball was organized by Bert and George Bebble and Carl Stotz of Williamsport, Pa. What they had in mind in organizing this kids' baseball

program, I'll never know. But I'm sure they never visualized the monster it would grow into.

(2) At least 25,000 teams, in about 5,000 leagues, compete for a chance to go to the Little League World Series in Williamsport each summer. These leagues are in more than 15 countries, although recently the Little League organization has voted to restrict the competition to teams in the United States. If you judge the success of a program by the number of participants, it would appear that Little League has been a tremendous success. More than 600,000 boys from 8 to 12 are involved. But I say Little League is wrong—and I'll try to explain why.

(3) If I told you and your family that I want you to help me with a project from the middle of May until the end of July, one that would totally disrupt your dinner schedule and pay nothing, you would probably tell me to get lost. That's what Little League does. Mothers or fathers or both spend four or five nights a week taking children to Little League, watching the game, coming home around 8 or 8:30 and sitting down to a late dinner.

(4) These games are played at this hour because the adults are running the programs and this is the only time they have available. These same adults are in most cases unqualified as instructors and do not have the emotional

strength or balance — **stability** to work with children of this age. The dedication and sincerity of these instructors cannot be questioned, but the purpose of this dedication should be. Young-

continued — sters eligible for Little League are of the age when their concentration lasts, at most, for five seconds—and without **sustained** concentration organized athletic programs are a farce.

(5) Most instructors will never understand this. As a result there is a lot of pressure on these young people to do something that is unnatural for their age—so there will always be hollering and tremendous disappointment for most of these players.

inadequate — For acting their age, they are made to feel **incompetent**. This is a basic fault of Little League.

(6) If you watch a Little League game, in most cases the pitchers are the most mature. They throw harder, and if they throw strikes very few batters can hit the ball. Consequently, it makes good baseball sense for most hitters to take the pitch. Don't swing. Hope for a walk. That could be a player's instruction for four years. The fun is

sensible — in hitting the ball; the coach says don't swing. That may be **sound** baseball, but it does nothing to help a young player develop his hitting. What would seem like a basic training ground for baseball often turns out to be a program of negative

slows down — thoughts that only **retards** a young player.

(7) I believe more good young athletes are turned off by the pressure of organized Little League than are helped. Little Leagues have no value as a training ground for baseball fundamentals. The instruction at that age, under the pressure of an organized league program, creates more doubt and eliminates the naturalness that is most important.

(8) If I'm going to criticize such a popular program as Little League, I'd better have some thoughts on what changes I would like to see.

(9) First of all, I wouldn't start any programs until the school year is over. Any young student has enough of a schedule during the school year to keep busy. These programs should be played in the afternoon—with a softball. Kids have a natural fear of a baseball; it hurts when it hits you. A softball is bigger, easier to see and easier to hit. You get to run the bases more and there isn't as much danger of injury if one gets hit with the ball. Boys and girls could play together. Different teams would be chosen every day. The instructors would be young adults home from college, or high-school graduates. The instructor could be the pitcher and the umpire at the same time. These programs could be run on public playgrounds or in schoolyards.

(10) I guarantee that their dinner would be at the same time every night. The fathers could come home after work and relax; most of all, the kids would have a good

time playing ball in a program in which hitting the ball and running the bases are the big things.

(11) When you start talking about young people playing baseball at 13 to 15, you may have something. Organize them a little, but be careful; they are still young. But from 16 and on, work them really hard. Discipline them, organize the leagues, **strive** to win championships, travel all over. Give this age all the time and attention you can.

try hard

(12) I believe Little League has done just the opposite. We've worked hard with the 8- to 12-year-olds. We overorganize them, put them under pressure they can't handle and make playing baseball seem important. When our young people reach 16 they would appreciate the attention and help from the parents, and that's when our present programs almost stop.

(13) The whole idea of Little League baseball is wrong. There are alternatives available for more sensible programs. With the same dedication that has made the Little League such a major part of many of our lives, I'm sure we'll find the answer.

(14) I still don't know what those three gentlemen in Williamsport had in mind when they organized Little League baseball. I'm sure they didn't want parents arguing with their children about kids' games. I'm sure they didn't want to have family meals disrupted for three months every year. I'm sure they didn't want young athletes hurting their arms pitching under pressure at such a young age. I'm sure they didn't want young boys who don't have much athletic ability made to feel that something is wrong with them because they can't play baseball. I'm sure they didn't want a group of coaches drafting the players each year for different teams. I'm sure they didn't want unqualified men working with the young players. I'm sure they didn't realize how normal it is for an 8-year-old boy to be scared of a thrown or batted baseball.

(15) For the life of me, I can't figure out what they had in mind.

Questions for Investigation and Discussion

1. What point is Roberts making in this essay? Who is the audience for his argument, and how would they feel about it? How does Roberts shape the organization and writing style to address these issues?
2. Does Roberts think that motives of the founders of Little League were bad? How does he feel about the motives of the parents involved in the program?
3. What point does Roberts make through the analogy in the third paragraph?
4. What are Roberts's main objections to Little League? What explicit transitional device introduces these objections?
5. What changes to the program does Roberts propose? What explicit transitional device introduces these changes?
6. What is the effect of the repeated sentence structure in the next-to-last paragraph?
7. Compare the first and final paragraphs of the essay. What device is Roberts using, and what is its effect?

SUGGESTED TOPICS FOR WRITING

As this chapter has stressed, you will be most persuasive when writing on topics you care about and know well. Therefore, the first suggestion in the following list, although very general, is intended to spur your thinking about such a topic:

1. Like Robin Roberts, choose a policy or practice that you disagree with, something you feel is wrong or unfair. It could be something in school, in an

organization you belong to, in your dormitory, or in society at large. Then compose a letter to the people most responsible for the policy (the school administration, the leaders of the organization, the governing body of the dormitory, or members of Congress), suggesting or demanding that they change the policy. Don't just criticize the existing policy; recommend specific changes.

For each of the remaining suggestions, assume you are writing a letter, either to the audience specified or to the editor of the college or local newspaper, which will reach a much larger audience.

2. Argue for or against minimum competency tests as a requirement for high school graduation. (*audience:* school administrators)
3. Argue for or against fraternities and sororities. (*audience:* college administrators)
4. Defend or attack the emphasis on sports in colleges or universities. (*audience:* college administrators)
5. Recommend what should or should not be taught in elementary or high schools. (*audience:* students, teachers, parents, or specific interest groups opposing or supporting such matters as sex education, consumer education, or evolution)
6. Defend or attack the widespread use of lawyers in our society. (*audience:* members of the American Bar Association)
7. Argue for or against the use of handguns. (*audience:* members of Congress)

Composing an Essay Examination Answer or an Impromptu Theme

The essay examination and the impromptu theme are inevitable facts of college life. In the classroom, in a limited amount of time, you must plan and write compositions that demonstrate your knowledge and writing ability and earn you high grades—without the aid of notes and without much opportunity to revise your work. Writing well under such conditions is a challenge, but one that you can meet. It requires many of the same invention, organizing, and composing practices you have come to know, combined with an extra measure of thoroughness and discipline. This chapter treats the essay examination and impromptu theme much as earlier chapters have treated other writing tasks:

- ☞ preparing;
- ☞ exploring and organizing your ideas in the examination and impromptu theme;
- ☞ composing the essay or theme; and
- ☞ revising and proofreading your work.

THE ESSAY EXAMINATION AND IMPROMPTU THEME DEFINED

All writing is done for a purpose, and the essay examination is no exception. *Essay* comes from a French word meaning both "to attempt" and "to lead." These meanings apply to the *essay examination,* during which you attempt single- or multiparagraph compositions that convincingly explain and interpret subject matter for a specific audience: your instructor. As with all writing, you must lead to a point—and make it clearly—whether by simply restating or arranging the material in some way or using the material to support your own interpretation. Your purpose, then, is both to inform your instructor of what you know and to persuade him or her that you deserve a high grade. And the composing process you follow in class requires quick organization, quick drafting, and then quick editing and proofreading.

Although an *impromptu theme*—an in-class composition on a topic announced at the time of the writing—doesn't allow for preparation outside of class, it still shares a number of similarities with the essay examination answer. Again, your purpose is to inform and persuade your instructor of your ability to write clearly and thoughtfully. Likewise, the composing process demands the same quick organizing, drafting, editing, and proofreading. Don't be intimidated by the impromptu theme or the essay examination, however, for the process of composing in both cases is actually rather simple. This chapter will guide you through the process, beginning with an explanation of how to prepare for an essay examination.

PREPARING AT HOME FOR AN ESSAY EXAMINATION

Since each answer on an essay examination must be a paragraph or composition, the better prepared and organized you are, the better your grade on the examination will be. However, the first part of that preparation occurs in the invention stage, long before you enter the classroom.

The invention stage begins at home with studying, continues with studying, and ends with studying. You should know the topics you will discuss on the examination as well as any you would write about on your own. You can't bluff your way through; there is simply no substitute for a thorough grasp of the materials.

Many students, however, don't understand how to study for an examination. They think—wrongly—that reviewing their notes and their textbooks is enough. Preparation for the examination should be much more systematic and thorough. The most important steps are outlined next.

Identifying and Then Restating Main Points in Your Own Words. As you read textbooks during the term, *identify* the information you might need to know for the examination. Underline or highlight all of these sections:

- previews, summaries within chapters, and summaries at the ends of chapters, which supply and reinforce the main points of each lesson;
- headings within the text (usually capitalized and in darker print), which outline the chapter for you; and
- main supporting points within the text, which you can find in the topic sentences of most paragraphs.

When studying for the examination later, reread the material you have underlined or highlighted and reread your classroom notes—but don't stop there. Divide the material into smaller, easy-to-remember sections (for example, four or five main points from your text or a page or more of notes). Read each section and then try restating it aloud in your own words. Don't stop trying until you succeed. If you can't explain the material while studying, you certainly won't be able to do so during the examination. As you move from section to section, stop periodically to review the earlier ones and finish only when you can restate all the material at one time. Afterward, have someone test you on the material; or study with someone else and take turns explaining it to each other. (Often the best way to learn a subject is by teaching it.)

Memorizing Key Definitions, Facts, and Figures. Make a list of important facts and definitions and commit them to memory as you study. Citing short quotations or pieces of specific information will show your instructor that you really know your stuff (and, in fact, you do). For example, you can write a sentence that follows this pattern:

Term	Authority	Definition
Macroeconomics,	which John Reilley defines as	"a study of the workings of every sector of the economy," is important for at least three reasons.

An easy way to remember important details you can use to develop an essay examination answer is to devise memory games. In a physics course, for instance, you could memorize the colors of the light spectrum by remembering the name ROY G. BIV, which stands for red, orange, yellow, green, blue, indigo, and violet. Or, in a music course, you could memorize the letters of the treble clef by remembering the sentence, "Every good boy does fine," which stands for E G B D F. Make up your own phrases or sentences to stand for important concepts.

1   Preparing for the Examination by Restating Material

Read each paragraph or section from the following textbook passages several times, and then restate its main points (including definitions of important terms) in your own words. Try not to look back at the passage until you have restated as many points as possible.

Passage A.   (from a psychology textbook)

Paragraph 1:   Although there is much that psychologists do not know about memory, they are fairly well agreed that there are three different memory systems within the overall system of remembering and recalling information: sensory memory, short-term memory, and long-term memory. **Sensory memory** preserves fleeting impressions of sensory stimuli—sights, sounds, smells, and textures—for only a second or two. **Short-term memory** includes recollections of what we have recently perceived; such limited information lasts only up to 20 seconds unless special attention is paid to it or it is reinstated by rehearsal. **Long-term memory** preserves information for retrieval at any later time—up to an entire lifetime. Information in long-term memory constitutes our knowledge about the world.

Restatement: *There are three basic types of memory: (1) sensory memory—very short impressions of sights, sounds, and the like; (2) short-term memory—slightly longer memories of what we see or hear; (3) and long-term memory—those things that we can remember even throughout our lives and that give us our real knowledge of life.*

Paragraph 2:   For examples of these three kinds of memories, imagine that as you are passing a movie theater, you notice a distinctive odor and hear loud sounds from inside (fleeting *sensory memories*). When you get home you decide to check the time of the next show, so you look up the theater's number and then dial the seven digits. Your *short-term memory* holds these digits for a brief period between looking up the number and dialing it; however, you will probably have to look up the number again if the line is busy because your memory of the number will fade very soon unless you work at remembering it. Once you are given the show times, you will have to rely on your *long-term memory* to get you to the theater on time. . . .

Restatement: _____

_____

_____

_____

_____

Paragraph 3: These three memory systems are also thought of as stages in the sequence of processing information. They differ not only in how much information they can hold and how long they can hold it but also in how they process it. Memories that get into long-term storage have passed through the sensory and short-term stages first. In each stage, the information has been processed in ways that made it eligible for getting into the next one. Sense impressions become ideas or images; these, in turn, are organized into patterns that fit into existing networks in our long-term memory.

Restatement: _____

_____

_____

_____

_____

_____

Passage B. (from an introductory business textbook)

1. A *business* is a competitive, profit-seeking organization that produces and sells goods or services.
2. Goods and services are produced by transforming inputs into outputs. The most basic inputs are the factors of production: labor, capital, and natural resources.
3. Profits are calculated by subtracting a firm's costs from the revenues it brings in by selling the goods or services it produces. To earn a profit, a firm must turn inputs into outputs that are worth more than the inputs were worth at the beginning. Profits serve a number of useful functions: they signal the best places to put resources to work, provide incentives to use resources wisely, and screen out mistakes.

Restatement: _____

_____

_____

_____

_____

_____

4. All firms compete both in selling outputs and in buying inputs. A firm that faces no competitors in the marketplace where it sells its outputs is called a *monopoly.* In the real world, pure cases of monopoly are rare, if they exist at all.
5. Successful competition requires a constant search for product improvements and better production techniques. The art of competition is known as *entrepreneurship.* Competition is not limited to business firms. Not-for-profit firms and government agencies also compete, both in buying outputs and in serving clients.
6. Business managers have a duty to obey the law and to fulfill the terms of contracts they enter into. They have a duty to earn as much profit as they can for the owners of their firms. Businesses have responsibilities toward the environment, employees, and consumers.

7. The major responsibility of government toward business and society is to establish a set of rules that minimize conflicts between profits and social responsibility. Ideally, a business would be able to do well only by doing good.

Restatement: _____

_____

_____

_____

_____

_____

Anticipating Questions.   When you study for an examination, study your instructor as well. Most instructors try to be fair, so they ask questions on material they have stressed in class. Many times they even tell you the material they expect you to know or the type of questions they will ask, so anticipate and try to answer those questions as you prepare. Nothing is more reassuring than finding an examination question similar to one you have answered several times the night before.

Most answers to questions use one or more of the methods of development examined in earlier chapters of this book: description, narration, process analysis, cause-effect, comparison-contrast, definition, or classification. Therefore, as part of your preparation, think about the methods of development you would use when writing definitions, drawing comparisons, explaining processes, and so on.

IN SUMMARY

To study for an examination,

1. identify and then restate the main points in your own words;
2. memorize key definitions, facts, and figures; and
3. anticipate questions.

✍ **2 Anticipating Questions on an Examination**

Return to the textbook passages from Exercise 1 and formulate three or four likely questions based on each passage using one of the following methods of development: description, process analysis, cause-effect, comparison-contrast, definition, or classification.

Passage A.

1. *Define and illustrate the three types of memory.* _____

2. _____

3. _____

4. _____

Passage B.

1. *Describe the process of calculating the profits of a business.* _____

2. _____

3. _____

4. _____

COMPOSING AN ESSAY EXAMINATION ANSWER OR IMPROMPTU THEME

As part of your preparation for either the essay examination or impromptu theme, be sure to bring the right equipment with you to class: at least two pens (in case one breaks or runs out of ink), some scratch paper for making notes (get your instructor's permission for this beforehand), and a watch if you can't easily see a clock in the room. If you are well prepared mentally and physically, you should be reasonably confident and relaxed. Keep a clear head so you can read the directions, budget your time, organize your papers, and write, develop, and then briefly revise and edit them.

Preparing to Write

Reading the Directions Carefully.   As soon as you receive the instruction sheet for the exam or topic for the impromptu, don't just jump right in and write. *Stop and read all the directions.* You will learn exactly what to do and how much time you have to do it in. For example, although an exam contains six questions, the directions may tell you to answer only three of them. Many a student has failed an examination or impromptu by ignoring the directions.

Budgeting Your Time.   Then allocate the time you can devote to each answer. Most essay examinations indicate how much each question is worth, so a typical three-part exam might divide its 100-point total in this manner:

Part I	20 points
Part II	40 points
Part III	40 points

In a 50-minute class period, the divisions translate into these percentages and amounts of time:

Part I	20 percent, or 10 minutes
Part II	40 percent, or 20 minutes
Part III	40 percent, or 20 minutes

Stick to those time limits. If you waste 25 minutes answering the first question, which can earn you only 20 points, you then have only 25 minutes—instead of 40 minutes—in which to earn the other 80 points.

On an impromptu theme, plan to give yourself 5 or 10 minutes at the end of the period to read over your paper, revise a few sentences (generally by crossing out and writing above the lines), and edit your work.

Answering the Easiest Question First.   Start with the question you can answer best while overcoming your test-taking jitters. Then you will be better able to answer the other questions.

Taking Organizational Keys from the Question or Topic.   Remember that an essay or impromptu theme is a composition, so it uses the same methods of development you have practiced throughout this book. Therefore, make sure you understand exactly what an essay examination question or impromptu topic is asking you to do. Underline the verbs, since they usually reveal the method of development to follow, and then underline other key words. For example, underline the verbs in the following essay examination question:

> Define the computer terms *bit* and *byte,* and compare the capabilities of a 16-bit byte system with a 32-bit byte system.

Did you underline *define* and *compare?* These familiar verbs suggest the two methods of paragraph development to employ in your answer. But, since the two types of systems apparently have both similarities and differences, a rough outline of your answer would take this form:

I. *Definition of bit and byte.*
II. *Comparisons of 16-bit and 32-bit*
    A. *Similarities*
    B. *Differences*

You will often find equally familiar verbs that reveal the method of development needed to answer other examination questions or develop impromptu theme topics, but not always. In fact, the question or topic sometimes implies rather than states the method of development. Here is a short list of synonyms for the verbs and phrases you already know:

Familiar verb	*Synonyms*
describe	show, indicate, discuss, summarize
narrate	tell, trace the development of (or history of), explain, What happened . . . ?
analyze (a process)	explain, describe, or discuss (especially with phrases the *process of* or *the steps in*), How does ____ work?
compare	show the similarities, draw parallels, make a comparison, How are ____ alike (similar)? What are the similarities between . . . ?
contrast	show the differences, establish the points of difference, How are ____ different? What are the differences between . . . ?
compare and contrast	evaluate, judge, show (explain) the similarities and differences between . . .
define	explain the meaning of, identify, What is the meaning of . . . ?
classify	identify, group, categorize, What are the kinds (types) of . . . ?
illustrate	provide (cite) examples (illustrations, instances) of, exemplify, demonstrate
show causes	explain (trace) the reasons (causes), What created (brought about, produced, gave rise to, led to, determined) . . . ? What are the reasons for . . . ?
show effects	What were the results of (resulted from, sprung from, happened because of) . . . ? trace the results

Planning Your Paper.   You won't have time for extensive revisions of your essay or theme, so you must ensure it is well organized and comes directly to the point. Spend a minute or two structuring your ideas. Jot down or outline the main points you wish to cover—on the back of the exam booklet, on the instruction sheet, or on a piece of scratch paper (provided the instructor allows you to use one). Then follow the order of the notes or outline as you write. Skip this step only when you are sure of your organization and feel confident enough to begin writing immediately.

3   Planning Answers to Essay Questions

For each of the sample essay examination questions, do the following:

1. Underline the key terms in the question (paying special attention to the verbs).
2. Identify the primary method(s) of development you would use in your answer.
3. List the steps you would follow in your answer.

Notice that the first sample question includes classification, since the question implies but does not state the necessity of discussing the separate needs and viewpoints of each country and how those were taken into account in the treaty.

Question A.   Describe the major provisions of the 1978 treaty between the United States and Panama, and explain the reasons for each provision.

Method(s) of development: description, cause-effect, and classification

Steps: 1. description of the major provisions

2. reasons for certain provisions based on the needs and viewpoints of the

Panamanian government

3. reasons for certain provisions based on the needs and viewpoints of the

American government

Question B.   Define an *escrow account,* and explain how it can be used in the purchase of stocks.

Method(s) of development: _____

Steps: _____

_____

_____

_____

Question C.   Describe child-rearing practices in the United States, and compare and contrast them to practices in *two* of the following countries: Japan, Israel, Poland, and Mexico.

Method(s) of development: _____

Steps: _____

_____

_____

_____

Question D.   Identify the primary regions of the brain and explain the function or functions of each.

Method(s) of development: _____

Steps: _____

_____

_____

_____

Question E.   What is a *value added tax* and how does it resemble and differ from a sales tax?

Method(s) of development: _____

Steps: _____

_____

_____

_____

IN SUMMARY

As first steps in preparing your answers to an examination,

1. read the directions for the whole examination carefully;
2. budget your time;
3. choose the easiest question to answer first;
4. follow the directions on each question; and
5. plan your answer.

Composing an Examination Answer or Impromptu Theme

Once you have decided on an approach and an outline to follow in answering a question, you can write the answer itself. Because time is limited, you must handle each step involved efficiently, with virtually no changes of mind or plan.

Beginning with a Thesis Statement and (If Possible) a Preview.   The difference between high and low grades on an essay examination answer or impromptu theme is often the degree to which a writer can make clear the answer's outlines and main ideas. Your instructor must read a great many examination booklets or compositions and probably won't spend much time on each. Therefore, the main points of your answer should almost jump off the page. Remember the advice from Chapter 1 of this book: tell your audience what you are going to say, then say it, and then tell him or her what you have said. Begin your answer with a straightforward thesis statement or topic sentence and include a preview if you can, outlining the main ideas.

Look at the language of the examination question or impromptu topic to guide your composing of the thesis statement and topic sentences. You can often establish your thesis by simply turning an examination question into a statement. Look at the following example:

What were the major stages of the civil rights movement in the 1950s and 1960s?

You can convert the question into a thesis statement or topic sentence by making only a few changes:

> *There were three major stages of the civil rights movement in the 1950s and 1960s.*

Even when the examination question doesn't convert so easily, you can still include much of its language in the opening sentence of your answer. For example, suppose the question above were phrased this way:

Trace the development of the civil rights movement in the 1950s and 1960s.

Your thesis sentence or topic sentence might look like this:

> *The development of the civil rights movement in the 1950s and 1960s can be classified into three stages.*

More often than not, the wording of an examination question supplies you with material for your first sentence.

The language of the impromptu theme topic often provides similar opportunities for restatement as your thesis or topic sentence. Suppose, for example, you encountered this theme topic:

Recently, many people have argued that the number of orphanages in the country should be expanded to replace what they regard as a failed system of placing orphans and troubled children with foster parents. State your opinion on this subject, explain your reasoning, and illustrate your explanations with examples.

You could begin your composition by incorporating much of the language of the theme topic:

> *I do not believe that the number of orphanages in the country should be expanded to replace the system of placing children with foster parents. I do not think that the foster-parent system has failed and I see some real dangers in putting orphans and troubled children in orphanages. Let me explain and illustrate my reasons.*

In-class writing time is precious, however, so don't waste any struggling with a preview. The main ideas will probably occur to you along the way. But if a preview comes quickly to mind, add it to the thesis statement. Not only will the preview clearly outline the answer, but it should impress your instructor with your command of the material. Here is one such preview added to one of the thesis statements you just read:

> The development of the civil rights movement in the 1950s and 1960s can be classified into three stages: (1) early legal challenges to discrimination in the early and mid-1950s, (2) nonviolent protests in the first part of the 1960s, and (3) the Black Power movement of the mid- and late 1960s.

Composing a Topic Sentence for Each Supporting Point.   Whether or not you write a preview for a multi-paragraph essay or theme, you can still reveal its outlines as you go along. Begin each paragraph in the body of your paper with a signpost—that is, a topic sentence—introducing the main point. For example, the three paragraphs in the body of your answer to the question on the civil rights movement could each start with the following topic sentences:

> The first stage of the civil rights movement, which took the form of legal challenges to unjust laws, occurred in the early and mid-1950s.
>
> The second stage, at the beginning of the 1960s, was characterized by nonviolent protests against both unjust laws and unofficial practices of discrimination throughout the South.
>
> The third stage, the Black Power movement, occurred in the mid- and late 1960s.

There is nothing fancy about any of these topic sentences; they repeat much of the language of the preview. Nevertheless, they unmistakably identify each main point of your argument.

In a one-paragraph essay or theme, transitional phrases would replace topic sentences to signal the main points.

> The first stage of the movement, the legal challenge to unjust laws . . .
> The second stage, of nonviolent protest, . . .
> Finally, the Black Power movement . . .

4   Outlining Full Essay Answers

After each of the following questions, write a thesis statement. Then, based on the information supplied as well as your own knowledge of the subject, write several topic sentences introducing main points.

1. In what ways were explorers of the fifteenth and sixteenth centuries like or unlike the early astronauts? [a. great distances traveled; b. danger involved; c. unknown conditions; d. astronauts in communication with technicians on earth]

Thesis statement: *The explorers in the fifteenth and sixteenth centuries resembled the early astronauts in three important ways and differed from them in one important way.*

Topic sentences: *First, both the explorers and astronauts traveled great distances. Second, both took dangerous journeys. Third, both faced unknown conditions on the oceans or in outer space. However, the astronauts had one major advantage over the early explorers: they could communicate with technicians on earth, who supported their efforts.*

2. Identify the three branches of the U.S. government and explain the role of each. [a. legislative branch (Congress): makes laws; b. executive branch (president and cabinet): enforces laws; c. judiciary branch (the courts): interprets laws]

Thesis statement: _____

_____

_____

Topic sentences: _____

_____

_____

_____

_____

_____

_____

3. Contrast the reproduction system of a single-celled organism with that of a mammal. [a. sexual differentiation: none in single-celled organism, male and female in mammals; b. sexual mating: none in single-celled organism; c. birth: single-celled organism duplicates itself, mammal produces embryo/infant]

Thesis statement: _____

_____

_____

Topic sentences: _____

_____

_____

_____

_____

_____

_____

4. Discuss the role of advertising in marketing a new product, using one such product as an example. [a. create consumer awareness; b. establish need for product; c. differentiate product from others]

Thesis statement: _____

_____

_____

Topic sentences: _____

_____

_____

_____

_____

_____

Supporting Topic Sentences with Specific Details and Explanations.   The best in-class papers aren't necessarily the longest ones. Instead, they are the most unified and specific. Don't waste time and words trying to pad your work with irrelevant information or repeated generalizations. Stick to the point and the facts that count. When you stray off the subject or merely repeat yourself, most likely you will annoy rather than impress your instructor.

Here is an example of a good essay answer, based on the first examination question from Exercise 4. It never strays off the point, which it develops specifically.

1. In what ways were explorers of the fifteenth and sixteenth centuries like or unlike the early astronauts?

thesis statement

The explorers in the fifteenth and sixteenth centuries resembled astronauts in three important ways and differed from them in one important way. The similarities involved the relatively great distances both traveled, the dangers in both journeys, and the unknown conditions both faced. The difference involved the ability of the astronauts to communicate with many technicians on earth, who could support their efforts. I'll discuss those similarities and differences below.

First, both the explorers and the astronauts traveled great distances, relative to the times in which they lived. In the fifteenth and sixteenth centuries, the known world was limited to Europe and parts of Asia and Africa. The longest journeys up to that point were only a few hundred miles, and most of those were over level ground or in calm seas. However, Columbus, Magellan, and other early explorers set out to travel thousands of miles in uncharted waters, using ships that were untested for journeys of that length. Similarly, before the astronauts went into space, the distance of journeys was limited to the face of the earth, which the astronauts would orbit many times during their voyages in the air or which they would leave completely as they traveled the quarter of a million miles to the moon.

A second similarity between the explorers and the astronauts is that both encountered many dangers. For the explorers, there were the high seas and storms, the possibility of meeting dangerous animals or hostile natives, and the possibility of running out of food and water far from land. For the astronauts, there were the unknown conditions of outer space, the extreme heat generated by friction as the rocket left and reentered the earth's atmosphere, and the possibility of running out of oxygen in space.

Third, both explorers and astronauts faced unknown conditions on the oceans or in outer space. The explorers took their journeys during a time of almost complete ignorance of the conditions they would face, but during a time when there were many superstitions about those conditions. While most educated people didn't believe in the possibility of sailing off the edge of the earth or being attacked by sea monsters, no one knew for sure what would happen. Furthermore, there were no accurate maps to guide the explorers, who could only estimate the distances involved (which, incidentally, turned out to be completely wrong). No one knew what the climate would be like, what food the explorers would find, or even how long the journeys would take. The astronauts knew more than the explorers: they had very precise measurements of distances to be traveled, the amount of food and oxygen they would need, and so on. Nevertheless, no one knew whether anything would happen to the body during long periods of weightlessness, whether there were objects or even living beings they would encounter in outer space or on the surface of the moon, or whether the surface of the moon would be rock hard or powdery soft. No one knew whether the moon might contain unusual types of bacteria that could be harmful to life forms on earth.

However, the astronauts had one major advantage over the early explorers: they could communicate with technicians on earth, who supported their efforts. These technicians were equipped with the most sophisticated technology available: computers, measuring devices, and so forth. Therefore, when something unexpected did happen, both the astronauts and hundreds of specialists on earth could devise ways of dealing with the problem. On the other hand, the early explorers were on their own, and many of them died or simply disappeared, never to be heard from again.

Editing and Proofreading Your Work.   You know the pain of looking back and criticizing something you have written, and that pain is worse under the pressures of an in-class test. Nevertheless, if you can finish writing the paper before time runs out, force yourself to read it over. You may discover phrases that make no sense or remember things you should have said. Make the changes by crossing out the errors and writing corrections or additions above the lines or in the margins. Instructors expect such revisions and won't penalize you for them, but try to make them legible. If you use a pen with erasable ink, your corrections will be even easier to read.

Of course, proofreading is a luxury you can afford only when you have time to spare. What can you do, though, if time runs out before you finish? Rather than simply turning in your paper, take an extra moment to add a few phrases that out-line the main points you still want to include. This will show the instructor that you studied and could have said more. Many instructors will give full or partial credit for this outline.

IN SUMMARY

When you write an essay examination or impromptu theme,

1. begin with a thesis statement and (if possible) a preview of the main points you will make;
2. write very clear transitions and topic sentences introducing main ideas;
3. develop your ideas with specific details, but don't pad it; and
4. take time to proofread when you finish writing.

5   Composing a Full Response to an Essay Question

Choose one of the examination questions from Exercise 4 and write a full answer to it. Don't worry about getting all the facts right; concentrate on organizing and devel-oping it clearly. Be sure to begin with the thesis statement and add a preview of the main ideas if possible. Use a topic sentence at the beginning of each paragraph in the body of your answer. Don't write for longer than half an hour, and leave yourself five or ten minutes for the analysis and revision.

6   Analyzing Your Work

Now quickly reread the examination answer you composed in Exercise 5 and respond to each of the following questions—not in writing but in your head. Use the re-sponses as guidelines for revising your answer, and then make the revisions above the lines and in the margins.

Revision Guidelines

1. Is the thesis statement clear? _____ If not, how should it be revised?

2. Have you followed a logical method of development? _____ Is its organization clear? _____ If the organization is not clear, where should you add transitional expressions? _____

   _____

3. Are the main ideas supported with details and examples? _____ If not, what details or examples could you add quickly? _____

   _____

   _____

4. Is every sentence clear? _____ If not, what should be revised? _____

_____ After revising your

answer, respond to this question in writing:

5. If you had had more time, what would you have changed? _____

_____

_____

_____

SUGGESTED TOPICS FOR WRITING

Use any of the following examination questions for additional practice in identifying specific instructions, outlining answers, writing thesis statements and topic sentences, or (if you are familiar with the subjects) writing examination answers themselves.

1. What major effects did the Crusades have on religious practices, everyday life, and the relationship between the nobility and serfs during the Middle Ages?
2. Explain the process by which the quadratic equation is derived.
3. Compare the views of the Imperialists with those of the Anti-Imperialists before and after the Spanish-American War of 1898.
4. Define and describe the process of *photosynthesis*.
5. What are the major effects of insufficient sensory stimulation of infants? Describe each.
6. Compare and contrast *common stock* to *preferred stock*.
7. What are the *humanities* and why are they important?

Editing to Improve Grammar and Mechanics

Writing Complete Sentences

Previous units of this text concentrated on the larger concerns of writing—the writing process, revising skills, drafting and revising paragraphs, and drafting and revising compositions. This unit focuses on a smaller division—the sentence itself—and some fundamentals of grammar and punctuation. This initial chapter of Unit Five acquaints you with the role of such fundamentals in paragraphs and compositions and then turns your attention to writing complete sentences. The chapter begins by defining key terms:

- a *sentence fragment;*
- a *clause;*
- the *subject* of a clause;
- *action verbs;* and
- *linking verbs.*

Then the chapter shows you how to identify and correct these matters:

- *simple fragments* (which are missing a subject, verb, or both); and
- more complex fragments formed from *dependent clauses.*

EXAMINING THE ROLE OF GRAMMAR, PUNCTUATION, AND SPELLING IN WRITING

Earlier units in this book encouraged you to develop your own practices for creating paragraphs and compositions: from discovering and planning, to drafting, revising, editing, and proofreading. You should determine what you have to say and then say it clearly, convincingly, and interestingly. You should organize, refine, and polish your writing so readers can concentrate on the content of your ideas, not on how you express (or misexpress) them.

Although this unit addresses the seemingly smaller concerns of grammar and punctuation, these concerns are important for the same reason: so readers may understand and respect your ideas. Errors often call attention to themselves, even suggesting to some readers that you aren't "smart" (although the errors have nothing to do with intelligence). Eliminate the errors, therefore, and be judged on what you have to say—not on what the errors say about you.

The usual time to search for and correct grammatical and mechanical errors is during revisions. Too much concern for these matters in first drafts can slow you down, stifle your ideas, and freeze your creativity. You shouldn't have to stop to check the spelling of every word or the punctuation of every sentence in the heat of composing. Let your writing cool for a while and then return to it with clearer eyes and mind. The better you eventually become at identifying and eliminating errors during revisions, the fewer errors you will make in the early drafts.

THE FRAGMENT DEFINED

Even if you don't know a great deal about grammar, you probably communicate in full sentences most of the time. The reason is simple: A *sentence* makes a complete statement, and complete statements are easily understood. Every sentence includes at least these two important parts, which together are called a *clause:*

◆ *a subject* (someone or something that the sentence discusses); and
◆ *a predicate* (the discussion of the subject, beginning with a *verb*).

Since every sentence must contain a subject and predicate, every sentence must contain a clause. However, as you will soon see, most sentences contain more than one clause.

A *fragment* is an incomplete statement—or only part of a sentence. Most fragments are incomplete clauses; they lack a subject, verb, or both. Some fragments contain a subject and verb but are incomplete statements for reasons you will see later in this chapter.

Fragments are not necessarily incorrect. In the give-and-take of conversations, incomplete statements ("Fine, thanks" or "Right here") may make sense in response to what other people have said. Although not everyone agrees that fragments are permissible in writing, many experienced writers employ them occasionally for emphasis or variety—provided their meaning is clear—but unintentional fragments are likely to confuse or annoy readers and muddle meanings.

These accidental fragments usually occur for two reasons: (1) writers may not feel comfortable discussing their topics, and (2) writers may punctuate (or mispunctuate) by ear. In the first case, writers struggling to express themselves may produce awkward and unnatural expressions—half thoughts in half sentences. In the second case (also when writers grapple with words to fit their ideas), they may hear a pause and write a period—signaling the end of a sentence that hasn't ended.

The first step in eliminating fragments, therefore, is to choose a topic that you feel comfortable discussing and to revise your paper until the sentences flow naturally. You can often hear that flow by reading your papers aloud. The second step is more mechanical—that is, to check each sentence during revisions, identify complete statements, and examine the way you punctuate them. With experience, you will compose complete sentences even in first drafts.

IDENTIFYING COMPLETE CLAUSES

Since every sentence contains at least one complete clause, you should learn to identify the subject and verb of every clause. And since subjects and verbs must go together, you can most easily identify the subject when you look for the verb at the same time.

Identifying Subjects

For a moment, concentrate on the *subject*—the word or words representing someone (who) or something (what) the clause makes a statement about. You usually (but not always) find the subject at or near the beginning of the sentence and before the verb, which tells what the subject does or is.

subject (who or what) + *verb*

For example, the following sentence makes a statement about *Deborah Sampson*. Notice that the verb *was* begins the predicate (or statement about the subject):

Deborah Sampson was a very unusual Revolutionary War heroine.

Underline the subjects at the beginning of each of the following sentences:

1. Miss Sampson was born in Plympton, Massachusetts, on December 17, 1760.
2. She came from a long line of Puritans, all the way back to the *Mayflower*.
3. However, her father had lost all of his money and deserted the family.
4. Deborah and her mother could not survive on their own.
5. Teaching infant school became Deborah's only alternative.

Are these the words and phrases you underlined? Each one reveals an important trait about subjects.

1. <u>Miss Sampson</u> (This subject is a *noun.*)
2. <u>She</u> (This is a *subject pronoun.*)
3. <u>father</u> (The word before this, *her,* is a possessive word and not part of the subject.)
4. <u>Deborah</u> and her <u>mother</u> (These two subjects are joined by *and.*)
5. <u>Teaching</u> (This subject is an *-ing word.*)

IN SUMMARY

The subject of a clause

1. is someone or something that the clause makes a statement about;
2. usually comes at or near the beginning of a clause and before the verb;
3. can be a noun (but not all nouns are subjects);
4. can be a subject pronoun (*I, we, you, he, she, it,* or *they*);
5. cannot be a possessive word (such as *my, our, your, his, her, its,* or *their*) before a noun;
6. can be two or more subjects joined by *and;* and
7. can even be an *-ing word* (even though such a word expresses an action).

1   Identifying Subjects

Underline the subjects of each of the following sentences.

1. <u>Deborah Sampson</u> taught for a short time in an infant school.
2. Nonetheless, she longed to travel and see the world.
3. Freedom was her goal—the kind of freedom only allowed young men.
4. Therefore, she decided upon a bold project.
5. A tailor made her a gentleman's suit.
6. In this disguise, Deborah went to a nearby village and enlisted in the Continental Army under the name of Timothy Thayer.
7. That night, her joyous drinking and loud singing in a tavern caused a scene.
8. Out of embarrassment, she crept back home, hid her man's suit, and resumed her post as a schoolteacher.
9. The authorities found her and made her refund her army pay.

Identifying Action Verbs (or *Does* Verbs)

Now turn your attention to verbs. A *verb* is one or more words coming directly after the subject and beginning the predicate (that is, that statement about the subject). Most verbs express action; they tell what the subject *does*. Verbs usually have a *tense* (past, present, future, and so on), and some verbs are *phrases* (that is, they contain more than one word).

Subject	Verbs
Tom	*works*
	slept
	walked
	is talking
	will go
	could have driven

Thus, one way to identify a verb is to change its tense and see if the clause still makes sense:

Deborah Sampson *served* in the Revolutionary War.
(With the tense of the verb changed, the clause still makes a complete statement: Deborah Sampson *serves* [or *will serve*] in the Revolutionary War.)

If the result sounds like something spoken by a Martian, look for the verb elsewhere in the clause or consider the possibility that the clause is missing the verb.

Deborah Sampson in her *fighting* gear.
(This is an incomplete statement, a sentence fragment. The "tense" of the italicized word cannot be changed: Deborah Sampson in her *fought* [or *will fight*] gear.)

Locate and circle the action verbs that follow the subjects in each sentence here:

1. Deborah's neighbors ridiculed her behavior.
2. They were criticizing her behind her back and to her face.
3. She could not tolerate such embarrassment.
4. Perhaps someone else would have stayed in the village.
5. However, Deborah again dressed herself as a male and left.

Are these the words you circled? (Again, each reveals a trait about action verbs.)

1. (ridiculed) (a *past-tense* verb)
2. (were criticizing) (a *two-word verb phrase*)
3. (could . . . tolerate) (The adverb *not* comes between these words.)
4. (would have stayed) (A *three-word verb phrase*)
5. (dressed . . . and left) (The word *and* joins these two verbs.)

IN SUMMARY

An action verb

1. usually comes after the subject;
2. shows what the subject *does* or *did*;
3. usually has a *tense* (past, present, future, and so forth);
4. can be a *phrase*—more than one word;
5. can have an adverb between the words of the phrase; and
6. can be one of several verbs joined by *and.*

✍ **2   Identifying Subjects and Action Verbs**

Underline the subjects and circle the action verbs in each of the following sentences.

1. A boat captain offered Deborah a job as a waiter.
2. But his friendliness on land changed to harshness at sea.
3. She quit the job and continued northward.
4. Upon her arrival at Bellingham, Massachusetts, she enlisted in the Continental army again and used the first and second names of her brother, Robert Shurtleff Sampson.
5. Her second enlistment began on May 20, 1782.
6. By that time, the war had practically ended.
7. Consequently, new recruits did not expect any combat duty.

Identifying Linking Verbs (or *Is* Verbs)

Some verbs do not express action. Instead, they *link* the subject to words that describe or name the subject in some way. The most important linking verb is *to be* (*is, am, are, was, were*), but there are others: *become, appear, seem, look, smell, taste, feel, sound, remain, get, act*, and *stay*.* Notice how they link a subject to the descriptive words *a doctor, sad, bad,* or *married*.

Subject	Linking verb	Descriptive words
Tom	*is*	
	was	*a doctor/sad.*
	became	
Judith	*appears*	
	seems	
	looks	
	feels	
	sounds	*sad.*
	remained	
	acts	
	stayed	
The soup	*tastes*	*bad.*
	smells	
Tom and Judith	*got*	*married.*

IN SUMMARY

A linking verb

1. begins a statement of what a subject *is* or *was*; and
2. is followed by words that describe the subject.

✍ **3   Identifying Linking Verbs**

Underline the subjects and circle the linking verbs in each of the following sentences. (Not every verb is a linking verb.)

---

* Many of these words are often action verbs, too.

1. Private Deborah's <u>uniform</u> (was) a handsome blue coat with white trimmings.
2. In it, she appeared quite masculine.
3. Her normal female bulges looked flat in their tight corsets.
4. Her movements were quick and strong.
5. Her deep voice sounded manly.
6. Thus, she felt quite confident in her disguise.

4 Composing Sentences with Linking Verbs

Write five sentences with a different linking verb in each, followed by any of these descriptive words or phrases: *weird, wet, a bit strange, embarrassing, impossible to understand, dazzling, uncontrollable, 300 pounds overweight, impressive, challenging, cuddly and affectionate.* You may add additional words to the predicate.

1. _____

2. _____

3. _____

4. _____

5. _____

Identifying the Subject and Verb Together

You have seen that in every sentence *someone* or *something does* something or *is* something. One simple question will help you spot the subject and verb.

> *Who* or *what does* something or *is* something?

Who or *what,* of course, will reveal the subject of the sentence. *Does* or *is* will reveal the verb.

Subject	Verb
Who	does
or	or something?
What	is

5 Completing Sentences with Missing Subjects or Predicates

Supply a subject or a verb, along with any other words needed to form a complete statement in each sentence provided.

1. Blue ice cream _____

2. _____ circled _____

_____

3. A large, slobbering dog _____

_____

4. _____ could have taken _____

_____

5. Grinning broadly, my younger brother _____

and _____

✍ 6 **Composing Complete Sentences**

Write five sentences of your own, and then underline the subjects and circle their verbs.

1. _____

2. _____

3. _____

4. _____

5. _____

ELIMINATING SIMPLE FRAGMENTS

During the final stages of revising and editing your papers, look for and try to eliminate fragments by identifying subjects and verbs of your sentences. If you discover that a subject, verb, or both are missing, supply the words that will make the statement complete.

✍ 7 **Identifying and Eliminating Fragments**

Label each of the following groups of words *F* (for fragment) or *S* (for sentence). Then rewrite each fragment to form a full statement.

___F___ 1. The United States Army fighting the enemy. *The United States Army*
was fighting the enemy.

_____ 2. The battle was bloody. _____

_____

_____ 3. A terrible sight to witness._____

_____ 4. A barrage of cannon fire, an exchange of rifle fire, and a charge of men

on horses. _____

_____

_____ 5. The number of dead and wounded seemed enormous. _____

_____

_____ 6. What a terrible waste of young lives! _____

_____

IDENTIFYING CLAUSES IN COMBINED SENTENCES

Quite often you write *combined sentences*, sentences formed by joining two or more sentences into one. Underline the subject and circle the verb of each clause in the following examples.

1. Deborah Sampson maintained her disguise, but she experienced some diffi-cult moments.
2. Although the soldiers bathed in the river together, she would always remain apart from the others.

Is this what you found?

1. Deborah Sampson (maintained) . . , but she (experienced) . .
2. Although the soldiers (bathed) . . , she (would) always (remain) . . .

In sentence 1, the joining word *but* combines the clauses; in sentence 2, the joining word *although* combines them.

This next example demonstrates another method of combining sentences. Un-derline the subjects and circle the verbs in each of its two clauses.

3. The chief dangers to her masquerade were the medical examinations, which could uncover her secret.

Is this what you underlined and circled?

3. The chief dangers . . . (were) (examinations), which (could uncover) . .

The pronoun *which* combines the two clauses, while relating the information in the second clause to the word *examinations* in the first. *Which* also serves as the sub-ject of the second clause. Two other pronouns—*who* and *that*—can function like *which* in similar combined sentences.

8   Identifying Clauses in Combined Sentences

Underline the subject and circle the verb of each clause in the sentences provided. Then put a box around the word that combines the clauses. One sentence has three clauses.

1. The fighting (continued) after Deborah's enlistment, [and] she (saw) plenty of ac-tion.
2. The British in New York stole food from the farmers, so the farmers com-plained to the American army.
3. The army would raid the British sympathizers who had protected them from harm.
4. Such raids were difficult to stop, for the soldiers needed stolen food to survive.
5. On one of these expeditions, Deborah received several wounds, but she could still conceal the secret of her sex.
6. Although her thigh was pierced by a bullet, which caused her right boot to fill with blood, she pulled the bullet out with a penknife and recovered from the wound.

Chapter 20 further discusses all three methods of sentence combining. Let's focus here only on eliminating fragments that result from improperly used joining words.

ELIMINATING DEPENDENT CLAUSE FRAGMENTS

Identifying Independent Clauses

Some combined sentences contain clauses that can be written as separate sen-tences. Look again, for example, at sentence 1 at the top of this page.

Deborah Sampson maintained her disguise. But she experienced some dif-ficult moments.

Each clause can be a sentence independent of the other, so each clause is called an *independent clause*. In combined sentences, the joining words *and*, *but*, *or*, *nor*, *for*, *so*, and *yet* link independent clauses together.

Identifying Dependent Clauses

Examining *Although, Because, If,* and *When* Clauses.   Not every clause can be a sentence by itself. The first clause from sentence 2 on p. 320 is an incomplete statement, a fragment:

Although the soldiers bathed in the river together.

As a reader, you are probably asking "What happened?" but receive no answer. The second clause of the sentence is absolutely necessary to form a complete statement:

> Although the soldiers bathed in the river together, *she would always remain apart from the others.*

Notice that the second clause is independent; it could stand alone as a sentence.

> She would always remain apart from the others.

Notice, too, that this independent clause can come first or last in the combined sentence.

> Although the soldiers bathed in the river together, *she would always remain apart from the others.*
> She would always remain apart from the others *although the soldiers bathed in the river together.*

Therefore, the clause beginning with the joining word *although* is called a *dependent clause* because it depends on the independent clause to complete its idea. A dependent clause that is not joined to an independent clause will be a sentence fragment.

Some other dependent clause fragments follow. Their joining words—*if, when, because,* and *after*—demand that the clauses be attached to an independent clause.

> *If* I am not busy . . .
> *When* you really enjoy yourself . . .
> *Because* Juan received a scholarship . . .
> *After* we went to the movies . . .

Now make these dependent clause fragments into complete statements:

If I am not busy, _____

When you really enjoy yourself, _____

Because Juan received a scholarship, _____

_____ after we went to the movies.

IN SUMMARY

To eliminate a *when-where-why* dependent clause fragment,

1. look for words such as *although, if, when, after,* and *because* at the beginning of the clause;
2. if the clause is not attached to an independent clause, join it to the preceding or following sentence—whichever one completes the meaning of the statement; and
3. if the preceding or following sentence does not complete the meaning of the statement, add the words that will make it complete.

✍ 9   **Adding Independent Clauses to Sentence Fragments**

Make each of the following dependent clause fragments into a complete sentence by adding an independent clause.

1. Although Deborah Sampson disguised herself a man, *no one in the army* _____ *detected the disguise.*

2. When the Revolutionary War began, _____

   _____

3. _____

   because the British Army had more soldiers and guns.

4. _____

   after Deborah was wounded in battle.

5. Because the Declaration of Independence was signed on July 4, 1776, _____

   _____

✍ 10   **Composing Complete Sentences with Dependent Clauses**

Write four complete sentences of your own that include a dependent clause after the joining word supplied. Be sure that each clause contains its own subject and verb.

1. *Our family always goes downtown on July 4 because the fireworks display is* _____ *spectacular.*

2. Although _____

   _____

3. _____

   if _____

4. When _____

_____

5. _____

because _____

Examining *Which, Who,* and *That* Clauses.   Another type of dependent clause sometimes sneaks its way into people's writing as a fragment. For example, look at part of sentence 3 on p. 320.

Which could uncover her secret.

This clause makes no sense by itself; it is an incomplete statement. The rest of the sentence, which contains an independent clause, has to be reattached.

> The chief dangers to her masquerade were the medical examinations, which could uncover her secret.

Therefore, almost every clause beginning with *which* (or *who* or *that*) is dependent.* It cannot be written as a separate sentence and must be attached to the words that complete its meaning. Here are some further examples of dependent clause fragments:

The woman *who smiled at you . . .*
The issue *that interests me most . . .*
A complete physical examination, *which people over 35 should have each year, . . .*†

Rewrite these fragments as complete sentences:

The woman who smiled at you_____

The issue that interests me most _____

A complete physical examination, which people over 35 should have each year,

_____

IN SUMMARY

To eliminate a *who-which-that* dependent clause fragment,

1. look for words such as *which, that,* or *who* at the beginning of the clause;
2. if the clause is not attached to an independent clause, join it to the preceding sentence that completes the meaning of the statement; and
3. if the preceding sentence does not complete the meaning of the statement, add the words that will make it complete.

* There are a few important exceptions. *Who* and *Which* can begin questions that consist of a single independent clause:
　　Who has joined the armed forces?
　　Which army wears brown uniforms?
And *that,* when it refers to an idea in a previous statement, can also begin an independent clause:
　　The soldiers destroyed crops and other private property. *That behavior* is not permitted under the articles of war.
† Chapter 20 discusses the punctuation of dependent clauses beginning with *who, which,* and *that.*

11 Identifying and Eliminating Dependent Clause Fragments

Label each of the following groups of words *S* (for sentence) or *F* (for fragment). Then add independent clauses to the sentence fragments to form complete sentences.

_F_ 1. Deborah Sampson, who was born to a wealthy family. *Deborah Sampson, who was born to a wealthy family, lived a difficult life as a soldier.*

_F_ 2. Her father lost all of his money in an investment that proved unlucky.

_____

_____

_____ 3. Deborah, who could have remained a teacher. _____

_____

_____ 4. A wound, which punctured her thigh just below the groin, still did not betray her disguise. _____

_____

_____ 5. The army officers who eventually discovered the true identity of their recruit were astonished. _____

_____

12 Composing Complete Sentences with Dependent Clauses

Write four complete sentences of your own that include a dependent clause beginning with the joining word supplied. Be sure that each clause contains its own subject and verb.

1. The Revolutionary War, which began in Massachusetts, *soon spread throughout the 13 colonies.*

2. _____

who _____

3. _____

that _____

4. _____

which _____

5. _____

because _____

IN SUMMARY

> **A dependent clause fragment**
>
> 1. incorrectly ends with a period;
> 2. contains a subject and a verb, but doesn't make a complete statement;
> 3. needs another clause to complete the statement;
> 4. often begins with words such as *if, when, because, after, although;* or
> 5. begins with the words *who, that,* or *which.*

13   Editing a Passage to Eliminate Sentence Fragments

The next passage contains several fragments. Find and eliminate them by following this procedure:

1. Underline the subject(s) and circle the verb(s) in every clause.
2. Make any necessary changes above the lines. These changes can include
   a. supplying the missing subject or a missing (or incomplete) verb;
   b. joining an incomplete sentence to another sentence (usually by removing a period between two sentences); or
   c. eliminating a word from a dependent clause to make the clause independent.

The first correction has been made for you as an example.

The Discovery of Deborah Sampson's Secret

❑   (1) In June 1783, <u>Deborah Sampson</u> was sent with some troops to put down a

who

mutiny of soldiers. (2) ∧ ~~Who~~ were demanding their pay. (3) Here she was

seized by a terrible fever. (4) After she had been carried to a hospital. (5) She

was examined by a doctor. (6) He put his hand on her bosom to feel her pulse.

(7) And found a tight corset compressing her chest. (8) After tearing it off, he

was even more shocked. (9) Not only that the soldier was alive, but that he was

quite obviously a female. (10) The doctor concealed his discovery from every-

one but the nurse. (11) Who helped bring Deborah back to health. (12) When

Deborah left the infirmary. (13) The doctor gave her some words of caution.

(14) He also entrusted her with a letter. (15) Which was addressed to her com-

mander at West Point.

(16) The letter contained the news of his discovery. (17) The good gen-

eral, who was amazed at this information. (18) He summoned Private Deborah to his quarters and addressed her. (19) "Since you have continued in my service and have always been vigilant, vivacious, faithful, and, in many respects, distinguished from your fellows. (20) I would only ask one question. (21) 'Does that martial attire, which now glitters on your body, conceal a female's form?'" (22) As he finished his sentence. (23) Tears came to his eyes, and Deborah fainted.

(24) The general gave Deborah an honorable discharge in October 1783, and she returned to Massachusetts. (25) Still in men's clothing. (26) She spent the winter doing farm work in a village, where she finally assumed the role of a woman once again. (27) Here she met a hard-working farmer, Benjamin Gannett. (28) Who stirred some long suppressed emotions in her heart. (29) She married Gannett on April 7, 1784.

✍ **14 Editing Your Own Work**

Look at a paragraph or composition you are now writing or have previously written and check it carefully for fragments. Begin by underlining each subject and circling each verb, and then check carefully for dependent clauses that are not attached to sentences completing their meanings.

Combining Sentences Through Coordination and Subordination

As Chapter 19 showed, you often combine sentences, for, if you didn't, your writing would sound childish and overly simple. Thus, this chapter teaches you not so much how to combine sentences as how to combine them with sophistication and variety. It examines two types of sentence combining: *coordination* and *subordination*.

The section on coordination demonstrates two ways of combining sentences:

- *coordinating conjunctions*, such as *and* or *but;* and
- the *semicolon* and *conjunctive adverbs*—words that explain the relationship between the combined ideas.

The section on subordination also demonstrates two ways of combining sentences:

- *subordinating conjunctions*, such as *when* or *because;* and
- *relative pronouns*, such as *who, which,* or *that.*

Both sections also explain how to punctuate combined sentences.

COMBINING SENTENCES THROUGH COORDINATION

Even without knowing why, readers recognize that certain words and punctuation marks combine sentences and signal logical relationships between ideas. One such method of sentence combining is through coordination. Master this process so you can send your readers the right signals.

Coordination Defined

Each of the following pairs of italicized words is grammatically equal:

- *he* and *Bill* (two subjects)
- *runs* or *jogs* (two present-tense verbs)
- a *graceful* yet *powerful* animal (two words describing *animal)*
- talked *quickly* but *clearly* (two words describing *talked*)

Grammatically equal structures are said to be *coordinate* (*co* = equal; *ordinate* = level), so *coordination* is the joining of grammatically equal structures.

Joining Independent Clauses with Coordinating Conjunctions

A *conjunction* is a joining word (like a *junction* that joins two roads), and the words that join grammatically equal structures are *coordinating conjunctions.*

327

There are only seven coordinating conjunctions, which you can memorize by remembering the words FAN BOYS:

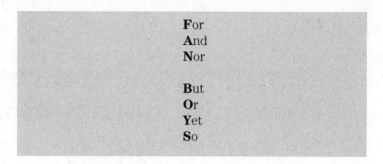

For
And
Nor

But
Or
Yet
So

You may recall from Chapter 19 that every sentence must have at least one subject-and-verb combination called an *independent clause,* which could be a sentence by itself. If you join two sentences with a coordinating conjunction, you create a single sentence (called a *compound sentence*) with two independent clauses, either of which could be a sentence by itself. Notice in the following examples that each conjunction not only joins two clauses but also *explains the relationship between them:*

1. A Sioux (Dakota) Native American boy was born sometime around 1842, *and* he was known at first as Curly. (*And* adds the second clause to the first.)
2. His mother was the sister of Spotted Tail, the chief of the Brule tribe, *but* his father was a medicine man for the Oglala tribe. (*But* contrasts the second clause to the first.)
3. His childhood should have been happy, *yet* tragedy struck when his mother died in the early years of his life. (*Yet* signals an unexpected contrast between the two clauses.)
4. Fortunately, Curly's father married his deceased wife's sister, *or* the infant would have had no one to take care of him. (*Or* presents the second clause as an alternative to the first.)
5. Before he was 12, Curly showed his bravery in killing a buffalo, *so* he received his own horse as a reward. (*So* signals that the second clause is a result of the first.)
6. He soon developed a hatred toward whites, *for* they killed a tribal leader, destroyed Sioux villages, and grabbed Native American land. (*For* signals that the second clause explains the first.)
7. These white men could not anticipate the fierceness of their future opponent, *nor* could they anticipate the fame of the man who would later be known as Crazy Horse. (*Nor* presents the second clause as a negative alternative to the first.)

In many combined sentences, the content of the clauses determines the choice of the conjunction:

Crazy Horse was only a boy, *but* he fought like a man. (The ideas obviously contrast.)

But in other combined sentences, you must determine the logical relationship between the two clauses. Different conjunctions convey different messages:

> Crazy Horse was a ruthless fighter, *and* the white soldiers greatly respected him.
>> (*And* merely joins two somewhat related ideas about the same person.)
>
> Crazy Horse was a ruthless fighter, *so* the white soldiers greatly respected him.
>> (*So* establishes that Crazy Horse's fighting ability caused the soldiers' respect.)
>
> Crazy Horse was a ruthless fighter, *yet* the white soldiers greatly respected him.
>> (*Yet* establishes that the soldiers respected Crazy Horse despite his ruthlessness.)

Notice that in every combined sentence *the coordinating conjunction is preceded by a comma*, which is necessary unless both clauses are very short. But remember: *The coordinating conjunction—not the comma—joins the clauses.*

IN SUMMARY

> **To join two clauses in a compound sentence (method 1),**
>
> 1. place one of the following coordinating conjunctions between the clauses:
>   **for** (to introduce a reason)
>   **and** (to introduce an addition)
>   **nor** (to introduce a negative alternative)
>   **but** (to introduce contrast)
>   **or** (to introduce a choice or alternative)
>   **yet** (to introduce an unexpected contrast)
>   **so** (to introduce a result)
> 2. place a comma before the coordinating conjunction, except when both clauses are very short.

 1   Combining Sentences with Coordinating Conjunctions

Rewrite each of the following pairs of sentences, joining them with a comma and a coordinating conjunction. Use each conjunction (*for, and, nor, but, or, yet, so*) at least once.

1. Soon after the killing of the Sioux leader, Curly had a strange experience. He underwent a Vision Quest in which he dreamed about a horseback rider in a storm. *Soon after the killing of the Sioux leader, Curly had a strange experience, for he underwent a Vision Quest in which he dreamed about a horseback rider in a storm.*

2. The rider had flowing long hair. Drawings of lightning and hail decorated his body. _____

_____

3. The rider was clearly a warrior. He carried no scalps. _____

_____

4. The storm faded. A red-backed hawk flew over the rider's head. _____

_____

5. Curly's father was a medicine man. He understood the meanings of dreams.

_____

_____

6. His father said that the dream predicted his son's future greatness in battle. The boy should now take his father's name, Crazy Horse. _____

_____

7. Four years later, Crazy Horse must have been highly respected. He couldn't have fought with the adults in a battle against the Crow Indians. _____

_____

8. As in his dream, his long hair flowed freely. He wore a red-hawk feather in his headdress. _____

_____

9. His face was painted with a lightning bolt. Hail-like dots adorned his body.

_____

_____

10. Crazy Horse fought bravely in the raid. He was wounded in the leg because, his father said, he had ignored the message of the dream and taken two scalps.

_____

_____

11. Crazy Horse never again took a scalp. He never sustained another wound in battle. (Use *nor*, and adjust the word order of the second sentence.) _____

_____

_____

✍ **2   Forming Combined Sentences Through Coordination**

Complete each of the following compound sentences by adding an independent clause. Be sure that the clause includes both a subject and a verb, not just a verb.

1. Many jobs are available in high-tech industries, *so many students are majoring in fields such as computer programming and engineering.*

2. Well-trained programmers often start at good salaries, but _____

_____

3. Several high-tech companies come to college campuses to recruit employees,

and _____

_____

4. In today's competitive job environment, new workers had better be well pre-

pared, or _____

_____

5. Modern corporations will not tolerate inefficient employees, nor _____

_____

6. One very popular high-tech field is the airline industry, for _____

_____

7. More than half of today's college students want to major in business or high-

tech fields, yet _____

_____

8. Subjects such as literature, history, and the humanities still attract a large

number of students, so _____

_____

3   Composing Your Own Combined Sentences

Write seven compound sentences, using each of the coordinating conjunctions. Be sure that the conjunctions join two full clauses—each containing both a subject and verb: *and, but, or, yet, so, for, nor.*

Eliminating Errors with Coordinating Conjunctions: The Run-on Sentence and Comma-Spliced Sentence

You must join independent clauses with *both* a coordinating conjunction and comma. Otherwise, your combined sentences may not be clear, as in the following examples:

1. I have a very good friend his name is Brad.
2. The answer seemed perfectly obvious to me, it couldn't have been hard for others to see.

◆ In the first sentence, *nothing* joins the two clauses, causing a type of error called a *run-on sentence.*
◆ In the second sentence, only a comma joins the two clauses, causing a type of error called a *comma-spliced sentence.*

Rewrite both sentences to include both a comma and a coordinating conjunction:

1. _____

2. _____

✍ 4 Identifying and Correcting Errors in Coordination

Label each of the following sentences as a comma-spliced (C.S.) sentence or a run-on (R.O.) sentence. Then correctly join each sentence by inserting the proper conjunction (*and, but, or, nor, for, so, yet*) and a comma where necessary.

The Beginnings of War

_C.S._   1. In 1848, gold was discovered in California, ^*and* trouble soon brewed between the American government and Northern Plains Native Americans.

_R.O._   2. Within a year, thousands of wagons clogged the Oregon Trail through South Dakota ^*, so* the Sioux hunting grounds were overrun with fortune hunters called "forty-niners."

_____   3. Garbage, dead animals, and disease fouled the land, white hunters drove away the buffalo.

_____   4. In 1851, the American government and a united council of tribes signed a treaty for the rights to the Oregon Trail, suspicion and bad will between the two parties continued.

_____   5. Then in 1854, a Native American killed a settler's cow, a foolish lieutenant named Grattan and 30 soldiers went looking for the Sioux.

_____   6. A good-natured Indian leader tried to settle the matter the soldiers shot him.

_____   7. A battle broke out, Native Americans killed Grattan and all but one of his men.

_____   8. The following summer, 1300 troops raided a small village, they slaughtered 86 Sioux, including many women and children.

_____   9. Gold was discovered in Montana, the army began building the Bozeman Trail through South Dakota in 1866.

_____ 10. The Oglalas, led by Chief Red Cloud, attacked and killed the entire army, Crazy Horse gained fame for his courage and brilliant battle tactics.

Joining Independent Clauses with Semicolons

If two independent clauses are closely related in meaning, you can combine them with a semicolon (;). Notice that the semicolon is a combination of a period and a comma—sort of a halfway mark between the two. It signals the end of the first clause while joining it to the second.

> A treaty finally resolved the conflict; the army abandoned the Bozeman Trail in exchange for an end to the fighting.
> Red Cloud retired from his warrior role; Crazy Horse was soon to take his place.

The two clauses joined by the semicolon make one sentence, so the first word after the semicolon is not capitalized (unless it is the pronoun *I* or a proper noun).

5   Composing Combined Sentences with a Semicolon

Complete each of the following compound sentences by adding a second independent clause after the semicolon. Use the hints supplied in parentheses if you wish.

1. The Black Hills of South Dakota are famous for their Native American history; *they were home to the Oglala and Brule branches of the Sioux.*

2. Native Americans and whites fought many battles; (whites/most often/ winners) _____

    _____

3. Whites traveled through Native American territory along the Oregon Trail; (for California/hunting for gold) _____

    _____

4. Wagon trains created many problems for the Native Americans; (ruined land/garbage) _____

    _____

5. The army and the Native Americans signed many treaties; (army/ not honoring) _____

    _____

6. To the Northern Plains Native Americans, the buffalo was vitally important; (many uses) _____

    _____

Placing Conjunctive Adverbs After Semicolons.   While the coordinating conjunctions (*for, and, nor, but, or, yet, so*) join two independent clauses, they also explain the relationship between the clauses. A semicolon doesn't explain anything, which is fine if the relationship between clauses is clear, but look at this sentence:

> Crazy Horse was a member of the Sioux Nation; he married a woman from the Cheyenne Nation.

◆ Because the two clauses don't seem logically related, *an explanatory word after the semicolon must establish that relationship:*

> Crazy Horse was a member of the Sioux Nation; *nevertheless,* he married a woman from the Cheyenne Nation.

◆ This explanatory word is called a *conjunctive adverb* because it is partly a conjunction and partly an adverb. It is not a true conjunction that joins the two clauses; the semicolon joins them.

Here are a few more examples of compound sentences with conjunctive adverbs after the semicolons:

> The soft-spoken Crazy Horse gained many friends and followers among the Cheyenne; *consequently,* they supported him in later battles. (*Consequently* shows a result; it is similar in meaning to *so.*)
>
> The whites called the Battle for the Bozeman Trail a massacre; *however,* it was actually a brilliant and overwhelming victory by the Native Americans. (*However* shows contrast; it is similar in meaning to *but.*)

◆ Notice in each example that a comma comes after the conjunctive adverb.

The following list of the most common conjunctive adverbs compares their meanings to those of the coordinating conjunctions:

Conjunctive adverbs	*Coordinating conjunctions*
also, additionally, furthermore, moreover	and
however	but
nevertheless	yet
therefore, consequently	so
instead, otherwise	or

Almost any adverb can follow the semicolon, especially if it establishes a logical relationship between clauses that a coordinating conjunction cannot express. Here are two more examples:

> The famous warrior was given the name Curly at birth; *later,* he took the name Crazy Horse. (*Later* expresses a time relationship.)
>
> The memory of Crazy Horse is greatly respected by the Sioux Nation; *in fact,* members of the nation are constructing an enormous monument to him in South Dakota. (*In fact* shows that the second clause emphasizes and expands on the first.)

In any case, semicolons and conjunctive adverbs are more formal than coordinating conjunctions; they dress up your writing and strongly emphasize logical relationships between ideas. Therefore, use them only occasionally. Don't try to substitute them for every comma in comma-spliced sentences, or your writing will appear stiff and unnatural.

IN SUMMARY

> **To join clauses in a compound sentence (method 2),**
>
> 1. place a semicolon (*;*) between clauses;
> 2. when necessary, use a conjunctive adverb (for example, *however, nevertheless, furthermore,* or *consequently*) after the semicolon to explain the logical relationship, and follow the conjunctive adverb with a comma; and
> 3. when necessary, use another adverb (for example, *later on, sadly, in fact,* or *hesitantly*) after the semicolon to explain the logical relationship, and follow the conjunctive adverb with a comma.

CHAPTER

20

✍ **6   Combining Sentences with Semicolons and Adverbial Conjunctions**

Combine each pair of sentences into one compound sentence. Join them with a semicolon and insert an appropriate conjunctive adverb followed by a comma.

1. Crazy Horse desperately wanted to protect the Black Hills area from white settlers and travelers. He joined in every major battle fought by the Oglala Sioux.

   Crazy Horse desperately wanted to protect the Black Hills area from white settlers and travelers; therefore, he joined in every major battle fought by the Oglala Sioux.

2. Several tribes agreed to a treaty in 1868 that would send them to a reservation in western South Dakota. Crazy Horse, Sitting Bull, and other prominent Native American leaders refused to sign the agreement. _____

   _____

   _____

3. After Red Cloud's retirement, Crazy Horse became warrior chief of the Oglala. He joined with his wife's people, the Cheyenne, in attacks against whites. _____

   _____

   _____

4. Everything in the outer world was changing. The nontreaty Native Americans in the Powder River country of South Dakota and Montana tried to live in the past.

   _____

   _____

   _____

5. The chiefs would not allow the Northern Pacific Railroad to build a new line through the Native American's only remaining buffalo range. The railroad immediately sent a team of a surveyors to the Sioux and Cheyenne lands.

_____

_____

6. The Native Americans were not heavily armed. The surveyors were accompanied by 1500 soldiers, including a lieutenant colonel named George Armstrong Custer. _____

_____

_____

7. The soldiers and Sioux and Cheyenne clashed several times. The surveyors completed their work without a large number of casualties on either side.

_____

_____

8. General Philip Sheridan hated the Native Americans and would not honor the treaty of 1868. He began to construct an army fort in the Black Hills, right in the middle of the Great Sioux Reservation. _____

_____

_____

IN SUMMARY

> **To join two independent clauses, use one of the following methods:**
>
> 1. place a comma and a coordinating conjunction (*for, and, nor, but, or, yet, so*) between the two independent clauses; or
> 2. place a semicolon (*;*) between the two independent clauses. After the semicolon, if necessary, use a conjunctive adverb (for example, *however, therefore, nevertheless*) followed by a comma.

7 Combining Sentences with Conjunctions or Semicolons

Combine each pair of sentences. Achieve sentence variety by using either coordinating conjunctions (*for, and, nor, but, or, yet, so*) or semicolons and conjunctive adverbs (*however, therefore, nevertheless,* and so on), if needed.

1. General Sheridan sent Lieutenant Colonel Custer to the Black Hills in 1874 to find more than a site for a fort. Scientists and geologists also were exploring for gold. *General Sheridan sent Lieutenant Colonel Custer to the Black Hills in 1874 to find more than a site for a fort; scientists and geologists also were exploring for gold.*

2. The Native Americans provided no opposition. Most of them did not even know what was happening until it was all over. _____

_____

3. By then, their last hope of keeping the Black Hills for themselves was doomed. The expedition had indeed found gold. _____

_____

4. Custer, who loved to brag, greatly exaggerated the size of the gold deposits. The whole country was burning with gold fever. _____

_____

5. The U.S. government could not keep its citizens out of Sioux lands. Government officials brought the chiefs to Washington and offered to buy the Black Hills. _____

_____

6. The meeting was unsuccessful. The government tried again the next year.

_____

_____

7. A distinguished group of commissioners arrived at the Sioux Reservation to negotiate. The commissioners came close to being the central figures in a massacre. _____

_____

_____

COMBINING SENTENCES THROUGH SUBORDINATION

Subordination lets you combine sentences and establish logical relationships between clauses that cannot be expressed as well through coordination. Even if readers can't explain why or how, they depend on subordination to help them perceive these relationships.

Subordination Defined

As you will recall from Chapter 19, a dependent clause cannot be a sentence by itself. It depends on and must be joined to an independent clause to complete its meaning. In other words, the dependent clause is *subordinate* (*sub* = lower; *ordinate* = level) to an independent clause.

A sentence that combines a dependent clause with an independent clause is called a *complex sentence,* and you write such sentences for two reasons. First, because two ideas are not always equally important, you should deemphasize the less important one within dependent clauses. Second, you should include complex sentences to add variety and interest to your writing. The remainder of the chapter examines two main types of dependent clauses:

◆ *when-why-where* (adverb) clauses, and
◆ *who-which-what* (adjective, or relative) clauses.

Forming *When-Why-Where* (Adverb) Clauses

Adverbs usually answer the questions *when? why? where?* or *how?* in a sentence.* Therefore, *when-why-where* clauses function as adverbs. Suppose, for example, you want to join these two sentences:

> The commissioners arrived.
> Several armed and angry Native Americans surrounded them with leveled guns.

◆ The coordinating conjunction *and* would suggest that the ideas in both sentences are equally important. However, the second idea is clearly more important than the first. A better solution, therefore, is to place a subordinating conjunction—*when*—at the beginning of the first clause, making it dependent on the second:

> *When* the commissioners arrived, several angry Native Americans suddenly surrounded them with leveled guns.

◆ Now the first clause establishes *when* the action of the second clause occurred. Since the first clause now functions as an adverb, it cannot be a sentence by itself.

Here are two more examples of complex sentences, with the dependent clauses italicized:

> After the Native American leader Little Big Man announced that this was as good a time as any to start a war, . . . (what happened?)
> (What happened?) . . . because cooler heads were able to prevail.

Again, the dependent clauses cannot be sentences by themselves:

> *After the Native American leader Little Big Man announced that this was as good a time as any to start a war,* the U.S. cavalry responded by drawing their guns.
> Bloodshed was avoided *because cooler heads were able to prevail.*

Punctuating Adverb Dependent Clauses.   Adverbs can be moved around in a sentence, so an adverb dependent clause can come first or last. Punctuate dependent clauses according to these rules:

◆ When the dependent clause begins a sentence, it requires a comma (such as in this sentence).
◆ A comma is usually unnecessary when the dependent clause comes last (as in this sentence).

---

* For a definition and discussion of adverbs, see Chapter 15.

◆ You can place a comma before final *although* or *since* clauses if you hear a pause before them.

Here is a list of subordinating conjunctions that express a variety of logical relationships:

When conjunctions:

After	After the play had ended . . .
As	After the audience stood and applauded . . .
Before	Before you leave . . .
Since	Since the semester began . . .
Until	Until I have finished studying . . .
When	When my relatives came to visit . . .
While	While the music was playing . . .
As soon as	As soon as he heard the news . . .

Why conjunctions:

Because	Because the telephone wasn't working . . .
Since	Since most revisions take more than a few minutes. . .

Where conjunctions:

Where	Where the sidewalk ends . . .
Wherever	Wherever you go these days . . .

Contrast/Concession Conjunction:

Although	Although some people prefer violent movies, I cannot tolerate them.
	(*Although* concedes and then contrasts a point—in effect saying "Yes, this is true, but . . .")

Conjunctions Establishing Conditions:

If	If the weather is good, we'll have a cookout.
	(*If* establishes the condition that allows the cookout.)
Unless	Unless it rains, we'll have a cookout.
	(*Unless* establishes the condition that prevents a cookout.)

IN SUMMARY

To join two clauses through subordination (method 1),

1. place a subordinating conjunction (such as *because, where,* or *as*) at the beginning of the less important idea, making it dependent (or subordinate);
2. write the dependent clause either at the beginning or end of the sentence; and
3. place a comma after the dependent clause at the beginning of the sentence, but usually not before a dependent clause at the end of the sentence.

8   Combining Sentences with Subordinating Conjunctions

Join each of the following pairs of clauses into a complex sentence. Place a subordinating conjunction in front of the less important idea. (You may wish to consult the list of subordinating conjunctions.) Insert a comma where necessary.

1. Whatever calmness the government commissioners still possessed must have been shaken. They sat down with Red Cloud to discuss the purchase of the Black Hills. _Whatever calmness the government commissioners still possessed must have been shaken when they sat down with Red Cloud to discuss the purchase of the Black Hills._

2. Red Cloud calmly proposed that $600 million seemed like a fair price. The region was so valuable to the Native Americans and appeared even more valuable to the commissioners. _____

3. The Native Americans had reconsidered their price tag. They suggested that $6 million would be a reasonable offer. _____

4. The commissioners were too intimidated to negotiate. They returned to Washington and angrily recommended teaching the Native Americans a lesson. _____

5. The government immediately ordered all Native Americans to come onto the reservation at once. The demand was both illegal and impossible to comply with. _____

6. Most of the Native Americans could never know about the order. They were spread out all over the Black Hills. _____

7. The deadline came. One small band of Native Americans had come in. _____

8. The other Native Americans were now assumed at war with the government. The Indian Bureau turned the matter over to General Philip Sheridan. _____

9. It was a totally unprovoked war. No Sioux or Cheyenne had ever violated a treaty or actually attacked a U.S. citizen. _____

_____

_____

Eliminating *When-Why-Where* Clause Fragments. As Chapter 19 showed, you can easily mistake a *when-why-where* clause for a sentence, since the clause contains a subject and a verb. Remember, however, that a clause beginning with a subordinating conjunction must be joined to an independent clause.

> *Incorrect:* When General Sheridan planned his strategy of attack. He expected an easy victory.
> *Correct: When General Sheridan planned his strategy of attack,* he expected an easy victory.

> *Incorrect:* However, the Native Americans overwhelmed the army forces. As Crazy Horse led his men into battle with his famous war cry: "Come on, Dakotas; it's a good day to die."
> *Correct:* However, the Native Americans overwhelmed the army forces *as Crazy Horse led his men into battle with his famous war cry: "Come on, Dakotas; it's a good day to die."*

The easiest way to avoid writing *when-why-where* dependent clause fragments is to read your draft aloud as you revise. Most people can hear when one clause should be joined to another. You may also want to review Chapter 19 for additional practice in avoiding such fragments.

Joining Sentences with *Who-Which-That* (Adjective, or Relative) Clauses

Here is how you form the second kind of dependent clause, which begins with *who*, *which*, or *that*. Suppose you wanted to combine these sentences.

> I have always wanted a car.
> It would be both practical and attractive.

Notice that the second sentence begins with the pronoun *it*, which refers to *a car*. You can replace the pronoun with another one, *that*, and create a complex sentence.

> I have always wanted a car *that would be both practical and attractive.*

◆ The pronoun *that*—the subject of the italicized dependent clause—relates the information of the clause back to "a car." Therefore, *that* is called a *relative pronoun*, and the dependent clause is called a *relative clause*. The clause functions as an adjective describing the car.

Here are two more combined sentences with relative clauses:

> Most watches today have an all-quartz movement, *which is very accurate and inexpensive.*
> The man *who just left the store* seemed very nervous.

Notice in the first sentence that the relative pronoun *which* refers to *movement*, and in the second the relative pronoun *who* refers to *man*.

◆ Use *which* or *that* to refer to *things*.

◆ Use *who, that,* or *whom*[*] to refer to people.

Finally, notice that the relative clause comes directly after the noun it describes.

> . . . *movement,* which is very accurate and inexpensive.
> . . . *man* who just left the store . . .

An incorrectly placed relative clause can create confusion.

> *Poor:*   I saw a dress for my wife that would look beautiful. (What would look beautiful, the dress or your wife?)
> *Better:* I saw a dress that would look beautiful on my wife.

IN SUMMARY

> **To join two clauses in a complex sentence (method 2),**
>
> 1. place a relative pronoun (*who, which, that,* or *whom*) at the beginning of the less important clause, making it a relative (or adjective) clause;
> 2. place the relative clause directly after the noun it describes;
> 3. use *who, that,* or *whom* to refer to people; and
> 4. use *which* or *that* to refer to things.

✍ **9   Combining Sentences with Relative Pronouns**

Combine each of the following pairs of sentences by making the second sentence into a relative clause beginning with *who, that,* or *which.* Place the relative clause directly after the noun it describes.

1. After the battle, the man camped out and considered his strategy for the next day. He had led the forces against Crazy Horse. *After the battle, the man who had led his forces against Crazy Horse camped out and considered his strategy for the next day.*

---

[*] Use *whom* when it is an object of a clause.

      O.   S.   V.
   The man whom you met at my house . . .

However, most of the time you can drop *whom* from the clause completely:

   The man (whom) you met at my house was Mr. Rodriguez.

See Chapter 23 for more discussion and practice with *whom.*

2. But Brigadier General George Crook didn't realize he had encountered a new kind of warfare. It differed completely from the Native Americans' charge-and-run tactics of the past. _____

_____

_____

3. The Sioux and Cheyenne nations had developed a new spirit of cooperation and determination. It led to a surprising victory against the stronger enemy.

_____

_____

_____

4. Nevertheless, General Crook devised a strategy. It would send one group of soldiers up the Little Bighorn River and the Seventh Cavalry down and around the river from the south. _____

_____

_____

_____

5. The action had been used successfully many times before. It would trap the hostile Native Americans between the two forces. _____

_____

_____

_____

6. The leader of the Seventh Cavalry had often bragged that his unit could whip all the Native Americans on the plains. He was a hotheaded and arrogant lieutenant colonel named George Armstrong Custer. _____

_____

_____

_____

Punctuating *Who-Which-That* Clauses.   The following sentence with a *who* clause contains no commas:

> The man who died in 1876 along with all of his troops in the Battle of Little Bighorn had earlier gained fame in the Civil War.

If the *who* clause is removed from the sentence, we don't know the identity of the man it discusses:

The man . . . had earlier gained fame in the Civil War.

◆ The *who* clause *identifies the man and is essential to the meaning of the sentence.* Thus, it should not be enclosed in commas.

No Commas:			
Beginning of + sentence	*who/which/that* +	*necessary information* +	remainder of sentence.
The person	who	led the attack	made a grave error.

However, the next sentence presents a different issue.

> Lieutenant Colonel George Armstrong Custer, who at 23 was temporarily promoted to brigadier general during the Civil War, further enhanced his reputation for fearlessness during the Indian Wars.

Notice what happens when the *who* clause is removed:

> Lieutenant Colonel George Armstrong Custer . . . further enhanced his reputation for fearlessness during the Indian Wars.

◆ The clause does not identify the man; his *name* identifies him. *Thus, the information in the clause is not essential. Therefore, the clause should be enclosed in two commas, which function almost like parentheses.*[*]

Commas:			
Beginning of sentence, +	*who/which* +	*extra information,* +	remainder of sentence.
George Custer,	who	acted foolishly,	paid dearly for his headstrong behavior.

Two other pieces of advice should help you determine when to enclose a who-which-that clause in commas:

◆ When in doubt, leave the commas out.
◆ *Never* place commas around a clause beginning with *that.*

IN SUMMARY

To punctuate *who-which-that* (relative) clauses,

1. do not place commas around clauses that identify a person or thing;
2. place two commas around clauses that do not identify a person or thing—in the same location where you would place parentheses. (In general, place two commas around a *who* or *which* clause that follows a capitalized noun.);
3. when in doubt, leave the commas out; and
4. do not place commas around clauses beginning with *that.*

---

[*] Of course, a relative clause at the end of a sentence requires only *one* comma because a period or question mark must be the final punctuation:

> Playing a major role in the fight against the Sioux was Lieutenant Colonel George Armstrong Custer, *who at 23 was temporarily promoted to brigadier general during the Civil War.*

✏️ **10 Adding Punctuation to Relative Clauses**

Underline the relative clauses in the following sentences. Then place commas around the *who-which-that* clauses that need punctuation.

Custer's Last Stand

1. In 1876, Lieutenant Colonel George Armstrong Custer's regiment joined troops <u>who had been directed to locate the Sioux and Cheyenne Native Americans and force them onto reservations.</u>
2. On June 22, as Custer left with the Seventh Cavalry before the remaining troops that would meet him on June 26, Colonel Gibbon called out to him, "Now, Custer, don't be greedy; wait for us."
3. From that point on, Custer ignored (some say arrogantly defied) his orders which were to scout the area thoroughly and follow the route south of the Little Bighorn.
4. Early on June 25, Custer's scouts discovered a Native American village that lay about 15 miles further away in a valley along the Little Bighorn River.
5. Custer who commanded 650 troops expected to find about 1000 warriors in the village, but he was convinced his men could easily encircle and capture them.
6. However, this group which included Crazy Horse, Sitting Bull, and other great leaders was probably the largest gathering of Native American warriors of all time, numbering at least 2000 and as many as 5000.
7. Deciding to attack at once, Custer split his regiment into three divisions which were led by Captain Frederick W. Benteen, Major Marcus A. Reno, and himself.
8. The divisions headed in three directions, so Custer lost contact with his commanders who could not join or rescue him.
9. Reno's troops were badly defeated by the Native Americans and withdrew to the other side of the river. Benteen's group who still had not seen or heard from Custer joined Reno's men there.
10. They asked why Custer had deserted them. The answer to their question came later that day. Scouts reported finding the dead bodies of Custer and all of his 210 men in a field that lay about four miles away.
11. They had probably been killed in fighting that lasted less than an hour.

Eliminating *Who-Which-That* Clause Fragments. As you saw in Chapter 19, people sometimes write *who-which-that* clause fragments.

> The wallet that I lost yesterday . . . (was or did what?)
> . . . which always looks bad when it happens. (What does *which* refer to?)

◆ To eliminate these fragments during revisions, look for the signal words *who, which,* or *that.** If they begin relative clauses that are not attached to nouns they describe, *attach the clauses, or rewrite the fragment completely.*

---

* Be careful, though, for some complete sentences begin with these words. For example, *who* and *which* can begin questions:

> *Who* was that masked man?
> *Which* horse was he riding?

And *that* can begin some statements:

> *That* man was the Lonesome Ranger.
> *That's* his horse, Silverware.

IN SUMMARY

To combine sentences, use one of these methods:

Coordination

1. Method 1

	, for	
	, and	
	, nor	
Independent clause	, but	independent clause.
	, or	
	, yet	
	, for	

Example: Crazy Horse was a great warrior, but he never was a tribal chief.

2. Method 2

	;	
	; also,	
	; additionally,	
	; furthermore,	
	; moreover,	
	; however,	
	; nevertheless,	
Independent clause	; instead,	independent clause.
	; still,	
	; therefore,	
	; consequently,	
	; thus,	
	; then,	
	; otherwise,	

Example: Crazy Horse was a great warrior; *however,* he never was a tribal chief.

Subordination

1. Method 1

After	
Although	
As (soon as)	
Before	
Since	
Until	
When	dependent clause, independent clause.
While	
Because	
Where	
Wherever	
If	
Unless	

	after	
	although	
Independent clause	as (soon as)	dependent clause.
	before	
	since	
	until	

Independent clause	when	dependent clause.
	while	
	because	
	where	
	wherever	
	if	
	unless	

Examples: **Although** Crazy Horse was a great warrior, he never was a tribal chief.
Although Crazy Horse never was a tribal chief, he was a great warrior.

2. Method 2

Independent clause	who	relative clause.
(noun)	which	
	that	
	whom	

Example: **Crazy Horse was a great warrior** *who* **never was a tribal chief.**

CHAPTER

20

✍ 11   Editing a Passage for Errors in Coordination and Subordination

The following passage contains many errors related to joining sentences. Some sentences use inappropriate conjunctions or relative pronouns to join clauses. Some sentences are actually fragments. The passage also contains comma-spliced or run-on sentences and sentences with other punctuation errors, including unnecessary commas or incorrectly used semicolons. Correct each error by writing your changes above the lines.

The Death of Crazy Horse

❑ (1) After they had won the Battle of Little Bighorn / (2) ∧ ~~The~~ *the* Native American

bands split up, and Crazy Horse led his people back to the Rosebud River. (3)

Then General George Crook sent off a new fighting force, which was led by

Colonel Nelson A. Miles to pursue the Cheyenne and Sioux during the coldest

months of the year. (4) As Miles's troops wore the Native Americans down and

starved them out; many of the reservation Native Americans returned to their

agencies. (5) Nevertheless; Crazy Horse, Sitting Bull, and most of the other

nontreaty Native Americans continued their hopeless fight for freedom and in-

dependence. (6) On January 8, 1877, when Crazy Horse and 800 braves at-

tacked Miles in southern Montana. (7) Miles opened fire with cannons and

then counterattacked. (8) The Native Americans withdrew to the hills then

they retreated in a blinding snowstorm.

(9) Finally, General Crook who the Native Americans respected for his integrity proposed a deal. (10) Through Chief Spotted Tail, who served as his emissary, Crook promised Crazy Horse that if he surrendered, his people would have a reservation of their own. (11) The proud warrior agreed because his people were weary and starving, on May 5, 1877, he led his 800 followers into the Red Cloud Agency in northwestern Nebraska.

(12) Although General Crook traveled to Omaha, Chicago, and Washington to secure a reservation for Crazy Horse. (13) He was unable to make good on his promise. (14) Crazy Horse remained at the Red Cloud Agency and married an Oglala woman which bore him a baby daughter. (15) Nevertheless, he soon grew to hate his life behind boundaries, so then his wife fell ill. (16) After some false rumors spread, that he was planning another rebellion, Crazy Horse left with his family for the Spotted Tail Agency on September 4, 1877. (17) When Crook sent some Native American scouts to stop him; Crazy Horse agreed to return, and he entered Camp Robinson the next day.

(18) Although Crazy Horse had surrendered peaceably, soldiers and their Native American helpers took him to a stockade instead of letting him rejoin his own people. (19) What happened as they entered the stockade. (20) That is not entirely clear. (21) The warrior chief apparently realized that he was about to be locked up and tried to break away. (22) According to some accounts, he grabbed a knife from his belt and lunged through the door, however, an army captain seized his left arm and Little Big Man seized his right arm. (23) Swift Bear and other Brule Native American police rushed to help Little Big Man, and one of the soldiers plunged a bayonet into Crazy Horse's abdomen.

(24) The Native Americans, who had helped the soldiers, immediately released Crazy Horse, but the damage had been done. (25) On September 7, 1877, Crazy Horse died, after asking his parents that his heart be returned to

his homeland. (26) They were given his body the following morning, and soon vanished into the hills. (27) To this day, no one knows where the great Oglala warrior lies buried; some white hunters later said that they had seen two elderly Native Americans carrying an empty wooden stretcher. (28) They were near Wounded Knee.

12   Editing Your Own Work

Look at a paragraph or composition you are writing or wrote earlier and check it carefully for correct use of coordination and subordination. Check for run-on sentences, comma-spliced sentences, and fragments. Look at the coordinating conjunctions and subordinating conjunctions to see if each one expresses the appropriate logical relationship between clauses. Check for correct use of semicolons, and see if any combined sentences might be strengthened by the use of semicolons and conjunctive adverbs. Finally, check the relative clauses for correct use of relative pronouns and correct punctuation.

CHAPTER

20

Checking Subject-Verb Agreement and Noun Plurals

As you wrestle with your ideas in early drafts of your writing, you may not pay close attention to word forms, especially word endings. Consequently, your paper may contain errors in subject-verb agreement and the plural forms of nouns that need to be corrected during revisions. This chapter familiarizes you with ways to make those corrections. After defining *subject-verb agreement,* the chapter explores the following matters:

- verb agreement with *noun subjects;*
- verb agreement with *pronoun subjects;* and
- verb agreement with *compound subjects.*

It then examines subject-verb agreement with three important present tense verbs:

- *to be;*
- *to do;* and
- *to have.*

Finally, the chapter addresses special problems in subject-verb agreement:

- collective nouns;
- sentences beginning with *there;*
- phrases between the subject and verb; and
- phrases representing a part of the subject.

SUBJECT-VERB AGREEMENT DEFINED

Subject-verb agreement primarily applies to the *present tense,* * which discusses habitual states or actions or actions that are happening now. Almost every present tense verb has two different forms—one without final *-s* and one with final *-s.* The following list provides some examples:

---

* It occurs in the past tense with only one verb, *to be.* See Chapter 22 for further discussion of the past tense forms of this verb.

make	makes
buy	buys
have	has
fly	flies
go	goes
walk	walks
do	does
display	displays
communicate	communicates

The form of the verb changes according to the subject of the sentence.

I work part time in a bank.
My friend works there, too.

CHAPTER

21

These sentences probably look fine to you; they meet your expectations about the forms of words you see in edited written English. When the subject is *My friend,* the verb form is *works*—with an -s ending. When the subject is *I,* the verb form is *work.*

◆ Thus, the *subject and verb agree* when the forms of the subject and verb are the ones most readers would expect to find together in written English.

Now look at another sentence:

One of the students *are* failing.

According to the sentence, how many students are failing? The sentence probably confuses you for a moment because the verb *are* agrees with the wrong word, *students.* Correct subject-verb agreement clears up the problem:

One of the students *is* failing.

You want readers to pay full attention to the *ideas* you write; you don't want them distracted by confusing or unexpected word forms. During revisions, then, check your subjects and verbs for agreement. With practice, you will make fewer agreement errors in first drafts.

FORMING AGREEMENT WITH NOUN SUBJECTS

The form of the verb depends on the subject, which can be singular or plural. *Singular,* of course, means only one, so nouns that name only one person or thing are singular. A singular noun almost never ends in -s,* but the present tense verb after every singular noun subject does end in -s.

---

* Only a few singular nouns end in -s, such as *bus, alumnus,* and *news.* A few more end in -ss: for example, *mess, fuss,* or *stress.* But these are exceptions.

> *Mr. Wilson* teaches geography.
> *My friend* plays bass guitar in a rock group.
> *The rule* applies to everyone.
> *Exercise* builds strong bodies.

Plural means more than one, and you probably know that most plural nouns end in *-s* or *-es* (*cars, birds, cities, potatoes, knives,* and thousand-dollar *bills*). However, the verb after a plural noun subject never ends in *-s.*

> *The Wilsons* both *teach* geography.
> *My friends play* guitar in a rock group.
> *The rules apply* to everyone.
> Certain *exercises build* strong leg muscles.

Applying the Rule of One *-s*

Plural verbs never end in *-s,* but most plural nouns do. Therefore, if the noun subject ends in *-s,* the verb will usually not. Likewise, if the verb ends in *-s,* the noun subject normally will not.

IN SUMMARY

> **The rule of one *-s* for nouns and verbs**
>
> *Singular:* noun (no *-s*) + verb with *-s*
> (The *boy plays* in the park after school.)
> *Plural:* noun with *-s* + verb (no *-s*)
> (The *boys play* in the park after school.)

1   Establishing Verb Agreement

Write the appropriate present tense form of the verb supplied in each of the following sentences.

A Mouthful of Crocodiles

❑ (1) A popular myth (hold) _____*holds*_____ that crocodiles (eat) _____ their young. (2) Although incorrect, the belief (come) _____ from the unusual practices of the mother crocodile. (3) After the young crocs (hatch) _____, their mother gently (take) _____ them into her huge jaw and (shake) _____ them down into a special pouch in the floor of her mouth. (4) The mother (create) _____ a strange and misleading picture with such a mouthful. (5) Perhaps 18 baby crocodiles (peer) _____ out from between her teeth as she (travel)

_____ along. (6) Mommy finally (carry) _____ them

down to the water, where the babies (try) _____ out their swim-

ming skills.

Forming Irregular Noun Plurals

A few nouns do not form their plurals in the regular way. The following is a list of some of the most important irregular nouns:

Singular form	*Change in the plural form*
child	children (not childrens)
man	men (not mens)
woman	women (not womens)
foot	feet (not feets)
medium	media
person	people (not peoples)

Singular form	*No change in the plural form*
deer	deer
fish	fish (or fishes)

CHAPTER 21

✐ **2   Editing to Correct Noun-Plural Errors**

Some of the noun-plural forms in the following passage are missing or incorrect. (Not every noun is the subject of a sentence.) Find and correct the errors.

The World's Best Dad

❑   (1) The temperature during the long Antarctic winter plunges as low as −80
degree∧ Fahrenheit. (2) Under these condition, only an amazing—even
heroic—combination of patience and acrobatics allows the emperor penguins
to hatch their eggs. (3) The emperors are magnificent bird, with feather covering most of their bodies. (4) The female lays a single egg in midwinter and immediately leaves on a long fishing trip, leaving her mate in charge of the egg.
(5) The egg would freeze almost immediately in the bitter cold if it touched the
ground. (6) To protect it, the male stands for 60 day on one foot, holding the
egg next to his warm underbelly with the other foot. (7) Occasionally, he
switches feets, but throughout this period he eats nothing at all. (8) Finally,
when the chick is about ready to hatch, the female returns to take over the
child rearing, and the famished male waddles off to the ocean to find some
fishes of his own.

FORMING AGREEMENT WITH PRONOUN SUBJECTS

Pronouns substitute for nouns, and only the third-person singular subject pronouns (*he, she, it*) agree with verbs that end in *-s*.

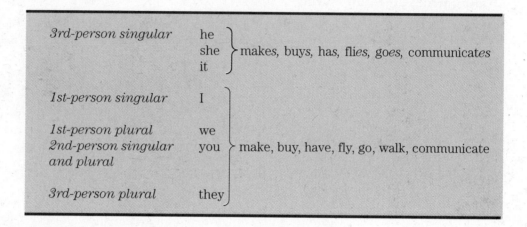

3rd-person singular	he she it	makes, buys, has, flies, goes, communicates
1st-person singular	I	
1st-person plural 2nd-person singular and plural	we you	make, buy, have, fly, go, walk, communicate
3rd-person plural	they	

3   Establishing Verb Agreement with Pronoun Subjects

Fill in the appropriate present tense verb form after each pronoun.

1. She (go) _____*goes*_____ to Hawaii every winter for a month.

2. Therefore, I (admire) _____, (respect) _____, and
    (despise) _____ her greatly.

3. You (need) _____ only two things for a trip to Hawaii: a lot of
    suntan lotion and a lot of money.

4. It (sound) _____ like a wonderful place to visit.

5. We (wish) _____ you luck with raising the funds to get there.

6. Why not check with John? He (make) _____ money the old-
    fashioned way; he (print) _____ it in his basement.

FORMING AGREEMENT WITH COMPOUND SUBJECTS

A second kind of plural subject is the *compound subject*—two or more subjects combined by *and*, whether nouns, pronouns, or nouns and pronouns. Here are some examples:

> John *and* I
> a man *and* his dog
> the plants *and* animals
> Sam, Pam, Bill, Will, Judy, *and* Trudy

These subjects always take a present tense verb form without -s because they are plural:

> John and I *study* for examinations together.
> The plants and the animals *look* beautiful.

The rule of *and* for nouns and pronouns

subject and subject = verb without -s

🖋 **4   Establishing Verb Agreement with Compound Subjects**

Write the appropriate present tense form of the verb supplied in each of the following sentences.

Facts About Aging

❑ (1) Instead of occurring suddenly when someone (reach) <u>reaches</u> 60 or 70, old age and its complications (come) _____ about in gradual steps. (2) As adults, you and I (die) _____ a little every day. (3) Most tissues, organs, and physical processes (begin) _____ to deteriorate when we (become) _____ about 25 years old, but these body parts and functions (decline) _____ at different rates. (4) The blood that (flow) _____ to the brain of a 75-year-old is 20 percent less than the amount the same person had at age 30. (5) Furthermore, the older person's brain weight (equal) _____ only 56 percent of what it was. (6) During short bursts of activity, old people (work) _____ at less than half of their former maximum speed. (7) An elderly man and a woman (lose) _____ almost two-thirds of the taste buds they had at age 30. (8) Why he and she (experience) _____ such a dramatic decline in the ability to taste is a mystery.

In present tense subject-verb agreement,

1. only the pronouns *he, she,* and *it* and all singular nouns agree with verbs ending in -s;
2. all other subject pronouns (*I, we, you,* and *they*) and all plural nouns agree with verbs without -s endings;
3. almost all plural nouns end in -s, but the verbs that agree with them do not; very few singular nouns end in -s, but the verbs that agree with them do; and
4. all compound subjects (two or more subjects joined by *and*) are plural and take verbs without -s endings.

CHAPTER
21

FORMING AGREEMENT WITH IRREGULAR PRESENT TENSE VERBS

The verbs *to be, to do,* and *to have* deserve special attention for two reasons: (1) you use them more often than most verbs, and (2) you use them as *helping verbs* in verb phrases—that is, as the verbs that come before main verbs. The following list provides examples of such verb phrases:

To be	*To do*	*To have*
is going	*doesn't* go	*has* gone
are talking	*don't* talk	*have* talked
am known	*does* know	*have* known.

Forming Agreement with *To Be*

To be is the only English verb with three present tense forms—*am, is,* and *are.* The form used depends on the subject with which it agrees.

Subject	Verb	Contractions
I	*am*	
he, she, it (or singular noun)	*is*	*he's, she's, it's*
we, you, they (or plural noun)	*are*	*we're, you're, they're*

Because *to be* is the most common verb in English, you will find it everywhere in your writing. It always precedes a verb ending in *-ing* in a verb phrase.

I *am counting* my millions right now.
My friend Lionel *is taking* a vacation in Pago Pago for a month.

To be often serves as a linking verb. (See Chapter 19.)

Those spotted green sandwiches *are* very appetizing.
The university *is* a great fountain of knowledge where many students come to drink.

Note that, in contractions of *to be,* the apostrophe replaces the letter that has been omitted.*

✏️ 5   Choosing Appropriate Forms of *To Be*

Write the present tense form of *to be* in each sentence.

---

* Don't confuse the apostrophes in these contractions with the apostrophes used to form possessive nouns. See Chapter 24 for more on apostrophes.

A Belly Full of Information

❑   (1) Your stomach growls because a lot of physiological activity _____*is*_____ taking place. (2) As you _____ eating, drinking, or swallowing saliva, you also
swallow gas. (3) Imagine that your stomach and intestines _____ like a
front-loading washing machine in a laundromat. (4) Instead of clothes, water,
and detergent whooshing around, there _____ solid foods, liquids from
your diet, water, digestive fluids, and gas constantly churning and contracting.
(5) This churning _____ important because it kneads and mixes the food
and enzymes as part of the digestive process. (6) But just as it _____ necessary to eliminate excess water and suds from the washer, the food left in
your stomach _____ moved into the intestines, where it _____ made
ready for disposal. (7) As the bubbles of gas and liquids _____ mixed together and then pushed out of the stomach, the result _____ gurgling,
splashing, and squeaking of all kinds—which you describe as "growling." (8)
The stomach seems to growl more when you _____ hungry because the
muscular activity in the abdomen increases as it anticipates a new meal.

CHAPTER
21

Tips on Avoiding Errors with *To Be* Contractions

1. Don't leave off the -*'s*, the -*'m*, or the -*'re* in contractions. If during proof-
    reading you see "*He* working" or "*She* a good teacher," change it to "*He's*
    working" or "*She's* a good teacher."
2. You can confuse *we're* with *were*, *you're* with *your*, *it's* with *its*, and
    they're with *their* and *there*. Since these words sound or look similar, you
    may write one when you mean the other.* Only the contraction forms
    contain apostrophes.

✐ **6   Editing for Errors in *To Be* Forms**

Many—but not all—of the following sentences contain errors in the use of *to be.* In
some sentences *to be* is missing. In other sentences, the form of *to be* does not agree
with its subject. And in still other sentences, there is an incorrect contraction using *to
be.* Correct each error above the line.

The Bear Facts

    We're
1. ∧~~Were~~ used to thinking of humans as left-handed or right-handed, but we don't
    think of animals in those terms.

2. Strangely enough, however, all polar bears is left-handed.

3. When their attacked, they use only their left paws to strike out or defend
    themselves.

---

* See Chapter 26 for more practice with these look-alike and sound-alike words.

4. A fully grown polar bear weighs as much as 1000 pounds, and its often 9 feet tall.

5. Very high concentrations of vitamin A is in the livers of polar bears.

6. In fact, all the members of a nineteenth-century Arctic expedition we're poisoned by eating the liver of a polar bear they'd killed.

7. The koala bear and the panda is not members of the bear family.

8. The panda is actually a type of giant raccoon.

9. The koala is more closely related to the kangaroo, since there both marsupials (animals that carry their young in pouches).

Forming Agreement with *To Do*

Aside from functioning as a main verb, *to do (do, does)* serves as the helping verb in most present tense questions or negative statements:

> *Do* you like pets?   I *don't* want two elephants—only one!
> *Does* she ever drive?   She *doesn't* drive a car, but she has a pilot's license.

Here are the affirmative and negative forms of *to do*:

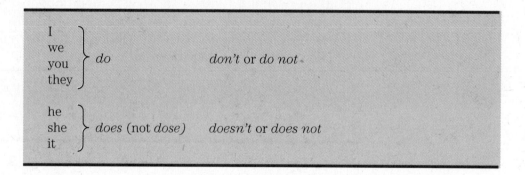

| I
we
you
they | *do* | *don't* or *do not* |
| he
she
it | *does* (not *dose*) | *doesn't* or *does not* |

Doesn't creates special problems. Many people say and write "He don't" instead of "He doesn't." If you are one of those people, proofread your papers carefully to find and correct the error.

7   Choosing Appropriate Forms of *To Do*

Supply the appropriate present tense form of *to do* in each blank space below.

The World's Most Boring Animals

❏   (1) Sloths may be the laziest land animals in the world; they

_____*do*_____n't do anything fast—but there isn't very much that they do

anyway. (2) For all intents and purposes, a sloth _____n't have any

reflexes. (3) Sloths _____n't even flinch, let alone jump, at a sudden loud noise. (4) A sloth that falls from a tree _____n't try to stand up; instead, it sags to the ground like a bag of flour.

(5) Moreover, only a female sloth can maintain a constant body temperature, and it _____ that only when pregnant. (6) The animals can turn their breathing on and off at will, and they _____n't suffer any ill effects. (7) Even the food sloths eat _____n't get digested fast. The process takes at least two weeks. (8) _____ this animal sound like the kind you would want to invite to a dinner party?

Forming Agreement with *To Have*

In addition to functioning as a simple verb, *to have* often acts as a helping verb.

> They *have fulfilled* all the certification requirements to become lifeguards.
> Albert *has eaten* the whole pizza.

Here are the present tense affirmative forms, contractions, and negative forms of *to have*:

Affirmative	*Contraction*	*Negative*
I we you they } *have*	I've we've you've they've	I we you they } *have not, haven't,* or *do not have*
he she it } *has*	he's she's it's*	he she it } *has not, hasn't,* or *does not have*

8   Choosing Appropriate Forms of *To Have*

Fill in the appropriate present tense form (affirmative or negative) of *to have* in each of the following sentences.

A Few Swift Facts

❏   (1) The European bird called the *swift* _____*has*_____ a number of unique and extraordinary behaviors. (2) It feeds exclusively on flying insects and _____ never been seen on land or in trees except when nesting.

(3) Apparently it also _____ real talent as a weather predictor.

(4) The birds _____ been observed flying hundreds of miles to the

---

* The contraction for *has* (*'s*) is the same as the contraction for *is*.

north or south well in advance of an approaching cyclone. (5) Swifts know that they _____n't a chance of finding insects in the air during the storm. (6) Meanwhile, their young, who _____ to be left in the nest, immediately hibernate until their parents return.

ADDRESSING SPECIAL PROBLEMS WITH SUBJECT-VERB AGREEMENT

Forming Agreement with Collective Nouns

Collective nouns represent a group of two or more persons, things, or ideas.

class	family	Sears, Roebuck, and Company
audience	team	jury

Deciding whether a collective noun is singular or plural is a problem for even the most experienced writers. The following rules govern the use of collective nouns.

Rule 1. Most of the time, collective nouns are singular when they represent the whole group of persons, things, or ideas acting together.

> My *family* (together) *has* a reunion each year in May.
> The baseball *team* (together) *practices* at 3 o'clock.

There is an exception to this rule. Collective nouns are plural when they represent a group of people, things, or ideas acting individually.

> The *family* (individual members) *are* seated around the table.
> The baseball *team* (individual members) *come* from all over the country.

However, this situation doesn't occur very often. When it does, the best way to treat it is to rewrite the sentences with plural subjects.

> The *members* of the family *are* seated around the table.
> The *players* on the baseball team *come* from all over the country.

Rule 2. A few collective nouns are always plural.

> The *police patrol* this area regularly. (Others in this category include *the faculty* and *the staff.*)
> The Atlanta *Braves* usually *have* a strong team. (All team names are plural, even if they do not end in -*s*, such as the Chicago *Sting.*)
> The *French are* proud people. (All nationalities are treated as plural.)

✍ **9   Establishing Verb Agreement with Collective Nouns**

Write the appropriate present tense form of each verb in parentheses.

1. The jury (have) ___*has*___ reached a decision.

2. The class (meet) _____ at 9 o'clock.

3. The police (come) _____ into this area often.

4. The Dutch (produce) _____ beautiful tulips, delicious chocolate, and wonderful beer.

5. The Chicago Bulls (win) _____ most of their games year in and year out.

6. The audience (be) _____ enjoying the play.

Determining Agreement After *There Is* and *There Are* Sentence Openers

When you begin a sentence with *there*, look at the subject following the verb before you decide whether to use *are* or *is*. If the subject is singular, use *is*. If the subject is plural, use *are*.

> There *is a player* on the basketball team who is 7 feet tall.
> There *are three players who are over 6'8".*
> There *are a center, two forwards, and two guards* on every team.

Notice in the last example that *and* joins more than one subject, so the verb is *are*.

Try not to overuse *there is* or *there are*, for they waste words and bury grammatical subjects in the middle of sentences. You can usually revise a sentence to omit these constructions.

> *Poor:*   There *are* some students in Professor Wilson's class *who never understand* his lectures.
> *Better:*   Some students in Professor Wilson's class *never understand* his lectures.

IN SUMMARY

To determine subject-verb agreement with sentences beginning with *there*, choose the verb form that agrees with the subject appearing *after* the verb.

1. *There is* + singular subject.
2. *There are* + plural subject.

✍ **10   Establishing Verb Agreement in *There Is/Are* Constructions**

Complete each of the following sentences with the appropriate present tense form of *to be* (*is* or *are*).

CHAPTER

21

The Problems with Wine Buying

☐ (1) Although many wealthy Americans buy wine, there _____*are*_____ very few sales of wine to people of moderate incomes (2) There _____ two explanations why average people won't buy much wine except wine coolers.

(3) These people themselves would probably say there _____ only one reason: Wine is too expensive. Yet these same people are quite willing to spend $1.50 for a bottle of imported water that tastes remarkably like tap water. (4) There _____ too much rigmarole surrounding wine, and the average person is afraid of it all. (5) At a French restaurant, for example, there _____ all those names of wine to (mis)pronounce and all that uncertainty about which wines go with which foods. (6) "Was that white wine with fish? And what do we order if I get steak and she orders fish—pink wine? Come to think about it, there _____ a pink wine, _____n't there?" (7) And then there _____ the moment when the server pours the wine in the patron's glass for inspection. The embarrassed customer, who can't even pretend to be judging the quality of the wine, is trying to avoid looking like an idiot.

Determining Agreement When Phrases Separate the Subject and the Verb

When a phrase comes between the subject and the verb, you may accidentally make the verb agree with a noun or pronoun in the phrase instead of the actual subject. Most of these phrases begin with a preposition—a small word such as *in, with, to, of,* or *from.* For example, what verb form is required in the following sentences?

The box of crayons (is/are) on the table.
The answers to the question (is/are) not difficult.

You should have chosen (1) *is* and (2) *are.* With the prepositional phrases removed, the sentences appear like this:

The box . . . is on the table.
The answers . . . are not difficult.

When you aren't sure of the verb form as you proofread, try drawing a line in pencil through the prepositional phrase so you can locate the true subject of the sentence.

The box ~~of crayons~~ is on the table.
The answers ~~to the question~~ are not difficult.

Cross out the prepositional phrases in the following sentences and then circle the correct verb form:

The top and bottom of the carton (have/has) to be handled carefully.
A female dog with seven puppies (make/makes) quite a mess.

Were these your answers?

> The top and bottom . . . (have) to be handled carefully.
> A female dog . . . (makes) quite a mess.

IN SUMMARY

> **To determine subject-verb agreement when a phrase comes between the subject and verb,**
>
> 1. draw a line in pencil through the phrase; and
> 2. choose the verb form that agrees with the subject.

CHAPTER

21

✍ **11   Determining Subject-Verb Agreement**

Draw a line through the prepositional phrase after the subject of each sentence and then fill in an appropriate present tense verb.

Dust and Skin

❑   (1) Pieces (make) ___*make*___ up 70 percent of common household dust, according to Dr. Raymond Clark of London's Clinical Research Centre. (2) Dr. Clark claims that 5,000 flakes of skin (be) _____ shed by the human body every minute. (3) In all, 40 pounds of skin (be) _____ shed during the average person's lifetime. (4) The entire outside layer of our bodies (be) _____ replaced every 7 to 10 days. (5) The pieces of discarded skin from this shedding action (be) _____ small enough to pass through most forms of clothing. (6) Columns of rising hot air (surround) _____ the body, (lift) _____ these tiny particles above a person's head, and (create) _____ household dust.

Determining Agreement When *of* Phrases Precede the Subject

Certain expressions with *of* are important exceptions to the rule about prepositional phrases.

> *Some of the glasses . . .*
> *All of the material . . .*
> *Most of the students . . .*

These sentences discuss *a part of the subject* (or even all of it), so the subject-verb agreement depends on whether the true subject is singular or plural.

Part markers	True subject	Verb	
Some of	*the glasses*	*are*	broken.
All of	*the material*	*is*	here.
Most of	*the students*	*are doing*	very well.

IN SUMMARY

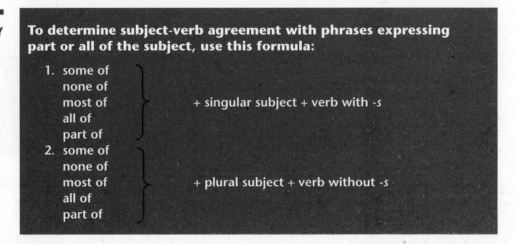

To determine subject-verb agreement with phrases expressing part or all of the subject, use this formula:

1. some of
   none of
   most of
   all of
   part of
   } + singular subject + verb with -s

2. some of
   none of
   most of
   all of
   part of
   } + plural subject + verb without -s

12   Establishing Agreement

Write the correct form of the verb in each of the following present tense sentences.

Age and Skin

❏ (1) Why (do) ___*does*___ all of our skin become dried with age? (2) As we grow older, all of the dead skin cells from the outer layer—the epidermis—(be) _____ replaced more slowly by new cells from the layer below, the dermis. (3) Most of the dermis gradually (shrink) _____ and (harden) _____. (4) Some of the secretion from sweat and oil glands also (decrease) _____. (5) As a result, a lot of our skin (begin) _____ to dry out and crack.

13   Editing for Agreement and Noun-Plural Errors

The sentences that follow contain a variety of errors: incorrect subject-verb agreement, incorrect noun plurals, missing verbs, and incorrect contractions with the verb *to be*. Find and correct each error by making your changes above the lines.

Food for Thought

1. A gourmet service in England offer ∧ this dish: a dormouse, electrocuted and
   then skinned, which are prepared either by braising in honey or wine or lightly
   fried in butter. The mouses are said to be delicious.

2. There is a live-minnow-eating festival that held every year in a town in Belgium. The contestants drop minnows into a silver goblet full of red wine and then drinks them.

3. Every year in Japan, about 200 people dies from eating the fu-gu, a fish that is considered a delicacy. The fish have a poison in its guts, and a cook who don't have a license is not allowed to prepare it.

4. Chicken feathers is 97 percent protein, and researchers at the University of Georgia has found a way of turning them into a fine white powder they claim is easy to digest. A panel who have tasted cookies made from this powder describes them as "pretty good to eat."

5. In 1868, a horse meat banquet for 160 peoples was held at London's Langham Hotel. The highlight of the meal was a 280-pound slab of horse carried on the shoulders of four chef.

6. In 1978, the movie director Herb Robbins held a worm-eating competition at Rialto College, California, to promote his movie *The Worm Eaters*. The winner, Rusty Rice, ate 28 worm.

7. A cookbook by Martha Wapensky describe the correct way to cook African Flying Ants. First, a cup of ants are fried in a dry pan. The next step in preparing the ants are to remove the pan and dry the ants in the sun. After their dry, any wing and stones are removed. Then the ants is fried again, with or without a little oil, and a bit of salt is added. When the ants is fully prepared, there served over a bed of rice.

✍ **14 Editing Your Own Work**

Look at a paragraph or theme you are writing in the present tense—or return to one you have written earlier—and check it carefully for subject-verb agreement and noun plurals. Be sure to look carefully at the contractions of *to be* with pronouns, and pay special attention to collective nouns, expressions beginning with *there,* and phrases between the subject and the verb that may cause errors in agreement.

Checking Past Tense and Past Participle Forms

You probably write in the past tense more than in any other, especially when you discuss your own experiences—things you did, saw, or heard at some point before the present. Most past tense verb forms and their close relations, the *past participles,* aren't difficult to master. They simply end in *-ed,* and only the verb *to be* changes to agree with its subject. Nevertheless, many people make errors in these forms in early drafts of their writing, so this chapter looks at ways to eliminate such errors as you edit your work. After defining the *past tense,* the chapter discusses its use with two types of verbs:

✐ regular verbs; and
✐ three special irregular verbs: *be, could,* and *would.*

The chapter then examines these matters:

✐ the present perfect tense;
✐ the past perfect tense;
✐ *to be* in these perfect tenses; and
✐ a complete list of the most common irregular verbs.

Finally, the chapter examines the uses of the past participle:

✐ after *have* in verb phrases;
✐ in the *passive voice;* and
✐ as an *adjective* after a linking verb, before a noun, or after a noun.

THE PAST TENSE DEFINED

You write in the *past tense* to discuss actions or events that took place before the present. Most often, but not always, these actions occurred at a specific time in the past. Here are some examples:

> The Soviet Union *launched* the first satellite into space on October 4, 1957.
> Its Russian name, *Sputnik,* immediately entered the vocabulary of the United States.
> A month later, *Sputnik II,* carrying a little dog Laika, *orbited* the earth.

Some people make two errors when writing in the past tense: shifting illogically to the present tense or using nonstandard past tense forms of verbs. We focus on both errors on the following pages.

EXAMINING THE PAST TENSE OF REGULAR VERBS

Each past tense verb in the preceding examples is a *regular verb,* which ends in -*ed* no matter what its subject.*

IN SUMMARY

To form the past tense of regular verbs,

add -*ed* to the present tense verb (without -*s*).
Examples: talk + *ed* = *talked*
                      happen + *ed* = *happened*
Note: If the present tense verb ends in -*e*, merely add -*d* to the past tense.
Examples: like + *d* = *liked*
                      bake + *d* = *baked*

✎ **1   Identifying Past and Present Tense Statements**

Write *Pr* before each present tense sentence and *P* before each past tense sentence.

  Pr   1.   Rockets launched into space are routine occurrences.
  _____ 2.   The Russian Yuri Gagarin circled the earth in a space capsule on April 12, 1961.
  _____ 3.   The American Alan Shepard piloted a space capsule beyond the earth's atmosphere soon afterward but did not orbit the earth.
  _____ 4.   John Glenn accomplished that feat almost a year later.
  _____ 5.   The space shuttle usually takes off from and lands in Cape Canaveral, Florida.
  _____ 6.   From its headquarters in Colorado Springs, Colorado, a government agency called NORAD tracks satellites and assorted junk left in space from previous launches.

✎ **2   Transforming the Tense of a Passage**

The following passage is written in the present tense. Change the passage to the past tense by writing the proper past tense form of each verb above the line. Be careful not to place -*ed* endings on infinitives (action words preceded by *to,* such as *to go*), for infinitives do not function as verbs and cannot have a tense.

The Beginnings of Manned Space Flights

                                                                                                    convinced
❑   (1) The flights by both Russian and American astronauts ∧ ~~convince~~ scientists

that a weightless environment presents no serious dangers to humans over ex-

tended periods of time.(2) People enter orbits around the earth, conduct use-

ful observations and experiments, and then return home to tell the tales of

their exploits. (3) The American Gemini and Russian Voskhod manned pro-

grams demonstrate the ability of humans to maneuver a spaceship and dock

---

* If the verb ends in -*y* or in a single consonant, its spelling may change slightly when it adds -*ed*. For example, *reply* becomes *replied,* and *slip* becomes *slipped.*

with another vehicle. (4) The programs also allow humans to walk and work in the vacuum of space. (5) These flights provide the experience and knowledge that prepares the United States' space program for manned landings on the moon.

FORMING THE PAST TENSE OF THREE IMPORTANT IRREGULAR VERBS: *TO BE, COULD,* AND *WOULD*

Using *To Be* in the Past Tense

An *irregular verb* does not end in *-ed* in the past tense. By far the most often-used irregular verb is *to be*—which is also the only verb that changes form for subject-verb agreement:

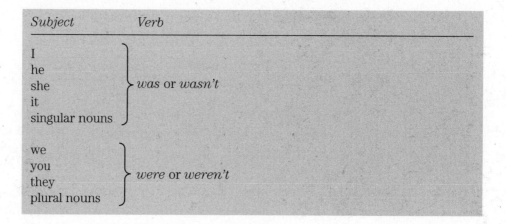

Subject	Verb
I he she it singular nouns	*was* or *wasn't*
we you they plural nouns	*were* or *weren't*

Notice that, like its present tense forms, *to be* takes a form ending with *-s* to agree with third-person singular subjects—but also with the pronoun *I.* You may want to review the section on *to be* in Chapter 21, which discusses present tense agreement, before you complete the following exercises (or consult that chapter as you go along).

3 Forming Past Tense Agreement with *To Be*

In each of the following sentences, write the proper past tense form of *to be.*

1. I ____was____ a good swimmer as a child.

2. Albert _____ reluctant to eat more than three full orders of ribs.

3. _____ you able to keep his plate full?

4. There _____ three cars involved in the accident.

5. _____ the police called?

6. It _____ a big problem.

7. All of you folks _____n't singing from the same music.

8. The jury _____ unanimous in its verdict.

9. The boa constrictor and the mouse _____ very close after they met.

10. _____ question-and-answer period interesting?

Using **Could** and **Would**

Two other important irregular verbs—*could* and *would*— are worth noting.

◆ *Could* is the past tense of *can,* so *could* refers to ability in the past. Compare these clauses:

> *Past ability*
>
> In 1969, the United States *could afford* to send manned missions to the moon,
>
> *Present ability*
>
> but now we *can only talk* fondly about those missions.

◆ *Would* is the past tense of *will,* so *would* refers to the future from a point in the past. Compare these clauses:

> *Past*
>
> At Christmas time in 1968, an American manned spacecraft *circled* the moon in preparation
>
> *Future from a point in the past*
>
> for a flight that *would take place* the following year.

Make sure you understand the difference between the present tense and past tense of these verbs.*

4   Transforming the Tenses of *Can* and *Will*

Rewrite each of the following sentences in the past tense.

Present	*Past*
1. We hope that the landing on the will be successful.	1. We hoped that the landing on the moon would be successful.
2. The astronauts can walk in space.	2. _____
3. They can live outside the earth's atmosphere for extended periods of time.	3. _____

---

* *Would* is also used in conditional statements, in which *if* is stated or implied. Notice that *if* establishes a condition that is contrary to fact, a remote possibility, or a very polite request:

If I were you, I *would be* careful. [Contrary to fact, since I cannot be you.]
If I won the lottery, I *would buy* my parents a house. [An unlikely possibility.]
Tom *would like* to play football next year [*if* it is possible].
Would you please *help* me [*if* you don't mind]?

CHAPTER

22

4. They realize that there will be
   many dangers.

5. On July 20, 1969, astronauts
   Neil Armstrong and Buzz Aldrin
   can land their space vehicle on
   the moon's surface just a few
   seconds before their fuel supply
   will run out.

4. _____
   _____
5. _____
   _____
   _____
   _____
   _____
   _____

FORMING THE PERFECT TENSES WITH REGULAR VERBS

Forming the Present Perfect Tense

The *present perfect tense* refers to actions in the past, but it doesn't function in the same ways as does the simple past tense. Here is how you use the present perfect tense:

Describing an Action That Began in the Past But Continues to the Present.   Compare these two sentences, the second of which is in the present perfect tense:

> The United States placed a communications satellite in orbit in 1958.
> The United States has placed communications satellites in orbit since 1958.

Notice that the second sentence means the United States continues to place the satellites in orbit—*the sentence refers to both the present and past.*
    The present perfect tense is formed from two verbs:

> ◆ the helping verb, a present tense form of *to have* (*have* or *has* or their contractions *'ve* or *'s*)
> ◆ a main verb called the *past participle*, which for regular verbs looks exactly like the past tense form ending in *-ed*

Also notice that the words *for* or *since* show when the action began.

> The Hubble space telescope has been orbiting the earth *since April 18, 1990*
> The Hubble space telescope has been orbiting the earth *for several years.*

Describing an Action in the Indefinite Past (Without Mentioning a Specific Time) That Relates to the Present.   Even when talking about the present, you can relate a statement to the past, as in the following examples:

> Astronauts *have brought back* moon rocks that *are* on display at the Air and
>   Space Museum in Washington.
> The Viking space project *has gathered* a great deal of data about Mars that
>   we still study today.

Statements about actions that ended just before the present often include the word *just, recently, already,* or *yet.*

> The prices of home satellite dishes have *recently* dropped dramatically.
> The Internet and other satellite-linked communications media have *already*
>   changed the way they gather and exchange information.
> Have you learned to go on-line *yet?* *

When editing, look carefully at each use of *have* or *has* and the word following it, for the verb may be in the present perfect tense. Have you used the tense cor-

---

* Use *yet* for questions and negative statements, but use *already* for affirmative statements.

rectly, and does the word following *have* take the appropriate past participle form? (You will see these forms of irregular verbs later in the chapter.)

IN SUMMARY

> **To form the present perfect tense with regular verbs,**
>
> 1. begin with a present tense form of *to have* (*have, has,* or their contractions *'ve* and *'s*) that agrees with the subject of the sentence; and
> 2. then use the past participle (*-ed* for regular verbs) as the main verb.

✏️ **5   Transforming Verb Tenses**

Change each past tense sentence into one using the present perfect tense. Then compare the difference in meaning between the two versions of each sentence.

1. We planned to visit the museum on our trip. *We have planned to visit the museum on our trip.*

2. I memorized only half of the dictionary so far. _____

_____

3. My friend Claudio worked overtime a lot this month. _____

_____

4. He remained in close touch with his wrestling coach. _____

_____

5. Elmer bathed every Saturday, whether he needed to or not. _____

_____

Forming the Past Perfect Tense

Like the present perfect tense, the *past perfect tense* is a combination of two words: (1) *had* (the past tense of *to have*); and (2) the past participle. However, the past perfect tense is a *past* tense that describes an action that occurred *before* another time in the past. Most past perfect tense statements occur in sentences that discuss two events that happened at different times in the past.

> Both Germany and the Soviet Union *had begun* rocket research programs 10 years before the United States *started* its program.
> Several German scientists, who *had worked* for Hitler during World War II, *continued* their rocket research in the United States after the war.

The present perfect tense and the past perfect tense can easily be confused, so remember these important differences:

> ◆ The present perfect tense occurs in present tense writing. Its helping verbs are *has* and *have*.
> ◆ The past perfect tense occurs in past tense writing. Its helping verb is *had*.

As you edit your work, make sure you haven't used one of these tenses when you intended the other, and look for past participle forms after *had*.

IN SUMMARY

> **To form the past perfect tense with regular verbs,**
>
> 1. **begin with the past tense form of *to have* (*had*); and**
> 2. **then use a past participle as the main verb.**

✍ **6 Writing Perfect Tenses**

Write either the present perfect or past perfect tense of the verb supplied in each of the following sentences.

1. After we (cross) __had crossed__ the bridge, we discovered the flat tire.

2. After you (boil) _____ the eggs, let them cool for a while.

3. We (danced) _____ for hours, but we don't want to stop.

4. They said to me that they (expect) _____ trouble earlier.

5. He is a fine gymnast because he (practice) _____ for many years.

6. Michael (study) _____ for three days before he took the final examination.

Using *To Be* in Perfect Tenses

The past participle of *to be* is *been.* Notice its use in the following sentences written in the present perfect tense:

> People have probably *been interested* in space travel since they first gazed at the stars.
> The existence of an atmosphere on Mars *has already been proven.*

Always use *have, has, had,* or their contractions before *been* in the present perfect and past perfect tenses. *Been* by itself cannot be a verb. Check carefully for errors in these verb phrases as you revise your papers.

✍ **7 Composing Perfect Tense Sentences with *Been***

Complete each of the following sentences with a verb phrase in the present perfect or past perfect tense using *been.*

1. The space shuttle ____has been____ operating since April 12, 1981.

2. All the shuttle flights _____ manned.

3. The flights were suspended after seven crew members of the Challenger

   _____ killed on January 28, 1986.

4. The flights resumed after the O-rings on the rocket boosters of the shuttle

   _____ redesigned and thoroughly tested.

5. Unmanned launches of satellites _____ successfully

   accomplished by many countries.

USING THE PAST TENSE AND PAST PARTICIPLE OF IRREGULAR VERBS

Remember that *irregular verbs* do not end in *-ed* in the past tense or past participle. You have already seen three irregular verbs in this chapter—*be, could,* and *would.* Now let's look at the remaining most common irregular verbs.

Examining the Irregular Verb Forms

Many errors in the past tense occur with irregular verbs, especially with those whose past tense forms also differ from their past participle forms. You probably know most of the irregular verbs, but the following list reviews the most common ones. Read through the list and put a check mark next to those you need to memorize.

Simple form	Past tense	Past participle
be	was, were	been
beat	beat	beaten
become	became	become
begin	began	begun
bend	bent	bent
bet	bet	bet
bind	bound	bound
bite	bit	bitten
bleed	bled	bled
blow	blew	blown
break	broke	broken
breed	bred	bred
bring	brought	brought
build	built	built
burst	burst	burst
buy	bought	bought
cast	cast	cast
catch	caught	caught
choose	chose	chosen
come	came	come
creep	crept	crept
cut	cut	cut
dig	dug	dug
do	did	done
draw	drew	drawn
drink	drank	drunk
drive	drove	driven
eat	ate	eaten
fall	fell	fallen

Simple form	Past tense	Past participle
feed	fed	fed
feel	felt	felt
fight	fought	fought
find	found	found
fit	fit (or fitted)	fit (or fitted)
flee	fled	fled
fly	flew	flown
forget	forgot	forgotten (or forgot)
forgive	forgave	forgiven
freeze	froze	frozen
get	got	gotten (or got)
give	gave	given
go	went	gone
grind	ground	ground
grow	grew	grown
hang	hung	hung
have	had	had
hear	heard	heard
hide	hid	hidden
hit	hit	hit
hold	held	held
hurt	hurt	hurt
keep	kept	kept
know	knew	known
lay*	laid	laid
lead	led	led
leave	left	left
lend	lent	lent
let	let	let
lie	lay	lain
lose	lost	lost
make	made	made
meet	met	met
pay	paid	paid
put	put	put
quit	quit	quit
read	read	read
ride	rode	ridden
ring	rang	rung
rise	rose	risen
run	ran	run
say	said	said
see	saw	seen
sell	sold	sold
send	sent	sent
set	set	set
shake	shook	shaken
shed	shed	shed
shine	shone (or shined)	shone (or shined)
shoot	shot	shot
shut	shut	shut

CHAPTER

22

* Many people confuse the verbs *lay* and *lie*. See Chapter 26 for practice with these verbs.

Simple form	Past tense	Past participle
sing	sang	sung
sink	sank (or sunk)	sunk
sit	sat	sat
slay	slew	slain
sleep	slept	slept
slide	slid	slid
slit	slit	slit
speak	spoke	spoken
speed	sped	sped
spend	spent	spent
spin	spun	spun
spread	spread	spread
spring	sprang (or sprung)	sprung
stand	stood	stood
steal	stole	stolen
stink	stank (or stunk)	stunk
strike	struck	struck
strive	strove (or strived)	striven (or strived)
swear	swore	sworn
sweep	swept	swept
swim	swam	swum
swing	swung	swung
take	took	taken
teach	taught	taught
tear	tore	torn
tell	told	told
think	thought	thought
throw	threw	thrown
thrust	thrust	thrust
understand	understood	understood
wake	woke	woken
wear	wore	worn
weave	wove	woven
win	won	won
wind	wound	wound
write	wrote	written

Whenever you are unsure of a verb form, refer to this list or look up the verb in a dictionary. There you will find the verb listed alphabetically in its present tense form; the past tense and past participle will be included before the definitions. (If you see no such forms, that means the verb is regular.)

8 Writing Past Tense and Past Participle Verbs

Write the correct past tense or past perfect tense form of each verb in the following passage.

The First Tragedy in the Space Program

❏ (1) Until January 27, 1967, the safest form of transportation in history (be) _had been_ the space capsule. (2) Dozens of American astronauts and Soviet cosmonauts (ride) _____ into space in giant rockets, fueled by explosive mixtures of oxygen and hydrogen. (3) They (spin)

_____ around the earth, covering millions of miles.
(4) They (go) _____ outside the capsule for space walks,
protected only by the thin fabric of their spacesuits. (5) They (come)
_____ back to earth in fiery capsules, splashing down in
the ocean or parachuting down to the land with amazing accuracy. (6) The
United States and the Soviet Union (build) _____ space
vehicles from marvelous new metals, computers, and electronic circuitry that
(withstand) _____ every challenge.

   (7) A failure (have) _____ to happen, however, and
it finally (do) _____ that day in January during a test run
for the Apollo project. (8) The project (will) _____ try to
land the first men on the moon, and the crew of the first _Apollo_ spacecraft,
Virgil "Gus" Grissom, Ed White, and Roger Chaffee, (know) _____
how to handle a spacecraft better than anyone else. (9) Grissom and White
(fly) _____ in space before, and Chaffee (be)
_____ a highly skilled pilot.

   (10) All three men (rise) _____ early that morning to
rehearse their upcoming flight inside the space module on Launch Pad 34 of
the Kennedy Space Center near Cocoa Beach, Florida. (11) They (spend)
_____ five long hours in their space suits as they (keep)
_____ repeating their drills. (12) Gus Grissom, a 40-year-
old veteran of two previous space missions, (lie) _____
on his back strapped to his seat as he (give) _____ responses to the ground control's request for information.

   (13) Then a ground control technician (catch) _____
the first sign of trouble. (14) The inside of the Apollo capsule suddenly
(become) _____ pure white and then (grow)
_____ dark on his television monitor. (15) He (try)
_____ first to adjust the brightness and contrast controls
on the screen. (16) But he soon (hear) _____ a voice
screaming over the headphones: "Fire . . . I smell fire! . . . " (17) There (be)
_____ a short silence, and then Ed White (speak)
_____ : "Fire in the cockpit! . . . "

   (18) The three men in the capsule (beat) _____ on
the hatch before the voice of Roger Chaffee (can) _____
be heard: "We're on fire . . . get us out of here! . . . " (19) Following that, there
(be) _____ silence.

(20) In just four minutes, an emergency crew (burst) _____ from the control room on the ground level and (shoot) _____ _____ up to the entrance to the capsule by high-speed elevator. (21) The hot surface of the capsule (burn) _____ their hands as they (tear) _____ open the main hatch. (22) But the billowing smoke and gases (make) _____ entry impossible, so they (draw) _____ back from the hatch.

(23) Meanwhile, as the smoke (blow) _____ out of the hatch, the pictures on the television cameras in ground control (become) _____ clearer. (24) Technicians (see) _____ the motionless bodies of the three astronauts. (25) The technicians (cut) _____ off all power supplies to the capsule, and the launch control director (tell) _____ the emergency teams to leave for fear that the capsule might explode.

(26) The crew of the *Apollo* (lose) _____ their lives in a matter of seconds—the victims of the first space disaster right here on earth. (27) At midnight, after the capsule (cool) _____ down, the ground control personnel (can) _____ take the bodies away.

USING THE PAST PARTICIPLE IN OTHER WAYS

Aside from its use in perfect tenses, the past participle also functions as part of a verb phrase or as an adjective.

Placing the Past Participle After *Have*

Most three- and four-word verb phrases contain *have* plus the past participle.

could have gone	may have been	could have been working
should have seen	might have stolen	should have been gone
must have done	would have driven	might have been sleeping[*]

Remember this simple rule: When *have* is a helping verb, the main verb following it must be a past participle.[†] As you edit your work, therefore, look for the helping verb *have,* which signals that a past participle follows.

---

[*] Don't confuse *'ve* (the contraction of *have*) with *of* in these verb phrases. See Chapter 26.
[†] The only exception to this is *have to,* as in "They have to study for a test."

IN SUMMARY | **To form most three- or four-word verb phrases,**

use *could, should, must, may, might, would* + *have* + past participle
(+ *-ing*)

9   Composing Phrases with Helping Verbs

Complete each of the following sentences using *have* and an appropriate past participle.

1. Maria had an accident. She should _have been more careful._

2. I don't know what happened to my notebook. I could _____

    _____

3. If I had known that you had to walk to school, I would _____

    _____

4. Walter got another perfect score on an examination. He must_____

    _____

5. Homer wore a striped tie, a polka-dot shirt, and checked polyester slacks. He

    might _____

    _____

Placing the Past Participle After *To Be* (Passive Voice)

The past participle follows *to be* in the *passive voice,* when the subject of a sentence does not perform the action but instead receives the action:

> The first airplane to break the sound barrier *was flown* by Chuck Yeager.

Notice that the subject of the sentence—*the airplane*—didn't do the flying. *Chuck Yeager did.* In other words, the subject of the sentence is passive; it did not act but was acted upon. Here's the same sentence in the *active voice,* in which the subject performed the action:

> Chuck Yeager *flew* the first airplane to break the sound barrier.

Don't confuse voice with tense, for passive voice ideas can apply to any time in the past, present, or future. Compare the following sentences:

	Passive voice	*Active voice*
Past tense:	The flying saucers were seen by several people.	Several people saw the flying saucers.

CHAPTER

22

	Passive voice	Active voice
Present tense:	New satellites are launched every month.	We launch new satellites every month.
Future tense:	Our society will be transformed by this new technology.	This new technology will transform our society.

As you edit your work, check for correct past participle forms after the verb *to be* in the passive voice sentences. Also consider whether to rewrite a passive voice statement in the active voice, which is usually less awkward and more direct. Use the passive voice only when the action you describe is more important than the person performing it:

Tickets will be sold on a first-come first-served basis. (Notice that the sentence does not—and need not—mention who will sell the tickets.)

✍ 10 Composing Passive-Voice Sentences

Complete each of the following sentences in the passive voice by supplying an appropriate verb phrase. Be sure the verb tense is logical for the context of the action.

1. I _____*was told*_____ that the restaurant didn't take reservations.

2. Final grades _____ to students two weeks after the end of the semester.

3. The lecture _____ in Robinson Hall last Wednesday.

4. This wallet _____ in room 2301 earlier in the day.

5. Applications must _____ by the first week of the coming month.

6. Walnut Street _____ repaired now.

Placing the Past Participle After a Linking Verb

Sometimes a past participle doesn't express an action. Instead, it functions as an *adjective* describing a noun or even a pronoun. Thus, check for correct past participle forms after verbs such as *is/are, become, feel, sound, taste, appear,* and *seem* as you edit your work. These are linking verbs, which link adjectives to the subjects of sentences. (See Chapter 19.) Notice the past participles after linking verbs in these sentences:

Subject	Linking verb	Past participle
Sammie	*looks*	*tired.*
That record	*sounds*	*worn out.*
Everyone	*is*	*excited* about the championship game.

These sentences are descriptive; nothing *happens* in them. The subject does not act, and the past participle does not act upon the subject.

✍ **11   Composing Sentences with Past Participle Adjectives**

Write the past participle adjective form of a verb from the following list in each of the sentences. Do not use the same past participle twice.

do	prejudice	disgust
know	shake	satisfy
annoy	shock	encourage
disappoint	please	sadden
thrill	delight	amuse
enrage	offend	frighten

1. I waited for a long time, so I was quite _annoyed_ when you didn't show up.

2. Everyone is _____ about the good news.

3. Don't be _____ if you don't win; there are a lot of talented people in the competition.

4. He is well _____ for his acting ability.

5. I was _____ to hear the news.

6. Paul says he is not upset, but he certainly acts _____ .

7. He is very _____ against minorities, but he should know better.

Placing the Past Participle Before a Noun

Like all adjectives, past participles often appear before nouns.

> That is a *stolen* watch; don't buy it.
> *Used* cars are cheaper than new ones.

Errors in past participle forms before nouns can confuse or annoy readers, as demonstrated by the following example:

> He was a tire man.

Is this sentence supposed to mean that the man was tired or that he sold tires? Look carefully for past participles before nouns and make sure you have used them correctly.

✍ **12   Writing Past Participles Before Nouns**

Write an appropriate past participle in each of the following sentences.

1. When you visit Washington, be sure to see the Tomb of the _Unknown_ Soldier.

2. Roland can't walk; I think he has a _____ leg or a _____ ankle.

CHAPTER

22

3. I usually have _____ eggs, but the rest of my family

likes _____ eggs.

4. The _____ bear chased after the

_____ camper.

5. That old _____ suit looks terrible on you.

Placing the Past Participle After a Noun

As you saw earlier, a one-word adjective (including a past participle) comes before the noun it describes. However, an *adjective phrase* (two or more words that function as an adjective) comes *after* the noun it describes. Many of these phrases begin with a past participle.

	Adjective phrase	
A man	*named John*	called a while ago.
I've just received a letter	*written by Mr. Lampley.*	

13 Writing Past Participles in Adjective Phrases

Complete each of the following sentences with a past participle.

1. I saw a man *robbed* by thieves in broad daylight.

2. It is often hard to understand the words _____ by rock performers these days.

3. Mr. Gonzalez is a businessperson _____ for his honesty.

4. At all the clubs, everyone is doing a dance _____ the Sloppy Shuffle.

5. At the Ritz restaurant, you will enjoy food _____ by Chef Rudolfo.

IN SUMMARY

Write past participles in the following places, and check these places during revisions:

1. after *have* or *has* in the present perfect tense, or after *had* in the past perfect tense;
2. after *have* in many verb phrases, such as *could have gone* or *should have been going;*
3. after *to be* in the passive voice;
4. after a linking verb;
5. before a noun; and
6. at the beginning of a phrase after a noun.

✍ **14   Editing for Past Tense and Past Participle Errors**

The following passage contains many errors in past tense and past participle verb forms. Correct each error by writing the necessary changes above the lines.

The First Moon Walk (July 20, 1969)

❑ (1) It ∧*begbegan* on July 16, 1969, when three astronauts—Neil Armstrong,

Michael Collins, and Edwin Aldrin—lifted off from earth in *Apollo 11,* a space-

ship power by the *Saturn V* rocket. (2) They was on their way to the moon,

where man will set foot on its surface for the first time. (3) The spacecraft

shooted along at a speed of 24,300 miles per hour. (4) On the second day of

the flight, the astronauts started to broadcast a live television picture back to

earth. (5) Over 500 million people was watching what the three men done.

(6) On July 19, three days after takeoff, the astronauts had travel 244,930

miles, and the ship was send into an orbit around the moon. (7) It circle the

moon twice before taking an orbit closer to the surface. (8) Then, while the

Apollo was on the far side of the moon, they undocked the *Eagle,* the Lunar

Module, from the *Columbia,* the Command Module. (9) Armstrong and Aldrin,

who will walk on the moon while Collins flied the *Columbia,* crawled through

the tunnel between the two modules, and open the hatches to enter the *Eagle.*

(10) The *Apollo* come back into radio contact with earth, and Armstrong an-

nounce, "*Eagle* has wings." (11) The Lunar Module was free from *Columbia.*

(12) The *Eagle* then drawed closer toward the moon until it was about 500

feet above the surface. (13) Armstrong and Aldrin watch the terrain and

choose the best place to land. (14) Shortly afterward, an alarm showed that

the on-board computer had began to fail, so the astronauts switched the ship

off semiautomatic pilot and brung the ship down themselves. (15) In a tense

moment, Armstrong saw that the *Eagle* was headed for a rocky crater, and he

fire the engines to carry the ship another 4 miles farther. (16) The maneuver

worked. (17) As the Lunar Module touch down on the surface, Armstrong, looking out the window, can see a sheet of moon dirt being blowed upward by the rocket exhaust. (18) He shut off the engine and reported, "The *Eagle* has landed." (19) He seem calm, but his heart beated at twice the normal rate.

(20) The two men were suppose to spend eight hours checking the ship out, eating, and then resting, but they was anxious to leave the *Eagle* and explore the moon. (21) They were certainly too excite to sleep, so Houston agreed that they can skip the rest period. (22) They spend 6 1/2 hours putting on their equipment and depressurizing the cabin before they open the hatch. (23) Slowly, Armstrong lead the way down the nine-rung ladder. (24) When he reached the second rung, he letted down a television camera. (25) On home-viewing screens all over the earth, people seen the image of his foot. (26) A moment later, that foot—encased in a size 9 1/2 boot—maked contact with the moon's surface. (27) It was July 20, 1969, at 10:56 P.M. eastern daylight time. (28) The world then heared Armstrong's now famous words, "That's one small step for a man, one giant leap for mankind."

✍ 15 Editing Your Own Work

Look at a past tense paragraph or composition you are writing or one that you have previously written and check it carefully for errors in past tense or past participle verb forms. Look for omitted *-ed* endings. Examine the verbs *was* and *were* to ensure that they agree with their subjects. See that you have used the appropriate forms of the past tense and the past participle for irregular verbs, and be sure that you have correctly used the present and past perfect tenses.

Using Pronouns

Pronouns are among the most common words, and most people employ them effectively most of the time. However, readers can be confused when pronoun forms are misused or when the antecedents of pronouns are unclear. This chapter helps you spot and correct pronoun errors as you revise and edit your work. We look at the following matters:

- ✏ *pronoun case,* especially in comparisons;
- ✏ problems with multiple, missing, or troublesome antecedents;
- ✏ the use of *who* and *whom;*
- ✏ the use of *reflexive pronouns;* and
- ✏ the use of *demonstrative pronouns*

PRONOUN CASE DEFINED

The word *pronoun* literally means "for a noun," and pronouns are in fact substitutes for nouns. They add coherence to your writing by referring to preceding ideas called *antecedents.* They provide variety by minimizing the repetition of nouns. And they increase clarity by taking different *cases*—grammatical relationships to the other words in a sentence—because pronouns can serve as subjects, objects, or possessive words.

These are the subject-case and object-case pronouns:

Plural object	*Singular subject*	*Plural subject*	*Singular object*	
First person	I	we	me	us
Second person	you	you	you	you
Third person	he	they	him	them
	she		her	
	it		it	

As their name suggests, *subject-case pronouns* function only as subjects of sentences.* Likewise, *object-case pronouns* function as objects of action verbs, words formed from verbs, or prepositions.

---

* Subject-case pronouns can also occur after linking verbs. (See Chapter 19.) This is why in formal English careful writers and speakers say, "It is *I,*" not "It is *me.*"

After action verbs	He hit *me*.
	You saw *them*.
	I told *her* the answer.
After -ing words	After seeing *him*, they ran away.
	Bradley picked up the puppy without hurting *it*.
After prepositions	some of *us*
	with *me*
	to *you* from *him*

DETERMINING CASE WITH TWO OR MORE PRONOUNS

Determining the appropriate pronoun case is easy when a clause contains only one subject or object:

Incorrect	*Correct*
Her is busy.	*She* is busy.
Bill gave it to *I*.	Bill gave it to *me*.
What is wrong with *they?*	What is wrong with *them?*

However, when a clause contains more than one subject or object, the appropriate pronoun case may not be so obvious. The following sentences contain pronoun case errors, but do they sound incorrect?

Me and him like to play ball.
You and me can do this.
Let's keep this a secret between *you and I*.

If your eye or ear doesn't pick up the errors, here's an easy way the detect them. Remove all but one subject or object for a moment so you can hear what is correct or incorrect.

Incorrect:	*Me* . . . like to play ball. *Him* . . . like to play ball.
Correct:	*I* . . . like to play ball. *He* . . . likes to play ball.*
Incorrect:	. . . *me* can do this.
Correct:	. . . *I* can do this.
Incorrect:	. . . between . . . *I*.
Correct:	. . . between . . . *me*.

Then you can correct these errors by rewriting the full subject or object.

IN SUMMARY

To choose the correct pronoun case in a sentence with two or more subjects or objects,

1. temporarily remove all but one subject or object from the sentence;
2. ask yourself if the remaining pronoun sounds correct alone or whether it can be a subject or an object; and
3. if the remaining pronoun is not in the correct case, change it.

---

* The incorrect *"Me and my friend* like to play ball" sounds better than *"I and my friend* like to play ball" because in the second version the pronoun *I* is in the wrong position. It should come second, not first. Here is a revised and correct version of the sentence: *"My friend and I* like to play ball."

✍ **1   Correcting Errors in Pronoun Case**

Some—but not all—of the following sentences use incorrect pronoun case. Cross out each error and write the correct form above the line. If a sentence has no errors, do not make any changes.

1. The Hendersons have always been friends with my wife and ∧ ~~I~~. *me*

2. When we were kids, me and my brother swam almost every day during the summer.

3. My parents always knew that he and I were at the beach.

4. You and her are welcome anytime.

5. Call me or him whenever you want.

6. There will never be a problem between you and I.

DETERMINING PRONOUN CASE IN COMPARISONS

Notice in the following comparisons that a simple clause—a subject pronoun and a helping verb—comes after the word *than* or *as*.

> My brother is taller than *I am.*
> Judith's mother wears the same size dress as *she does.*

You can drop the verb from these clauses, but you must still retain the subject pronoun after *than* or *as*.

> My brother is taller than *I (am).*
> Judith's mother wears the same size dress as *she (does).*

But suppose you compare objects instead of subjects:

> Bob talked to *her* as much as *me.*

In this case, the incorrect pronoun case is not only inappropriate but misleading. Does the sentence say that *Bob* talked to *me* or that *I* talked to *her?* The best way to resolve the problem is to include an additional clarifying word.

> Bob talked to him as much as *to me.*

CHAPTER

23

IN SUMMARY

> **To determine the correct pronoun case after *than* or *as* in a comparison,**
>
> 1. temporarily insert the omitted words after *than* or *as*
>   *Incorrect:*   They did better on the test than *her.*
>   *Correct:*   They did better on the test than *she (did).*
>   *Incorrect:*   Tim drove them to school as often as *we.*
>   *Correct:*   Tim drove them to school as often as *(he drove) us.*
> 2. then remove the words you inserted or leave them in to avoid possible confusion.

2   Using Pronouns in Comparisons

Write a sentence making a comparison based on the information in each of the following sentences.

1. Tom is 6 feet tall, but she is 5 feet 6 inches tall. *Tom is taller than she.*

2. Lonnie is very tall. He is also very tall. _____

3. José runs fast. They run more slowly. _____

4. Jerold is very friendly. She rarely says hello. _____

5. Mom always liked you a lot. She didn't like me as much._____

USING PRONOUNS WITH MULTIPLE OR MISSING ANTECEDENTS

Pronouns must refer clearly to their *antecedents*, the words that the pronouns represent or replace. Here are some examples:

Antecedent	Pronoun
Juan and I	we
Juan and me	us
someone	he/she; him/her
he and Katrina	they
Katrina and him	them
Carlos and you	you

Sometimes, however, it's better to repeat or use a synonym for an antecedent instead of writing a pronoun. Too many pronouns can become monotonous and boring, and a pronoun with more than one possible antecedent can be confusing. Note the repeated words or substitutions for them (both in italics) in the following paragraph:

The Amazing Guru

❑   (1) In India, a religious brotherhood of warriors called the Sikhs tell the story about one of their early *leaders,* a *guru* named Gobind *Singh,* who lived in the seventeenth century. (2) *He* gathered the Sikhs together during a crisis and said that the times required supreme loyalty. (3) Drawing *his* sword, *he* asked for volunteers to give *him* their heads. (4) There was a long silence. (5) Finally, one man stepped forward and was led into the *guru's* tent. (6) *Singh* reappeared soon after— alone, and with a bloody sword. (7) *He* asked for a second volunteer, and then a third and a fourth and a fifth. (8) Each time, a man was led away and, each time, the *guru* returned with blood on *his* sword. (9) "Now," said the *leader* to *his* followers, "you have proven your courage and devotion to our cause, so I will restore the men to life." (10) *Singh* returned to *his* tent and brought the five men back, unharmed—the result of either a miracle or a trick, for some say that a goat had been sacrificed in place of the men.

Notice that after Gobind Singh is identified as a leader, or guru, in the first sentence, the paragraph refers to him in sentences 2, 3, 7, 8, 9, and 10 with the pronouns *he, him,* and *his.* However, the paragraph does not use these pronouns when their antecedents are unclear, as in sentence 8:

> Each time, *a man* was led away and, each time, *the guru* returned with blood on his sword.

The sentence discusses two people: *a man* and *the guru,* so the pronoun *he* could be confusing, saying that the man—not the guru—returned with blood on his sword.

> Each time, a *man* was led away, and each time, *he* returned with blood on his sword.

Similarly, the paragraph avoids confusion by repeating the name *Singh* in sentences 6 and 10, repeating the word *guru* in sentence 5, and repeating the word *leader* in sentence 9.

Another problem with clarity occurs when pronouns have no antecedents. For example, what does *they* refer to in the following sentence?

> *They* are replacing the curbs on my block this week.

A noun should replace the pronoun to avoid confusion. Here are two possible revisions:

> *City workers are* replacing the curbs on my block this week.
> *The city is* replacing the curbs on my block this week.

CHAPTER

23

IN SUMMARY   **When the antecedent of a pronoun isn't clear,**

rewrite the sentence, usually replacing the pronoun with a noun.

✍ 3 Revising a Passage for Pronoun Variety

The following passage repeats the same words too often. Provide more variety by substituting nouns or pronouns for the italicized words. Write your substitutions above the line.

The Amazing Boy General

❑ (1) When *Galusha Pennypacker,* a U.S. Civil War hero of the

Union army, was awarded the rank of major general, ∧ *Pennypacker* ^{he} was too

young to vote. (2) The tall ∧ *Pennypacker* ^{recruit} first joined the ∧ *Union army* ^{army} in 1861 as a quartermaster sergeant at the age of 16. (3) That August, he was elected captain of the Ninety-seventh Pennsylvania Volunteers. (4) *Penny-packer* was a colonel by 1864, for his men loved their brave leader. (5) At Fort Gilmer, Pennypacker led troops across a mile of brush in full view of the *Con-federate army.* (6) Though the *Confederate army* killed Pennypacker's horse and wounded *Pennypacker, Pennypacker* kept on fighting. (7) *Penny-packer's* twentieth birthday was spent convalescing from three battle wounds, but *Pennypacker* was soon back in action.

(8) On January 15, 1865, at Fort Fisher, North Carolina, Pennypacker led a brigade across the Confederate army's defenses and was the first to reach the top of the hill where *Pennypacker* triumphantly planted his brigade's flag. (9) Standing in plain sight of the Confederate army, Pennypacker watched as *a Confederate army* soldier took aim, shot, and badly wounded *Pennypacker* in the side and hip. (10) A month later the 20-year-old *Pennypacker* was ap-pointed a brigadier general. (11) *Pennypacker* was the youngest soldier to achieve that rank on either side of the Civil War. (12) In March 1865, Penny-packer was appointed a major general, and *Pennypacker* was still not 21.

(13) The rest of Pennypacker's career was uneventful. (14) Throughout the Reconstruction period, *Pennypacker* remained in the army. (15) *Pennypacker* later refused an opportunity to run for governor of Pennsylvania and lived out a lonely retirement in Philadelphia, where *Pennypacker* died on October 1, 1916.

ESTABLISHING PRONOUN AGREEMENT WITH TROUBLESOME ANTECEDENTS

Indefinite pronouns and *collective nouns* create special problems as the an-tecedents of pronouns.

Establishing Agreement with Indefinite Pronouns

As you can guess from their name, *indefinite pronouns* do not refer to a specific person, place, or thing.

For people		_For things_	_For places_	_For people, things, or places_	
everyone	everybody	everything	everywhere	each	either
someone	somebody	something	somewhere	one	neither
anyone	anybody	anything	anywhere	any	
no one	nobody	nothing	nowhere		

As antecedents, indefinite pronouns present real difficulties with pronouns that refer back to them. For example, which pronoun should refer to _Everybody_ in the following sentence?

Everybody has turned in _____ paper.

The most obvious choice is the plural pronoun _their,_ which avoids sexual bias. However, _everybody,_ like all indefinite pronouns, is _grammatically singular._ (Notice that the verb after _everybody_ is _has,_ a singular verb.) Therefore, while _their_ has gained great acceptance among writers and readers, it may not be appropriate in formal writing.

Another choice is _his,_ which seems to exclude women.* A third choice is _his or her,_ but the phrase sounds awkward, especially in longer passages:

Everybody has turned in _his or her_ paper. _He or she_ . . .

So what do you do? One solution is to avoid the pronoun entirely:

> Everybody has turned in _a_ paper.

Another is supply a female pronoun:

> Everyone has turned in _her_ paper.

Yet another solution is to rewrite the sentence with a plural subject:

> _All of the students_ have turned in _their papers._ (Note that _papers_ is plural to establish consistency throughout the sentence.)

And a fourth solution is to use _their._ Since the handling of pronouns with indefinite pronoun antecedents is controversial, you may want to discuss the issue in class with your instructor.

---

* Of course, _his_ is quite appropriate when a sentence discusses only males.

     Everybody on the football team has done _his_ best.

And _her_ is the obvious choice when a sentence discusses only females.

     Everybody in the convent says _her_ prayers at 6 A.M.

CHAPTER

23

✍ **4   Revising Sentences to Avoid Sexual Bias**

Rewrite each of the following sentences, using a plural subject and making all other appropriate changes.

1. Everyone in the class has improved his grade.

   Rewritten: <u>All the students in the class have improved their grades.</u>

2. Everyone has reduced his or her weight during this exercise program.

   Rewritten: _____

   _____

3. Everybody involved is doing their best to make the party successful.

   Rewritten: _____

   _____

4. Anybody who uses this type of savings account can withdraw her money at any time.

   Rewritten: _____

   _____

5. No one has left their books on the desk.

   Rewritten: _____

   _____

Establishing Agreement with Collective Nouns

Most *collective nouns,* which represent a group (for example, a club, a team, or a class), are singular. Therefore, careful readers expect you to refer to a collective noun by using *it* or *its.*

> The *class* meets in room 214 on Monday, but *it* meets in room 210 on Wednesday.
> My hockey *team* won all of *its* (not *their*) games this season.

Some collective nouns are treated as plurals:

the police
the Chinese, the British, etc.
the staff
the faculty
the name of a sports team, whether plural (the New York *Yankees*) or singular (the Miami *Heat*)

✍ **5   Writing Sentences with Collective Nouns as Antecedents**

Complete each of the following sentences, referring back to its subject with an appropriate pronoun.

1. The police <u>sent five of their patrol cars to the scene of the crime.</u>

2. The group _____

   _____

3.   The committee _____

   _____

4.   Wal-Mart _____

   _____

5.   The Giants _____

   _____

USING *WHO* AND *WHOM*

You may recall from Chapter 20 that *who* serves as the subject of a clause in a combined sentence:

> Juan was the man *who spoke to you.*
> The woman *who left her package* will be back to get it soon.

Many people insist that in formal writing you use another relative pronoun—*whom*—as the object in a relative clause:

$$O. \quad S. \quad V.$$

> Juan was the man *whom you spoke to.*

Most of the time, you can eliminate *whom* from such clauses:

$$S. \quad V.$$

> Juan was the man [whom] *you spoke to.*

But you cannot eliminate *whom* when it follows a preposition (a somewhat rare and very formal structure).

$$P. \quad O. \quad S. \quad V.$$

> Juan was the man *to whom* you spoke.

✍ **6   Combining Sentences with Relative Pronouns**

Join each pair of sentences, using *who, whom,* or no relative pronoun.

1.   Mr. Bailey is the administrator. He handles student loans and grants.

   Mr. Bailey is the administrator who handles student loans and grants.

2.   Dr. Brown is the counselor. Students consult with her when they need advice on personal matters.

   Dr. Brown is the counselor [whom] students consult with when they need advice on personal matters.

   (Or)

   Dr. Brown is the counselor with whom students consult when they need advice on personal matters.

3.   You must talk to the person. She sets the policy for admissions. _____

   _____

CHAPTER

23

4. Washington and Lincoln were the presidents. Historians consider them our
   greatest. _____

   _____

5. We all need a close friend. We can discuss our problems with him. _____

   _____

USING REFLEXIVE PRONOUNS

In some sentences, the same person or thing is both the subject and the object.

> The wicked witch looked at *herself* in the mirror.
> I talk to *myself* when I want to have an intelligent conversation.

The objects in these sentences are called *reflexive pronouns* because they reflect
back to the subjects like mirrors. Note that all the singular reflexive pronouns end
in *-self;* all the plurals end in *-selves.*

	Singular	*Plural*
First person	myself	ourselves
Second person	yourself	yourselves
Third person	himself (not hisself)	themselves (not theirselves)
	herself	
	itself	

You can also use a reflexive pronoun to repeat and thus emphasize a subject or
object.

> I *myself* don't want to drive that far, but my best friend insists that we do it.
> If you want to exchange this merchandise, you will have to talk to the manager
>   *himself.*

However, you cannot use a reflexive pronoun as the subject of a sentence.

> *Incorrect:*   Rudolfo and *myself* would like to thank you for your help.
> *Correct:*   Rudolfo and *I* would like to thank you for your help.

IN SUMMARY

When you use reflexive pronouns,

1. end singular pronouns in *-self* and plural pronouns in *-selves* (for example, *yourself* = singular, *yourselves* = plural);
2. use *himself* (not *hisself*) and *themselves* (not *theirselves*); and
3. never use reflexive pronouns as subjects—only as objects—but you
   can emphasize a subject or an object by repeating it with a reflexive
   pronoun.

✎ **7   Writing Reflexive Pronouns**

Write the correct pronoun in each of the following sentences.

1. Does John ever do any of the repairs by <u>himself</u> ?

2. You and Sheila should help _____ to whatever you want to eat.

3. Thanks. We can prepare it _____.

4. My children walk to school by _____ .

5. My parents, my brothers, and _____ manage to arrange our schedules so that we actually eat dinner together every Sunday.

USING DEMONSTRATIVE PRONOUNS

This/that and *these/those* are called *demonstrative* words because they demonstrate what they refer to. You can use demonstratives alone as pronouns:

This is the one I want.
I like *these* but not *those*.

Or you can place the demonstratives before nouns as adjectives:

This cake is delicious.
Would you hand me *those papers,* please?

Note that the demonstratives have both singular and plural forms.

Singular	Plural
this	these
that	those

As a general rule, use *this/these* to refer to things physically close but *that/those* to refer to things farther away.

These books (close by) belong to me; *those* (farther away) must belong to you.

However, don't use *this* when you mean *a.*

Incorrect: I have *this* friend who always gets into trouble.
Correct: I have *a* friend who always gets into trouble.

Also, don't use *this* alone to refer to the general idea of a previous sentence. Instead, place *this* before a noun.

Poor: Some of my friends always want to copy my homework. *This* bothers me.
Better: Some of my friends always want to copy my homework. *This dishonesty* bothers me.

CHAPTER
23

✍ **8   Writing Demonstrative Pronouns and Adjectives**

Write the correct word—*this, that, these,* or *those*—in each blank space provided.

1. As a child, I swam in the pond near our house in the country. I loved <u>*those*</u>

   times.

2. Would you give _____ letter to Mr. Turner and bring

   _____ one to Ms. Green?

3. _____ chairs in the other room might look nice in

   _____ spot.

4. Who was _____ masked man? I wanted to thank him.

5. Keep _____ in mind: The test will begin at 9 A.M. sharp.

✍ **9   Editing for Errors with Demonstratives**

Eliminate the error in the use of *this* in each passage by rewriting the appropriate section of the passage.

1. I saw this movie last night that was terrific.
   Rewritten: <u>I saw a movie . . .</u>

2. The underground wells do not have enough water to supply all the houses in
   the area. This is a problem.
   Rewritten: <u>This water shortage is a problem.</u>

3. This car in front of me had a flat tire.
   Rewritten: _____

   _____

4. I saw this dog biting this man right in front of this crowd of people who just
   stood and watched.
   Rewritten: _____

   _____

5. People should not charge more on their credit cards than they can afford to
   pay each month. If people would do this, they would avoid a lot of financial
   problems.
   Rewritten: _____

   _____

✍ **10   Editing for Pronoun Errors**

The following passage contains many errors related to pronoun use. Correct these errors by making any necessary changes above the lines.

The Amazing Machine

❑   (1) Perhaps the most famous robot in history was the Terrible Turk, ∧ ~~whom~~ *who*

All the people

was a robot chess player. (2) ∧ ~~Everyone~~ who saw this fantastic adult toy was

amazed, but they were the victims of a brilliant fraud. (3) Baron Wolfgang von

Kempelen built this for Maria Theresa, the empress of Austria. (4) The robot

looked like a man with a mustache that was made out of wood. (5) It wore Ori-

ental robes and a turban and sat at a chest, that had a built-in chessboard.

(6) You could open the doors of the robot to reveal brass machinery inside.

(7) After the baron died in 1804, it was sold to Johann Nepomuk Maelzel.

(8) Him and the robot then went on tour, first in Europe and then in America.

(9) People were amazed that it could play so much better than them.

(10) However, while they were in France in 1809, Napoleon Bonaparte seemed

to frustrate it by deliberately making false moves. (11) The robot swept the

pieces from the board in a very unmachinelike display of temper. (12) On it's

second tour in 1826, as Maelzel took the robot across the United States accom-

panied by a friend, chess champion William Schlumberger, who's shoulders

were suspiciously stooped. (13) It was a big hit, with whirring and rackety ma-

chinery, rolling eyes, and its cry of *"Echec!"* ("Check!"). (14) They wondered,

however, why Schlumberger was so often absent when the Turk played.

(15) In 1834, the secret workings of the automaton were revealed; this

parts proved it was not a robot at all. (16) Jacques Mouret, a chess player from

Paris that had worked for Maelzel, explained that once they closed the doors, a

human player (usually Schlumberger) concealed hisself inside it, behind the

display machinery. (17) He could see the chess pieces and move it with rods

leading to the robot's arms. (18) This had been kept a secret for nearly 60

years. (19) After Schlumberger and Maelzel both died in 1838, there machine

ended up in Philadelphia's Chinese Museum, where it was destroyed by fire at

age 85.

✍ **11   Editing Your Own Work**

Look at a paragraph or composition you are writing, or return to one you have written previously, and check it carefully for pronouns in the wrong case, pronouns that
could refer to more than one antecedent, pronouns that do not agree with their antecedents, pronouns that do not have antecedents, and reflexive pronouns used as
subjects. Then rewrite the paper and correct these errors.

CHAPTER

23

24

Using Apostrophes and Hyphens

The *apostrophe* (') and the *hyphen* (-) may seem like small things, but they signal important relationships among words. Although the rules for their use are rather simple, you may confuse or forget them in the heat of composing early drafts. This chapter will help you apply the rules, especially in revisions, when you can examine your sentences more carefully. Specifically, we examine the three uses of the apostrophe:

- to form possessive nouns;
- to make contractions; and
- to make a letter or group of letters plural.

Then we look at the two uses of hyphens:

- to join words two or more words; and
- to signal that words divided at the end of the line are still joined.

USING APOSTROPHES

Apostrophes serve two main functions: to signal possession with nouns or to indicate contractions. We examine each function here.

Forming Possessive Nouns

You can express *possession or ownership* in several ways:

> the dog that belongs to Henry
> the stereo my friend owns
> the house of my brother

However, a simple *apostrophe + s* added to a noun signals the same relationship in a shorter and more direct way.

> Henry's dog
> my friend's stereo
> my brother's house

Notice that although a dog, a stereo, and a house are concrete and easy to visualize, abstract concepts can also be possessed:

Brad's suggestion
the doctor's opinion

People don't own these concepts, but the people are responsible for them. "The doctor's opinion" really means "the opinion *of* the doctor." "Brad's suggestion" really means "the suggestion *made by* Brad."

IN SUMMARY

Form the possessive by adding *apostrophe* (') + s to

1. concrete nouns
   the gloves that belong to the man = the man's gloves
   the bicycle that my son owns = my son's bicycle
2. abstract nouns
   the contribution of Ms. Pearson = Ms. Pearson's contribution
   the frown made by Juan = Juan's frown

1 Establishing Possession with Apostrophes

Rewrite each of the following expressions, using 's.

1. the hat that belongs to Susan *Susan's hat*

2. the jewelry that Tom owns _____

3. the friendliness of Lonell _____

4. the mistake made by Elizabeth _____

5. the radio that belongs to Mr. Lorenzo _____

6. the question asked by Adam _____

Using Apostrophes with Nouns Ending in -s.   As you know, many nouns end in -*s*, especially plural nouns.

books	students	glas*ses*	the Pearson*s*
chairs	dollars	cit*ies*	the Lopez*es*

Even some singular nouns end in -*s* or -*ss*.

bus	class	business	news

Because these nouns already end in -*s*, you make them possessive merely by adding the apostrophe after the -*s*.

the apartment that belongs to the Pearsons = the Pearson*s'* apartment
the behavior of my brothers = my brother*s'* behavior
the teacher of the class = the clas*s'* teacher

The position of the apostrophe is important. It shows whether you mean that the possessive noun is singular or plural:

my brother*'s* behavior = singular
my brother*s'* behavior = plural

CHAPTER

24

One important exception to these rules is singular proper nouns ending in *-s*, such as *James*, John *Keats*, and Ms. *Williams*. These words take possessive forms by adding the apostrophe and *-s*:

> the mother of James = James's mother
> the poems of John Keats = Keats's poems
> the work of Ms. Williams = Ms. Williams's work*

IN SUMMARY

To form possessive nouns:

1. add *'s* to nouns that do not end in *-s:*
   one boy's room
   Tom's brother
   Mr. Thompson's house
   Mrs. Reilley's desk
2. add *only* ' to singular common nouns and plural nouns that already end in
   -s or -ss:
   the girls' room (more than one girl)
   the Thompsons' house
   the boss' desk
3. add *'s* to singular proper nouns that end in *-s:*
   James's friend
   Dr. Jones's lecture

2 Forming Possessives of Singular and Plural Nouns

Rewrite each of the following expressions, using *'s or s'*.

1. the friend of the man _____ *the man's friend* _____

2. the responsibility of the children _____

3. the uncle of the boy _____

4. the uncle of the boys _____

5. the briefcase that belongs to Carlos _____

6. the new car that the Simpsons bought _____

7. the Day that celebrates Father _____

Forming Possessives of Things and Time. You can use *'s or s'* not only to show that people possess things, but also to show that objects possess things:

> the car's right headlight = the right headlight *of* the car
> the trees' top branches = the top branches *of* the trees

---

* Many handbooks now recommend that common nouns ending in *-s* also use the apostrophe plus *-s* to form possession, as in *the class's teacher.* You may wish to ask your instructor about his or her preference.

You can even use *'s* or *s'* in some time expressions. Notice in the following examples that the ones with *'s* or *s'* sound better than the ones with *of:*

> a month's vacation = a vacation *of* a month
> several years' work = the work *of* several years*

A Tip About Using Apostrophes

As some people learn to use the apostrophe, they mistakenly put it before or after almost every final *-s*. Don't confuse the possessive *'s* or *s'* with the final *-s* on plural nouns or third-person singular verbs.

Possessives:	my *friend's* hobby (not *friends*)
	the *nurses'* responsibilities (not *nurses*)
Plurals:	Three of my *friends* go to other colleges. (not *friend's*)
	The *nurses* have many responsibilities. (not *nurses'* or *nurse's*)
Verbs:	Lawrence *works* in a large bank. (not work's)
	Who *owns* the blue Mercedes? (not own's)

---

3   Placing Apostrophes Correctly

Insert apostrophes to establish possession where necessary in the following sentences. (Do not use apostrophes to form plural nouns.) Not every sentence requires an apostrophe.

1. On the island of Yap in western Micronesia, one bank∧s doors are always unlocked, and the money is unguarded.
2. In fact, all of the depositors money is openly displayed and may be handled and studied by anyone with the village chiefs permission.
3. The bank, called Stone Money Bank of Balabat, contains only 30 large donut-shaped stones, which are the traditional form of currency for Yap.
4. While the people purchase most items with American dollars, the stone moneys purpose is reserved for expensive purchases.
5. However, because of the stones great size, no one can steal them, and when ownership changes, the money remains in the bank.
6. The moneys value is actually based not on size but on the difficulty involved in bringing it to Yap; most of the stones came from the Palau Islands, which are 275 miles away and many days journey by sea.

Using Apostrophes in Contractions

A *contraction* is a shortened word that is missing one or more letters, usually when combined with another word. By replacing the missing letters with an apostrophe, you signal to readers where you have shortened the word.

---

* Only possessive nouns (Tom's, the man's, the Wilsons') use apostrophes. Possessive adjectives never use apostrophes. The form of the adjective itself indicates possession:

> <u>*possessive*</u>
> it = its
> they = their
> you = your

For more practice with contractions, possessive adjectives, and their other look-alike or sound-alike words, see Chapter 26.

does not = does*n't* (' replaces *o*)
it is = it*'s* (' replaces *i*)
you are = you*'re* (' replaces *a*)
we have = we*'ve* (' replaces *ha*)
I would = I*'d* (' replaces *woul*)

When you write a contraction, be sure to insert the apostrophe in place of the missing letters.

Incorrect:	do'nt	*Correct:*	*don't*
	its'		*it's*

Another Tip

Be careful to distinguish between the contractions and their look-alike and sound-alike words. Note these comparisons:

Contraction	*Possessive adjective*	*Place word*	*Other word*
it's	its		
you're	your		
they're	their } house	there	
who's	whose		
we're		where	were

🖎 **4 Forming Contractions**

Make the following pairs of words into contractions, placing apostrophes in the proper locations.

1. she is *she's* _____   6. could not _____

2. they are _____   7. who is _____

3. I have _____   8. you would _____

4. we are _____   9. it has _____

5. does not _____   10. you are _____

🖎 **5 Identifying Correct Placement of Apostrophes**

Add apostrophes where necessary in the following sentences.

1. That∧s my coat.

2. The elevators arent working today.

3. Dont you know whats the matter?

4. Whos the fellow whose shirt is torn?

5. Your letter doesnt say what youre interested in.

6. I cant help you when you wont help yourself.

Forming Plurals of Letters or Groups of Letters

Add apostrophe plus *s* to make a lowercase letter or group of letters plural, so readers won't mistake the *s* for one of the letters:

Be sure to dot your i's and cross your t's.
How many A's did you get this term?
My youngest child already knows her ABC's. *

An Important Tip

Only *letters* are made plural with apostrophe + *s*; nouns need only the final *s* or *es*.

the *Jeffersons*
the *books* that you want

✏ **6   Forming Plural of Letters**

Rewrite each of the following sentences, making the letter or letter group plural. Use the words in parentheses as guides.

1. She got a B last semester. (all) *She got all B's last semester.*

2. One student in my class has a very high I.Q. (several students) _____

_____

3. You need at least one I.D. to cash a check. (two) _____

_____

4. The word *traveled* can be spelled with one *l*. (two) _____

_____

5. The army wants to produce a new ICBM. (three) _____

_____

IN SUMMARY

Use an apostrophe

1. *to show possession* by adding *'s* to nouns that do not end in *-s,* or by adding just *'* to nouns that already end in *-s;*
2. *to make contractions* by putting *'* in place of the omitted letters; or
3. *to make letters or groups of letters plural* by adding *'s* to them.

✏ **7   Editing for Errors in Apostrophe Use**

The following passage contains many errors in the use of apostrophes. In some places, apostrophes have been omitted. In other places, unnecessary apostrophes have been included. Make all necessary corrections above the line.

---

* The apostrophe could be omitted in this group of letters, for the lower-case final s clearly means a plural:

My youngest child already knows her ABCs.

The Other Jonah

❑   (1) Is the biblical tale of Jonah being swallowed by a whale just an ancient fish story? (2) Don∧t be too sure, for it∧s not the only case on record. (3) Theres another that occurred about a century ago.

(4) It happened in February 1891 when a young English sailor named James Bartley was a crew member on the whaling ship *Star of the East* near the Falkland Island's in the South Atlantic. (5) Suddenly three miles' out, the sailors spotted a sperm whale that later proved to be 80 feet long and to weigh 80 ton's. (6) Two boats with crew members—one of them Bartley—were sent out to kill the whale. (7) As the whale was struck with a sailors harpoon, the whale struck back with it's huge tail, which was shaped like two Vs joined at the point. (8) The force of the blow lifted the boat into the air and capsized it. (9) Fortunately, sailor's on the other boat didnt panic and soon killed the wounded mammal.

(10) When the boat was righted, Bartley and another crewman had disappeared and were presumed to have drowned. (11) The crew pulled the animals carcass alongside *Star of the East* and worked until midnight removing its' blubber. (12) The next morning, using the ship's crane, they hoisted the stomach up on deck. (13) According to one newspaper report, the men then noticed some movement in the whale's belly. (14) They opened it and found Bartley unconscious. (15) Several sailor's immediately carried him away and bathed him in seawater. (16) Although this action revived Bartley, he was delirious and needed two weeks rest in the captains quarters to regain sanity.

(17) Within a month Bartley was fully recovered and able to describe what living in the belly of a whale had been like. (18) He remembered seeing total darkness and then slipping along a smooth passage. (19) His hand's felt slime all around him. (20) In the unbearable heat of the stomach, he lost consciousness, and when he awoke he was in the captains' cabin.

(21) Bartley recovered his full mental powers, but he carried around physical evidence of his experience for the rest of his life. (22) His' face, neck, and hand's remained white—bleached by the whales digestive juice's.

USING HYPHENS

Hyphens serve two functions: to join words or to establish syllable breaks at the end of a line.

Joining Words with Hyphens

Hyphens join two or more words (or a prefix and a word) to function as a single word. Typically, these combinations form numbers, add certain prefixes to nouns, or create single adjectives that precede nouns. Let's examine all three types of joined structures.

Hyphenating Two-Word Numbers.   In formal writing, you should hyphenate numbers from twenty-one through ninety-nine:

sixty-two
twenty-seven*

However, don't hyphenate two-word numbers for one hundred or above, and express numbers of three or more words as numerals.

six thousand
five million
427
6,901

Finally, hyphenate any fractions written as words:

three-fifths
seven-eighths

✍ 8   **Joining Numbers with Hyphens**

Hyphenate the following numbers where necessary.

1. thirty∧four
2. seven thousand
3. two thirds
4. fifty one
5. five hundred

Hyphenating Prefixes Before Nouns.   A *prefix* is a short structure added to another word, called a *root word,* as in these examples:

unhappy
disagree

However, the prefixes *self-, all-,* and *ex-* (meaning "former") require hyphens:

self-control
all-world
ex-wife

Hyphens connect any prefix to a capitalized noun:

pro-German
anti-American

And hyphens must join all expressions with *-in-law:*

brother-in-law
my in-laws
sisters-in-law (Note how the plural is formed.)

✍ 9   **Using Hyphens with Prefixes**

Rewrite each of the following prefix/noun combinations, using hyphens when necessary. Not all items require hyphens.

1. self awareness   _____*self-awareness*_____

2. ex police officer   _____

3. brothers in law   _____

---

* Many newspapers and book publishers now use numerals for numbers of more than one digit. Addison Wesley Longman Publishers, who publish this book, use a modified form of this system.

CHAPTER

24

4. trans American   _____

5. non violence   _____

6. all conference   _____

7. un natural   _____

Hyphenating Phrases Acting as Single Adjectives.   When two or more words form a single adjective before a noun, the groups are hyphenated as if they were one word. Consider, for example, the expression *a four-hour trip.* It is not a *four* trip or an *hour* trip, but a four-hour trip. The two words act as one and therefore must be joined. Here are further examples:

> a simple-minded idea
> a two-car accident (Note that *car,* as part of an adjective, is not plural since adjectives are never plural.)
> a better-than-average runner

However, do not hyphenate these word groups if they come after linking verbs:

> As a runner, he is better than average.

10   Hyphenating Phrases as Adjectives

Rewrite each of the following word groups, creating a two- or three-word adjective requiring hyphens. Eliminate plural noun forms where necessary.

1. a job for two persons _____ *a two-person job* _____

2. a suit with three pieces _____

3. a job that is long overdue _____

4. a board that is 10 feet long _____

5. a situation meaning life or death _____

Hyphenating Compound Words.   A compound word is formed from two complete root words (such as *background).* Be careful how you form a compound, however, for they can be written in three different ways:

1. As a single word:

Root word	Root word	New word
hand	made	handmade
help	less	helpless
head	ache	headache
note	book	notebook

Note that these compound words retain all the letters from their root words.

2. As hyphenated words (usually as nouns; verbs generally aren't hyphenated):

Root word	Root word	New word
president	elect	president-elect
give (and)	take	give-and-take
send	off	send-off (noun)
		send off (verb)

3. As two words (these are really not compound words):

master builder	heat wave	grand piano

Whenever you are unsure about the hyphenation of a compound word, consult an up-to-date dictionary.

IN SUMMARY

> **Use hyphens to join**
>
> 1. all two-word numbers from twenty-one to ninety-nine and all fractions;
> 2. a prefix and a capitalized noun;
> 3. the prefix *self-*, *all-*, or *ex-* to a noun;
> 4. all words with *-in-law;* and
> 5. many—but not all—compound words. Consult a good up-to-date dictionary when you are unsure whether to use a hyphen.

✐ **11   Forming Compound Words**

Combine a root word with each root word, using hyphens when necessary. Check a dictionary if necessary.

1. night*time*_____

5. eye _____

2. house_____

6. _____ work

3. _____ worker

7. war _____

4. _____ ground

8. _____ book

CHAPTER

24

Hyphenating Divided Words

When you must divide a word at the end of a line, use a hyphen to signal that the two parts of the word are still joined. Divide the word only between *syllables*—one or more letters that include a single vowel sound (such as the three single vowel sounds in *un-der-stand*) or a vowel blend (such as *-sion* in *div-i-sion*). Don't divide single-syllable words such as *worked, through,* or *speak.*

　　intell-igent
　　com-munity
　　pic-ture
but not
　　sty-le (one syllable)
　　walk-ed (one syllable; the *-ed* has no vowel sound)

Determining Syllable Breaks. Syllable breaks often come after complete root words:

> *camp*-ing
> *like*-ly
> *spell*-er
> *sad*-ness

Syllable breaks also occur after prefixes or before suffixes:

> *un*-natural
> agree-*ment*
> usual-*ly*

Syllable breaks also come between two consonants—unless the consonants form a blended sound, such as *-ph, -th, -sh, -sc,* or *-ch,* or unless the consonants are part of a root word:

> win-ning
> pen-cil
> paral-lel
> real-ly
> ac-custom
> *but*
> graph-ic
> wash-ing
> north-ern

Avoiding Confusion and Errors with Hyphens. Since two hyphens in the same word are confusing, break a hyphenated word only at its hyphen:

> ex-wife   self-confidence

Never hyphenate a contraction, and don't leave a single letter at the end of a line:

> | *Wrong:* | does-
n't | *Right:* | doesn't |
> | *Wrong:* | a-
bandon | *Right:* | aban-
don |

Consult your dictionary if you are unsure of where a hyphen break occurs.

IN SUMMARY

Use a hyphen to divide a word at the end of a line

1. only between syllables; or
2. only where a word is already hyphenated.

Do not use a hyphen to divide a word

1. if the word is a single syllable;
2. if the word is a contraction; or
3. if you leave only one letter at the end of a line.

✍ **12   Dividing Words Between Syllables**

Rewrite the following words, dividing them between syllables. If a word cannot be divided, do not rewrite it.

1. unnatural   _____*unnat-ural*_____

2. reply   _____

3. stopped   _____

4. self-awareness   _____

5. communication   _____

6. happiness   _____

7. truthfully   _____

✍ **13   Editing Your Own Work**

Look at a paragraph or composition you are now writing or have previously written, and check your use of apostrophes with possessive nouns, contractions, or plurals of letters. Also check your use of hyphens to join or to separate words or word parts. Correct any errors you find.

CHAPTER

24

CHAPTER

25

Checking Punctuation

Punctuation marks—commas, periods, semicolons, and the like—are the stop and go signs that guide readers along their journey through your ideas. Some punctuation marks separate ideas; other punctuation marks join ideas. Therefore, incorrect punctuation can both annoy and confuse readers. You must know the punctuation rules that this chapter explores:

- ✏ the five rules for the comma;
- ✏ the rule for the question mark;
- ✏ the two rules for the semicolon;
- ✏ the rule for the colon;
- ✏ the rule for the dash;
- ✏ the rule for parentheses; and
- ✏ the rules for quotation marks.

USING THE COMMA ,

Contrary to what many people think, commas (,) do not merely indicate pauses in speech. Commas have five main uses—some to separate ideas, others to enclose them. Learn these uses and you will know the proper signals to send your readers.

Punctuating Three or More Items in a Series

When you write three or more items in a series, separate them with commas and place *and* or another coordinating conjunction (*but, or, for, so, nor,* or *yet*) before the last item. A comma before the conjunction is optional, but be consistent in using it. Either include or omit the comma each time.

> *José, Sammy,* and *I (subjects)*
> I *ran* to the station, *bought* my ticket, and *caught* the train just in time.
>   *(verbs)*
> He is *short, ugly, obnoxious,* but *rich. (adjectives)*
> *not on the grass, on the beach,* or *in the water (phrases)*

> item in a series, item, *and* item

✍ **1   Adding Commas**

Place commas where they are needed in the following groups of words. Some groups need no commas.

410

1. a jug of wine∧ a loaf of bread∧ and you
2. The Mad Dipper at the amusement park is exciting funny and scary.
3. You can take the crosstown bus the elevated train or the subway.
4. All I see in the mail are bills bills bills.
5. The government of the people by the people and for the people shall not perish from the earth.
6. The dog ran wildly around the kitchen crashed into a chair in the dining room tore a curtain in the living room and wet the bedroom rug.

Punctuating Two Independent Clauses Joined by a Coordinating Conjunction*

Remember that an independent clause contains a subject and a verb and can be a sentence by itself. When you join two independent clauses, signal to your readers that the clauses are separate by placing a comma before the conjunction that joins them.

California was a remote area with very little population, *but* the gold rush of 1849 changed that situation in a hurry.

Word of the discovery of gold spread quickly, *so* thousands of fortune hunters journeyed west to find the "gold in them thar hills."

Don't confuse two independent clauses with two *verbs*, which are simply two items in a series and should not be separated by a comma.

Incorrect: People made fortunes in a day, *and* then gambled them away at night.

Correct: People made fortunes in a day *and* then gambled them away at night.

Correct: People made fortunes in a day, *and* then they gambled them away at night.

independent clause	, *and* independent clause
	, *but*
	, *or*
	,*for*
	, *so*
	, *yet*
	, *nor*

✍ **2   Joining Independent Clauses**

Join each of the following pairs of independent clauses by inserting an appropriate coordinating conjunction from the box above, preceded by a comma. You need not use every conjunction.

* See Chapter 20 for more explanation of and practice with such clauses.

CHAPTER
25

Joshua Abraham Norton (1819–1880): "The Emperor of the United States"

1. During and after the gold rush of 1849, San Francisco attracted many odd character _____, *but* _____ one man rose to become perhaps the most successful eccentric in American history: Norton I, emperor of the United States and protector of Mexico.

2. In the first 40 years of his life, Joshua Abraham Norton did not behave oddly _____ he was both a shrewd and respected businessperson.

3. He was born in England _____ he lived and worked in South Africa and Brazil until the age of 30.

4. Hearing of the discovery of gold in San Francisco, he arrived there in 1849 with $40,000 _____ he opened an office on the town's main street.

5. He may have been new to town _____ he was no stranger to investing wisely.

6. Other men trusted his sharp judgment _____ they asked him to be their agent in business deals.

✍ **3 Punctuating Joined Independent Clauses**

Some—but not all—of the sentences in the following paragraph contain a conjunction that joins two independent clauses and require a comma before the conjunction. Place commas where they are necessary.

The Collapse of Norton's Business Career

❏ (1) Joshua Norton bought property and goods at cheap prices and then sold them at large profits. (2) Within a few years, he had earned a quarter of a million dollars so the town leaders greatly respected him. (3) In the end, however, one of Norton's risky investments led to his downfall but it also led to his rise to royalty. (4) In 1853, he was sure that he could corner the market in rice so he bought every grain of it already in the city or on its way there. (5) When unexpected shiploads of rice sailed into port, prices crashed and Norton and his friends lost a fortune. (6) Up to that point, no one in San Francisco had more energy or ambition but during the long, painful lawsuit that followed, Norton seemed to lose heart.

Enclosing Sentence Interrupters

You often write words, phrases, or clauses that interrupt the flow of a grammatically complete sentence. Note, for example, the two versions of the following sentence, the first without the interrupter and the second with it:

Joshua Norton dropped out of sight for two years.
Joshua Norton, *therefore,* dropped out of sight for two years.

Alert your readers to a sentence interrupter by enclosing it in two commas—in the same spots where parentheses would go, as in these examples:

One day, looking and acting quite differently, Norton suddenly reappeared.
(*looking and acting quite differently*)

A true sentence interrupter can be removed without seriously affecting the sentence's meaning. Therefore, you can use these tests to help you decide whether to enclose a structure in commas:

◆ See if the structure fits logically in parentheses; or
◆ Temporarily remove it and see if the sentence still makes sense.

Be careful to enclose an interrupter in *two* commas. Many people mistakenly punctuate by ear, putting in only one comma where they hear a pause. Only one comma, however, can confuse readers.

Incorrect: Norton, who had been a conservative in dress and action was a strange sight to behold. (This looks like a sentence fragment.)

Incorrect: Norton who had been a conservative in dress and action, was a strange sight to behold. (The comma in this sentence seems to separate the subject and verb: *Norton . . . was.*)

Correct: Norton, who had been a conservative in dress and action, was a strange sight to behold.

, sentence interrupter,

---

 4   Editing for Missing Commas

The following sentences contain only one comma before or after a sentence interrupter. Place the second comma where it is needed.

1. Depressed about his bad luck, Norton had spent two years in a cheap

   boardinghouse. As time passed, however ⋀he became deeply troubled by the worsening political condition of the country.
2. Because of growing tensions between the North and South, a war, it seemed to him was unavoidable.
3. A democracy, which was loose and inefficient could not handle the conflicts between the slave states and the free states.
4. Only a king, such as the one that Norton had lived under as a British citizen could guarantee peace.
5. What America needed Norton concluded, was a ruler with strong powers.
6. He had made this argument so often to his friends that they began to refer to him, jokingly of course as "His Gracious Highness" and "Emperor."
7. One day, therefore he asked himself: Why not?

Punctuating Introductory or Concluding Words, Phrases, or Clauses

When a sentence begins with an introductory expression, a comma signals to your readers that the rest of the grammatical sentence will follow. The expression may be a single word, a phrase, or a dependent clause.

Single word

However, Norton seemed to have lost his mind.

Phrase

In San Francisco's business community, he had been a prominent and re-spected figure.

Dependent clause*

After Norton reappeared, all of that changed.

> Introductory words, complete sentence.

A comma is usually unnecessary at the end of a sentence, unless it precedes an afterthought or a contrasting idea:

The city had changed considerably *in those two years.*
Norton seemed to have lost his mind, *however. (a contrast)*
Norton had never been married, *incidentally. (an afterthought)*

If you are not sure whether a word or group of words needs one or more com-mas—no matter where the word or group is placed—remember this simple rule: *When in doubt, leave the commas out.*

✍ 5   Punctuating Sentence Interrupters

Rewrite each of the following sentences, inserting the sentence interrupter (indicated in parentheses) in the most logical place. Be sure to use commas where they are needed.

The Rise of the Emperor

1. A dignified gentleman appeared in the offices of a San Francisco newspaper. (one day in September 1859) *One day in September 1859, a dignified gentle man appeared in the offices of a San Francisco newspaper.*

2. He gave the editor a proclamation that began: "At the . . . request and desire of a large majority of the citizens of these United States, I, Joshua Norton . . . de-clare and proclaim myself emperor. . . ." (quietly and seriously) _____ _____ _____

3. The editor ran it without comment. (amused by this unusual feature story) _____ _____

4. Very few people in the city paid much attention, even though the proclamation also abolished Congress and the Supreme Court. (at first) _____ _____ _____

5. When Norton began appearing in the streets in an odd uniform, the townsfolk began to take notice. (however) _____ _____

---

* See Chapter 20 for more explanation of and practice with such clauses.

Emperor Norton I. *Bancroft Library, University of California, Berkeley.*

6. There was some jeering, but people soon stopped. (of course) _____

_____

7. The emperor created a sensation. (in his blue jacket with gold epaulets and brass buttons, red general's cap, and navy boots) _____

_____

6   Punctuating a Passage

Correctly punctuate the sentence interrupters where necessary in the following passage.

❑   (1) Soon growing used to this oddly dressed monarch, the public gave him "appropriate" respect. (2) He marched up and down the streets showing himself to his subjects and accepting their ironic bows with the dignity of a true ruler.

(3) Without fail each day he attended public gatherings and continued to issue proclamations concerning his empire. (4) Furthermore his concern for the people, his dignity, and his graciousness soon completely won over the city. (5) For 20 years the citizens of San Francisco cheerfully supported him in his madness. (6) The royal bonds he issued in the amount of 50 cents were always honored by the local merchants. (7) And the taxes always small amounts of money that he levied against his former business associates were paid.

Punctuating Two or More Adjectives

Don't separate all adjectives. Use this test: If you can reverse the order of the adjectives, separate them with a comma.

a handsome, charming man (a charming, handsome man)
a shy, awkward child (an awkward, shy child)

If you cannot reverse the adjectives, don't separate them with a comma.

a large red pencil (*not* a red large pencil)
a powerful fastback car (*not* a fastback powerful car)

adjective, adjective (when their order can be reversed)

✍ **7   Separating Adjectives with Commas**

Place commas where they are needed in the following phrases.

1. a good-looking ∧talented singer
2. a clever old thief
3. a disgusting slimy worm
4. a dirty worn-out shirt
5. a magnificent still-life drawing

IN SUMMARY

Use commas

1. to separate three or more items in a series;
2. to separate two independent clauses joined by *and, but, or, for, so, nor,* or *yet;*
3. to enclose a sentence interrupter;
4. to separate most introductory words or phrases (and some concluding words or phrases) from the rest of a sentence; and
5. to separate two or more adjectives before a noun when their order can be reversed.

✍ **8   Editing for Comma Use**

Some commas are missing or misplaced in the following passage. Insert commas where they are needed and cross out those incorrectly placed.

Emperor Norton's Reign

❑   (1) Norton I ate and drank for free at the best restaurants and saloons in the city. (2) Furthermore he was often invited to speak at political rallies where he received, often ironically of course the applause of his admiring subjects. (3) When the state legislature met a large comfortable chair was always reserved for him. (4) The city directory, listed him as "Norton, Joshua, Emperor." (5) And when the genuine Emperor Dom Pedro II of Brazil, visited the city in 1876 San Francisco proudly presented its own emperor to him with fitting pomp and circumstance.

(6) Once when the emperor's uniform wore out the public, contributed money for a replacement. (7) On a similar occasion, later the board of supervisors voted city funds. (8) Several tailors, who made and contributed uniforms proudly displayed cards in their windows that read: "By appointment to His Majesty." (9) His loyal subjects gave him a variety of hats a magnificent walking stick, and a big three-color, Chinese umbrella to keep his imperial self dry on rainy days. (10) When someone, attempted to have him committed, the judge dismissed the hearing into the emperor's sanity with the remark that Norton was "just about the best going in the king line."

USING THE QUESTION MARK ?

A question mark (?) indicates that you are writing a question; it cannot signal anything else. Therefore, place a question mark at the end of a direct question, but do not use a question mark at the end of an indirect question.

> Why *did* this change in Norton *occur?* (A direct question, using the word order of *verb-subject-verb*)
>
> *but*
>
> I'd like to know *why this change occurred.* (Indirect question, using the order of a statement: *subject-verb*)

> direct question?
> indirect question.

✎ 9   **Punctuating Direct and Indirect Questions**

Place a question mark or a period at the end of each of the following sentences.

1. Just who was that masked man⌃
2. I want to know what is supposed to happen at the meeting
3. Paul asked if we could meet next Thursday
4. Is it possible to change the date of the meeting
5. He wanted to know how long the meeting would last
6. Is this the end of the exercise, or are there more sentences

USING THE SEMICOLON ;

Placing Semicolons Between Independent Clauses

You can use a semicolon (;) to show you have joined two independent clauses whose ideas are closely related. (See Chapter 20.)

> We cannot afford any further delay; the problem must be stopped immediately.
> Everyone agrees upon the solution; however, no one can agree about how best to implement it.
> Our records indicate a billing error on your last statement; consequently, we are enclosing a corrected statement with our apologies.

Notice in the last two examples that a comma follows the introductory words *however* and *consequently* after the semicolon. You should treat these and similar introductory words just like sentence interrupters at the beginning of sentences.

> independent clause; independent clause
> independent clause; *however*, independent clause

Using Semicolons with a Series of Items Containing Internal Commas

As you know, commas separate three or more items in a series. However, the items in a series can also contain commas used for other purposes, such as commas to separate city names from state names.

> New York, New York
> Los Angeles, California
> Chicago, Illinois
> Houston, Texas
> Philadelphia, Pennsylvania
> San Diego, California
> Detroit, Michigan
> Dallas, Texas

To avoid confusing readers, retain commas between city and state names, but use semicolons to separate items in a series.

> The only eight cities in the United States with populations larger than one million are New York, New York; Los Angeles, California; Chicago, Illinois; Houston, Texas; Philadelphia, Pennsylvania; San Diego, California; Detroit, Michigan; and Dallas, Texas.

> item, in a series; item, in a series; and item, in a series

10   Punctuating with Semicolons

Place semicolons and commas where they are needed in the following sentences.

1. Our reading list for this term includes Herman Melville, *Moby-Dick*; Mark
   Twain, *The Adventures of Huckleberry Finn*; Nathaniel Hawthorne, *The
   Scarlet Letter*; and Henry James, *The Europeans*.

2. We will be visiting St. Louis Missouri Springfield Illinois Louisville Kentucky and Jackson Tennessee.

3. The winners of the election were Wendell Smith president Laury Jackson vice president Casey Redlinski secretary and Billy Hanson treasurer.

4. The most popular songs last year were "Boogie Boogie Hot and Heavy" "All I Want Is You You You" "Susie Lulu and Me" "Let's Do It Again Again and Again" and "I Can't Get No Education."

5. Mr. and Mrs. Williams adopted six children: Jon who was born in South Africa Ahn who was a native of Vietnam Marita who grew up in Argentina and Chile Tanveer who left Pakistan when he was 4 months old Eleni who was a victim of famine in Ethiopia and Frank who was born in San Francisco California.

USING THE COLON :

Use the colon (:) to show readers that you are introducing a long quotation or a list.

Long quotation: When the federal government ignored Emperor Norton's decree to abolish Congress, he issued a second decree: "We do hereby Order and Direct Major General Scott, the Commander-in-Chief of our Armies, immediately on receipt of this our Decree, to proceed with suitable force and clear the halls of Congress."

List: Norton's room in the boardinghouse contained only a few simple pieces of furniture: a table and a chair set on a faded rug, an outdoor camping cot, and a pitcher and a basin resting on a broken stand.

However, use a colon only after a complete statement.

Incorrect: Norton's room in the boardinghouse contained: a table and a chair set on a faded rug . . . (*Norton's room in the boardinghouse contained* is not a complete statement because *contained* requires an object after it.)

Don't use a colon after any form of *to be,* since *to be* doesn't end a complete statement.

Incorrect: The three winners of awards *were:* Wilson Rand, Judi Johnson, and Diego Ramos.

Correct: The three winners of awards *were* Wilson Rand, Judi Johnson, and Diego Ramos.

complete introductory statement: list or long quotation

Be careful not to confuse semicolons with colons. Readers expect semicolons to join independent clauses or to separate items that have internal commas, and colons to introduce lists or long quotations.

Semicolons: Ask not what your country can do for you; ask what you can do for your country.

CHAPTER
25

> You can visit the most famous cities of the world without leaving the United States if you go to Paris, Texas; Cairo, Illinois; New London, Connecticut; Venice, Illinois; or Toledo, Ohio.

Colons: On your world tour, be sure to visit these cities: Paris, Cairo, London, Venice, and Toledo.*

11   Punctuating with Colons and Semicolons

Use either a colon or semicolon—whichever is required—in each of the following sentences.

Emperor Norton's Continuing Rule

1. Emperor Norton paid virtually nothing for all of his necessities and entertainment ∧ his lodgings, meals, streetcar fares, laundry, and even his drinks in saloons.

2. Each day, he followed a rather leisurely routine rising late, permitting a fellow boarder to help dress him, strolling to the nearest bar for a light meal, and setting out on foot to observe his subjects.

3. Once an elderly lady, a fellow passenger on a streetcar, could not find her five-cent fare however, Norton rescued her by announcing to the conductor, "Let her be a guest of the empire."

4. On his daily walks he rarely went without company wild-eyed children and two faithful old dogs of less than aristocratic pedigree followed along.

5. One dog, a black mongrel, was known as Bummer for his habit of begging meals at taverns the other, a dark-yellow collie, was known as Lazarus because he had risen to life after a near fatal fight.

6. On his strolls, the emperor fulfilled a number of kingly duties inspecting civic improvements, chatting with attractive women, discussing law enforcement with police, worshipping in a different church every week, and attending all political discussions and meetings.

USING THE DASH —

Dashes (—) usually come in pairs and function like two commas that enclose sentence interrupters. However, dashes are more dramatic; they tell readers that you want to emphasize and call attention to the sentence interrupter. Note the following example:

> Norton's evening meals—*always at the best restaurants and free of charge*—were full-course affairs.

---

* The only time a colon can join independent clauses is when the second clause explains the first.

Peter knew what he must do: he had to report the murder to the police.

Some handbooks now recommend that the clause after the colon begin with a capitalized letter.

An interrupter can come at the beginning or end of a sentence, of course. When that happens, use only one dash.

> Norton's evening meals were full-course affairs—*always at the best restaurants and free of charge.*
> *Eating well*—that was one luxury Norton often enjoyed.

On most typewriters and word processors, you must create a dash by striking the hyphen key (-) twice: (—).

USING PARENTHESES ( )

Parentheses ( ) work in just the opposite way from dashes. They signal to readers that you are de-emphasizing a sentence interrupter. Parentheses indicate that some information is merely incidental to a sentence (a short explanation, a definition, or some examples—such as the material you are reading right now). Notice the parentheses in the following sentences:

> On his daily walks, Emperor Norton was sure to chat with his subjects (especially attractive women).
> Joshua Norton's father, John Norton, helped found the city of Algoa Bay (now known as Port Elizabeth) in South Africa.

The parentheses are part of the sentence in which they appear, so the period that ends the sentence goes after the final parenthesis (like this one).

IN SUMMARY

> **Use dashes**
>
> to enclose a sentence interrupter you want to emphasize;
>
> **but use parentheses**
>
> to enclose a sentence interrupter you want to deemphasize.

12 Punctuating Sentence Interrupters

Each of the following sentences contains an interrupter. Enclose it in two dashes (or use one dash for an interrupter at the end of the sentence) if the interrupter should be emphasized; enclose it in parentheses if it provides incidental information and should be deemphasized.

1. As emperor, Norton issued many proclamations∧on every subject, whether national or international ∧and sent them off to newspapers or other leaders.
2. Early in his reign, he decided that Mexico was unfit to govern itself it was in fact fighting for independence at that time and declared himself "protector of Mexico."
3. However, after Mexico's actual ruler was brutally executed a rather dangerous precedent Norton withdrew his protectorship on the grounds that the people were too "unsettled" to deserve it.
4. During the Civil War 1861–1865 he ordered President Lincoln and the leader of the South to come to California so Norton could negotiate an end to the fighting.

CHAPTER

25

5. When they ignored his imperial command, he addressed a similar proclamation to the leaders of the two armies Generals Grant and Lee.

USING QUOTATION MARKS " "

Quotation marks (" ") tell readers that you are borrowing someone else's exact words. Use quotation marks in the following situations.

Quoting Titles of Short Works

Put quotation marks around the titles of poems, magazine articles, newspaper articles, songs, and other short works.

"The Road Not Taken" (poem)
"Yesterday" (song)

But underline the titles of complete books, the names of magazines, the names of newspapers, and other complete longer works. If you are composing on the computer, you may italicize (instead of underlining) these titles.

or

Life (magazine)	*Life*
The New York Times (newspaper name)	The *New York Times*
Tom Sawyer (book title)	*Tom Sawyer*
The Lion King (movie title)	*The Lion King*

Here are some titles of short works contained within longer ones.

"A Rising Star in the East," *Life*
"President Proposes Tax Cut," *the New York Times*
"Using Important Punctuation Marks," in *Composing with Confidence*

> "Title of Short Work"
> Title of Long Work

Because quotation marks and underlining tell readers that you are discussing someone else's work, don't use them with the titles of your own compositions.

13   Punctuating Titles

Underline or quote the following titles.

1. The New York Daily News
2. Time (magazine)
3. Pretty Woman (movie)
4. Fierce Storm Strands Thousands (title of article) in the Los Angeles Times (newspaper)
5. My favorite poem from Modern American Poetry (book) is Walt Whitman's I Sing the Body Electric.
6. Did you see the play The Phantom of the Opera when it appeared here?

Quoting Definitions

Quote (or underline) the word you want to define and quote its definition. (Either practice is acceptable.)

"Villain" once meant "a resident of a village," but the meaning of the word has since changed.

Paleontology is "the study of early life forms as revealed in fossils."

---

word to be defined and "definition"

Quoting Speech and Other People's Writing

Use quotation marks to let readers know when you are borrowing a speaker's or writer's exact words. Put quotation marks around direct quotations, but do not put quotation marks around reported speech.

Direct quotation: Norton once told a candidate for office who rose to appeal for votes: "You don't have to speak further because I hereby appoint you United States senator."

Reported speech: Norton once told a candidate for office who rose to appeal for votes that the candidate didn't have to speak further because Norton was appointing him a United States senator.

Direct quotation: During a political debate, an uninformed citizen once rose and asked, "Who is Emperor Norton the First, I would like to know?"

Reported speech: During a political debate, an uninformed citizen once rose and asked if someone would tell him just who this emperor Norton the First was.

The words that identify the speaker or writer are not part of the quotation, so don't place them in quotation marks. The words *that* or *if* introduce reported speech. (*Whether* can also introduce a reported speech question.)

"speaker's or writer's exact words" in direct quotation

---

14 Punctuating Quotations and Reported Speech

Put quotation marks around only the direct quotations in the following sentences.

1. Early in Norton's reign when a few newspapers made fun of him, he responded angrily, calling the attacks ∧scurrilous and untrue articles."
2. At another time when the emperor's authority was challenged, a local newspaper wrote, Since he has worn the imperial purple, he has shed no blood, robbed nobody, and despoiled the country of no one, which is more than can be said of any of his fellows in that line.
3. Once a newly hired policeman said that he was going to arrest Norton on a charge of vagrancy.
4. However, the officer changed the charge to insanity after the enraged Norton shouted that he was not a vagrant since he had five dollars in his pocket.

CHAPTER

25

5. The moment that the chief of police heard of the mistaken arrest, he personally released the monarch and said Your Majesty, I apologize for this indignity visited upon your royal personage.

Capitalizing Words and Punctuating Within Quotations.   Capitalize the first word of a quoted sentence—regardless of whether it precedes or follows the identification of the speaker or writer.

> Robert Louis Stevenson wrote, "**O**f all our visitors, I believe I preferred Emperor Norton."
> "**O**f all our visitors, I believe I preferred Emperor Norton," wrote Robert Louis Stevenson.

Place commas and periods in quotations as follows:

◆ When the identifying words introduce a quotation, place a comma after the introduction and place a period inside the final quotation mark. (See the first example above.)

◆ When the sentence begins with the quotation, place a comma inside the quotation marks. (See the second example above.)

◆ However, when the quotation is a question or an exclamation, replace the end comma with a question mark or exclamation point, as in these examples:

> "Who is Emperor Norton the First, I would like to know**?**" a politician asked.
> "I don't pay for my meals**!**" Norton shouted at a waiter who was ignorant of the royal stature of the person he was serving.

◆ When you quote only part of a sentence after the identifying words, do not capitalize the first word of the quotation.

> On December 31, 1879, Norton published a proclamation welcoming in the new year and offering up **"p**rayers of thanksgiving to Almighty God."

Note that all periods and commas go inside the final quotation mark, whether they are part of the quotation or not. Question marks and exclamation points go inside the final quotation mark when they are part of the quotation but outside the final quotation mark when they are not part of the quotation.

> Have you read the poem, "Sailing to Byzantium"**?**
> He asked, "Have you read any poems by William Butler Yeats**?**"

> Identifying words, "**Q**uoted sentence."
> "**Q**uoted sentence," identifying words.
> "**Q**uoted question?" identifying words.
> "**Q**uoted exclamation!" identifying words.
> Identifying words, "**p**art of a sentence."

Punctuating Longer Quotations.   When quoting more than one sentence, use only two quotation marks—one at the beginning of the quotation and the other one at the end. Do not quote each sentence separately, for your readers may think that the sentences are spoken by different persons.

> In praise of San Francisco, Robert Louis Stevenson wrote, **"I**n what other city would a harmless madman who supposed himself emperor of the two Americas

have been so fostered and encouraged? Where else would even the people of the streets have respected the poor man's illusion**?"**

> "Quoted sentence. Quoted sentence."

However, you can split a quotation from the same speaker. Notice the punctuation and capitalization used in the following quotations:

> "There were many hats**,"** reported a newspaperman who visited Norton's room after the emperor's death. **"T**here was an old stovepipe hat. Directly above, hanging in a row on the wall, were three more."
> "On the wall opposite, over the bed**,"** the reporter added**, "h**ung the well-known sword of the emperor."

In the first example, the quotation is split between sentences, so the first word of the second sentence is capitalized. In the second example, the quotation is split in the middle of the sentence so the first word is not capitalized.

> "Quoted sentenc**e**," **h**e said. **"Q**uoted sentence."
> "Part of a quoted sentenc**e**," **h**e said, "remainder of the quoted sentence."

Paragraphing Quotations Involving More Than One Speaker.   In quoted dialogue between two or more speakers, change paragraphs each time the speaker changes so readers can distinguish between the speakers.

> Once a streetcar conductor said to an elderly woman, "Lady, if you can't pay the five-cent fare, you'll have to get off."
>
> "Let her be the guest of the empire," Norton said, and he advised the conductor to move on.

> "Quotation from one speaker." (end of paragraph)
> (a new paragraph) "Quotation from another speaker."

15   Punctuating Quotations and Reported Speech

Correctly punctuate and capitalize the following passages containing quotations or reported speech.

1. ∧When the genuine Emperor Dom Pedro II of Brazil visited the city in 1876,∧
   "
   Joan Parker wrote in *American Heritage*, ∧San Francisco proudly presented its
   "
   own to him with fitting pomp and circumstance.∧

2. Once Norton participated in a discussion of free love sponsored by a local organization. He began by claiming that 82 percent of infants born in America were destroyed. Said Norton take 25 miles of land. let it rain on that land 24 hours. then turn every one of those drops of water into a baby. how many babies will there be? Norton expected an answer to this question, but when the dazed audience offered none, the emperor marched out of the meeting.

3. When Norton was arrested by the rookie cop, the chief of police personally released the monarch and asked that Norton accept his apology.

4. Why are you wearing the uniform you have on an old friend of Norton's from South Africa once asked.

5. After the friend had promised to keep the secret, Norton confided that he had been born of French royalty and had been sent to South Africa for safety, with one John Norton as his guardian.

IN SUMMARY

Use quotation marks

1. around the titles of short works or works contained within longer works (but underline the titles of longer or complete works);

2. around words you are defining and around their definitions;

3. around the speaker or writer's exact words when you quote them, paying attention to the following rules:

   a. Begin these quotations with a capital letter if they are complete sentences or if they are the first words of a sentence.

   b. Place a comma after the words that introduce a quotation.

   c. If the identifying words come after the quotation, end quoted statements with a comma, quoted questions with a question mark, and quoted exclamations with an exclamation mark. Do not capitalize the identifying words.

   d. Place all periods and commas inside the final quotation mark.

   e. Place question marks and exclamation points inside the final quotation mark if they are part of the quotation, outside the final quotation mark if they are not part of the quotation.

   f. Place quotation marks around the entire quotation, not around each sentence of the quotation.

   g. Each time you quote a new speaker, begin a new paragraph.

 16   Editing for Punctuation Errors

The following passage contains a number of errors in punctuation and matters related to the use of the quotations:

1. missing punctuation;
2. incorrect punctuation;
3. words not capitalized at the beginning of quotations;
4. words incorrectly capitalized in quotations; and
5. punctuation marks placed incorrectly inside or outside final quotation marks.

Cross out incorrect punctuation and insert correct punctuation by using the caret symbol [∧].

The Death of the Emperor

❑   (1) On the evening of January 8, 1880 ∧ Norton went out in a drizzle to attend a debate. (2) He was in full uniform, and in a fine mood. (3) Even as a 62-year-old man he still walked confidently. (4) Those who saw him observed, as Robert Louis Stevenson had written a portly rather flabby man, with the face of a gentleman, rendered unspeakably pathetic and absurd by the great saber at his side and the peacock's feather in his hat. (5) As he approached the building where the debate was held; he suddenly tumbled and collapsed. (6) A passerby ran to his aid and propped him up while shouting for others "That they should get a carriage." (7) Norton was unconscious, when he was taken to the hospital; he was dead a few minutes later. (8) In the morgue, his pockets were emptied. (9) The contents spoke more eloquently than any biography; $3 in silver coins a gold piece worth $2.50 a French franc note dated 1828, a batch of cables signed by many foreign rulers a certificate of ownership of 98,200 shares of stock in a mine, and several copies of his own imperial writing.

(10) The next morning, the San Francisco "Chronicle's" headline announced, "Le Roi Est Mort" that is, The King Is Dead. (11) As he lay in the morgue a crowd began to gather. (12) All classes of people were represented—from the rich to the poor, from the well dressed to the ragged, and by noon the crowd was so large that the police had to be called. (13) He is dead, wrote the Morning Call, And no citizen of San Francisco could have been taken away who would be more generally missed".

(14) Reportedly, 30,000 attended his first funeral. (15) However more than 50 years later, there was another funeral. (16) In 1934, when the city expanded to swallow up the Masonic Cemetery the emperor's remains were dug up, and buried at another cemetery. (17) The mayor placed a wreath on the grave, while the municipal band played and a military battalion fired a volley in salute. (18) A fine granite monument was set in place. (19) It read;

NORTON I, EMPEROR OF THE UNITED STATES,
PROTECTOR OF MEXICO,
JOSHUA A. NORTON 1818–80

(20) As one historian has noted, there were no quotation marks around the inscription.

17   Editing Your Own Work

Look at a paragraph or composition you are now writing or have previously written, and correct any errors related to punctuation and quoting. Look for the types of errors outlined in Exercise 16.

CHAPTER

25

Checking Sound-Alike and Look-Alike Words

Many people confuse words that look alike or sound alike, writing one when they mean the other. The result can be equally confusing and annoying to readers, who may have to reread a sentence before they can understand its meaning. Therefore, be sensitive to such errors as you revise and proofread—especially if you know the errors you are most likely to commit. This chapter helps you distinguish between the most common (and troublesome) look-alike and sound-alike words. It begins by examining the three most frequent errors:

✏ the contractions and their look-alike and sound-alike words;
✏ final -d omitted on *used, supposed,* and *prejudiced;* and
✏ the incorrect use of *of* instead of *have* after helping verbs.

The remainder of the chapter examines these matters:

✏ other commonly confused words, arranged alphabetically.

You may want to study the entire chapter or just the words that give you the most trouble.

AVOIDING THREE COMMON ERRORS WITH LOOK-ALIKE AND SOUND-ALIKE WORDS

Distinguishing Between Contractions and Their Look-Alikes or Sound-Alikes

Certain contractions deserve special attention because so many writers confuse them with similar looking or sounding words:

Contractions	Possessive words	Place words	Other
it's = *it is* (and *it has*)	its		
who's = *who is* (and *who has*)	whose		
he's = *he is* (and *he has*)	his		
they're = *they are*	their	there*	
you're = *you are*	your		
we're = *we are*		where	were (past tense of *are*)

* *There is* or *There are* at the beginning of a sentence usually does not refer to a specific place.

◆ Notice that each contraction contains both a subject pronoun and a verb (*is*, *are*, or *has*), so each is always the subject and the verb of a sentence or clause.

◆ Notice that the possessive words do not contain an apostrophe ('), which, as you may recall from Chapter 24, signals a contraction.

◆ Notice that the place words contain the word *here*.

there
where

1   Identifying Contractions and Their Look- and Sound-Alikes

Label each of the italicized words in the sentences provided as *C* (contraction), *P* (possessive), *Pl* (place), or *PT* (past tense). If the word is a contraction, write out the words the contraction represents.

___C___ 1. *It's* eight o'clock. _____It is_____

_____ 2. The cat lost *its* collar. _____

_____ 3. *They're* friends of mine. _____

_____ 4. They got *their* grades yesterday. _____

_____ 5. It was *there* a while ago. _____

_____ 6. *You're* just in time for dinner. _____

_____ 7. Is *your* biology class interesting? _____

_____ 8. *Who's* seen my book? _____

_____ 9. *Whose* hat is this? _____

_____ 10. *We're* happy to see you. _____

_____ 11. *Where* is it? _____

_____ 12. *Were* you in the house? _____

2   Composing Your Own Sentences

Use each of the following words in a sentence.

1. (their) *Their friends invited them to dinner.* _____

2. (it's) _____

3. (your) _____

4. (who's) _____

5. (they're) _____

6. (whose) _____

7. (its) _____

8. (we're) _____

9. (where) _____

10. (who's) _____

CHAPTER

26

11. (were) _____

12. (you're) _____

Placing Final -d on Three Common Words

Because the sounds of the letters *d* and *t* are almost identical, many people drop the final -*d* on a word when the next word begins with *t*. But notice the spelling of the following phrases:

> suppose**d** *to*   I'm suppose**d** *to* work later.
> use**d** *to*   He use**d** *to* get up late, but now he's use**d** *to* getting up early.

Be careful to distinguish between *use* and *used to*. *Use* can be a verb in any tense—or even a noun.

> I *use* at least eight sheets of paper every time I write a one-paragraph com-
>   position. (present tense verb)
> In fact, I revised the last paragraph so often that I *used* a dozen sheets of
>   paper. (past tense verb)
> But I find a *use* for the scrap paper; I give it to my children to draw on. (a
>   noun)

Used to, however, has two meanings.

> ◆ It can describe an action in the past that no longer occurs.
>
>   When I was a child, I *used to* swim every week, but I don't swim anymore.
>
> ◆ Or it can mean *accustomed to.*
>
>   Bill is *used to* working a double shift on Friday.

Many people also confuse the adjective *prejudiced* with the noun *prejudice.* You must put a final -*d* on the adjective.

> *Adjective:*   He is *prejudiced* against many people.
> *Noun:*   Racial *prejudice* shouldn't exist in this country.

✍ **3   Writing Correct Word Forms**

Supply the appropriate form of *use, suppose,* or *prejudice* in each sentence.

1. (use) For centuries, sap from the rubber tree _____*used*_____

   to have only a few _____*uses,*_____ and very few Europeans knew

   about them.

2. (use) The Indians of Central and South America, who weren't

_____ to the clothes that Europeans wore,

_____ the hardened juice to make clothes and bottles.

3. (suppose) One day around 1820, Thomas Hancock of London devised another

use for the rubber bottles, which were only _____
to hold water.

4. (suppose) He _____ that if he sliced the bottle into
strips, they could be put into garters and waistbands.

5. (prejudice) About 25 years later, another Englishman named Stephen Perry,

who wasn't _____ against stealing someone else's
invention, patented the rubber band.

✍ 4   **Composing Your Own Sentences**

Write a sentence of your own that correctly uses *used to,* another that correctly uses
supposed to, and one more that correctly uses *prejudiced.*

1. _____

2. _____

3. _____

Avoiding the "of" Error After *Could, Should, Would, Might,* and *Must*

In speech, many people contract *have* as -'*ve* after a helping verb.

> could've = could have
> should've = should have
> would've = would have
> might've = might have
> must've = must have

Because this contraction sounds like the preposition *of,* some people mistakenly write *could of* when they mean *could have,* and so forth. However, *of* cannot
follow the words *could, should, would, might,* and *must.*

Incorrect: He must *of* done it.
Correct: He *must have* done it.
Incorrect: I *might of* gone.
Correct: I *might have* gone.

✍ 5   **Writing Correct Word Forms**

Complete each of the following sentences using *might have, would have, could have,
must have,* or *should have.*

1. If I had known you were coming, *I would have baked a cake.* _____

2. It started to rain while I was walking to work. I _____

_____

CHAPTER

26

3. Barry wasn't in school yesterday. He _____

_____

4. You didn't have to take a cab to my house. You _____

_____

5. Susan's tennis game is much better than it was. She _____

_____

✍ 6 **Composing Your Own Sentences**

Write a sentence of your own using each of the following phrases.

1. could have *If I hadn't been slow, clumsy, and weak, I could have been a major*
   *league baseball player when I was younger.*_____

2. should have _____

_____

3. might have _____

_____

4. must have _____

_____

5. would have _____

_____

AVOIDING ERRORS WITH OTHER COMMONLY CONFUSED WORDS

Distinguishing Between *Accept* and *Except*

Accept means *to agree to receive.*

> We are happy to *accept* your invitation.

Except means *excluding* or *but.*

> All my brothers and sisters *except* one have been to college.

✍ 7 **Writing Correct Word Forms**

Supply the appropriate word in each of the blank spaces.

1. When the fork was introduced in England in 1608, the English were slow to
   _____*accept*_____ the new invention.

2. The English ate with their hands and did not use any silverware,

   _____ knives for cutting meat they couldn't tear with

   their teeth.

3. They gradually began to _____ the fork after King James
(1566–1625) began eating with one.

4. In the American colonies, however, forks were not _____
until the eighteenth century.

✍ **8   Composing Your Own Sentences**

Write a sentence of your own that correctly uses *accept* and another that correctly
uses *except*.

1. _____

2. _____

Distinguishing Between *Advice* and *Advise*

Advice is a noun.

> What *advice* can you offer me?

Advise is a verb.

> He *advised* me to get a lawyer.

Remember this rhyme. *Advice* is *nice,* but only the *wise advise.*

✍ **9   Writing Correct Word Forms**

Supply the appropriate word in each of the blank spaces.

1. In Florence, Italy, in 1306, a priest named Giordano ____*advised*____
the members of his monastery to improve their eyesight by getting "disks for
the eyes" from a glassmaker whose name today is unknown.

2. His _____ is the earliest record of what later were called
eyeglasses. Giordano claimed he had met the glassmaker about 20 years earlier, which would put the date of the invention at around 1280 to 1286.

3. Giordano's _____ didn't help every person with poor eyesight, however, for the spectacles were only for the farsighted.

4. Today, if you are both farsighted and nearsighted, you would be well
_____ to wear bifocals, which were invented in 1785 by a
famous American, Benjamin Franklin.

CHAPTER

26

✍ **10   Composing Your Own Sentences**

Write a sentence of your own that correctly uses *advice* and another that correctly uses *advise*.

1. _____

2. _____

Distinguishing Between *Affect* and *Effect*

Affect, a verb, means *to influence or change*.

> The cold *affected* her breathing ability.

Effect, a noun, is *the result of a cause*.

> We don't know what the *effect* of his decision will be.

✍ **11   Writing Correct Word Forms**

Supply the appropriate word in each of the blank spaces.

1. In 1827 an English chemist named John Walker accidentally struck a stick coated with potash and antimony against the floor and created a surprising _____*effect*_____ .

2. The stick burst into flames, and the resulting invention has greatly _____ our lives.

3. Seeing how _____ively he could light a fire, Walker began to manufacture the first friction matches.

4. Although Walker never patented his invention, this did not _____ his success, for he continued to produce and sell matches throughout his life.

✍ **12   Composing Your Own Sentences**

Write a sentence of your own that correctly uses *affect* and another that correctly uses *effect*.

1. _____

2. _____

Distinguishing Between *Buy* and *By*

Buy means *to purchase*.

> We *buy* our groceries at Save-A-Lot.

By, a preposition, has several meanings.

> He is standing *by* the door.
> I will be home *by* nine.
> He finished his term paper *by* working all weekend.

13   Writing Correct Word Forms

Supply the appropriate word in each of the blank spaces.

1. False teeth were invented_____*by*_____ the Etruscans around 700 B.C.E.

2. These early dentures were carved from bone or ivory or were taken from the mouths of young cattle. They were held together _____ gold bands.

3. _____ the eighteenth century C.E., certain improvements had been added. A Parisian dentist named Pierre Fauchard joined together upper and lower false teeth _____ using steel springs.

4. However, not everyone would _____ his invention, for the springs made it difficult for a wearer to close his mouth.

5. Porcelain teeth were introduced into the United States in 1785 _____ Dr. John Greenwood of New York City.

6. George Washington was one of the first to _____ Greenwood's product.

14   Composing Your Own Sentences

Write a sentence of your own that correctly uses *buy* and another that correctly uses *by*.

1. _____

2. _____

Distinguishing Between *Conscience* and *Conscious*

Your *conscience* monitors your behavior.

> My *conscience* bothers me about telling a lie.

Conscious means that you are *awake and aware*.

> The man was *conscious* for only a few minutes after his stroke and then fell into a coma.

15   Writing Correct Word Forms

Supply the appropriate word form in each blank space.

1. Locks and keys have been around so long that few people are

    _____ conscious _____ of how or when the first were invented.

2. Devices have always been needed to stop people whose

    _____ won't prevent them from breaking into houses.

3. _____ of the problem, a man named Joseph Bramah in-

    troduced the padlock in 1784. He offered a large reward to anyone who could

    open the 4-inch iron device; many tried, but no one succeeded.

    (See Exercise 17 for more about the padlock.)

16   Composing Your Own Sentences

Write a sentence of your own that correctly uses *conscience* and another that correctly uses *conscious.*

1. _____

2. _____

Distinguishing Between *Fine* and *Find*

As an adjective, *fine* means *acceptable* or *excellent.* As a noun, it means *a penalty to pay.*

> This desk is *fine* for my purposes.
> We had a *fine* meal at Maxwell's restaurant.
> There is a $25 *fine* for parking here illegally.

Find means *to discover or locate.*

> Did you *find* the watch you lost?

17   Writing Correct Word Forms

Supply the appropriate word in each of the blank spaces.

1. No one could _____ find _____ a way to pick Bramah's padlock be-

    cause there were 494 million combinations of the notches.

   2. Finally, 67 years later, an American locksmith named Alfred Charles Hobbs was

     able to _____ a way to pick the lock, after a month's

     work.

   3. So _____ is Bramah's original design that variations of it

     are still in use today.

18   Composing Your Own Sentences

Write a sentence of your own that correctly uses *fine* and another that correctly uses *find*.

   1. _____

   2. _____

Distinguishing Among *Know* and *No*; *Knew* and *New*

Know means *to be familiar with* or *understand*. Its past tense is *knew*.

> I *know* a lot about skiing. I *knew* how to ski when I was 8.

No is a negative word, and *new* is *the opposite of old*.

> We have *no* car at the moment. We have sold our old car and are going to buy a *new* one soon.

19   Writing Correct Word Forms

Supply the appropriate word in each of the blank spaces.

   1. As we all _____*know*_____ there is nothing more sinfully delicious

     than a Swiss chocolate bar.

   2. But chocolate originated in France and Italy in the late eighteenth century.

     This _____ delicacy was made in rolls and sheets that

     were cut into smaller pieces for sale to local consumers.

   3. Then in 1819, a Swiss named François-Louis Cailler, who

     _____ of the public's great desire for the sweet stuff,

     mass-produced chocolate in a _____ block shape.

   4. Cailler's son-in-law added milk to chocolate in 1875, and thus perfected the

     candy that _____ one can resist.

20   Composing Your Own Sentences

Write a sentence of your own that correctly uses each of the following words.

   1. (know) _____

   2. (knew) _____

CHAPTER

26

3. (no) _____

4. (new) _____

Distinguishing Between *Led* and *Lead*

Led is the past tense of the verb *lead*.

> The trail *led* to a riverbank.

Lead is a heavy metal.

> The pipe is made of *lead*.

21 Writing Correct Word Forms

Supply the appropriate word in each of the blank spaces.

1. In 1908, women in Paris began wearing wrist bracelets with watches attached to them. Men continued to carry pocket watches made of gold, silver, or even _____*lead*_____.

2. It was war, not fashion, that _____ men to change their habits.

3. In World War I, the generals who _____ the troops realized that soldiers could consult wristwatches more quickly than pocket timepieces during battle.

22 Composing Your Own Sentences

Write a sentence of your own that correctly uses *led* and another that correctly uses *lead*.

1. _____

2. _____

Distinguishing Between *Lie* and *Lay*

Lie doesn't take an object.

> I am going to *lie* down.
> The pen is *lying* on top of the book.

Its forms are as follows:

Present tense	Past tense	Past participle
lie, lies	lay	lain

Lay is something you do to an object.

I am going to *lay* this book on the table.

Its forms are as follows:

Present tense	Past tense	Past participle
lay, lays	laid	laid

23   Writing Correct Word Forms

Supply the appropriate word in each of the blank spaces.

1. Would-be inventors have long dreamed of creating a machine so efficient that, once it was started, would keep going indefinitely with no consumption of fuel. The beginning of the search for such an invention _____*lies*_____ at the very beginning of civilization.

2. In Egypt around 3500 B.C.E., slaves aboard ships _____ down their oars when wind filled the newly invented sails.

3. In northern Greece during the first century B.C.E., water turned the blades of a wheel that _____ in a stream, powering the first water mill.

4. In England in 1191 C.E., Dean Herbert invented the first English windmill and used it to grind corn. Prior to then, corn had to be ground slowly by hand, resulting in the loss of many bushels that had simply _____ unharvested in the fields.

5. The sail, the water mill, and the windmill depend on external and unreliable energy sources, so the true secret of perpetual motion still _____ undiscovered. (See Exercise 25 for more about the search.)

CHAPTER

26

✍ **24   Composing Your Own Sentences**

Write a sentence of your own that correctly uses each of the following words.

1. (lie) _____

2. (lay, present tense) _____

3. (lay, past tense) _____

4. (laid) _____

5. (lain) _____

Distinguishing Between *Lose* and *Loose*

Lose, a verb, means *to misplace* or *not to win.*

Did you *lose* your wallet?
Who *lost* the game?

Loose is an adjective meaning *not tight.*

These pants are very *loose* on me.

✍ **25   Writing Correct Word Forms**

Supply the appropriate word in each of the blank spaces.

1. In Italy around 1500, Leonardo da Vinci envisioned a large and delicate wheel with flat, curved spokes, which would never _____lose_____ momentum.

2. Inside the rim and between each pair of spokes was a heavy metal ball. When the wheel turned, the balls on the high end of the rim would be set _____ and would roll toward the rim on the low end.

3. In theory, this would create enough force to carry the balls on the low side back to the top, turning the wheel indefinitely. However, each time Leonardo spun the wheel, it would _____ speed and then grind to a halt.

✍ **26   Composing Your Own Sentences**

Write a sentence of your own that correctly uses *lose* and another that correctly uses *loose.*

1. _____

2. _____

Distinguishing Between *Mine* and *Mind*

Mine is a possessive word.

> This book is *mine*.

Mind as a noun means your *intellect*. As a verb, it means *to object*.

> The human *mind* is still much smarter than a computer.
> Do you *mind* if I smoke?

27   Writing Correct Word Forms

Supply the appropriate word in each of the blank spaces.

1. We don't _____*mind*_____ paying for traveler's checks when we take a vacation because the checks protect our money.

2. If the checks are lost or stolen, you can get your money back, and I can get

   _____.

3. Prior to 1792, an inefficient system of "letters of credit" existed to protect travelers. Then, a better idea popped into the _____ of an Englishman named Robert Harries. He introduced "circular notes," which were accepted in 90 cities throughout the world.

4. However, Marcellus Berry was the master _____ of the modern system of traveler's checks. In 1891, he devised the idea of signing the checks twice.

28   Composing Your Own Sentences

Write a sentence of your own that correctly uses *mine* and another that correctly uses *mind*.

1. _____

2. _____

Distinguishing Between *Passed* and *Past*

Passed is the past tense and past participle of the verb *pass*.

> I *passed* the sign without noticing it.

**CHAPTER
26**

Past as a preposition means *beyond.* As a noun or adjective, *past* means *before the present.*

> Be careful not to go *past* Seventh Street, or you will get lost.
> You can't forget the *past,* but you have to live in the present.

✍ **29   Writing Correct Word Forms**

Supply the appropriate word in each of the blank spaces.

1. Sixty-one years _____*passed*_____ between the conception of the ballpoint pen and its production.

2. In 1888, an American named John Loud patented a pen that used a rotating ball to deliver ink, but he never got _____ the technical problems that made its writing messy and blurred.

3. In 1919, the Hungarian brothers Lasalo and Georg Biro reintroduced the ballpoint, but it still leaked and smeared. After fleeing France and setting up shop in Argentina during World War II, they introduced a new design that overcame many of the defects of _____ versions.

4. Finally, in 1949, Franz Seech of Austria joined their company and perfected a new ink, which was highly concentrated and dried on contact with the page. That same year, ballpoint sales sur_____ those of fountain pens.

✍ **30   Composing Your Own Sentences**

Write a sentence of your own that correctly uses *passed* and another that correctly uses *past.*

1. _____

2. _____

Distinguishing Between *Quiet* and *Quite*

Quiet means *not noisy.*

> The children were very *quiet* as they watched the movie.

Quite means *very.*

> Stretch Johnson is *quite* tall.

✐ **31**   **Writing Correct Word Forms**

Supply the appropriate word in each of the blank spaces.

1. There were _____ _quite_ _____ a few inventors responsible for the modern escalator, which has changed considerably since its inception.

2. The first escalator was patented in March 1892 by an American named Jesse W. Reno and was known as the Reno Inclined Elevator. The grooved wooden slats attached to its inclined conveyor belt made it less _____ than modern ones, but the rubber cleats on the slats dampened the sound a bit.

3. Two years later, Harrod's department store of London installed a Reno Elevator, complete with a porter at the top serving brandy to _____ down passengers who were nervous from the ride.

4. Charles A. Wheeler patented a model in August 1892 that added flat steps, but its ride still wasn't very _____ or smooth. Six years later, Charles D. Seeberger further improved the design to create the first practical "moving staircase."

5. The Otis Elevator Company of New York exhibited this model at the Paris Exhibition of 1900, where it was _____ a hit. Parisians called this device the *escalator.*

✐ **32**   **Composing Your Own Sentences**

Write a sentence of your own that correctly uses *quiet* and another that correctly uses *quite.*

1. _____

2. _____

Distinguishing Between *Rise* and *Raise*

Rise means *to get up without help.*

> The sun *rises* in the morning.

Raise as a verb means *to lift something* or *to increase something.* As a noun, it means *an increase in pay.*

> He *raised* the window to let in more air.
> The Ritz restaurant has *raised* prices again. I will need a *raise* in salary before I can afford to go there.

CHAPTER
26

✍ **33   Writing Correct Word Forms**

Supply the appropriate word in each of the blank spaces.

1. Its first appearance at a Paris fashion show on July 5, 1946,

    _____*raised*_____ a public outcry.

2. This explosive debut came four days after the first atomic mushroom cloud fin-

    ished _____ing above Bikini Atoll, so the creator of the

    two-piece bathing suit, Louis Reard, named it the *bikini*.

3. The first bikini was cotton and was worn by dancer Micheline Bernardi. Each

    time a newspaper printed her photograph, it would _____

    the number of fan letters she received.

✍ **34   Composing Your Own Sentences**

Write a sentence of your own that correctly uses *rise* and another that correctly uses *raise*.

1. _____

2. _____

Distinguishing Between *Sit* and *Set*

Sit means *to seat yourself*.

> Please *sit* over here.

Set means *to put something down* or *to establish something*.

> You can *set* your books on this chair.
> The rules were *set* many years ago.

✍ **35   Writing Correct Word Forms**

Supply the appropriate word in each of the blank spaces.

1. People have been _____*setting*_____ words on paper for a long time,

    but the developing commercial world at the beginning of the nineteenth cen-

    tury needed fast and easy "duplicates of writing."

2. One day in 1806, Ralph Wedgwood of England decided to

    _____ down and invent a way to satisfy the need.

3. He soaked thin paper with ink and dried it between sheets of blotting paper, producing a substance he patented under the name *carbon paper.* He _____ up a shop at 4 Rathbone Place, Oxford Street, London, where he sold his product in the 1820s.

36   Composing Your Own Sentences

Write a sentence of your own that correctly uses *sit* and another that correctly uses *set.*

1. _____

2. _____

Distinguishing Between *Then* and *Than*

Then is a time expression meaning *afterward* or *later.*

> We stayed for a while and *then* we left.

Than is used in a comparison.

> He smells worse *than* a goat.

37   Writing Correct Word Forms

Supply the appropriate word in each of the blank spaces.

1. There has been no more important advance in the treatment of ordinary pain _____ *than* _____ the development of aspirin.

2. It was formulated in 1853 by Karl Gerhardt but _____ was ignored until 1899, when another scientist published a paper on its power to relieve pain.

3. _____ Dr. Felix Hoffman, who worked for a German firm, the Bayer AG, succeeded in manufacturing aspirin in a form pure enough to be used as a medical remedy.

4. Bayer began retailing aspirin tablets in 1915, and since _____ they have been used more _____ any other over-the-counter drug.

CHAPTER

26

✍ **38 Composing Your Own Sentences**

Write a sentence of your own that correctly uses *then* and another that correctly uses *than*.

1. _____

2. _____

Distinguishing Among *Too, To,* and *Two*

Too means *more than enough* or *also*.

> He is *too* fat; he must lose weight.
> His brother should lose weight, *too*.

Two is the number.

> He ate *two* whole chickens.

To is used in all other cases.

> I walked all the way *to* the library.
> I want *to* talk *to* you.

✍ **39 Writing Correct Word Forms**

Write the appropriate word—*too, two,* or *to*—in each blank space.

1. In 1867, a chef at the Saratoga Springs hotel in Florida was paying

   _____*too*_____ little attention _____*to*_____ his work;

   consequently, he dropped a small quantity of thinly sliced potatoes into hot

   cooking oil.

2. _____ the rich and fashionable people who came to the

   Saratoga, it was a new delicacy that they called the Saratoga chip.

3. One or _____ chips were never enough, so these elegant

   people would eat large quantities of them at a time. (See Exercise 41 for more

   about the chips.)

✎ **40 Composing Your Own Sentences**

Write a sentence of your own that correctly uses each of the following words.

1. (too) _____

2. (two) _____

3. (to) _____

Distinguishing Between *Whether* and *Weather*

Whether suggests a choice; it is used in the same way as *if* in indirect questions.

> I don't know *whether* it will rain or not.
> He asked me *whether* I could come.

Weather refers to the temperature and atmospheric conditions.

> It is supposed to rain tonight, but the *weather* will be better tomorrow.

✎ **41 Writing Correct Word Forms**

Supply the appropriate word in each of the blank spaces.

1. _____*Whether*_____ strolling down the wide avenues or sitting on the huge porch of the famous hotel, such rich and fashionable people as the Vanderbilts daintily ate potato chips from paper cups.

2. Each year, the wealthy would return to the Saratoga Springs hotel to escape the winter _____ and enjoy their chips.

3. Finally, in 1925, the first plant devoted exclusively to the making of potato chips was built in Albany, New York. Without mass production, who knows _____ the elegant potato chip would have ever become a commonplace household item.

✎ **42 Composing Your Own Sentences**

Write a sentence of your own that correctly uses *whether* and another that correctly uses *weather.*

1. _____

2. _____

CHAPTER 26

LITERARY

Chapter 2

From *Panati's Extraordinary Origins of Everyday Things* by Charles Panati, pp. 22–24, 267. Copyright © 1987 by Charles Panati. Reprinted by permission of HarperCollins Publishers, Inc.

From *Significa* by Irving Wallace, David Wallechinsky, and Amy Wallace. Copyright © 1983 by Irving Wallace, David Wallechinsky, and Amy Wallace. Reprinted by permission of Irving Wallace.

Chapter 3

From *The People's Almanac #3* by David Wallechinsky and Irving Wallace. Copyright © 1978 by David Wallechinsky and Irving Wallace. Reprinted by permission of William Morrow & Company, Inc.

Adapted excerpts from *1500 Fascinating Facts* by Simon Goodenough, et al. Copyright © 1983 Octopus Books Ltd. Reprinted by permission.

Chapter 4

From *Don't Know Much About History* by Kenneth C. Davis. Copyright © 1990 by Kenneth C. Davis. Published by Avon Books.

From *I Love Paul Revere, Whether He Rode or Not* by Richard Shenkman, pp. 2, 8–9. Copyright © 1991 by Richard Shenkman. Reprinted by permission of HarperCollins Publishers, Inc.

From *The People's Almanac #3* by David Wallechinsky and Irving Wallace, p. 262. Copyright © 1978 by David Wallechinsky and Irving Wallace. Reprinted by permission of William Morrow & Company, Inc.

From *Panati's Extraordinary Endings of Practically Everything and Everybody* by Charles Panati, p. 71. Copyright © 1989 by Charles Panati. Reprinted by permission of HarperCollins Publishers, Inc.

From *The People's Almanac* by David Wallechinsky and Irving Wallace, pp. 113–14. Copyright © 1975 by David Wallechinsky and Irving Wallace. Reprinted by permission of the author.

Chapter 7

From *Significa* by Irving Wallace, David Wallechinsky, and Amy Wallace, p. 20. Copyright © 1983 by Irving Wallace, David Wallechinsky, and Amy Wallace. Reprinted by permission of Irving Wallace.

Adapted excerpts from *Panati's Extraordinary Origins of Everyday Things* by Charles Panati. Copyright © 1987 by Charles Panati. Reprinted by permission of HarperCollins Publishers, Inc.

Chapter 5

From *Significa* by Irving Wallace, David Wallechinsky, and Amy Wallace, p. 165. Copyright © 1983 by Irving Wallace, David Wallechinsky, and Amy Wallace. Reprinted by permission of Irving Wallace.

Adapted excerpt from *1500 Fascinating Facts* by Simon Goodenough, et al. Copyright © 1983 Octopus Books Ltd. Reprinted by permission.

From "Plato's Atlantis" from *Mystery, Intrigue and the Supernatural* by Roger Boar and Nigel Blundell. Reprinted by permission of Reed International Books Limited.

"The Beauty of My Town" by Max Rodriguez-Reyes. Reprinted with permission of the author.

"I Remember . . . My Little *White* Schoolhouse" by K. W. Carter, as it appeared in *Down East Magazine*, April 1979, p. 108. Reprinted by permission of Lorena Carter.

Chapter 10

From *Significa* by Irving Wallace, David Wallechinsky, and Amy Wallace, p. 270–71. Copyright © 1983 by Irving Wallace, David Wallechinsky, and Amy Wallace. Reprinted by permission of Irving Wallace.

From *The Dictionary of Misinformation* by Tom Burnam. Copyright © 1975 by Tom Burnam. Reprinted by permission of HarperCollins Publishers.

Adapted excerpt "ax to grind" from *Loose Cannons & Red Herrings: A Book of Lost Metaphors* by Robert Claiborne. Copyright © 1988 by Robert Claiborne. Reprinted by permission of W.W. Norton & Co., Inc.

From *Fatherhood* by Bill Cosby. Copyright © 1986 by William H. Cosby, Jr. Used by permission of Doubleday, a division of Bantam Doubleday Dell Publishing Group, Inc.

"I Want a Wife," by Judy Brady. Copyright © 1970 by Judy Brady. Originally appeared in *Ms. Magazine*, December 20, 1971. Reprinted by permission of the author.

Chapter 11

From *Imponderables: The Solution to the Mysteries of Everyday Life* by David Feldman. Copyright © 1986 by David Feldman. Reprinted by permission of William Morrow & Company, Inc.

From *Significa* by Irving Wallace, David Wallechinsky, and Amy Wallace, p. 270–71. Copyright © 1983 by Irving Wallace, David Wallechinsky, and Amy Wallace. Reprinted by permission of Irving Wallace.

From *Imponderables: The Solution to the Mysteries of Everyday Life* by David Feldman. Copyright © 1986 by David Feldman. Reprinted by permission of William Morrow & Company, Inc.

From *Why Do Dogs Have Wet Noses?* by David Feldman, pp. 60–61, 113–14. Copyright © 1990 by David Feldman. Reprinted by permission of HarperCollins Publishers, Inc.

From *Panati's Extraordinary Origins of Everyday Things* by Charles Panati. Copyright © 1987 by Charles Panati. Reprinted by permission of HarperCollins Publishers, Inc.

"Magic's Revelation Transcends Sports," by Alison Muscatine, November 10, 1991. Copyright © 1991, *The Washington Post.* Reprinted with permission.

"Mother Tongue" by Amy Tan. Copyright © 1990 by Amy Tan. First appeared in *The Threepenny Review.* Reprinted by permission of Amy Tan and the Sandra Dijkstra Literary Agency.

Chapter 12

From *The People's Almanac #3* by David Wallechinsky and Irving Wallace. Copyright © 1978 by David Wallechinsky and Irving Wallace. Reprinted by permission of William Morrow & Company, Inc.

From *Curious Trivia* by John May. Copyright © 1980 by Clanose Publishers. Reprinted by permission of Henry Holt and Company, Inc.

From *Panati's Extraordinary Origins of Everyday Things* by Charles Panati, pp. 14–15. Copyright © 1987 by Charles Panati. Reprinted by permission of HarperCollins Publishers, Inc.

Excerpts from *The Dictionary of Misinformation* by Tom Burnam. Copyright © 1975 by Tom Burnam. Reprinted by permission of HarperCollins Publishers, Inc.

From *Significa* by Irving Wallace, David Wallechinsky, and Amy Wallace, p. 98. First published by E. P. Dutton, Inc. Copyright © 1983 by Irving Wallace, David Wallechinksy, and Amy Wallace. Reprinted with permission of the authors.

Chapter 14

Excerpts from *Panati's Extraordinary Origins of Everyday Things* by Charles Panati, pp. 78–82. Copyright © 1987 by Charles Panati. Reprinted by permission of HarperCollins Publishers, Inc.

Chapter 15

Adapted excerpts from *Humbug: The Art of P. T. Barnum* by Neil Harris. Copyright © 1973 by Neil Harris. Reprinted by permission of the author.

From *The People's Almanac* by David Wallechinsky and Irving Wallace, pp. 701–02. Copyright © 1975 by David Wallechinsky and Irving Wallace. Reprinted by permission of the author.

Chapter 16

From *The People's Almanac* by David Wallechinsky and Irving Wallace, pp. 521–23. Copyright © 1975 by David Wallechinsky and Irving Wallace. Reprinted by permission of the author.

Chapter 23

From *Legends of the World*, edited by Richard Cavendish, p. 37. Copyright © 1982 by Little, Brown & Co., London. Reprinted with permission.

From *Significa* by Irving Wallace, David Wallechinsky, and Amy Wallace, pp. 145–46, 202–03. Copyright © 1983 by Irving Wallace, David Wallechinsky, and Amy Wallace. Reprinted by permission of Irving Wallace.

Chapter 24

From *Significa* by Irving Wallace, David Wallechinsky, and Amy Wallace, pp. 33, 325–26. Copyright © 1983 by Irving Wallace, David Wallechinsky, and Amy Wallace. Reprinted by permission of Irving Wallace.

Chapter 25

"Emperor Norton I" by Joan Parker, *American Heritage*, December 1976. Copyright © 1976 Forbes, Inc. Reprinted by permission of American Heritage Magazine, a division of Forbes, Inc.

From *The Square Pegs: Some Americans Who Dared to be Different* by Irving Wallace. Copyright © 1957 by Irving Wallace. Reprinted by permission of the author.

Chapter 26

From *The People's Almanac #2* by David Wallechinsky and Irving Wallace. Copyright © 1978 by David Wallechinsky and Irving Wallace. Reprinted by permission of William Morrow & Company, Inc.

PHOTO CREDITS

p. 28 Walker Evans/Library of Congress. **p. 34** Walter Chandoha. **p. 41** Charlie Wunder/Monkmeyer Press Photo Service, Inc. **p. 42** Dali, Salvador, THE PERSISTENCE OF MEMORY, 1931. Oil on canvas, 9 1/2 x 13". Collection, The Museum of Modern Art, New York. Given anonymously. Photograph © The Museum of Modern Art, New York. **p. 47** Walker Evans/Library of Congress. **p. 58** © The Metropolitan Museum of Art/Culver Pictures Inc. **p.62** Don & Pat Valenti. **p. 63(T)** John Moore. **p. 69** Don & Pat Valenti. **p. 71** Metropolitan Museum of Art, Harris Brisbane Dick Fund, 1932. (32(124)). **p. 80** Rohn Engh/Image Works. **p. 108** Goldberg, Rube (see United Features Syndicate). Reprinted with special permission of King Features Syndicate, Inc. **p. 111** Illinois State Historical Library. **p. 128** Mark Newman/Photo Network. **p. 146(BR)** G. L. Kooyman/Animals Animals. **p. 146(TR)** Ewing Galloway, Inc. **p. 146(TC)** Miami Seaquarium. **p. 164(B)** Volvo of North America. **p. 164 (TR)** Ford Motor Company. **p. 164(TL)** Ford Motor Company. **p. 240** Granger Collection. **p. 371** NASA. **p. 415** Bancroft Library, University of California, Berkeley.